DAY OF THE ASSASSINS

MICHAEL BURLEIGH

DAY OF THE ASSASSINS
A History of Political Murder

PICADOR

First published 2021 by Picador
an imprint of Pan Macmillan
The Smithson, 6 Briset Street, London EC1M 5NR
EU representative: Macmillan Publishers Ireland Ltd,
Mallard Lodge, Lansdowne Village, Dublin 4
Associated companies throughout the world
www.panmacmillan.com

ISBN 978-1-5290-3013-6 HB
ISBN 978-1-5290-3014-3 TPB

1 3 5 7 9 8 6 4 2

A CIP catalogue record for this book is available from the British Library.

Typeset in Sabon LT Std by Palimpsest Book Production Limited, Falkirk, Stirlingshire
Printed and bound by CPI Group (UK) Ltd, Croydon, CR0 4YY

Visit **www.picador.com** to read more about all our books
and to buy them. You will also find features, author interviews and
news of any author events, and you can sign up for e-newsletters
so that you're always first to hear about our new releases.

Contents

Second Murderer: 'I am one, my Liege,
Whom the vile blows and buffets of the world
Hath so incens'd, that I am reckless what
I do, to spite the world'

Shakespeare, *Macbeth* 3:1

'The important thing to know about an assassination or
an attempted assassination is not who fired the shot, but
who paid for the bullet'

Eric Ambler, *The Mask of Dimitrios* (1939)

'He wanted to carry himself with a clear sense of role,
make a move one time that was not disappointed . . . He
thought the only end to isolation was to reach the point
where he was no longer separated from the true struggles
that went on around him. The name we give this point is
history'

Don DeLillo, *Libra* (1988)

Prologue

Let us go on a journey, beginning with James Bond. The British Secret Intelligence Service (also known as MI6) are the best in the world at state assassinations – Bond, after all, has a licence to kill. British assassins are in high demand, in fiction at least. In Frederick Forsyth's 1971 thriller *The Day of the Jackal*, when French right-wing fanatics could not kill President Charles de Gaulle in 1962, they hired an expert rifle shot from London's Mayfair.

The classically educated elite are familiar with the murder of Julius Caesar, but know less about the Middle Ages and Renaissance, when ancient ideas on tyrannicide were expanded to permit inter-confessional killing of 'heretics'. A few might recall that nineteenth-century democratic leaders were assassinated: British Prime Minister Spencer Perceval in May 1812 and American President William McKinley in September 1901 plus a few Russian tsars. Next we come to the most consequential assassination of all time: the shooting of Archduke Franz Ferdinand in Sarajevo on 28 June 1914, a single event which handily simplifies the more impersonal causes of the First World War.

The Nazis assassinated many people, including former Chancellor Kurt von Schleicher and Austrian Chancellor Engelbert Dollfuss both in 1934, as one might expect from mass-murderers. No one knows much about Italian Fascists, let alone what the Soviet NKVD did far beyond Russia. But the Allies were also responsible for killings, as in wartime enemy commanders became legitimate targets. The icy SS General Reinhard Heydrich was killed by Czech SOE agents in Prague in 1942, while the Americans hit the Japanese Admiral Isoroku Yamamoto in 'Operation Vengeance', when his plane was ambushed over the Solomon

Islands in 1943. We can next move onto the murders committed by the CIA and KGB, a kind of warm-up for the assassination of John F. Kennedy, Martin Luther King and Robert Kennedy.

The assassinations of Anwar Sadat and Yitzhak Rabin in the Middle East damaged the Arab–Israeli Peace Process. Russia seems to kill critics and opponents with apparent impunity – though we should connect this to a lineage that stretches back to the NKVD and KGB, this might detract from the focus on President Putin. We cannot avoid the gruesome murder of the Saudi journalist Jamal Khashoggi in Istanbul, but what can we do with the killings of Daphne Caruana Galizia in Malta or Walter Lübcke in Kassel, other than to say that they were random? In fact, how do we make sense of assassination at all?

Like most people, I do not like being told I am going on 'a journey' whenever I watch a TV history documentary. Let's dispense with this version of assassination and see how it might be done more analytically, while allowing due space for events which are both random and inexplicable.

Nowadays, the James Bond films are little more than exotic travel adverts and opportunities for product placement. The twenty-five films in the franchise are filler for TV schedulers. The British Secret Service do not assassinate people and do not recruit would-be Bonds, and their sophisticated chiefs would be horrified if some out-of-control British politician asked them to do so.

The thirty-three attempts to kill President de Gaulle by the Organisation Armée Secrète did not actually include any foreign gunmen – they had French Legionnaires and paratroopers to do the business. The French DGSE (France's MI6) still maintains a training school for assassins, as an ongoing investigation has revealed. The overwhelming number of assassinations in this book do not involve remote rifle shots; most assassinations have been carried out with bombs, knives or handguns. This is not to claim that works of fiction do not influence reality. Both Mehmet Ali Ağca, who shot Pope John Paul II in 1981, and Yigal Amir, who murdered Yitzhak Rabin in 1995, were avid fans of Forsyth's *Day of the Jackal*.

•

Assassinations are designed to have direct political and symbolic effects, which is why we know about most of them. But technically speaking most successful assassinations must surely be those where it remains open to doubt whether the victim was assassinated at all. Air crashes over deep sea or rugged mountains are ideal since recovery of the physical evidence is very arduous. In 1955 Kuomintang nationalist agents in Hong Kong conspired to blow up Chinese Premier Zhou Enlai in a chartered Lockheed Constellation aircraft called *Kashmir Princess* as he flew from Bombay via Hong Kong to Jakarta. Fortunately for Zhou he missed the flight because of suspected appendicitis, though sixteen of his delegation died in the crash over the South China Sea which three people survived. The main suspect, a janitor at Hong Kong Aircraft Engineering Co. called Chow Tse-ming (he had three aliases), fled to Taiwan. A good example of an assassination that may or may not have happened at all, would be that of China's Vice Chairman Marshal Lin Biao, who in 1971 – after plotting to assassinate Chairman Mao in a train wreck – perished along with his wife and adult son in a plane crash in Mongolia as he sought to flee to the Soviet Union. Whether the plane was sabotaged or hit the ground while flying low trying to avoid radar remains a mystery. Likewise, there have been persistent claims that PLO Chairman Yasser Arafat was poisoned with polonium, after he was taken gravely ill at a dinner in his West Bank headquarters in October 2004, dying in a French hospital of a massive haemorrhagic stroke a month later. Israel denies having killed Arafat (though it plotted to kill him many times before then) and radiological tests on his remains nearly a decade after his death yielded differing results according to who commissioned the French, Russian and Swiss forensic pathologists. Others have pointed to Arafat's chronic ill health or claim that he died of Aids, though the stroke seems the most probable cause of death.

•

Thriller writers have long been obsessed with elaborate conspiracies to assassinate politicians; one of the finest is Eric Ambler's

Judgement on Deltchev, his 1951 novel set in an unnamed Balkan country. In the political struggle between the Agrarian Party which Deltchev leads and the Communists, it is increasingly unclear to the perplexed foreign narrator who is trying to assassinate whom. The killing of Julius Caesar shows us what a real conspiracy looks like: a conspiracy of elite social equals, where the secret stayed within the group until they publicly exulted in what they had done. There is nothing to suggest that something similar underlay the slaying of the Kennedys or Martin Luther King. Lee Harvey Oswald was a frustrated man with large pretensions who wanted his hour in the limelight, while King was killed by a racist criminal who sought a bounty. The shooting of Archduke Franz Ferdinand did not 'spark' the First World War. The Austro-Hungarians (and Germans) would have found other pretexts for war with Serbia (and France and Russia); indeed on 31 July 1914 the German Kaiser told the Austrians not to bother with war with puny Serbia but to focus on their main event. Even if Archduke Franz Ferdinand had lived, he might well have caused a war with Serbia himself. But some killings would have had major repercussions. Killing Hitler in November 1939, as Georg Elser nearly did, would have had huge global consequences and prevented many millions of deaths. Only moral absolutists would object to such an outcome.

Much of this book focuses on the assassins themselves, who except in a few cases gave no advanced warning of their plan. Lone assassins are therefore much more deadly than conspiracies, which as Machiavelli pointed out long ago tend to become fractious and porous. If the security around a leader is lax then they sometimes get through and sheer luck is also a part of it. Assassins risked being tortured and executed if they were caught – some were effectively committing suicide by their deed. What we know about them derives from interrogators and torturers or, more recently, from policemen, prosecutors and commissions of inquiry, though these can be shaped too. Henry Bellingham, the English trader with a grievance against Tsarist Russia where he was detained for fraud, spent eight years brooding on this injustice as a vexatious litigant before shooting Spencer Percival in the House of Commons in 1812. Whatever the problems of

Bellingham's trial, the judges did seriously discuss the differences between anger, resentment and insanity before sentencing him to death.

In modern times, criminologists and psychiatrists have added more to the picture, especially where assassins politicized their personal miseries by killing someone powerful. While we do not need to stray too far from these individuals, it is necessary to describe the context in which they emerged. Not all of them were unsympathetic figures, though many were deeply malign. We will encounter some highly professional killers, especially when 'business' and politics fused, but most of the assassins in this book did not act for pecuniary reasons, except in so far as some were salaried employees of states. These professional killers also include terrorists who have regularly resorted to assassination. This has a long history, of which the most striking examples come from nineteenth and early twentieth century Russia and some of the nationalist movements of that time. It has endured in the world of extreme Islamism. Most dramatically, on 9 September 2001 three Tunisian Al-Qaeda operatives masquerading as a Moroccan–Belgian TV crew blew up the Afghan Northern Alliance chieftain Ahmad Shah Massoud with the aid of a bomb built into their camera and battery unit. This pre-emptively knocked out the main threat to the Taliban regime a couple of days before Al-Qaeda carried out the attacks of 9/11. In August 2009 a 'surrendering' Al-Qaeda terrorist also unsuccessfully tried to murder the Saudi Interior Minister Prince Mohammed bin Nayaf with a remotely detonated phone inserted in his rectum. This led to the victim having health problems which eased his sidelining by his ascendant nephew Mohammad bin Salman, who replaced him as heir apparent to King Salman. Other terrorist assassinations have been motivated by vengeance, as when in December 2016 an off-duty Turkish policeman, Mevlut Mert Altintas, shot dead the Russian ambassador Andrei Karlo, at a gallery opening, allegedly in retaliation for Russian bombing of Aleppo in Syria. President Putin took this crime in his stride.

The wider political effects of assassination are also considered here. The killing of kings usually results in a name change or the heir adding another roman digit to the same one. Democratic politicians are replaced. Killing an autocrat can sometimes result in moves towards democracy, but failed bids on their lives tend to end in increased repression. Some assassinations reflect bitter social polarization. The shooting of President Abraham Lincoln in 1865 involved a group of Confederate sympathizers who could plausibly claim to represent a large part of American opinion in the defeated South. Something similar happened to Sadat and Rabin, whose killers represented visions of 'another' Egypt or Israel. Failed assassinations are included here too. Sometimes fate intervened, as when a grenade thrown at Ugandan dictator Idi Amin bounced off his huge chest, killing several bystanders but not Amin himself. Failed assassination attempts can also politically benefit the victim through a 'sympathy vote'. In September 2018 the Brazilian 'law and order' populist presidential candidate Jair Bolsonaro was stabbed in the abdomen by a lone religious maniac claiming to act in the name of God. Bolsonaro recovered, with his support boosted, and despite his manifest unfitness for high office, he became Brazil's thirty-eighth President. Among the assassinations which have also had political effects, one should include the bomb attack on Pakistani politician Benazir Bhutto in Rawalpindi in 2007. Her death increased support for her thoroughly corrupt widower Asif Ali Zardari and the Pakistani People's Party, with him becoming the nation's President two years later.

One of the other themes we will pursue is why assassinations seem to cluster in certain centuries and not in others, for as in music or paintings the silences and spaces are equally telling. The chapters on early modern Europe and the nineteenth century show a remarkable uptick in the frequency of assassinations before a long pause ensues. Both surges were related to sectarian tensions (albeit of a secular variety in the latter case) and the public visibility of the targets in more modern times. The long intervening pause is worth examining in some detail. Why did rulers succeeding kings who had paid contract assassins to murder their opponents decide that this was an immoral thing to do, and how was this established in international law? Then the pace picks up again in the late nineteenth and early twentieth centuries, before settling down to the post-1950 norm of a national leader assassinated in two out of every three years. Some countries have felt the need to repeat prohibitions of state-sponsored killings. Why did the United States introduce a ban on federal employees assassinating people in 1975? As President Trump blithely conceded, the US has killed many people around the world before and since the Al-Qaeda attacks on 9/11; how is this ban circumvented in the contemporary age of drone warfare? Does Trump bear some indirect responsibility for licensing assassinations by others? Some of his supporters who invaded the US Capitol on 6 January 2021 were found to have threatened leading Democrat politicians with death by hanging or 'a bullet'.

Few outside Russia would deny that President Vladimir Putin has been involved in having people murdered, though he sometimes disavows that of course. Unfortunately, that aberrant habit has proved catching, the most obvious example being the murder of Jamal Khashoggi in 2018, ordered by men working directly for the Saudi Crown Prince Mohammed bin Salman, as the February 2021 ODNI report confirmed. The Israelis seem to think they can go around like cowboys killing their enemies. The book ends with a warning about who else might be killed, whether journalists or politicians whose views offend various constituencies. In many democracies politics have become so angry and polarized that one wonders why it is still a comparatively rare occurrence. To clarify these main themes, we need to look in more detail at three major assassinations, two of which succeeded and a third that did not. These examples also draw the arc of the book in chronological terms. And this takes us first to Republican Rome, which in turn was suffused with memories of ancient Greece.

1

The Bright Day Brings Forth the Adder: Three Infamous Deeds

There are two assassinations that most people have heard of, though no one alive could conceivably remember them. Separated by two thousand years, the assassinations of Julius Caesar and Abraham Lincoln were strangely interlinked, and tell us much about the conditions that make high-level political murder more likely. These assassinations both involved conspiracies, the first by a disgruntled and at times idealistic elite, the second by a tiny group of nonentities, who claimed to act on behalf of half a nation.

After describing these killings we will turn to a failed assassination bid, when a twenty-three-year-old Turk, Mehmet Ali Ağca, tried to murder Pope John Paul II in 1981. Even though the assassin was captured on the spot and never denied the deed, Ağca's motives and whether there was a wider conspiracy remain as opaque now as at the time. Conspiracies suggest powerful hidden forces at work, though not quite as we imagine; the question of *cui bono* ('to whom is it a benefit?') can have many answers. We also need to understand that plausibility is related to how people thought at the time. In 1981, almost everyone was prepared to believe that the Bulgarian and Soviet secret services had recruited Ağca to shoot the anti-Communist Polish Pope.

So we begin with ancient Rome. While the emotions may seem strikingly like ours, the political context, the guiding ideas and the Romans' own sense of history were very different from our own experiences. First we need to visit a republican capital unlike what we know from endless Hollywood movies. The dominant colour was a browny-red rather than gleaming white, with more small bricks, bedsits and tenements than palaces with marble columns.[1]

It was a paradox of ancient Rome that it was a society that used assassination promiscuously at home, but regarded killing foreign kings with disdain, at least until they had them in captivity, when they strangled them. The most powerful military power on earth preferred the valour and heroism of its legions and their commanders to battlefield 'frauds and deceptions'. Ironically, one of those who most deplored 'treachery' in warfare was Cicero, who would write one of the earliest defences of tyrannicide. He was part of the plot to kill Caesar, and it cost him his own life.[2]

Gaius Julius Caesar was fifty-six at the time of his assassination – the same age as Lincoln, as it happens. On the morning of 15 March 44 BC, the Ides of March by the new 'Julian' calendar, Caesar ignored ominous warnings typical of an age alert to dreams, divination and strange portents, including from his wife Calpurnia. But his friend Decimus Junius Brutus Albinus offered reassurance: 'Will a man such as yourself place any trust in the dreams of a woman and the omens of brainless men?' The friend would be one of Caesar's killers, almost shepherding the victim to his violent fate.[3]

Half the ruling senate, roughly three hundred men, were waiting in a chamber in the cavernous theatre erected by Pompey the Great, arguably Rome's first proto-emperor. Together with the property tycoon Licinius Crassus, who had died fighting the Parthians in 53 BC, Caesar and Pompey had dominated Roman politics from 59 BC onwards, soaring above the 'best men' who were the elite within the senate. But since Pompey had been murdered, while fleeing defeat by Caesar at the Battle of Pharsalus in 48 BC, Caesar was the last man standing. Crassus had died with only the repression of Spartacus's slave revolt to his name, and crucifying insurgent slaves was not regarded as an act of conspicuous valour. By contrast, great deeds of war in Gaul and Britain had further underlined Caesar's singularity. His Twelfth Legion was known as the Thunderbolt, as depicted on their shields, and it was one of the best in the Roman Army.[4]

Despite there being no professional detectives to investigate crimes, nor policemen and only few prisons, Caesar's murder is known in astonishing detail, a result of the story being handed down by living witnesses. Arriving at the senate that March morning, Caesar recognized Spurinna, the Etruscan soothsayer who weeks earlier had warned him to 'beware the danger that would not pass until the Ides of March'. Laughing that the Ides had dawned without incident, Caesar moved on, perhaps not hearing Spurinna's response: 'They have come, but they have not gone.' He progressed into the senate, anticipating the extravagant flattery that had already led to his being showered with impressive titles. He had been granted the right to add a pedestal to his own house, as if it were a temple to the god inside. The historian Suetonius disapprovingly lists some of this flummery:

> Not only did he accept excessive honours, such as continual consulships, a life dictatorship, a perpetual censorship, the title of Imperator put before his name and the title of Father of His Country after it, a statue among those of the ancient kings and a raised seat in the orchestra of the theatre, but he took other honours which, as a mere mortal, he should certainly have refused. These included a golden throne in the Senate House and another in the Tribunal, a ceremonial wagon and litter carrying his statue in the religious procession around the Circus, temples, altars, divine images, a couch for his image at religious festivals, a *flamen*, a new college of Lupercali and the renaming of a month after him [July]. Few, in fact, were the honours which he was not pleased to accept or assume.[5]

With Caesar's antennae for danger blunted by the sycophancy of the elite, he did not glance at a rolled note pressed into his hand. It warned of a conspiracy to kill him. Caesar was so confident that he was untouchable that he had not brought the Spanish bodyguards who protected him during campaigns. Bodyguards were regarded with suspicion by, among others, Aristotle, who said 'one who is aiming at tyranny asks for a bodyguard'.[6] They were what kings and dictators had, namely dangerous slaves, gladiators or foreign mercenaries with no loyalty to the polity as a whole. Cicero concurred, especially when in 45 BC Caesar had come to dine with an entourage of two thousand retainers, which resembled being billeted on rather than private entertaining. As part of his political calculus, Caesar decided that bodyguards would send the wrong message. The historian Appian reports that during a discussion about body-guards, Caesar had said, 'There is no worse fate than to be continuously protected, for that means you live in constant fear.' His loyal legions loitered outside Rome, dreaming of the riches from the forthcoming enterprise against Parthia. Any troops in Rome would have been unarmed, as was the custom. Many more veteran legionaries were camped just beyond Rome's formal demilitarized boundaries awaiting resettlement in rural colonies.[7]

Seated on his gold and ivory chair, and wearing calf-length red boots – another sign of kingly pretensions – Caesar began hearing a plea from one Tillius Cimber. But matters took an unexpected turn when Cimber jerked Caesar's red and gold toga from his shoulder, enabling Servilius Casca to plunge his short S-shaped, double-edged dagger into him. Some senators had arrived with such blades concealed within their togas; others had retrieved them from the containers used to store rolled parchments.

Caesar moved before Casca's dagger could find his heart, so the blade glanced off his collarbone. A man used to commanding and fighting in the Roman legions was being stabbed to death himself, though his killers were from Rome's ruling senatorial elite rather than low-born soldiers. Over twenty senators drew their daggers and lunged at their victim. Caesar managed to puncture one of these assailants with his iron stylus, while some of the assassins missed their target in the melee, stabbing each other in the hand or thigh. Struggling to his feet, Caesar exposed his side and groin to their daggers, twisting and turning like a wild animal.

At some point, Caesar recognized Marcus Brutus, the son of his long-time mistress and a man whose life he had spared at Pharsalus. While Caesar did not exclaim, '*Et tu, Brute?*' he did say, '*Kai su, teknon?*' the Greek for 'You too, child?'[8]

Realizing that the fight was impossible, Caesar tugged his toga over his head and released his belt so it covered his lower limbs, falling to the ground in a shroud. He expired at the foot of a statue of Pompey, one of several he had restored to their positions after the senate had torn them down. There were between twenty and forty wounds to his corpse. At this point, the assassins may have exalted, waving their daggers in the air, as imagined in a famous nineteenth-century rendition by the French painter Gérôme.

The motives for killing Caesar were an all-too-human blend of idealism and moralism with the more mundane. In modern jargon, the killers were 'spinning' almost as they ceased stabbing. The genius of Shakespeare catches this spirit as his lead conspirator, Brutus, wrestles with the dilemmas of killing someone he knew in anticipation of what he might do in the future, while simultaneously pondering how the murderous deed could be sold to a credulous public:

> It must be by his death: and I for my part
> I know no personal cause to spurn at him
> But for the general. He would be crowned:
> How that might change his nature, there's the question.
> It is the bright day that brings forth the adder,
> And that craves wary walking [. . .]
>   And since the quarrel
> Will bear no colour for the thing he is,
> Fashion it thus: that what he is, augmented,
> Would run to these and these extremities.
> And therefore think him as a serpent's egg
> Which hatched, would as his kind grow mischievous.
> And kill him in his shell.[9]

Between celebrating an unprecedented four crowd-pleasing triumphs for past victories and embarking on a fresh war against Parthia, Caesar had basked in the approbation of a nervous senate. There his enemies were as numerous as his friends. His imperious manner antagonized some of them, though he was not regarded as haughty by the troops he fought alongside.

He caused much offence when he failed to stand when the senate entered, while as a busy man he had kept the likes of the self-important former consul Cicero waiting for appointments. But hatred of him also festered because his ostentatious clemency towards former opponents created deep resentments because of the future political obligations such mercy entailed. That the senate voted for a holy sanctuary devoted to his Clemency aggravated those twisted psychological processes.

Of the many honours and titles Caesar received in an indecorous rush, 'dictator in perpetuity' was the most significant. When Sulla had earlier been awarded the title for eighteen months there had been a bloodbath of punitive killings known as 'the proscriptions'. Perhaps rather too ostentatiously, Caesar rejected 'spontaneous' offers of a monarchical crown. But would the man who had reportedly marvelled at Egypt's hybrid Greco-Egyptian kingdom while in bed with its Greek queen Cleopatra return even more enriched from Parthia without even greater pretensions? In a venerable republic, founded on the historic expulsion of kings, whose contemporary foreign exemplars were sometimes led through Rome in chains and then ceremoniously strangled, kingship was a theme of almost toxic sensitivity.

Caesar's killers could manufacture precedents for slaying a ruler who had degenerated into a ravening beast – not just in Rome's deep history, but in that of ancient Greece. A king ruled with the consent of the governed through established laws and institutions; tyrants ruled oppressively because they were slaves to their own appetites. Both Plato and Aristotle concurred that tyranny was a degenerate form of monarchy, and that tyrants could be killed.[10]

A conspiracy lay behind Caesar's assassination. It fomented rapidly and involved social equals, so it stood a good chance of success, as Machiavelli would note many centuries later. It may have involved eighty or so people, with up to twenty-three of them actually assassins themselves, which remains unusual when conspiracies are involved. For some of its key members, tyrant-slayer was integral to their identity. For the elite 'best men' who ruled Rome, their ancestors were a constant presence, in the form of elaborate family trees drawn on the walls of the public atriums of their houses, where the death masks of illustrious forebears watched over the daily stream of political clients. At family funerals, mourners would don such masks to reanimate the dead, whose great deeds were a constant challenge to the living. Veneration of their ancestors drove ambitious men to distinguish themselves in the senate, on the battlefield and in the competition for elective offices that brought power, prestige and huge material rewards. Becoming one of the ruling consuls chosen each year was the ultimate accolade, though the senatorial oligarchy typically ensured that there were two, to check the danger of rule by one.[11]

Caesar himself could reach back to the mythical Trojan wanderer Aeneas, whose mother was the goddess Venus, though his clan, the historic Julii, were less distinguished. His assassin Marcus Brutus could not trump his victim's divine lineage, but in 510 BC a Lucius Brutus had deposed and expelled Rome's seventh and final king. On Brutus's maternal side, Servilius Ahala had slain an aspirant tyrant in 439 BC. Graffiti reminding Brutus of his brave ancestor was scrawled on the plinth of Servilius's statue in the weeks before Caesar's assassination: 'If only you were alive,' it read.

If one were so minded, the abolition of Rome's early monarchy could be blurred with a vivid example of ancient Athenian tyrannicide. Athenian aristocrats derived power and regard from warlike deeds but also through their performance at the Olympic games. Chariot racing and the like required money, which came from the accumulation of family lands, a competition that led to war between rival groups. The first putative tyrant, Cylon, in the mid-seventh century BC, was himself a winner at these games; others, including the benevolent and popular Pisistratos (561–527 BC), followed with intermittent frequency.

Pisistratos is relevant to our story since he attempted to entrench his sons, Hippias and Hipparchus, in power, by using looted gold to hire mercenaries. In 528 BC he died of old age, and the elder son Hippias took power. Hipparchus developed

an interest in a young man called Harmodios, which caused
ructions since he was committed to his older lover Aristogeiton.[12]

Spurned, Hipparchus decided to indirectly humiliate
Harmodios, by claiming that the youth's sister was unfit to
take part in a procession of sacrificial gifts during Panathenian
festivities. The clear insinuation was that she was not 'intact',
a charge that would prevent her future marriage to anyone
that mattered.[13] In response, Harmodios and Aristogeiton
attempted to kill the tyrant Hippias and his brother, stabbing
Hipparchus to death during the Panathenaic games of 514
BC.[14] Harmodios was killed on the spot by spearmen, while
Aristogeiton died under torture. Hippias ruled until 508 BC,
but as a much-weakened figure.

The assassins became central to the foundation myth of
Athens. They were immortalized in a famous bronze statue that
stood in the agora, and no slave could bear their names; their
descendants lived from public funds, in honour of what they
had done. As for Hippias, the last Athenian tyrant, he fled to
the Persians. Copies of their statue found their way to Rome,
where Greek artistry was much admired. The two fearsome
lovers are depicted in mid-stride, their swords raised to strike.
Originally they may have stood back-to-back.[15]

In reality, nothing connects the men in these sculptures to
Rome's own early history. Tarquinus Superbus, the last tyrant,
was expelled from Rome rather than killed, and the sculptures
may not have reached Rome until the time of Sulla, who was
popular in democratic Athens, where Roman domestic politics
were akin to foreign support for Manchester United or AC
Milan.[16]

The problem in the Roman Republic was not kings, but the
growing tension between the aristocratic families who filled the
senate and the voting plebs, freemen who elected the republic's
officials and approved the senate's legislation. From 493 BC
onwards, two upper-class tribunes were supposed to represent
the lower orders vis-à-vis the ruling elite senate.

When these tribunes took the plebs' grievances too much to
heart, the elite struck back hard, as with the brothers Tiberius
and Gaius Gracchus, who were slain in 133 and 121 BC. In 100 BC

another radical tribune, Saturninus, who wanted to distribute land to veteran legionaries and to lower the price of grain, was murdered in a vengeful aristocratic riot. These killings of men suspected of harbouring tyrannical ambitions were aggregated into a doctrine by the orator Cicero, who flitted in the wings during the plot to kill Caesar and played a major part in justifying it. While serving as consul in 63 BC, he had the senator Catiline prosecuted for attempting to overthrow the republic and for promising to cancel plebeian debts. Catiline was killed in battle, while his fellow conspirators were garrotted to death. At the time, Caesar had opposed these extra-judicial killings which Cicero ordered.

It may not have been Caesar's monarchical temptations that resulted in his murder, but unease among the elite about the reforms that earlier figures had proposed. Caesar was doubly dangerous as he had already achieved tremendous power, to the alarm of younger men who thought it was their birthright, and were he to return triumphantly from Parthia he would be unstoppable.

Not only was Caesar deranging the customary channels of aristocratic patronage and promotion – for everything increasingly ran through his hands – but he was also pitching for popular support from the plebs. A massive programme of land colonization in the Italian provinces benefited not only retired legionaries but also some of the poor in Rome's tenement slums. The original discrete ancient hill settlements had coalesced into a vast and teeming mess, with stark contrasts between the haves and have-nots.

Caesar scrutinized the lists of the large number of wealthy people claiming grain subsidies and cut the numbers of beneficiaries in half. Worse, he also increased the number of senators from six to nine hundred, including mere veteran centurions and nativized foreigners. The elite grew uneasy and members of the 'few' decided that Caesar would have to go, in the name of 'liberty' and in line with a republican tradition they had partly invented.

There was much moral posturing by men like Brutus, whose record involved starving to death foreign debtors for refusing to pay an extortionate 48 per cent interest on loans. He was bolstered by his wife Porcia, daughter of the austere Cato, who as the date set for the assassination neared, slashed her thigh to demonstrate her tolerance of torture should things go awry. As a woman she might be dubbed the honorary assassin.

Gaius Longinus Cassius was a capable military commander who, after switching from Pompey to Caesar's camp, had not been commensurately rewarded by a patron who paid more attention to neutralizing his enemies. He was one of the few senators who voted against Caesar being showered with honours and titles. Decimus was another military man who felt he was being marginalized in favour of Octavian, although he later figured in Caesar's will as a kind of second substitute heir. He was important to the conspiracy – as a trusted companion of Caesar, he could not only track his movements but help determine them. He also had his own small army of gladiators who would provide the assassins with security.[17]

Conversations among a group of men, roughly in their forties, established underlying commonalities; their time to succeed was running out under a dictator who had yet to reach his sixties. These were the lean and hungry men whom Caesar rightly feared. Moreover, although Caesar's will was a private affair, who could ignore the fact that with no legitimate sons and heirs, he seemed to look favourably on his sister's capable grandson Octavian?

The act of assassination became more attractive once Brutus had overruled Cicero's desire for a more general bloodbath that would include the hot-headed Mark Anthony. As Shakespeare put it, they were 'sacrificers but not butchers'. The silver-haired Cicero was co-opted to 'purchase us a good opinion and buy men's voices to commend our deeds'. It was Cicero who subcontracted another poet (and admiral), Cassius Parmensis (from Parma), who would be the final assassin whom Octavian would have killed.[18]

While the deed's scope was established in meetings in private houses, the more detailed matter of where, when and how arose. Killing Caesar on the prominent Via Sacra or at a public event would not have the political force of death amidst the massed senate. Since the next senate session was scheduled for the Ides of March, with Caesar scheduled to depart for Parthia three days later, the timing seemed to arrange itself. Although the eighty or so conspirators would be theoretically outnumbered by many hundreds of senators, they would enjoy the advantage of being secretly armed and after the deed many people's loyalties began to shift too. Various distractions were arranged to keep Mark Anthony at a distance, including engaging him in conversation about battles past.

Every assassination requires planning for the immediate aftermath, establishing physical control and fabricating a compelling story. In this case, the alarmed senators fled, while the conspirators went to the Capitoline Hill and joined the milling crowds in the forum, whose numbers were swelled by those leaving a gladiatorial show. Surrounded by bodyguards, Brutus and his self-styled 'Liberators' appealed to the crowd in a series of public gatherings. Their oratory fell on stony ground. Charges of Caesar's tyranny falsely assumed that he had already achieved monarchy, which in the eyes of many was not the case. The senate appeared to agree when on 17 March it granted both an amnesty to the assassins and a public funeral for the victim, falling well short of branding the dead man a tyrant. Although few were convinced that concord was restored, Lepidus hosted Brutus and Anthony hosted Cassius at dinners designed to symbolize reconciliation. The funeral was another matter.

Caesar's corpse was surreptitiously retrieved by his servants and returned to his grieving widow. His funeral took place on 20 March, with Mark Anthony brandishing Caesar's blood-spattered robe on the tip of his spear and whipping the crowd into hysteria. He was followed by an actor impersonating Caesar, who while listing the endless beneficiaries of his mercy ironically included his murderers. A mechanized wax effigy graphically exhibited Caesar's multiple wounds as the actor solemnly declaimed the names of Caesar's assassins. The crowd began to riot, setting fire to the senate house and hunting for the conspirators, killing an innocent poet, Cinna, by mistake.[19]

The assassins began to slip out of Rome, as a decade of

renewed civil war ensued. The conspirators' early loss of tactical initiative was compounded by their later physical separation; Decimus was in Cisalpine Gaul, Brutus was in Greece and Cassius was in Syria, while Cicero tried to manage the senate in Rome before fleeing south to the Bay of Naples.

Though deadly rivals themselves, Anthony and Octavian had few difficulties in rallying Caesar's troops to their respective illustrious names though they constantly needed land and money to retain their loyalty. After some tense standoffs, in the end they brokered a pact on a riverine island at Bononia. This made them co-equal triumvirs, for they had been joined by Marcus Lepidus, one of Caesar's top generals. Securing order in Rome was their first priority. They drew up lists of those to be proscribed, a fancy term for the extra-judicial killing of men whose heads were hacked off by soldiers seeking the reward. There were three hundred senatorial names on the lists, in other words suspected sympathizers as well as Caesar's actual assassins. Even before this commenced, the first assassin to die, Tribonius, was surprised in Smyrna – he was the newly appointed governor – where he died after two days of intensive torture. His head was used as a football before being deposited at the feet of a statue of Caesar.[20] Among the ensuing victims was Cicero, who in December 43 BC was betrayed by a slave and beheaded by a military killer working for a political rival near his villa by Naples. He died like a defeated gladiator; exposing his neck to their swords.

But what of the major conspirators rather than their useful mouthpiece? Decimus tried to move his legions from Cisalpine Gaul in northern Italy to Greece to join his fellow conspirators, but his men baulked at an arduous Alpine crossing to avoid the enemy blocking the coastal route and deserted. Somewhere in modern-day Switzerland, he was betrayed and executed, the task devolving on a Gaul.

The two chief conspirators, Brutus and Cassius, had 80,000 troops to meet Anthony and Octavian, who despite the late season converged on the Macedonian coast. It was probably to pay these troops that Brutus minted more coinage. One coin showed his profile with the inscription 'IMPERATOR', while on the other side two daggers accompanied the pileus cap awarded to emancipated slaves. It was stamped 'EID MAR', 'Ides of March'. The money to pay these troops came from a general rampage around rich coastal cities where Rome's would-be 'liberators' proved to be very effective extortioners.

Battle was joined in an inclement October near the coastal city of Philippi. Ten more of Caesar's assassins would perish in this epic battle or shortly afterwards as tents were combed and heads cut off. Cassius killed himself after falsely believing that Brutus had been routed, while Brutus died while on the run, falling on his own sword. While on the journey to Rome, his severed head – the ultimate trophy – was lost at sea. Although Octavian had not actually done much fighting at Philippi, the victory further boosted the reputation of this calculating twenty-year-old.

Of the remaining assassins, the last was the poet-admiral Cassius of Parma who had made the major error of penning savage verses about Octavian, while more illustrious turncoats like Horace had reverted to his service. In 30 BC, or thirteen years after Caesar's death, Cassius was tracked down to his final refuge in Athens, and beheaded amidst his poetry manuscripts. By then Anthony and Cleopatra were long dead, as was Caesar's illegitimate seventeen-year-old son Caesarion, who Octavian had murdered. In 27 BC the thirty-six-year-old Octavian 'son of the deified one' – from January 42 BC Caesar was declared a god – assumed the title Augustus Caesar, Rome's first emperor.

However high-minded some of Caesar's assassins claimed to be, jealousy and the self-interest of a narrow elite lay behind the murderous deed, which followed a decade of civil war in which 200,000 Romans perished – enmities abounded and were fresh in memory. The assassination plunged the republic into renewed civil war. Intended to prevent rule by a single individual, the killing perpetuated it. Many more Roman emperors would be slain, often by the praetorian guards protecting them, but the killing of Caesar was the most fateful of assassinations in terms of political consequences, since the republic was killed off, too. When we now think of ancient Rome, we think of its colourful emperors rather than the great republic that preceded it.

The conspirators might have learned from the ancient Greek historian Herodotus, who wrote about the killing of Hipparchus by Harmodius and Aristogeiton: 'The murder, however, did the Athenians no good, for the oppression they suffered during the four succeeding years was worse than before.' Much the same could be said of the ravaged towns and dead soldiers and sailors who were the main tragic consequences of Caesar's murder. Given that Brutus behaved in much the same way as Caesar had before him, it is remarkable that his myth assumed a life of its own, inspiring not just Shakespeare but also the actor who murdered Abraham Lincoln.[21]

·

In the greatest modern republic on Earth, the spirit of Brutus had a curious afterlife. The American Civil War (1861–65) resulted in an estimated 752,000 deaths, including 13 per cent of the South's military-age male population. Many others were incapacitated by war wounds – in 1866, 20 per cent of Mississippi's budget was spent on artificial legs. The war divided families and left quiet pools of grief. Mary Todd had three brothers and three brothers-in-law who had fought for the Confederacy, of whom two died in battle. Her husband, Abraham Lincoln, who led the Union forces, was assassinated in front of her in Ford's Theatre on 15 April 1865, which was the eve of Easter. The horrors of war prefigured those on the Western Front fifty years later, as did the total mobilization of two economies and societies.[22]

The opening of the 1859 song 'Dixie's Land' conveys what the war was about, and the song acquired a mythological purchase on the American racist right that would prove enduring: 'I wish I was in the land of cotton, old times there are not forgotten,' it trills jauntily. 'Dixie' was written by a Yankee composer from Ohio for blackface minstrels. A version cleansed of dialogue became the national anthem of the Confederacy, played as each rebel state voted to secede and then by its troops as they tramped off to war.

The Civil War was hardly a contest of equals, but its outcome was far from inevitable. Long before armies clashed, the issue of slavery caused burning passions. Congress spent much of the 1850s debating related issues with mounting acrimony. A Mississippi congressman pulled a gun on one from Missouri, who bared his chest and dared the 'assassin' to shoot. In May 1856, the South Carolina congressman Preston Brooks attacked the Republican senator Charles Sumner with a walking cane after he made a speech attacking slavery, causing traumatic brain injury. Two years later the anti-slavery radical Galusha Grow and the pro-slavery enthusiast Lawrence Keitt came to blows in Congress, which degenerated into a mass brawl.[23]

The South was less populous and its population was moving northwards. The northern Union states were far more industrialized than the rebellious Confederacy, and farming there rested on a productive yeoman class rather than vast estates worked by African slaves. Most advocates of abolition lived in the North, while most slaves were in the South. Most Republicans opposed slavery – without necessarily supporting racial equality – and most Democrats supported it. While the northerners were protectionists, the southerners were free traders. The big southern crop, cotton, depended on others to bring it to market and turn it into cloth, and it was also vulnerable to naval blockade and competition from places such as British India. The Union could equip and mobilize more troops, even before they considered arming some of the four million slaves, and could move these troops with the aid of railways and a larger navy. But these facts take no account of ideas or fighting spirit.[24]

A pseudo-aristocratic plantation economy prevailed in the 'Deep South', its idle oligarchs imagining themselves as latter-day Cavaliers nobly resisting grim northern Roundheads, while depending on slaves toiling on plantations. Not all poorer whites supported slavery, but the majority were easy to rally to the cause because racial superiority to Black slaves was all they had going for them. Slavery was integral to the conflict, though that fact had to be disguised since it was hard to reconcile with Christianity. The pious Virginia general Robert E. Lee thought slavery would disappear in time, but then he thought of God's time, when a day was two thousand years.[25]

Expanding frontiers raised the political heat. The acquisition of huge new territories from indigenous Cheyenne, Lakotas and Navajos – who were killed in huge numbers – in the south and west raised the vexed question of whether slavery would become legal in such new states as Kansas and Nebraska, whose cattle and wheat-based economies were unsuited to the 'peculiar institution'. Abolitionists got their way in both California and the New Mexico Territory in the Compromise of 1850. The federal government, increasingly sympathetic to militant abolitionists, was initially defied by seven southern states that saw slavery being constricted on land and sea while the balance in Congress was tilting against their interests. In early 1861 the seven seceded from the Union to form the Confederacy. They were joined by four others. There would have been more, but some of the four border slave states like Delaware and Maryland were occupied by Union forces.

Slave insurrections were very localized and rare, but 'San Domingo syndrome' – named after the Caribbean island where there was a slave revolt between 1791 and 1804 – haunted the southern imagination. One rash deed by a man in whose family insanity was epidemic tilted the balance between passive and violent abolitionism, which duly triggered a southern response. The attempt by the failed businessman and white abolitionist John Brown to spark a slave uprising by distributing arms from the federal armoury at Harpers Ferry to slaves had dreadful consequences. Brown's adventure was funded by the Secret Six, a group of wealthy and well-educated northern abolitionists, though he deliberately incriminated them by leaving a trail of evidence that made it look like a vaster conspiracy. Some of the key figures in the Civil War were involved in Brown's denouement; he was captured by marines led by Colonel Robert E. Lee, and one of his odder admirers, John Wilkes Booth, stood just a few feet from the future rebel general Thomas 'Stonewall' Jackson as he watched Brown hang. Even as Brown was repurposed as an abolitionist saint, his madcap raid spread terror among southerners, who feared not just a general slave revolt, but that northern abolitionist subversives were conniving in it, leading to expulsions, mass book burnings and a clampdown on the press.[26]

The election of Abraham Lincoln in November 1860, without the support of a single slavery-supporting state, was the final straw. The future Confederates feared Lincoln would check the expansion of slavery into new states, with adverse effects on the political representation of the slave-owning oligarchy. Until his election, southern Presidents had held office for fifty of the previous seventy-two years, a majority of judges on the Supreme Court, and for half of that period the House Speakership. In their minds, the 'honour' of a supposedly cultured southern aristocratic oligarchy was slighted by an increasingly assertive bourgeois and puritanical North, which sought to define the future identity of the nascent republic. A romantic vision of a transplanted feudal past confronted a progressive one of a democratic, republican future, though there were plenty of Democrats in the North, and many 'Negrophobic' northerners supported slavery.

Everything southerners hated was embodied in Abraham Lincoln, the tall, gaunt hard-working President whose stovepipe hat exaggerated his six-foot-four-inch stature. He was a self-educated country boy from Illinois, who after travelling widely across the States became a postmaster, a lawyer and then a politician. His approach was to slowly strangle slavery by cordoning the states where it was practised. He had no executive experience when he was elected President in 1860. He learned warfare from library books, and what he saw and heard of the art of it. It may be fashionable to depict him as a pragmatist, far removed from fervent abolitionists. Despite whatever tactical compromises he might make, he regarded slavery as morally corrupting and believed in the Union with a religious fervour. That was enough to win.[27]

Five years on, high office had taken its toll; Lincoln's face was creased beyond his years, his eyes were sunken and his hands were cold and clammy. Bouts of crippling depression gave him a haunted look – in war, his decisions could result in the deaths of tens of thousands of teenage factory workers and farm boys. Re-elected in 1864, Lincoln gave strategic direction to the war, outclassing his southern counterpart 'President' Jefferson Davis and his galaxy of generals.

The outcome of the war was not preordained, and the southern rebels fought with grim ferocity. But at the end, Union commanders like 'Fightin' Little' Phil Sheridan burned and looted their way along Virginia's Shenandoah Valley and southern plantations fell into desuetude, with 180,000 of their slaves joining Union armies to haul loads and to fight in segregated Black regiments. The game was up when the Confederate Congress had to offer slaves their freedom in return for joining its depleted forces. Southern armies suffered over a hundred thousand desertions – despite their belligerent public stridency, southern womenfolk urged their husbands and sons to return home. For some Confederate soldiers, the penny dropped that 'It is a rich man's war and a poor man's fight, at best.'[28] As the northern armies advanced, ragged lines of barefoot Confederate captives limped through ruined southern estates and small towns, leaving plagues of lice and venereal diseases in their wake. The poet Walt Whitman (a Union supporter) described the horrors he witnessed on battlefields, or in hospitals (he was a volunteer nurse) and in hellish Confederate prison camps where up to 11,000 men had died during their captivity. In field hospitals where as many men were dying of dysentery and pneumonia as of wounds, he noted a single cart piled high with amputated feet, hands, arms and legs. Many vacant-eyed young men wearing blood drenched rags expired in front of him.[29]

In its death throes, the southern imagination turned to guerrillas and terrorists. Lincoln was the natural focus of attention, simultaneously denounced as an oppressive tyrant by Confederate sympathizers, and for being too weak to exterminate the entire southern slave-owning South by his own more rabid supporters.

A week after General Robert E. Lee surrendered to Ulysses Grant at Appomattox, on the evening of Good Friday 1865, an exhausted Lincoln and his wife Mary sought brief respite in Washington's Ford's Theatre. There were many Union troops in Washington, a modest, muddy city of 75,000, where the ambient swamp frogs croaked all night. On his progresses about town, Lincoln was usually escorted by about twenty cavalrymen with their swords drawn, but going to the theatre, Lincoln had one bodyguard who he gave the night off. Although the US Secret Service was created in July 1865, it was only in 1901, after two more Presidents were slain, that it assumed responsibility for their close protection. The Lincolns were twenty minutes late arriving, with the play interrupted for a rousing 'Hail to the Chief' as they took their places in the flag-bedecked box.[30]

The audience at Ford's Theatre was heaving with armed Union soldiers, though Lincoln himself had had a woman body-guard supplied by the Pinkerton agency when he passed through Baltimore. Absorbed by a comedy about English and American manners, Mary did not notice when a man entered and jammed the door to the corridor containing their box. On stage, the actor playing the character Asa Trenchard in *Our American Cousin* brought the house down with the line: 'Don't know the manners of good society, eh? Well, I guess I know enough to turn you inside out, old gal – you sockdologizing old man-trap!'

John Wilkes Booth used a six-inch-long single-shot .44 calibre derringer pistol to shoot Lincoln in the back of the head. He then slashed Major Rathbone, a last-minute substitute for Ulysses Grant, with a short dagger engraved 'America' and 'Liberty', before leaping over the edge of the box and falling twelve feet onto the stage. He then stood up, turned into the lights and proclaimed: '*Sic semper tyrannis*' – 'Thus always to tyrants'. The actorly assassin fled through the wings and away on a waiting horse, with hardly anyone making a move to stop him.

Having been carefully extracted from the box, which was then thoroughly ransacked by memento-hunters, the unconscious Lincoln wheezed his last breaths in a nearby clerk's row house the following morning. A channel seven inches deep stretched from the base of his skull to his right eye socket, where the bullet had burrowed, and multiple doctors were unable to save him; two silver dollars were placed on his dead eyes.

Shortly after Lincoln was shot, a large man claiming to bring medicaments barged his way into the bedroom of the indisposed Secretary of State, William Seward, whose jaw had been broken when his carriage toppled over. The assassin slashed Seward's face and tried to cut his jugular vein, but fled as staff entered the room. It may have been the case that a third killer, stalking Vice-President Andrew Johnson at a reception, decided to cut and run.

John Wilkes Booth was a twenty-six-year-old actor. It seems significant that he was named after the eighteenth-century English mob orator Wilkes, and that his father and brother were both named Junius Brutus.

Born in Maryland to English émigré parents, Booth and his brother Edwin enjoyed successful stage careers, though Edwin was a bigger star, which rankled with Booth. He was also a conspiracist and fantasist, who falsely claimed to have played a role in suppressing John Brown's slave revolt. Politically he supported the populist Know-Nothing party, which opposed foreign immigration. Though he earned between $25,000 and $30,000 per year as an actor – double the salary of Robert E. Lee – he lost $6,000 in the 'Dramatic Oil Company' venture, and henceforth relied on charm, cadging and debt to maintain outward respectability.

Six months before he assassinated the President, Wilkes Booth joined his brothers Edwin and Junius Brutus in a Broadway performance of *Julius Caesar*. While Booth postured as a fake Roman, he was elaborating more sordid connections, included with the Confederate underground linking slavery-supporting Maryland to the South, and shady Confederacy supporters in neutral Canada.

Thus Booth came to devise a plot to kidnap Lincoln in Washington, and to deliver him in handcuffs to rebel Richmond. Quite apart from this being hard to accomplish, Booth's mind turned to murder when he heard Lincoln speak in Richmond after Lee had surrendered, promising to enfranchise African-American war veterans and literate Blacks. 'That means nigger citizenship. Now, by God, I'll put him through. That is the last speech he will ever make,' Booth said. 'Honest Abe' had long since become sinister in the eyes of southern and northern mob orators and gutter press, with the London *Times* joining hyster-ical denunciations of his alleged oppressions.

To accomplish the kidnapping, Booth recruited a small group of dregs and misfits, including a woman named Mary Surratt, whose son was in on the first kidnap plot. He deliberately laid trails of incriminating evidence, to ensure they kept their mouths shut. Many of his 'collaborators' imagined they were merely helping to liberate Confederate prisoners from hellish conditions. Booth elaborated his escape route, with the aid of long-established networks of smugglers to guide him through forests, creeks and snake-infested swamps with horses and boats.

In the aftermath of the assassination, Booth and his associates boldly slipped through perimeter sentries that locked down Washington. Having broken bones in his foot after a fall from his horse, Booth was in a desperate condition, hobbling about on crutches as he moved between safe houses. In one diary entry, scribbled by candlelight, he wondered why he was being denounced even in the South: 'I am here in despair. And why; For doing what Brutus was honoured for, what made [William] Tell a hero. And yet I, for striking down a greater tyrant than they ever knew, am looked upon as a common cut-throat. My action was purer than either of theirs.'[31]

One of the largest manhunts in history ended in a blazing barn in the middle of nowhere, as Booth decided to resist and was fatally shot in the neck by a Union trooper. His accomplices were also run to ground. A military tribunal – for Lincoln was commander-in-chief – sentenced four to hang, including Mary Surratt and Seward's assailant Lewis Powell, with the rest imprisoned on the Dry Tortugas in the Gulf of Mexico.[32]

Booth's actions accomplished nothing. His final words were 'Useless, useless,' though he may have been talking about his own hands, as his muscles failed. Lincoln became a secular saint, his funerary tour being one of the greatest public spectacles in US history. Some of his sanctity rubbed off on his Republican Party, which dominated the federal government until 1913.

The South drifted deep into the Democrat camp, and found ways to informally institutionalize African-American tutelage. Lincoln was automatically replaced by Andrew Johnson, a notoriously drunken Democrat and the first President to be impeached. He ensured that whatever constitutional measures introduced to further emancipation were frustrated. As a former slave-owner, Johnson said, 'This is a country for white men, and, by God, as long as I am President, it shall be a government for white men.'[33] African-Americans responded to his inauguration by asking, 'We going to be slaves again?' He tried and failed to veto the 1866 Civil Rights Act, which made African-Americans full citizens entitled to equal civil rights. Ten of the eleven former Confederate states opposed the Fourteenth Amendment that canonized this in the Constitution. The Reconstruction Act of 1867 put these states under military rule until they ratified this amendment.

Booth's violent actions were deplored by the vast majority of people in the South, though the Ku Klux Klan, founded in 1865 by the former Confederate general Nathan Bedford Forrest, emerged as the armed terrorist wing of vanquished traitors. A world had vanished. 'All gone, wealth, servants, comforts, all means of support for my family gone; all lost save honour' wrote the returning Mississippi veteran Samuel French. The Confederate currency was instantly worthless. Not a few of the defeated veterans committed suicide, took to drink or ended their lives in mental institutions.

The last five secessionist states didn't re-join the Union until 1870. The rabidly racist and violent strain of politics that Booth embodied found other channels during the era of Reconstruction. Had Lincoln lived, he would have had a finer grasp of the gap between constitutional amendments and realities on the ground than Johnson, and he might have balanced the punitive and forgiving side of things with greater skill.

Johnson had all the demerits of someone chosen to balance a political ticket. Between 1866 and 1868 Radical Republicans in Congress initially achieved their own version of what is called Radical Reconstruction, imposing military government and martial law on the South, with a Freedmen's Bureau to ensure that former slaves entered into their new rights. The 1866 Civil Rights Act was the first definition of citizenship rights in US history. The 14th constitutional Amendment enshrined birth-right citizenship and equality before the law, and the 15th extended voting rights to Black adult males. But obstruction by Johnson – 'the Union as it was, the Constitution as it is' being his slogan – and demobilization and cuts to the military budget left them unable to police an area the size of Western Europe. A war against slavery was deliberately misconceived as one primarily about states' rights, while many southerners resembled the Bourbon dynasty, who famously learned and forgot nothing. Since state governments had never gone out of existence, re-founded southern legislatures could reclaim their rights, including deciding who could vote or where people could live and work. Effectively African-Americans became serfs rather than slaves.[34]

As had been the case following the abolition of serfdom in Russia in 1861, land redistribution was botched. Isolated Black farmers were easy targets for lynch mobs, which took organized form with the gruesome Klan. Under the new contract labour arrangements, African-Americans who left their masters were liable to new Vagrancy Acts, which effectively led to their re-enslavement. Very few slaves had ever been imprisoned since their owners had 'disciplinary' powers, but convict leasing enabled white employers to exploit those jailed under these new laws.[35] Southern Democrats restored their power by disenfranchising Republican-supporting African-Americans, as constitutional adjustments ensured that Black turnout in the South fell from 61 per cent in 1880 to 2 per cent in 1912. Ironically, collusion in the exclusion of African-Americans until the 1960s led to the restoration of relative civility in politics.[36]

While the antebellum South was mythologically gilded in the 1880s, an idyll of white porticos, magnolias, blonde tresses and fancy frocks, the southern oligarchy reforged alliances with the poor whites, who Johnson regarded as the victims of a conspiracy by aristocratic planters and slaves. To ensure the 'liberated' African-Americans remained 'the lowest rail', the Klan was on hand to ensure that former slaves never voted, went to school or owned land. In 1868, the KKK shot thirty-four-year-old civil-rights-supporting Arkansas congressman James Hinds in the back with a shotgun, the first US Congressman to be assassinated. The murderer was the secretary of the local Democratic Party branch of the Klan, but he was never arrested or prosecuted. Some two thousand African-Americans were lynched between 1865 and 1877, and a further 4,400 between 1878 and 1950, according to a report by the Equal Justice Initiative.[37]

The spirit of Wilkes Booth would have eagerly ridden alongside the murderous masked men in white sheets. Though their first incarnation was suppressed by Ulysses Grant's troops, this spirit persisted through decades of Democrat-driven Jim Crow segregation, and it still lingers today. As I wrote this chapter, this element were threatening to take over state legislatures that did not support Donald Trump, perhaps the least fit person to occupy the highest office and a man incapable of comprehending the racist darkness at the heart of modern America. The Confederate flag appeared ominously in the halls of Congress during the January 2021 coup attempt while Republican politicians seek to suppress minority voters.

•

Historians have a good idea of who assassinated Caesar and Lincoln, and also understand their motives. The Roman conspiracy was elite-level and ramified, and virtually all its members were identified and slain under Octavian. Similarly, those involved in killing Lincoln were hunted down and either killed or executed following a trial. The perpetrators were extreme representatives of views held by a large number of Americans who may have regarded the slaying of Lincoln with horror.

It would be misleading to think that every assassination can be clarified in this way. A minority of prominent assassinations have not been resolved – for example, the shooting of Swedish Prime Minister Olof Palme in Stockholm in 1981. Then there are assassinations that seemed clear-cut at the time, largely because the explanation is what contemporaries wanted to believe. One notorious example of a failed assassination bid shows some of the complexities of uncovering a conspiracy or the motives of the killer, who in this case published an autobiography following his release from prison.[38]

On Wednesday 13 May 1981, Pope John Paul II was being driven across St Peter's Square in Rome as part of a general audience. He had been on the throne of St Peter for three years, and was celebrated as a supporter of freedom movements in Eastern Europe. As Karol Wojtyła, Bishop and then Cardinal of Kraków, he had long been a thorn in the side of Poland's Communist rulers. As a patriotic Pole, he encouraged Solidarity, a new unofficial trade union that sent shockwaves throughout the Eastern Bloc. The internal discussions about the Polish Cardinal turned Pope within the Polish secret services and the Soviet KGB reflected anger about this subversive new occupant of the throne of St Peter.[39]

Suddenly at 17.19 on this May evening, three shots rang out. One bullet grazed the Pope's elbow, the second smashed the index finger on his left hand and the third travelled through his large and small intestines, before lodging itself near his spinal cord.

With the Pope losing consciousness and a great deal of blood, the Popemobile rushed through cobbled courtyards until it reached an ambulance. Instead of taking John Paul II to the nearby Santo Spirito hospital, it travelled five kilometres to the Church's own Gemelli hospital. Following five hours of surgery, doctors said that John Paul was out of danger, though being shot at the age of sixty-one was obviously a major challenge – even to a man who had once been a keen footballer. He never fully recovered his strength.

The Pope's Vatican security guards had conspicuously failed to protect him. Various bystanders claimed to have apprehended the assassin, including a nun, one of the ceremonial Swiss Guards and two policemen, who thought they would enter paradise because *they* had apprehended the assassin.

The would-be killer was a twenty-three-year-old Turk called Mehmet Ali Ağca. Thanks to the bystanders and police, he had no opportunity to use a smoke-bomb to mask his getaway.

A Catholic news agency once calculated that there are at least 134 'theories' to explain his motives for shooting the Pope. Ağca's original trial lasted all of three days, though the judge concluded that a larger international plot was involved before sentencing him to life imprisonment. In 2000, President Ciampi pardoned Ağca on the express request of the Pope, who had visited his would-be assassin in prison in December 1983.

Ağca was born into a modest family in an Anatolian shanty-town in 1958. His father died when he was eight, which meant times were hard. Nothing in his childhood marked him out, but while at school he fell in with pan-Turkic nationalist extremists. It is very likely that he was simultaneously involved with Turkish mafia drug smugglers who infested the town; he seems to have gone further off the rails during the endemic political violence of the 1970s. As a Sunni Muslim, Ağca turned to the Right, partly because so many Shia Alevi were on the Left. He acquired a slightly younger 'mentor' in the shape of Oral Celik, who was a violent Rightist too and also from the Malatya region of Turkey.

By this time, Ağca belonged to a Rightist nationalist terror organization called the Grey Wolves, or 'Bozkurtia' in Turkish, a group that explicitly admired the Nazis. Their name derived from a mythical female wolf called Asena, who extreme Turkish nationalists revered as a symbol of the Central Asian origins of the Turkic peoples. Such beliefs were similar to other attempts to claim that some states were based on unique civilizational virtues, for example the 'Mongol' contribution to the Russians or the 'wolf-like' Manchus in China. The Grey Wolves were the muscular end of a small political party that fed into the National Action Party or MHP. Both groups were founded by the same man, Colonel Alparslan Türkeş. Between 1974 and 1980, the Grey Wolves murdered 694 people. Ağca was a cog in this machine.[40]

As a teenager, Ağca read Frederick Forsyth's *Day of the Jackal* (1971) several times. His other hero was the Venezuelan master terrorist Carlos 'the Jackal' Ramirez Sánchez, who had shot to global notoriety through the seizing of OPEC hostages in Vienna in 1975. Ağca claimed to have undergone training in terror tactics at a PLO camp in Lebanon, though there is no evidence that he ever went there. Instead, in 1978 he enrolled at the University of Istanbul to study economics – someone else sat the entrance exams – but never turned up to classes. He lived in a Rightist hostel, but seems to have received money from his criminal activities. After participating in attacks on Leftist and secular students, Ağca shot dead Abdi İpekçi, editor of the *Milliyet* newspaper, on 1 February 1979. His support group for this killing involved several friends from his school-days.

After going on the run, Ağca returned to Istanbul where an informer, a lottery ticket seller called Ramazan Gündüz, told the police of his whereabouts. He was arrested in the Café Marmara, a Grey Wolves hangout, only to be freed by fellow Grey Wolves supporters who worked as guards within Istanbul's Kartal-Maltepe military prison. After Celik paid a $4,000 bribe to a right-wing guard, Ağca escaped dressed as a soldier, walking through eight sets of unlocked doors.

Ağca was sentenced in absentia to life imprisonment. The day after his escape, he wrote to the new editor of *Milliyet* regarding the imminent papal visit to Turkey. If the visit was not cancelled, he warned, 'I will murder the Pope, the sole reason why I fled from prison.' The papal visit passed off without incident, under heightened security. Though Ağca did not strike, he did murder Ramazan Gündüz, the informer who had landed him in jail.[41]

Ağca embarked on a bewildering flurry of movements in the run-up to the assassination. He went to Erzurum near the Iranian–Turkish border, and in July 1980 travelled to Sofia, the Bulgarian capital. He spent two months in Room 910 of the city's shady Hotel Vitosha, which was where Bulgarian and Turkish gangsters met to arrange movements of weapons into Turkey in return for drugs that went the other way. Since the state-owned trading firm Kintex was used for exports, Darzavona Sigur'nost, the Bulgarian secret police, frequented the same hotel. Ağca would later claim that a Turkish businessman called Bekir Çelenk offered to pay him $1.7 million to kill the Pope. Çelenk was alleged to be the head of this arms-for-drugs mafia and linked to Abuzar Urgulu, the top mafia boss in Istanbul.

Travelling now on a forged Turkish passport as 'Faruk Ozgun', Ağca visited twenty-five places in six countries, despite being on most international arrest and watch lists. While in Germany he made use of the MHP and Grey Wolves network within the large migrant worker or *Gastarbeiter* community and participated in two more murders.

Ağca enrolled at the University of Perugia for a three-month

Italian course in April 1981, though he never attended. He spent at least 100,000 Deutschmarks that year, smartening himself up with nice clothes and a neat haircut. He eventually made his way to Rome and rented a room in the Pensione Isa. He strolled the streets, scouting out St Peter's. When on 10 May the Pope paid a visit to the pontifical university of San Tommaso d'Aquino, a chance photo taken by a tourist showed Ağca standing close to the pontiff. Maybe he did not shoot him then since it would be harder to escape in a small town; in Rome he could vanish into huge crowds.[42]

The Italian authorities made little progress in their interrogation of Ağca, who freely admitted that he had shot John Paul II. The Italian investigating magistrates were nonplussed by his claim that he shot the Pope because he was 'leading a crusade against my faith'. Ağca said that politically, he was 'red and black', a kind of national socialist. Concluding that he had received counter-interrogation training, the police recognized that 'the longer we questioned Ağca, the more mysterious he became to us'.

Pope John Paul's visit to Ağca in 1983 only served to cloud the waters. It seems possible that he told his would-be assassin that the day of the shooting was the sixty-fourth anniversary of the day in 1917 when three small girls in Fatima in Portugal saw the Virgin Mary, who communicated three messages. In 1941 the only surviving girl, Lúcia dos Santos, wrote down the first two, adding the third in 1944. One concerned the eruption of global war, which was at its zenith in 1917. The second spoke of the conversion of Russia to Christianity. The third, which John Paul II himself revealed in 2000, spoke of persecution of the Church, which he understood as referring to the attempt to kill him. Since Ağca knew nothing of these prophecies, he clearly was not acting with them in mind, though he noted that Fatima was derived from 'Fatma', his mother's name. On the first anniversary of the shooting, the Pope visited Fatima and placed the extracted bullet on the shrine to Lúcia dos Santos.[43]

Ağca claimed to be a devout Muslim believer; in his memoir, he wrote that he had gone to Tehran in May 1980 where

Ayatollah Khomeini had told him, 'Mehmet Ali, you must kill the Pope in the name of Allah.' One can blame Khomeini for many things, but ordering the death of a fellow divine is preposterous – in other words, Ağca was a total fantasist. He claimed to reveal this commission to John Paul II during his 1983 prison visit, though the Pope's private secretary denied that there was any discussion of this matter. Ağca also claimed that both the Pope and Cardinal Josef Ratzinger (the future Pope Benedict XVI) urged him to convert to Christianity, and that it was the powerful 'Goddess of Fatima' who deflected his bullets, though all three had of course hit the Pope.[44]

Ağca used a forged Indian passport to enter Bulgaria from Turkey in 1980. After his two-month sojourn there, he was flush with money, which has led to the theory that he was hired by the Bulgarian secret service, to whom the Soviet KGB sub-contracted the assassination of the Pope, in concert with Turkish mafiosi linked to the Grey Wolves. The problem with this theory is that Ağca himself only alighted on it a year into his detention and it is most insistently propounded by authors who worked for the CIA, at a time when the New Cold War flourished. Elements in the Bulgarian service engaged in drug-trafficking in Turkey, but that does not take us to the door of Leonid Brezhnev and Yuri Andropov. When it came to Poland, an exasperated Brezhnev was captive to a lot of mediocre Polish comrades who came and went with bewildering rapidity.

Ağca was initially blasé about his solitary confinement in Ascoli Piceno penitentiary. Perhaps he thought the Grey Wolves could spring him from there. A formal reinvestigation of any conspiracy behind his assassination bid was particularly interested in three Bulgarians: Todor Aivasov, treasurer of the Bulgarian Embassy in Rome, Zhelyo Vasilev, secretary to the military attaché, and Sergei Antonov, who worked for Bulgaria's Balkan Air. Four Turkish men were alleged to have been involved: Bekir Çelenk, Ömer Mersan, Musa Serdar Çelibi, and Ömer Bağci. Some of them were by then already also pointing the finger of blame at the Bulgarians and Soviets.

Aivasov allegedly first met Ağca in his Sofia hotel. When Ağca reached Rome, his first phone call was to the embassy, where Vasilev became his contact and introduced him to Antonov. According to Ağca, who the Italian press dubbed 'Il Pagliaccio', 'The Clown', the initial plot seems to have involved killing the Polish statesman Lech Wałęsa as well as John Paul II, but this was allegedly dropped as unfeasible. The Turkish mafiosi dealt with the money side of things; $400,000 would be split three ways, while Bağci acquired the gun from an Austrian arms dealer. After the shooting, Ağca would be driven out of Italy on a Bulgarian truck that was transporting a diplomat's household effects. These trucks were marked Transport International Routier and were never searched. The Italian magistrates found it odd that the only time the Bulgarian embassy ever used such a vehicle was on 13 May 1981, when such a truck pulled out of the embassy. This one may have hidden another Bulgarian allegedly involved in the plot.

Vasilev and Aivasov left for Bulgaria, and in any case had been covered by diplomatic immunity while in Rome. Oral Celik, who had been in Rome too that fateful day, vanished after reaching Bulgaria, and would die in a Turkish military jail while awaiting trial on drug-smuggling charges. Both Aivasov and Vasilev were interviewed by Bulgarian magistrates in December 1985 on behalf of the Italian authorities.

That left the lowly Sergei Antonov in Italian custody, along with the Turk Mersan, who was extradited from Germany. Although the Italian magistrates received much circumstantial detail from Ağca, who recalled the tiny wart on Vasilev's face and his hobby of collecting miniature liquor bottles, they wondered why the two Bulgarian secret service officers would have left the hapless Antonov selling air tickets in Rome while they fled home. They also knew that Ağca was a compulsive liar and capable of elaborate deceits.[45] Three Bulgarians and three Turks were put on trial, but it collapsed in 1985, not least because the star witness announced on the opening day that he was Jesus Christ. It also helped that two Italian tourists were detained in Bulgaria for allegedly photographing military airbases.[46]

The Bulgarian government responded by comparing lowly Antonov to Georgi Dimitrov, the Bulgarian Communist framed by the Nazis in 1933 for the Reichstag fire. But even the ailing

John Paul II himself dismissed the idea of Bulgarian Communist involvement in his shooting when he visited Sofia in 2002.[47]

A Russian defector claimed that KGB chief Yuri Andropov had ordered the elimination of the Pope to undermine Poland's Solidarity movement. In 1999, documents from the Czech and other Eastern Bloc security services seemed to confirm that the Soviet Central Committee had ordered 'special measures' to be taken against John Paul II, though Mikhail Gorbachev denied these claims. The Soviet leaders were appalled by how their Polish comrades were handling Solidarity, but their huffing and puffing about an invasion was bluff. They also knew that the Poles were not Czechs and that a bloodbath would ensue, as the Poles would have fought back.[48]

A document dump by the KGB defector Vasili Mitrokhin in 1992 proved that there was no internal evidence that the KGB had plotted to kill John Paul II, even if some parts of the KGB may have aired such thoughts. The Polish SB never entertained the idea of assassination and the Soviets would have been hesitant to kill a pope, especially using a flaky Turkish right-wing killer to do it.

But this world of mirrors yielded a further twist. The founder of the Grey Wolves, Alparslan Türkeş, was a colonel involved in NATO's murky Operation Gladio for 'stay-behind' operations of armed resistance in the event of a Soviet invasion of Western Europe. What if 'the Americans' had been responsible for a non-lethal attack on the Pope, to discredit the Eastern Bloc and consolidate Catholic support for the West? This theory relied on the dubious claim that Ağca was such a good shot that he could put a bullet close to the Pope's spinal cord without damaging it.

It is more likely, as a CIA official would reveal in 1991, that the CIA had taken the opportunity in their own report ten years earlier to smear the Bulgarians and Soviets, by leaving out any detail relating to the assassination attempt that did not confirm a Bulgarian and Soviet connection. They then ensured this information came into the greedy hands of various writers, so the falsehoods were recycled further.[49]

Of Ağca's Bulgarian contacts, Aivasov died of cancer in 2019 and Vasilev was killed in a terrible car crash a few years ago. After his acquittal, Antonov returned to a low-level job at Balkan Air, and played the Bulgarian national anthem every night before going to bed. Only in 2002 did a democratic Bulgarian government give him a modest pension. In 2007, aged fifty-seven, he fell down the stairs at home and died. He was exonerated in 2016 and his Italian defence lawyer Giuseppe Consolo suggested that Bulgaria should name a street or square in his honour. Former colleagues and friends who had worked with him in Rome claimed that he had turned down offers of money to blame Bulgaria.[50]

Ağca was released from an Italian jail in 2000, at the age of forty-eight. Deported to Turkey, he was jailed for his earlier political murders and released in 2010. The Turks tried to assess whether he should perform the military service he had avoided as a young man but concluded he suffered from an 'antisocial personality disorder'. In 2014 he travelled to Rome where he placed flowers on Wojtyła's grave in the grotto beneath St Peter's Basilica. Since he lacked a visa, he was arrested and deported back to Turkey, his wish to settle in Italy denied.

It might be that Ağca was a disciplined professional assassin who knew how to cover himself with a fog of lies. We will soon encounter more of them in this book, mainly from killers who worked for the Soviet NKVD. Equally, it is possible that Ağca did not know who had contracted him to shoot the Pope. There is no doubt that he squeezed the trigger, but he might have been a lowly element in a bigger conspiracy.[51]

It is, however, possible that Ağca regarded the Pope as the enemy of Islam and decided to kill him.[52] Although the MHP was nationalist and secular in origin, most Turks are conservative religious Muslims; along with anti-Communism and anti-capitalism, Islam was one of the constituent elements of MHP and Grey Wolf ideology. In July 1981, two months after he was captured, a letter from Ağca to Türkeş was published in *Milliyet*. It read:

> Illustrious Leader. First, I kiss your hands with my deep respects, and I want to express my debt of infinite thanks for

your paternal interest. I am in no difficulties, with help of all kinds of from my brother Idealists who have taken me into their hearts. I find myself in the happy condition of doing my duty with honour, with the pride of being a Turk . . . the duty of grand Ideals. May Tanri protect the Turks and make them Great.

Tanri was a pre-Islamic sky god and the letter was not a forgery. Perhaps Ağca did regard John Paul II as the Commander of the Crusaders after all – however, the world in 1981 was more attuned to a Cold War version of his motives so as to confirm the idea of a Soviet 'evil empire'.[53]

Before we turn to modern-day assassination, we must explore some other important matters, including how major world religions that otherwise condemned murders were able to justify them. That means encountering great poets, political philosophers and theologians. And that will lead us in turn to a universe we still inhabit, in which secularized versions of religion encourage political killing, though the highly religious are often murderous too. What Frederick Douglass once called the 'hell black spirit of revenge' in his oration to Lincoln assumed many forms.

2

A Knife Trenchant:
Europe's Era of Religious Wars

Rulers with absolute power have tended to use it to satisfy pathological urges, and the so-called 'Dark Ages' between the fall of the Western Roman Empire in the fifth century and the Renaissance in the fifteenth century were rife with examples of fratricidal and parricidal murder. The eastern, Byzantine Empire probably held the record for political murder. Of the one hundred and seven emperors who ruled in Constantinople between 395 and 1453, only thirty-four died of natural causes; eight were killed in battle or by accident and the remaining sixty-five were assassinated.[1]

Endemic murderousness did not mean there were no attempts to contain and moderate it. The ancient world left the powerful example that it was legitimate in specific circumstances to kill rulers who acted tyrannically, while at the same time deploring the assassination of an enemy. But how did that message fare under Christian governments, with their potent notions of sin and of submission to rulers who derived their authority from God? Christian Europe was also exposed to Islamic influences, not least during the Crusades after the first in 1095. Cultural influences accompanied horrific episodes of violence.

Caesar's violent death was such a richly consequential event that it inspired some of the greatest dramatists and poets a thousand years later. One of them was Dante Alighieri (1261–1321), an enthusiastic propagandist for imperial monarchy as the only means of securing the unity of the Italian peninsula and a regime of universal peace. *Inferno* was written some time between 1308 and 1320, long after he had been forced to leave

Florence for a life of exile. The treacherous municipal politics explain why he included Caesar's murderers Brutus and Cassius in his *Inferno*, as the most notorious traitors in history after Judas Iscariot. The poem imagines Hell as a steep subterranean cone, ringed with descending concentric circles formed when Lucifer was thrown down from the heavens.

In the ninth and last circle of Hell, all is cold and dark. In the centre, Lucifer himself is held rigid. His three ghastly mouths chew the worst sinners of all time, with the worst – Judas Iscariot – also perpetually flayed by Satan's claws. Dante's inclusion of Brutus and Cassius reflected how increased knowledge of ancient Greek and Roman thought had modified a simpler Christian view that secular power had to be endured because life on earth was fleetingly transient before eternal life in the heavenly kingdom. That was the view of St Augustine, who condemned the killing of any man, including tyrants, with the exception of those who interfered with the worship of God. Their slaying had to be authorized by lawful magistrates, but anyone commanded by God could also undertake this task. This left some scope for fanatics who saw themselves as God's executants.

Later medieval Christian thinkers addressed tyrannicide in theoretical treatises that grew out of the older 'mirrors of princes' genre, prescribing kingly conduct. One of the most influential was John of Salisbury's *Policraticus* (1160). A close associate of Thomas Becket, the Archbishop of Canterbury who in 1170 Henry II indirectly murdered with a casual word to his knights, John regarded himself and his contemporaries as standing on the shoulders of philosophical giants, which meant access to worldviews not bounded by the Sixth Commandment.

Policraticus reimagined the state as an organism, in which each organ and limb – from the ruling head and heart via the sword-bearing arms to the humble feet – had a vital function. Divinely inspired justice was the animating spirit for the whole body. But should the ruling mind go crazy, God would surely punish the tyrant, and his end could come about through sickness, natural disaster or by human hand. Appending a long list of historical examples from classical antiquity meant that John provided no more than a typology of tyrannicide, rather than an explicit justification. A good Christian, he also condemned tyrannicide when it involved betraying a friend or involved such underhand methods as poisoning.[2]

Thomas Aquinas (1225–1274) came to similar conclusions when he argued that the 'princes of the earth' were instituted by God to guarantee the common good of civil society. Using an old dichotomy, he argued that usurping tyrants could be killed by anyone, whereas legitimate tyrants who became oppressive over time had to be ousted by the appropriate authorities and following a trial. Like Augustine, he left the door ajar for the divinely inspired individual. Comparing tyranny to slavery, he wrote, 'When there is no recourse to a superior by whom judgment can be made [. . .] he who slays a tyrant to liberate his fatherland is praised and receives a reward.'[3] The nephew of an emperor and son of a count, the future Saint Thomas changed his mind as he grew older, coming to the conclusion in *The Rule of Princes* that since good kings were more likely than bad ones to be slain by 'evil doers' it was better to leave tyrannicide alone.

•

We enter clearer and colder air with Niccolò Machiavelli (1469–1527), the Florentine administrator and diplomat who wrote about what he had experienced in the politics of Renaissance city states. As an envoy to the young cardinal turned adult condottiere Cesare Borgia, Machiavelli heard from the duke himself how he had lured restive mercenary captains to dine with him, showered them with lavish gifts, and then had them strangled. Machiavelli admired the swiftness with which it was done. The longest of his Discourses deals with conspiracies to kill or eject a ruler. There is nothing here about what God may have thought, but instead a nuanced discussion of which conspiracies stood a chance of success, addressing the differences between an elaborate plan and how an assassination actually unfolds, as well as what one might call a 'cost-benefit analysis' of involvement in such an enterprise. The odds were not great.[4]

But the Florentines were novices compared to the Venetians in the matter of assassinations. Between 1415 and 1525, the oligarch republic's ruling Council of Ten plotted some two hundred assassinations for reasons of foreign policy, and also sought proposals from aspirant assassins on how to bring about these deaths. Meticulously kept records reveal the grim details of these plots, many of which involved the services of makers of poisons with which meats or sweets could be laced.[5]

The would-be assassins ranged from 'the scum of society' to murderous clergymen such as Brother John of Ragusa, who told the Council in 1513 that he could 'work wonders in killing anyone the Council chose'. He had a tariff list: 'For the Grand Turk, 500 ducats; for the King of Spain (exclusive of travel expenses), 150 ducats; for the Duke of Milan, 60 ducats; for the Marquis of Mantua, 50 ducats; for his Holiness, only 100 ducats. As a rule, the longer the journey and the more valuable the life, the higher would be the price.'[6] You would not have wanted to attract the attentions of Brother John.

•

There were similar debates about what to do with unjust or unrighteous rulers in Islamic societies, which resorted to political murder to simplify the number of rival claimants to high office. One tributary stream in Islam's great river inadvertently supplied the word 'assassin', which in some languages became the generic term for 'murderer' or used when the separate verb 'to murder' is lacking. Dante used 'lo perfido assassin' in his Inferno, a word sufficiently unfamiliar to need explaining as 'one who kills others for money'. He and many lesser poets wove assassins into love poems, though the romantic impact of 'I am your Assassin, who hopes to win paradise through doing your commands,' the words of an anonymous troubadour, seems doubtful.

The medieval equivalent of travel guides warned Crusaders that the Assassins were a sect devoted to a mysterious 'Old Man of the Mountains' that practised high-level murder. But the existence of such a sect inevitably led to further leaps of imagination among medieval writers, including from Sunni Muslim authors whose own rulers were the Assassins' targets. They claimed that the Old Man would impress his visitors by ordering Assassins to leap off towers to their deaths.

The Venetian merchant traveller Marco Polo conflated what he imagined as the customs of the Assassins with descriptions of paradise in the Koran. In Marco Polo's imagination the mythologized Old Man seduced his youthful recruits with the prospect of girls and wine in dreamy gardens within a walled valley, before despatching them on their suicidal missions to murder rulers and religious leaders.

It suited those who did not understand sectarian religious enthusiasm to think drugs were involved, especially because the Arabic plural *Asasiyeen* sounded like *hashshashin*, which had the same negative connotations as 'druggie' does today. However, there was no actual connection between the Assassins and hashish or any other drug. They were generally known as '*fedayeen*', devotees willing to sacrifice themselves for God.

The Assassins were from an esoteric Shia sect called the Ismailis, whose beliefs were an attractive blend of Islam and philosophy. They were detested by both the dominant Sunni caliphs and the 'Twelver Shia', who invested secular and spiritual power in a clerical imam rather than a caliph. The Ismailis originated after the death of Imam Ja'far in 765, when two of his sons, Musa and Ismail, competed for the succession.

The twelve imams who followed Musa ruled what is now Iran, while the Ismailis evolved into a proselytizing sect dotted around southern Iraq, Syria, Yemen and Fatimid Egypt. The advent of the warrior Seljuk Turks in the region gave a military impetus to Sunni orthodoxy, including in Persia, where a branch of the Ismailis defended themselves by creating an autonomous state.

During travels that took him to Cairo, the Yemeni Hassan-i Sabbah (1050–1124) adopted the Ismaili faith, before going on to the rugged Elburz Mountains in present-day Iran. There he proselytized among the region's warriors, identifying remote and defensible positions to fortify. He acquired the castle of Alamut, to which he added other forts with water supplies and deep caverns to hoard food and weapons. Hassan reminded his followers that after being expelled from Mecca, the Prophet himself had had to use many kinds of warfare – including assassination and raiding – from his own temporary refuge in Medina.[7]

Hassan's recruits formed a brotherhood akin to a military religious order of Crusaders, but without subordination to pope or monarch. Although high-level murder was their modus operandi, they also fought as a small army. Designating them 'proto-terrorists' seems anachronistic, and equally applicable to the Jewish Zealot Sicarii who had indiscriminately killed Romans and their Hebrew collaborators before the Romans destroyed Jerusalem in AD 70.

There was nothing indiscriminate about the daggers of the Assassins, who were distinguished by elevating targeted killings into their primary strategy for destroying the Sunni establishment. States that were little more than a collection of warlordships could quickly dissolve if the chief overlord was murdered. The first known victim of the Assassins was the Sultan's reforming vizier Nizam al-Mulk, stabbed to death in his litter while travelling to Baghdad in October 1092 by a man called Bu Tahir Arrani, who had disguised himself as an itinerant Sufi divine.

Successive Seljuk armies tried to crush the Assassins, to which the sect responded with a stream of killings. Powerful men took to wearing chainmail beneath their clothing, after a dagger was left stuck in the floor of one Sultan's bedchamber. A message explained 'Did I not wish the Sultan well that dagger which was struck into the hard ground could have been planted in his soft breast.'[8]

Hasan's supporters acquired other fortresses in northern Persia, and also sought out similarly inaccessible terrain in Quhistan, bordering Afghanistan, Fars and Khuzestan, as well as the rugged interior of Syria, where they came to control nine remote fortresses. Their first victim in Syria was the ruler of Homs, who in 1103 was knifed to death while praying by a group of Assassins masquerading as Sufis.[9]

By the second half of the twelfth century, the Syrian branch of the sect had eclipsed its Persian original, under the notorious Rashid al-Din (1131–1193), who for thirty years exploited Christian and Muslim rivalries to secure the existence of his sectarian state. Rulers including King Louis IX of France and Frederick Barbarossa of Hohenstaufen paid good money to avoid

being slain. Their first Christian victim was Count Raymond II
of Tripoli, who was stabbed to death in 1152.

However, the main threat to the Assassins was the great
Kurdish-Turkish warlord Saladin, who crushed the Latin
Crusaders and entered Jerusalem on 2 October 1197. The
Assassins twice attempted to kill him and he took to sleeping
on a raised wooden platform, with only men he knew well
allowed around him after Assassins infiltrated his entourage.
After Saladin's forces failed to exact revenge, he received written
warnings from the Assassins' leader. Eventually, the two
concluded that a pact made better sense. Saladin may have
contracted Assassins disguised as Christian monks to kill Conrad
of Montferrat, the Latin King of Jerusalem, in April 1192. Under
torture, one of the killers claimed that England's King Richard
the Lionheart had commissioned the murder, in an attempt to
deflect attention from whoever had really sought it.

Following Rashid's death, power passed back to the Persian
Assassins of Alamut, but they and the Turkish Seljuk rulers of
Persia both fell victim to an unexpected force that descended
like a vast storm over the entire region. In 1256 Alamut was
surrendered to Hülegü, the grandson of Genghis Khan.
Khwurshah, Hassan's final successor, was savagely kicked to
death by Mongol guards as he went to pay homage to Khan in
Karakorum, after which the Mongols took their time in the
difficult task of demolishing Assassin fortresses. Finally, after
roughly two centuries, the Assassins disappeared from history,
leaving only an ominous word as their legacy.[10]

•

The twentieth-century dissident Russian novelist Aleksandr
Solzhenitsyn was responsible for the observation that 'The imagination and spiritual strength of Shakespeare's evildoers stopped
short at a dozen corpses. Ideology – that is what gives evildoing
its long-sought justification and gives the evildoer the necessary
steadfastness and determination.' Solzhenitsyn's Orthodox faith
blinded him to the role that religion played in bringing about
a toleration of large numbers of murders in eras long before his
own. After all, the Old Testament is littered with mass murders.

Any medieval Christian inhibition about killing unjust or tyrannical rulers was abandoned during vicious sectarian wars in early modern Europe. The Renaissance brought deeper knowledge of ancient morality, while the Reformation intensified the confessional climate to fever pitch. Rulers were declared 'heretics' by their subjects and devastating interconnected religious wars erupted. While Lutherans tended to obey the royal princes who protected them, the more 'purist' Calvinists who tended to live in cities, absorbed many of the doctrines of corporate resistance already practiced by feudal lords, magistrates and urban oligarchs. On the opposing Catholic side, popes Pius V, Gregory XIII and Sixtus V explicitly condoned (and celebrated) the assassination of heretical rulers.[11]

There was a new means of killing too, with handguns available to everyone from aristocratic light cavalrymen to common thieves. In 1570 a Protestant, James Stewart, 1st Earl of Moray, was shot with a longer-barrelled 'carabine' from a high window by James Hamilton, a Catholic, in one of the intra-Scottish feuds that were so visceral that the young James VI of Scotland could not wait to get onto the English throne to escape multiple attempts on his life. Explosives also made their grim debut, most memorably in the November 1605 Gunpowder Plot to assassinate James I and the Westminster Parliament.

One of the earliest assassinations with firearms was of the Catholic François, Duke of Guise, who was ambushed and shot by the Calvinist convert Jean de Poltrot in 1563, an early indicator of how bloody France's Wars of Religion would become. Between 1562 and 1598 the eight conflicts that made up the Wars of Religion are estimated to have led to the deaths of three million people.

Though France was an overwhelmingly Catholic country, with Paris a bastion of orthodoxy, about 10 per cent of the population were Calvinist or Reformed Protestants. In France they gradually became known as Huguenots, most numerous in the south and west, and dependent on the safe havens provided by powerful aristocratic converts. Internationally, they enjoyed the support of England's Queen Elizabeth I, the Dutch provinces in their insurgency against Catholic Spain and German princes including the Elector of Saxony. Where they could, the Huguenots resorted to violent iconoclasm to wipe out every trace of Catholicism. The supporters of both sides organized themselves as leagues and associations, which 'massified' the sectarian conflict.

The Huguenots' most implacable opponents were the ruling Guise dynasty of Lorraine in eastern France, who claimed to be descendants of the Emperor Charlemagne. The Guise were reliably supported by the papacy and the Spanish Habsburgs. France's Valois rulers tempered their defence of Catholic orthodoxy with a recognition that they could not overwhelm the Huguenots with might. Instead they settled on episodic reconciliations and limited toleration within Huguenot areas, which periodically broke down into bouts of war.

In 1572, large numbers of Huguenot nobles came to Paris for the wedding of their champion, the Bourbon Henry of Navarre, with Margaret of Valois, daughter of the late French king and sister of his successor Charles IX. It was lost on no one that having been raised as a Huguenot, Henry of Navarre was pretending to be Catholic after a papal dispensation had permitted his mixed marriage. Dark hatreds also lurked beneath the lavish celebrations. A Catholic ruffian shot and wounded Admiral Gaspard de Coligny, a leading advisor to Charles IX and a prominent Huguenot, probably in revenge for the murder of the Duke of Guise; by midnight, an attack on one leading Huguenot had been reworked into a Huguenot plot to seize the King.

While Guise supporters hunted down their enemies, killing Coligny as he recovered from the earlier attack, mobs of ordinary Parisians turned on their Huguenot neighbours, killing more than two thousand before dawn broke. Henry of Navarre was lucky not to be murdered after he renounced his faith in a tense audience with King Charles while royal bodyguards combed the palace murdering other Huguenots. Within four years, he would escape what amounted to house arrest at the court of the new King Henry III and revert to his original Calvinist faith.[12]

In a climate of sectarian hatreds, rulers began to commission the murders of their religious opponents. In 1570 Queen Elizabeth I was declared an apostate and a heretic by Pope Pius V, and ten years later Gregory XIII told her English subjects that it would not be a mortal sin to kill the Queen; at least twenty attempts were made on Elizabeth's life in the 1570s and 1580s. In 1580, William the Silent, Prince of Orange, another leading Protestant and the de facto ruler of two insurgent provinces in the Dutch Netherlands, had the following bounty placed on his head by the Habsburg King Philip II of Spain:

> If there be any found, either among our own subjects, or amongst strangers . . . that knoweth any means how to . . . set us and himself free, from [William], delivering him unto us quick or dead, or at the lest taking his life from him, we will cause, to be given and provided, for him and his heirs, in good land or ready money, choose him whether, immediately after the thing shall be accomplished, the sum of 25 thousand crowns of gold.[13]

This was personal for Philip, since as a boy the Protestant Prince of Orange had been brought up at the court of the Emperor Charles V in Antwerp, which is why he was entrusted with the governorship of Holland and Zeeland. Known as the 'Silent', William had become one of the aristocratic leaders of the Dutch Revolt. This Protestant uprising diverted huge 'Spanish' armies – for many of the troops were mercenaries like Guido Fawkes – from the parallel Habsburg crusade against the Ottoman Turks in the Mediterranean.

William was key to diplomatic attempts to draw both the Protestant Elizabeth I of England and the Catholic Duke of Anjou into a war with the Spanish. Anjou intervened in the war, supported by Huguenot volunteers, and following his death, so did a reluctant Elizabeth, with an expeditionary force that was comprehensively defeated. Following that, Philip II launched the Armada invasion in 1588.

The first attempt on William's life was in 1582, when a Spanish merchant in Antwerp persuaded one of his young clerks, Juan de Jauregui, to shoot him, so that he might receive the bounty Philip II had placed on the life of this 'pest on the whole of Christianity and the enemy of the human race'. Jauregui shot

William in the head from close range as he presented him with a petition. The bullet passed through the right side of William's neck and out through his left jaw. Luckily, a flash from the overcharged gun set fire to the victim's hair and beard, cauterizing the entry wound and throwing the assassin off his feet. Jauregui was slain on the spot by William's retinue, which included William's son and heir Maurice. They discovered various lucky charms that had done the dead assassin no good, but which were used by the pamphleteers to connect Catholicism with black magic as well as murder. Parts of Jauregui's corpse adorned the gates and walls of Antwerp until the Spanish retook the city, while his two accomplices had their throats cut.

Perhaps emboldened by this near miss, and equally interested in Philip's huge bounty, a twenty-five-year-old Catholic from Burgundy called Balthasar Gérard tried to take William's life two years later. Gérard pretended to be François Guyon, a Protestant agent offering intelligence on the Spanish armies. He won William's confidence when he brought the news that the Duke of Anjou had died, inclining William to assume that he had 'the High and Government authority' of the Dutch provinces.

With astonishing audacity, Gérard cadged fifty crowns from William himself, while reconnoitring the royal palace in Delft, money he used to purchase new shoes and a pair of pistols. These weapons were short enough to conceal under a cloak, and most importantly, employed a coiled spring like a watch mechanism; they were self-igniting, meaning the gun was ready to fire when produced. On 10 July 1584, Gérard surprised William on the stairs of the palace and shot at him three times at point-blank range. Two bullets hit the wall, but one entered William's breast, fatally wounding him. Gérard fled, stumbling over some rubbish where his pursuers captured him.

Gérard's interrogation and trial were swift, since there was no doubt of his guilt. His execution did not happen for four days, for states sought to advertise the terrible fate that would befall regicides.

Since monarchs could determine the international diplomacy and confessional coloration of their countries, killing a king or queen could have major political and religious consequences;

some people began to argue that it was morally better to kill a single individual than to go to war, in which huge numbers of innocent people might perish. After William's assassination, Elizabeth I lived in dread of such a fate, and a kind of 'security state' of bodyguards and spies was established to deal with the Catholic enemy within. By contrast, although there had been three attempts on the life of Philip II, he went about the Escorial Palace without guards, rode his horse and would sometimes walk alone in city streets.

Having ordered the assassination of his brother Don Juan's secretary Juan de Escobedo, without success, Philip had commissioned the murder of William of Orange in 1584 but felt immune from harm himself. A reclusive, suspicious and pedantic man, he annotated an inaccurate report on the assassination of King Henry III of France that read: 'The manner in which he had been killed was that a Jacobin monk had given him a pistol shot in the head.' Philip underlined the word *'pistolle'*, adding in the margin 'This is some kind of knife; as for *"tayte"*, it can be nothing else but head, which is not *"tayte"* but *"tete"*, as you well know'.[14]

Theologians kept pace with this climate of threat, though sometimes Catholics and Protestants swapped places in terms of their reticence on the issue of assassination. A new word was coined – monarchomachy – to describe those 'fighters against monarchs' who had strayed from the 'pure' faith. Luther was an absolutist in defending the Sixth Commandment. Calvin advocated passive obedience to earthly authority, but if a ruler acted against God, rebellion was allowed. Other Calvinists pushed this idea further as religious wars became more barbaric.

In the rival Roman Catholic camp, the Spanish Jesuit Juan de Mariana argued that tyrants, whether usurpers or not, should be deposed by assemblies of the people, or failing that killed by any divinely guided individual. The Italian Jesuit and future Cardinal Robert Bellarmine advocated to the Pope the right to depose rulers and to make war against them. This was open to generous misreading, and conniving Jesuits were invariably seen as the brains behind various murderous plots. So much so that in 1610 the Jesuit Superior General Claudio Acquaviva felt

compelled to warn his fathers that they would be excommunicated if any of their subordinates wrote in support of
assassinations. Two events inclined Acquaviva to this stance.[15]

One such plot was the abortive attempt to murder King
James I & VI, his son Prince Henry and the House of Lords at
Westminster on 5 November 1605, the second the assassination
of France's King Henry IV in 1610.

The first did not have papal sanction since James was born
a Protestant, though his Danish wife Anne was a Catholic.
Being politically astute, he made soothing noises to English
Catholics to smooth his exit from ruling what he viewed as
the grimly barbaric Scots to the more civilized English. Since
his father Henry Stuart, Lord Darnley had been assassinated
in 1567, and a supporter of his mother Mary Queen of Scots
had been responsible for the carbine shot from within the
washing which killed the Earl of Moray three years later,
James had good reasons to take the low road to England and
to dedicate himself to peace. One of the first acts of his reign
was to enter a ceasefire with King Philip III of Spain, which
was confirmed with a peace treaty in June 1605. Like other
Catholic monarchs, Philip deplored the assassination of fellow
rulers.

These diplomatic masterstrokes had two significant consequences. Peace meant a surplus of unemployed mercenary
soldiers and weapons, especially gunpowder. English Catholics
hoped James might alleviate the onerous burdens that made
them third-class subjects, but he had to simultaneously pander
to the Puritans, another set of zealots who wanted greater
repression of these 'Papists'.

The Gunpowder Plot was hatched at the Duck and Drake
tavern on London's Strand on 24 May 1604 by five Catholic
zealots. Its leader was the charismatic Robert Catesby, who
had recruited a mercenary soldier from York called Guy Fawkes
(Italianized to 'Guido' while serving in Flanders). Since the inn
was a Catholic safehouse, the five men heard mass and took
communion in another room from Father John Gerard, a
clandestine priest. The five original conspirators recruited eight
more men from the Midlands gentry. The plotters were mainly

in their early thirties and had special swords engraved with pious exhortations.[16]

The wider group of plotters were supposed to lead an armed coup; with King James and his heir blown to pieces, they would snatch the nine-year-old Princess Elizabeth, who would be installed on the English throne under the guiding hand of a Catholic protector. The coup might be backed by foreign Catholic invasion, and England would rejoin the Catholic fold. Since the plotters possessed substantial country homes, this incriminated the Jesuits and other Catholic clergy, who were hidden all over them, in elaborately constructed 'priest holes'. The hidden clergy heard the confessions of some of the conspirators, as did their household servants. Not all of the latter were loyal.

Since parliament was repeatedly prorogued because plague was coursing through London, the plot was not activated until it reconvened in early November. By that time the plotters had rented a small house within the grounds of the Palace of Westminster, as well as a large store room beneath the Lords' chamber. In one corner, they piled up thirty barrels of gunpowder – rowed over the Thames from Lambeth – and covered them with bundles of firewood. There was no security around the palace, and people came and went through its chaotic precincts at will.

Intimations of a plot to kill the King came to the ears of his security chief Robert Cecil, who let the plot go the distance in order to catch Guido Fawkes in the store room. The main conspirators were tortured, which consisted of being hung from a wall in manacles, before sessions on the rack that dislocated shoulders and broke wrists and ankles. Armed men descended on the rural homes of the other conspirators. Gunpowder deteriorates and separates when wet, and Catesby had spread their stock in front of a fire to dry, with predictably fiery results as the hunters moved in, before he was shot dead along with some of his co-conspirators.

The first batch of malefactors had a swift trial in January 1606. There was no defence and the outcome was not in doubt.[17] The accused were hanged, drawn and quartered and their hearts were ripped out. The lucky ones suffered a broken neck in the initial stage, rather than being temporarily choked and revived for the rest of the ghastly performance. The corpses of Catesby and Thomas Percy were dug up and beheaded.

The second wave of trials focused on captured clergy. The trial of Henry Garnet, the chief clandestine Jesuit in England, was a more respectful affair, concerning such learned subjects as hiding one's true views – or 'equivocating' as a book by Garnet called it – and his duty to reveal what had been vouch-safed in the confessional by the other conspirators. After conviction for 'misprision of treason', he and his fellow accused were executed on 3 May 1606. Garnet acted with such dignity that the crowd helped break his neck by tugging on his legs, to spare him castration and disembowelment.

That year William Shakespeare alluded to these events in his new play *Macbeth*, written for his company, the King's Men. Two years earlier the dramatist had boldly addressed a real attempt on the life of James VI of Scotland (as the King then was) in 1600 in a play called *The Tragedy of Gowrie*. Two Scottish aristocratic brothers had either lured James to their house in order to kill him (the King's version of what happened) or more likely he had had the brothers killed to get his hands on their money and property and to liquidate the huge debt he owed them. This topical play had only two performances and then vanished since it was risky to portray living kings on stage or even to deal with relatively recent history. *Macbeth* revisited the theme of assassination, albeit with a setting in medieval Scotland. Apart from being a ringing endorsement of dynastic legitimacy, the play pandered to James's obsession with diabolic forces, which in 1591 had led the King to participate in the torture and trial of a group of witches in North Berwick who, it was alleged, had tried to shipwreck and drown his future wife Anne as she tried to sail from her native Denmark to Scotland for the nuptials. In the aftermath of the Gunpowder Plot the dark themes of *Macbeth* touched every nerve in James's agitated mind – he was too scared to dine in public – and there was even a nod to the executed Garnet when a gatekeeper answering a late-night knock on the door ruminates about 'equivocators' going straight to Hell.[18] James's terrors further increased in the course of 1610, after which he hardly ventured out at all.

The great Henry IV of France, like Caesar and Lincoln, was killed at the age of fifty-six. The essential problem for France's early modern monarchs was that Catholics and Protestants had established their respective states-within-the-state thereby subtracting royal power. Under French Salic law, Henry of Navarre was heir presumptive to King Henry III of France, but his manifest lack of 'Catholicity' was a major obstacle to his accession; in 1585, Pope Sixtus V excommunicated him as a relapsed heretic.

However, King Henry III himself feared domination by the Guise faction, behind whom stood the King of Spain and the papacy. Shortly before Christmas 1588, Henry III ordered the assassination of the two most powerful men in the faction. Royal bodyguards cut down the Duke of Guise as he crossed a court-yard while answering a specious summons; his brother Louis, the Cardinal of Guise, was hacked to pieces in a prison cell. This did Henry little good, for in the eyes of many of his subjects he was a murdering tyrant. Within nine months he was also dead, stabbed by a monk who gained admittance to his apart-ment at Saint-Cloud. He had already reluctantly designated Henry of Navarre as his successor.[19]

King in name only, Henry IV had to conquer his own kingdom, for only about a sixth of the country recognized him. The Guise Catholic League and the Habsburgs implacably opposed him, and he was an excommunicated heretic. He was only able to take control of his own capital after negotiating his way back to Catholicism in 1593, so as to win the allegiance of his suspicious subjects, and he was crowned a year later. It helped that his grasp of religious complexities was so superficial that in the eyes of the Church it seemed as if he had not strayed too far. The papacy was not convinced, though feared that he might emulate his English predecessor Henry VIII in a total rupture from the Church if there were no compromise. That is why in 1595 the heretic king was granted absolution, though for the next fifteen years he ignored a detailed ancillary agree-ment to reimpose Catholic orthodoxy on his Protestant subjects.[20]

Henry was a brave and resourceful military commander. Like an early modern Caesar, he was often in the thick of battle. Though he is falsely said to have joked that Paris was worth a mass, in reality his bluff affability had hidden depths – his friends included Michel de Montaigne, the greatest essayist of his day. Henry guaranteed an orderly succession by having six children with Marie de Medici, having set aside his previous wife to marry her. He would become an immensely popular ruler, showing concern for the poor. His major achievement was the 1598 Edict of Nantes, which reaffirmed Catholicism as the religion of state, while extending limited toleration to the Huguenots.

Given his complicated relationship with Catholicism and Protestantism, Henry suffered at least twelve assassination attempts in his lifetime. By ducking at the right moment, he was merely knifed in the lip by one young zealot in 1594. As punishment, the assassin was drawn and quartered, his family home was demolished, his mother and sister were turned onto the streets and his father was banished.

But in François Ravaillac, the King met his destroyer. Ravaillac was a loner whose dysfunctional branch of a moderately successful family had slid down the social order; by the age of thirty he was little more than a legal messenger boy who had spent time in prison for debt. He also came from Angoulême, an island of Catholic orthodoxy in a sea of Huguenots. Inspired by two uncles who had been cathedral canons, he made two attempts to join religious orders, but was quickly shown the door because of his propensity for lurid visions that the Catholic Church felt enabled enemies of the faith to detect hocus pocus and derangement.

Ravaillac's thoughts turned increasingly to the King. If only he could secure a personal audience, he would set Henry on the right path of extirpating the Huguenot enemy within. His desire to speak with the King was given added urgency when, to his horror, he learned that he was planning to intervene on behalf of the Calvinist claimant in a disputed succession in Jülich-Cleves. In the assassin's mind, this became an intent to wage war on the Pope, and on God himself; Ravaillac was convinced that Henry must make war on the Huguenots instead.

He took to stalking the King's carriage in the streets, crying out that he needed to speak with Henry in person, but every attempt was repulsed by the King's entourage. Clearly in a desperate state of mind, Ravaillac took to commuting back and forth from Paris, armed with a stolen knife. One day he came across a roadside shrine in Étampes; an image of the *Ecce Homo* broke through any residual psychological barriers to the temptation of killing the King. He now regarded himself as a messiah.

After loitering around the Louvre, Ravaillac caught up with the royal coach in the narrow Rue de la Ferronnerie on the afternoon of 14 May 1610. Henry had gone to inspect decorations for the lavish reception of Marie de Medici, crowned the previous day at Saint-Denis. The coach was blocked by two carts and tilted into a gutter in a street thick with pedestrians, and its blinds were open to let in light. This enabled Ravaillac to jump on a carriage wheel and reach inside to stab the King. One strike missed but two hit home, above his heart and through a lung. Henry IV died quickly, mumbling, 'It's nothing,' as blood filled his mouth.

Ravaillac surrendered meekly and was interrogated and tortured for two weeks, which is why we know so much about him. Indeed, fame might have been a motive, for suddenly the victim of a lifetime of slights was the centre of attention. Several authorities were anxious to know if a wider conspiracy was involved, though Ravaillac's main concern was whether he was an instrument of God or had been misled by the Devil. Rather archly, he warned one high-born inquisitor, 'Watch out that in the end I don't say it was you.'[21]

In fact, though Ravaillac had tried to communicate his mental anguish to various clerics, most of them were totally perplexed by his stream-of-consciousness musings. How could they know what he intended to do, if he was not clear in his own mind?

His death was a public spectacle on the Place de Grève, which went on for several hours in front of a baying mob. Ravaillac's legs were already broken and mangled through torture. His right arm was plunged into burning sulphur, then hot pincers were used to tear off strips of flesh, before a mixture of molten lead, sulphur and resin was poured into the wounds to prolong his agony. Having prepared for such a fate, Ravaillac kept insisting that 'It was I alone who did it.' He was tied to four horses and torn apart, before his body was chopped into smaller pieces by the furious crowd.

The demented assassin achieved nothing by killing Henry IV – the King's nine-year-old heir was crowned King Louis XIII. Queen Marie de Medici was regent and rapidly reconfirmed the Edict of Nantes. Even when Louis XIV revoked it, sending streams of Huguenots into exile, the lingering influence of Calvin was evident in the Jansenist wing of the French Catholic Church. Ravaillac's victim became part of the mythologized lineage of France's absolutist monarchs, heretic or not. Royal absolutism was endorsed by the Estates General of 1614, the assembly that would not be reconvened until 1789.

One effect of the slaying of Henry IV was to make assassination seem ignoble. We have seen that Europe's Catholic monarchs did not want to get involved in plots against James I, but this shift in attitudes cannot be solely ascribed to pioneering activists and moral crusaders – it also involved a spirit of precaution at the very top. Disdain for assassination developed from a sense of honour, from the attempts of jurists to codify acceptable international conduct and from structural changes in the European states system. Philip II's grandson protested against the 'disgraceful calumny' that he had been involved in plots to slay Henry IV, and both Emperor Ferdinand II and Philip IV of Spain declined to kill the Swedish warlord Gustavus Adolphus during the Thirty Years War.

The gradual adoption of normative prohibitions on assassination was also probably connected to the increasing organization of states for war, which downgraded the role of individuals, including the most exalted. Apart from the reputational costs of assassination, major powers could contemplate unleashing vast armies against each other. The Swedish monarch Gustavus Adolphus was the biggest threat since Martin Luther to Europe's Catholic great powers. They called this all-conquering northern warrior 'the Goth'.

But in 1631 Emperor Ferdinand II rejected a plot to assassinate him as 'neither Christian nor imperial' and a year later his cousin Philip IV declared in a 2 March 1632 letter to his envoy in Vienna that a 30,000 Hungarian ducts plot to rid the world of the Swede 'would be unworthy of a great and just king . . . there remain to us appropriate and legitimate means to resist and humiliate them according to what prudence and just intention will advise.'[22] Of course, there are several ways to skin cats. Emperor Ferdinand grew fearful of his most powerful military commander, the Bohemian Albrecht Wenzel Eusebius von Wallenstein, who was rich and in charge of a private army. In 1634, by which time Gustavus Adolphus was dead and no threat, Ferdinand organised a commission which stripped Wallenstein of his command and lands, with the Emperor appending 'seize him dead or alive' in his own hand on their report. Charges of crypto dealings with the Protestant enemy were cooked up too. Wallenstein was murdered on 25 February 1634 in a wintry billet at Eger in Bohemia. Irish and Scottish mercenaries killed his entourage and then finished off the ailing Wallenstein in his bedchamber with a half pike. The pseudo-legal proceedings point to why assassination was going out of fashion; rulers could judicially murder their enemies, the fate of many of Cardinal Richelieu's aristocratic foes and of the great Dutch patriot Johann van Oldenbarneveldt, who was executed for 'treason' by William of Nassau in 1619. While judicial murder continued apace, assassination went out of favour.[23]

Commencing in the late sixteenth century, international jurists argued that assassination would elicit a cycle of tit-for-tat killings, while also contributing to a more general descent into disorder. Hugo Grotius, whose tract *De Jure Belli ac Pacis* ('On the Law of War and Peace') was written under the patronage of Louis XIII, also disapproved of assassination, even as he tolerated the slaughter of people in besieged towns or those taken captive on battlefields. Such practices continued well into the Age of Enlightenment, but at least state assassination had ceased to be normative. When in 1806 the British Foreign Secretary Charles Fox was approached with a plan to kill Napoleon, he not only had the plotter arrested but revealed the scheme to his French counterpart.[24] When Prime Minister Spencer Perceval was shot dead in the lobby of the House of Commons in 1812 by John Bellingham, a businessman aggrieved by official indifference to his mistreatment for fraud, this seemed utterly aberrant. But later in the nineteenth century, such killings would occur across Europe, with stunning frequency.

Apart from terrorism, religiously inspired killing seems remote for many of us in the modern West. But before we assume that 'our' Enlightenment mitigated this strain of violence, we should recall that in the 'Age of -Isms', assassins flourished, not least in civilized Europe and uncivilized Russia. And in 1914, one of these political killings would indirectly trigger a global conflict in which ten million soldiers perished and by which Europe would be fundamentally transformed.

3

'We are being hunted like wild beasts': Murder by -ism in the Late Nineteenth Century

The late nineteenth century was notorious as an age of political assassinations. This was partly because it followed a long period in which killings of rulers were very rare. Between 1672 and 1792, only one major figure may have been assassinated; in July 1762, Tsar Peter III died after being overthrown by disgruntled Guards officers, a striking example of autocracy being tempered by assassination.

From about 1880 to 1910, however, many countries were touched by the violence of ideological '-isms' that proved as lethal as the confessional furies of the early modern religious wars. The perpetrators had renounced religious faith, and many of them were self-professed atheists. This was also the 'classical' age of terrorism, eclipsing memories of the state terrorism unleashed in France between 1793 and 1794. But the focus here will be on political assassination, rather than a promiscuous desire to murder every representative of the bourgeoisie wherever they gathered.[1]

Three of these -isms, anarchism, nationalism and nihilism, account for the violent deaths of, among others, Tsar Alexander II of Russia in 1881, King Umberto I of Italy in 1900, President Sadi Carnot of France in 1894, the Republican US President William McKinley in 1901 and Russia's Prime Minister Pyotr Stolypin in 1911. Lesser casualties included Lord Henry Cavendish and Thomas Henry Burke, the second and third most powerful British officials in colonial Ireland, who were stabbed to death in Dublin in 1882. In Russia there were repeated attempts on the lives of successive tsars, which broadened into attacks on every category of government official, from prison officers and village policemen to Prime Ministers. Between October 1905 and September 1906 alone, 3,611 Tsarist government officials were assassinated. As many as 17,000 people may have been killed in the last two decades of the Tsarist autocracy.[2]

Paradoxically, reforming rulers and politicians were just as vulnerable as more hard-line figures; their deaths underlined the impersonality of the killers' objectives, which were directed at systems of rule rather than good or bad individual rulers. Cultural changes made assassination easier, as monarchs moved from guarded palaces to represent their respective nations. Rulers had to balance reduced security with the need for public visibility. The creation of a cultural space for the public, with exhibitions, opera houses and theatres open to all, made it easier to kill rulers, especially as newspapers often published their precise whereabouts. Fear of assassination became so pervasive that Crown Prince Friedrich Wilhelm of Prussia once told a minister that 'Whenever I get out of my coach, I wonder whether the shot will come from the right or the left.' Even Britain's Queen Victoria was subject to eight assassination attempts, a couple of which were potentially serious.[3]

It made little difference that some of the victims had no power themselves, since they embodied a hated idea. In 1898 Luigi Lucheni, an Italian anarchist who had hoped to kill the Duke of Orleans, alighted instead on Empress Elizabeth of Austria, the sixty-one-year-old wife of Franz Josef, after a Genevan newspaper revealed that she was travelling incognito in Switzerland.

As Elizabeth boarded a lakeside paddle steamer, Lucheni stabbed her in the heart with a sharpened file. She managed to stagger a hundred metres back to the ship, where she died. It did not matter to Lucheni that Elizabeth had spent her later years doing good works with the mentally ill, for he knew nothing about her as a person. 'It did not matter to me who the sovereign was whom I should kill . . . It was not a woman I struck, but an Empress; it was a crown that I had in view,' said the assassin. Coming as it did a few years after the suicide of his son and heir Archduke Rudolf, the assassination of Elizabeth was a hammer blow for the aged Habsburg emperor; it was not to be the last one.[4]

•

When the exiled Russian anarchist Prince Peter Kropotkin contributed the entry on 'Anarchism' to the *Encyclopaedia Britannica*, he omitted any reference to 'propaganda of the deed' which he himself had espoused. In 1879 he wrote in the Swiss anarchist paper he had founded: 'Permanent revolt by word of mouth, in writing, by the dagger, the rifle, dynamite . . . Everything is good for us which falls outside legality.' This was more than an oversight, since in 1879 his cousin Evgeny, the governor of Kharkov, had been assassinated by Grigory Goldenberg, a socialist revolutionary.[5]

Anarchism was the result of a schism in the International that came to a head between 1869 and 1871, involving the followers of Karl Marx and the devotees of Pierre-Joseph Proudhon and Mikhail Bakunin. It coincided with a final spasm of revolutionary violence during the 1871 Paris Commune, when the soldiers of the Third Republic massacred 25,000 people and arrested 40,000 more. Proudhon and Bakunin believed that only by rejecting all forms of control would humble people bring about their own social revolution. Since most of these people were illiterate, deeds spoke louder than printed words.[6]

In predominantly rural societies such as Italy, Russia or Spain, desperate peasants were prepared to take on authority. In its non-pacific forms, anarchism was dismissive of parliamentary politics, social meliorism and convoluted 'Germanic' theorizing. After acquiring international celebrity from long prison sentences, Bakunin dedicated his life in exile to causing destruction and chaos. Most of the conspiracies only existed in his fertile imagination, but one key relationship had consequences.

In 1869 Bakunin welcomed a young Russian revolutionary called Sergei Nechaev, a fugitive from Tsarist prisons, into his orbit. The pair were equally adroit at elaborating entirely imaginary conspiratorial networks. Bakunin made Nechaev Number

2771 in the Russian branch of an imaginary World Revolutionary Alliance, which had no other members.[7] Together they collaborated on such pamphlets as *Revolutionary Catechism* and *Principles of Revolution*. Nechaev had been influenced by the neo-Jacobin Pyotr Tkachev (1844–86) on the need for a puritanical revolutionary elite that would abandon notions of personal morality, law and 'sentimental' human relations.[8]

There was also a belief among them that violence was purifying and sacred: 'We recognize no other activity but the work of extermination, but we admit that the forms in which this activity will show itself will be extremely varied – poison, the knife, the rope etc. In this struggle, revolution sanctifies everything else.' It is to Bakunin's credit that he belatedly realized that Nechaev was not to be trusted.[9]

Nechaev was responsible for a single death. Having returned to Moscow in 1869, he strangled and shot a student member of his tiny group the Society of the Axe who he imagined was an informer. Trials of revolutionaries became occasions to publicly celebrate them; after being extradited from Switzerland, where he had sought refuge, Nechaev was lionized by Russian liberal opinion during his trial and his long years in the St Peter and Paul Fortress in St Petersburg. Clearly beguiling, he transformed his guards into admirers and managed to smuggle a letter to the woman who had masterminded the assassination of Tsar Alexander II in 1881.

Bakunin and Nechaev set in motion a particularly violent strain of anarchism, in which terror was used by those who sought vengeance for oppression, but also a means of bringing about wider upheaval. Both men idolized those who lived beyond the law, while anarchism in turn made it easy for criminals to justify their own sordid depredations.

The strange duo were not the sole propagators of anarchist violence; demented scribblers elsewhere contributed more straightforwardly psychotic renditions. There was Karl Heinzen, whose essay 'Murder and Liberty' elevated killing into the main force of history. Another was the German anarchist Johann Most, who was jailed in Britain for rejoicing in the death of Alexander II, and then emigrated to New York in 1882, having become hopeful about violent labour unrest in the US. Known to friends as 'Hans' and to critics as 'Dynamost', he dressed in a broad-brimmed black hat and red scarf and called for 'the death of a monarch a month'.

In the minds of the authorities of many countries, a murderous type of being was abroad, connected through unfathomably complex conspiracies. This was mostly fantasy, though as tiny groups of conspirators proliferated in dozens of countries, it is easy to see why some imagined that they were directed by a single controlling intelligence. The absurdity of this was satirized in G. K. Chesterton's *A Man Called Thursday*, in which a policeman hunts anarchists who turn out to be fellow policemen.[10] One result was that autocratic powers deployed secret policemen and spies in countries hosting anarchist, nihilist and nationalist exiles, though they had a professional interest in reporting criminal acts in the most hair-raising terms. The Anglo-Polish novelist Joseph Conrad (1857–1924) explained these sordid convolutions to incredulous Englishmen whose capital was a refuge for visiting foreign secret policemen and the resident terrorists they hunted.

In Italy and Spain, anarchist-inspired violence encompassed peasant insurgencies against oppressive landlords, which were met with military and police repression, and terrorist attacks on sites of aristocratic and bourgeois commerce or leisure, which also afflicted France. A cycle of attack and response ensued, followed by revenge attacks. Stock exchanges, restaurants and opera houses became sites of terror. In 1893, Santiago Salvador threw two bombs into the audience at Barcelona's Liceu Opera House as the second act of Rossini's *William Tell* began, killing twenty people and injuring many more. In the minds of terrorists, the targets were illimitable, though some more focused assassinations also caused 'collateral' casualties.

The fourth attempt to kill King Alfonso XIII of Spain, in 1906 during his wedding to Princess Victoria Eugenie of Battenberg, was a case in point. A young anarchist called Mateo Morral, the son of a wealthy textile industrialist, used his means to subsidize a variety of subversive groups. It is not known what prompted him to try to kill the King, who the year before had survived an attempted bombing of his coach after he returned from the opera. Morral rented a room in a hotel, insisting on a view of the street, and tossed a bouquet of flowers from his hotel balcony that landed next to the nuptial carriage and exploded. Though the newlyweds survived, fifteen spectators were killed, and fifty more were injured.

If the aim was to achieve notoriety and to inspire others to act, heads of state or government were optimal targets. In Italy, the monarchy held enormous symbolic importance in a super-ficially unified country. There were huge gulfs between north and south, rich and poor, and the educated and uneducated, with regional dialects adding to almost total incomprehension. It was important for the monarch to be seen by his new people.

Within a year of ascending the throne, King Umberto I was subject to an assassination attempt in Naples, during a visit with the Prime Minister Benedetto Cairoli. On 17 November 1878, a young anarchist called Giovanni Passannante attacked Umberto in his carriage, wounding his arm. When Cairoli tried to grab the attacker, he was stabbed in the leg. After Passannante was subdued, he was found to have a knife inscribed 'Death to the King! Long Life to the Universal Republic! Long Live Orsini!' After a brief trial, Passannante's death sentence was commuted to life imprisonment, which he served in a tiny cell below sea level, wearing chains that weighed 40lbs. He went mad and died in an asylum.[11]

Umberto was attacked again in April 1897, by an unem-ployed ironsmith. But it was the imposition of martial law following bread protests in Milan in 1898 that finally did for him; General Fiorenzo Bava Beccaris ordered troops to shoot at the demonstrators and the monarch was intimately associated with the armed forces. Estimates of fatalities ranged from 82 to 400, depending on who was counting. A Tuscan-born anarchist, Gaetano Bresci, who had emigrated to New Jersey, returned to his native country to kill Umberto in revenge for the massacre. He walked up to the King in Monza on 29 July 1900 and shot him four times with a revolver. Bresci was jailed for life and sent to Santo Stefano, the prison island in the Tyrrhenian Sea. He died less than a year later, either from murder or suicide.

As Bresci's story shows, anarchism thrived among European immigrants to the US in the late nineteenth century, though the movement also had many indigenous devotees. Labour relations in this era of predatory capitalism were extremely fraught, with more strikes and lockouts in 1880 alone than in the preceding hundred and forty years. Some strikes, such as that at the Carnegie Steel works in Homestead, Pennsylvania in 1892, developed into full-pitched battles between strikers, police and troops.[12]

One of those drawn to anarchism was the US-born son of Polish immigrants, Leon Czolgosz, who turned to anarchism when he lost his job in a steel-rolling mill during the 1893–97 credit panic. Czolgosz briefly met the anarchist intellectual Emma Goldman when she spoke at the Liberty Association in Cleveland, though his awkward manner led her comrade Abe Isaak, editor of the journal *Free Society*, to believe that he was a police plant.[13]

The twenty-eight-year-old Czolgosz was obsessed with Bresci's killing of King Umberto, and in the autumn of 1901 resolved to murder President William McKinley. Nine months into his second term, McKinley was an attractive and thoughtful figure, who had fought bravely as a major at the Battle of Antietam in the Civil War. He was conducting a national tour to encourage American exporters, after protective tariffs had led to a saturated domestic market, a policy that would lead him into war with imperial Spain and the US invasions of Cuba, Guam, Puerto Rico and the Philippines in 1898.

While sojourning in Chicago, Czolgosz read in a newspaper that the President planned to deliver a major speech at the Pan-American Exposition in Buffalo. On the day of his death, McKinley and his wife Ida visited Niagara Falls, before the President attended a reception in his honour at the fair's ornate Temple of Music. The idea was that visitors could shake his hand, while he stood before the Stars and Stripes and a display of potted plants.

McKinley was an expert hand-shaker; he would use one hand to close the person's fingers and the other to guide them away, thus managing to process fifty people every minute. While

Bach was played on an organ in the background, McKinley's modest security team did not pay much attention to a man who came up with his right hand wrapped in a white cloth.

As McKinley went to shake Czolgosz's left hand, he pulled the trigger of the .32 Iver Johnson revolver clutched beneath the cloth in his right. Two bullets hit McKinley in the abdomen. 'I did my duty,' said Czolgosz, as he fell to the floor under a flurry of blows from rifle butts. As McKinley was taken to hospital in an ambulance, he found a bullet in his clothing that had been deflected by a coat button. Although he seemed to be recovering during his last days in hospital, gangrene was spreading around a deep wound, and he died in the early hours of 14 September.

Czolgosz explained why he had acted: 'I don't believe in the republican form of government and I don't believe we should have any rulers. It is right to kill them. I fully understood what I was doing . . . I am willing to take the consequences.' He stood trial on 23 September,[14] and the jury took half an hour to convict. He went to the electric chair on 29 October, and his body was splashed with acid to hasten its decomposition before being buried in an unmarked grave inside Auburn Prison.

Vice President Theodore Roosevelt was sworn in on 14 September, and commenced his tail-end term by hitting anarchists hard. Although there was no evidence that Czolgosz had been part of any conspiracy, anti-anarchist legislation was introduced and several anarchists like Emma Goldman were briefly detained. Johann Most was pulled in because on the day of the murder he unwittingly used an 1849 article by Karl Heinzen titled 'Murder contra Murder' in his journal *Freiheit*. However, like Goldman, Most had nothing to do with the murder of McKinley. Although the anarchist scare abated within a few years, it flared up again after the Bolshevik revolution. In 1919 several anarchists were included among a cargo of 249 deportees on a ship known as the 'Red Ark'. Lenin would do this in reverse a few years later, with what became known as the 'Philosophy Steamer'.[15]

.

Assassinations by European or American anarchists were nothing compared to the violence that Nechaev's spiritual heirs unleashed in late-nineteenth-century Russia. But before considering terrorism, we should consider a much broader movement of Russian populism.

Between 1861 and 1864, populists formed a movement called Land and Freedom, based on the belief that because of the egalitarian nature of peasant communes, 'the basic character of the Russian people was socialistic'. This belief led in 1901 to the foundation of the Socialist Revolutionary Party. Unlike the Marxists, the Socialist Revolutionaries argued that Russia could miss out the capitalist phase of development, since the peasantry were already habituated to socialism.[16]

But this discovery by Russia's tiny number of educated and idealistic young people – there were three thousand university students in the entire country – often induced the disillusioning realization that patience was hopeless; the peasants were often barbarous, devious, anti-Semitic, superstitious and patriotic devotees of the Tsar.[17] They might accept ointments for their children's ailments from a populist medic, but they were not going to change their minds on fundamentals like their faith in a remotely benevolent tsar. Slowly, many revolutionaries lost faith in the utopian peasant.

An additional reason was that by the mid-1880s, Russia was embarking on rapid industrialization; factory workers were another pool for potential revolutionary activity, especially as they were ready to engage in strikes. This led to splits within the revolutionary movement between those focused on peasants or workers, those who regarded terrorism as the best means of overthrowing the autocracy and those who believed that larger socio-economic forces would play the essential role. This led to the foundation of revolutionary social democracy, in which Russians became part of a pan-European socialist movement of those who thought there was more mileage in terrorism. In addition to groups addicted to killing people, another halfway house was the Socialist Revolutionary Party. Unlike the Marxists, many of whom withdrew into exile, the Socialist Revolutionaries argued that terror was a useful destabilizing adjunct to the main matter of raising the revolutionary consciousness of Russia's workers. Of course, the boundaries between these groups were more fluid than Soviet historiography once maintained.[18]

Beyond these organizational developments, there was a hard core of people who readily thought that violence would collapse the regime and acted in a spirit of revolutionary vengeance against its more robust repressors. On the rebound from their unrequited love of the peasantry, the more implacable opponents of the Tsarist regime decided on violent action, in the hope that this would trigger fundamental progressive change. These tiny groups believed they were a vanguard whose spectacular deeds of violence would spark a general change in consciousness.[19]

When Land and Freedom was 'refounded' in 1876, it was as a tiny conspiratorial organization with two hundred adherents. Three years later it spawned a small group called People's Will, with thirty members at most, though it still had a grandiosely named Executive Committee.[20]

On acceding to the throne in 1855, Alexander II was widely admired as a reformer, but that changed when he adopted a harder line when his reforms fell short of expectations.[21] The essential problem was that while his reforms resulted in disillusionment, his repression was inefficient. Despite his pioneering legal reforms, he became the target of successive assassination attempts.[22]

Some radicals decided that the 'small deeds' of social improvement were inadequate to the task of transforming Russian society and that a decisive strike at the personification of autocracy would set in motion revolutionary change. In 1864 a few dozen disaffected youths formed The Organization. Two years later, its leader, Nikolai Ishutin, established a smaller group called Hell, dedicated to assassination, apparently after being inspired by John Wilkes Booth's murder of Lincoln. In April 1866, a member of the group called Dmitri Karakozov tried to shoot Tsar Alexander as he walked his hunting dog in St Petersburg's Summer Garden, but he was prevented by a loyal hatter's apprentice, who jogged his arm.[23] Alexander strode up to the captive assassin and asked, 'Who are you?' 'A Russian,' Karakozov replied. The hatter's apprentice was ennobled and given an estate where he lived for the next twenty-six years.[24]

On 26 August 1879, People's Will convened in a forest and formally decided to kill the Tsar. Although the group devoted enormous ingenuity to this task, they had virtually no followers and no idea what they would do when Alexander III succeeded the dead Alexander II. The gesture was all. One of Alexander II's achievements was the construction of thirteen thousand miles of new railway track, so the group chose to blow up the royal train when he returned from his 1879 summer sojourn at Livadia in Crimea. The assassins knew that he would have to travel either by ship to Odessa and then on by rail to St Petersburg, or all the way by rail from Simferopol, via Kharkov and Moscow. They also knew that he travelled in a three-train convoy, with one acting as an advance decoy and the other with baggage and entourage. He would be in the middle train.

Three teams of assassins went to extraordinary lengths to tunnel under the railway at three likely sites the Tsar would pass. The dedicated revolutionary Vera Figner managed to get a lowly confederate a job as a watchman on the railway line eight miles from Odessa. In the event, the Tsar did not take ship as the weather was rough and he was a fearful sailor. Her comrade Andrey Zhelyabov, posing as a northern merchant planning a tannery, rented a piece of land and buried two large bombs on the Zaporozhe stretch of the Simferopol–Moscow line. In the event, the explosives failed to detonate and the Tsar's train sped past.

A third team led by Alexander Mikhaylov spent weeks digging a fifty-yard tunnel from a small house near the railway entering the Moscow–Kursk Terminus. The excavated soil had to be stored in the small house, inside which sat a female revolutionary with a gun she could fire at a jar of nitroglycerine should the police burst in. Despite all the hard labour, the Tsar travelled in the first train; it hurtled past the bombers, who blew up the second train as planned. There was an explosion of viscous red liquid; the bomb had destroyed a carriage with a large consignment of jam for the imperial pastry chefs, which was attached to the train conveying Alexander's baggage and entourage.[25]

Four months later the People's Will tried again: Stephen

Khalturin, a carpenter, infiltrated the Winter Palace and assembled a massive bomb in his sleeping quarters. A skilled craftsman, he was the best kind of assassin – methodical, patient and meticulous in his work, though not without sudden eruptions of rage. On one occasion Khalturin found himself working in Alexander's study where he briefly pondered killing the Tsar with a hammer.[26]

Instead Khalturin focused on the fact that his own accommodation in the basement lay beneath a guardroom, above which was the Tsar's dining room. A powerful bomb would collapse these floors. At about 6 p.m. on 5 February 1880, Khalturin left an engagement party, returned to the palace and lit the fuse, before returning to the party. His bomb tore through the floor above, killing or maiming fifty members of the royal household but merely rocking the floor of the dining room above. The Tsar was not in the room; his guest Prince Alexander of Battenberg was late and he'd postponed the dinner until 6.30. Writing immediately after the bombing, Dariya Fedorovna Tyutcheva, lady-in-waiting to Empress Maria Alexandrovna, said: 'We are in great need of mercy, as we are being hunted like wild beasts. We do not know if we will wake up in this world or the next, where I hope there won't be any of these socialists.'[27]

Alexander never slept in the same bed for more than one night, not least because his mistress and illegitimate family lived in another part of the palace so he crept about a lot. When he ventured out, accompanied by uniformed Cossacks, he scanned faces in the crowd for suspected terrorists whose mugshots were listed in a book. However, on one day a week his movements were predictable; every Sunday morning he inspected troops at a military parade ground before returning to the Winter Palace, though he was careful to vary his return route.

The final plan, devised by Andrey Zhelyabov and Vera Figner, involved renting a ground-floor shop on St Petersburg's Little Garden Street, along which the Tsar would be driven to inspect his troops. A fifteen-foot-long tunnel from the shop would reach under the street and house a mine. Though the shop displayed cheese, the cheese barrels in the back were filled with earth excavated from the tunnel. In case Alexander took a different route, four men lurked in the street with homemade grenades. These weighed about five pounds each and had a blast radius of a yard.

The attack occurred in the early afternoon. One bomb hit the sleigh carrying the Tsar's bodyguards. This caused the Tsar to stop to see to the injured. A second assassin detonated another grenade between himself and the Tsar, whose lower torso and legs were mangled by the blast. Alexander died of blood loss shortly before 4 p.m., a couple of hours before he was due to issue major constitutional reforms, and in the same room where he had signed the Emancipation Edict of the Russian serfs in 1861. Five of the assassins were hanged – one the first woman to be executed in Russia. On the site where Alexander bled out into the snow, his son and heir began work on the Church of the Resurrection of Christ, which was completed in 1907.

Tsar Alexander III (1881–94) proved to be a more Victorian version of his louche father, but though he tried to repress revolutionaries, he was powerless to prevent the forces unleashed by industrialization from clashing with an unreformed political structure.[28] It was surely telling that the man appointed to supress revolutionaries, the Interior Minister Count Dmitri Tolstoy, could not go out for a walk, kept a loaded pistol at all times, and made his summer house blast-proof. Special guards were present on every train journey, and he fixated on such strange plots as his bodyguards being stupefied with drugged cigarettes to allow an assassin a clear run at him. Alexander also avoided appearing in public, cancelled balls and dinners, and ceased to ride a horse.[29]

Arguably, the most eventful assassination bid against Alexander III was one that did not succeed. On 1 March 1887, the police foiled a bomb plot on the streets of St Petersburg. After two bombers were caught red-handed it transpired that fifty people were involved. Most of them were teachers and students; Alexander wrote 'Education to be abolished!' shortly afterwards, though he only banned the education of 'dependants', the children of servants and the like.[30]

The plotters included not only Aleksandr Ilyich Ulyianov,

the twenty-year-old brother of Vladimir Lenin, but the brothers Bronisław and Józef Piłsudski, the future architects of independent Poland. The group acquired explosives and then made them into viable bombs, a task that devolved on Ulyianov, the only scientist among them. While awaiting the Tsar on Nevski Prospekt, they were seized by the police. Ulyianov took the leading oratorical role at the trial, and was hanged with four others; Bronisław Piłsudski was sentenced to twenty years' hard labour and Józef was despatched to Siberia. Shards of ice closed over the heart of Ulyanov's younger brother, already grieving for his father who died aged fifty-three the same year; that damaged sixteen-year-old boy would tear down not just the monarchy but Russian society as a whole.[31]

Other than of Alexander II, the most eventful assassination in Russia was the killing of Prime Minister Pyotr Stolypin in 1911. Stolypin came from a noble family, and married into an even more illustrious one; he moved effortlessly from governorships in Grodno and Saratov to Interior Minister and then, after only a few months in June 1906, to become Russia's third Prime Minister.

Within a month of his appointment, assassins from the Social Revolutionary Party struck. Founded in 1901, it had an exiled Central Committee with local committees around the country, as well as a secretive Combat Organization for killing Tsarist officials and to hang its own traitors and informers. It killed the nation's Interior Minister in 1902 and the Governor General of Ufa a year later. In July 1904 the party killed the new Interior Minister Vyacheslav von Plehve by throwing a bomb under his carriage. Neither the carriage's armour nor a squad of detectives on bicycles were any help.

Stolypin was a workaholic and was spending a rare weekend off at his dacha, combining paperwork with receiving petitioners. Three men entered, two of them in army uniform and holding briefcases. When guards became suspicious, this trio of Socialist Revolutionary assassins threw their cases, which exploded, demolishing the entire wooden facade of the house. The assassins died, along with twenty-seven others, while seventy people were injured, including Stolypin's fifteen-year-old daughter and his three-year-old son. Though the bombs exploded in the entrance hall, the top of Stolypin's desk was hurled thirty feet by the blast and he was wounded in the neck by a flying inkwell. Thereafter, he and his family lived in the Winter Palace rather than the official residence.

This murderous assault on Stolypin resulted in demented vengeful clamour from the more reactionary elements of Russian society who saw two stark alternatives: 'ruin or a dictatorship'. Many of them also detected Jews behind every bomb and bullet, claiming that 'in all the bloody events of recent years the instigators, organizers, and executors are more often than not Jews'.[32] That was not true, though 15 per cent of the Socialist Revolutionaries were of Jewish heritage, as were most Russian anarchists. One immediate result of the attack was a law that introduced small military tribunals to dispose of suspects, from trial to execution, inside four days. In the eight months before the law was rescinded, 1,102 people were executed; in the previous eighty years an average of nine people were executed per year. The expression 'Stolypin's neckties' in reference to hangman's nooses became common among revolutionaries, and sealed his fate.[33]

Though a conservative and nationalist, and a man of deep religious faith, Stolypin did not share the obsession with Jews and dedicated his five years as Prime Minister to preserving the autocratic empire and its Orthodox religion through careful reforms. The insoluble conundrum was how to balance a weak but autocratic ruler, Nicholas II, and the parliamentary arrangements introduced after 1905. When he adjusted the electoral system to minimize the number of liberals and socialists, he would add to the number of reactionaries who opposed his reforms. Stolypin's reforms included the privatization of peasant communes and a temperate foreign policy, since he thought war would ruin the empire. He also sought to 'adjust' the electoral franchise, so as to check liberals while filling the Duma with loyalist placemen. One minor success for Stolypin was the expulsion from court of the monkish intriguer Rasputin, who would eventually be assassinated in turn by right-wing fanatics.

A senior police director, sacked for failing to prevent the

assassination of the Tsar's uncle, revealed the extent of police collusion with the leader of the socialist Revolutionary Combat Organization. Evno Azef was a young Jew from Rostov-on-Don, who after fleeing Russia with the proceeds of fraud, studied engineering in Karlsruhe and Darmstadt. But from 1893 he was also a secret police spy reporting on Russian students, having volunteered his services in return for a monthly stipend and New Year bonuses.

Returned to Russia at police insistence in 1899, Azef rose through the ranks of the clandestine terror organization of the Socialist Revolutionaries, which enabled him to dip deeply into their secret funds. Despite providing warnings of an imminent attack on Plehve, the Interior Minister was killed. Ironically, Azef encouraged his comrades to think he had masterminded the attack, in order to allay their suspicions about his extra-curricular sources of income. A year later, Socialist Revolutionary assassins blew up the arch-reactionary Grand Duke Sergei Aleksandrovich on a Moscow street. There was so little of him left intact that a jester kicked something wet and quipped, 'Brothers, and they said he had no brains.'[34]

But after fifteen years as an agent provocateur, Azef's luck was out. One of the SR's more suspicious associates alighted on a disgruntled former director of Tsarist police and kidnapped the man's teenage daughter to force him to reveal Azef's under-cover role. In the ensuing scandal, it transpired that Stolypin himself was fully aware of Azef's dual role, which damaged both him and the image of the security forces. As for Azef, he abandoned his wife and two children in favour of his German mistress, the singer Hedwig Klöpfer, with whom he would establish a business making smaller corsets for emaciated wartime women. He died in 1918, with Hedy the sole mourner.[35]

Though the Socialist Revolutionaries abandoned terrorism in the wake of the Azef fiasco, the message did not reach all their supporters and the local committees killed with gusto. By the last year of his life, Stolypin's relations with the Tsar were strained and his reforms were blocked in a Duma that he ceased to be able to control. He suffered from liver and heart disease and was deeply weary.

In August 1911, he accompanied Nicholas II to Kiev to underline Ukraine's Russian identity. Under the direction of a senior police official, detectives closely inspected three hundred buildings. But while the Tsar was tightly protected, no such arrangements were made for the Prime Minister. On 1 September the two men attended a performance of Rimsky-Korsakov's *The Tale of the Tsar Sultan* at the opera house. During the interval, all eyes were focused on the royal box, while Stolypin stood in the front stalls chatting, with his back to the orchestra pit. A young man in evening dress walked towards him and shot him twice, once in the hand and then in the chest. The wounded man made the sign of the cross as he looked to the empty royal box and died four days later, of damage to his liver.

Thousands of Jews streamed out of Kiev as rumours spread that the assassin Dmitri Bogrov was a Jew, though in reality he was an atheist whose grandfather had converted to Christianity. Born in 1887 to a wealthy lawyer, Bogrov dropped out of law school and in 1905 became a Socialist Revolutionary, before turning to anarchism. A gambling addict, he became an agent for the secret police, which paid him a monthly retainer. After three years abroad reporting on radicals, Bogrov re-enrolled at Kiev University, before moving to the capital to work for a liberal law firm. Guilt about his informing may have led him to seek licence to kill Stolypin. When he returned to Russia from France, where he had received treatment for a nervous breakdown, an anarchist told him he was being suspected to be a police informer, intelligence he may have sought to expiate through killing Stolypin.

Bogrov brazenly decided to use the Okhrana in his plot. He invented a pair of husband-and-wife assassins who were coming to Kiev to kill the Prime Minister, tantalizing the police with the suggestion that they might capture them in the act, but only if he was used to entrap them. A gullible police chief volunteered a ticket to enable him to identify the assassins in the Kiev opera house. When Bogrov said the visiting pair had been to his apartment and shown him their guns, the police did not wonder how they evaded a tight perimeter of agents watching the building. With his own police escort trailing behind him, an armed Bogrov entered the opera house – alone – and walked down the stairs to shoot Stolypin.

Given the catastrophic failures of the police, it was not surprising that Bogrov's trial lasted just three hours and that he was hanged on 11 September. Although exhaustive investigations sought to discover a wider conspiracy, there was none; as Bogrov explained, he had acted 'without criminal intent and [that it was] even a surprise to me'. Like most of official Russia, the Okhrana also knew that Stolypin was politically finished and that Nicholas wanted to replace him with someone less competent who would change nothing. The sudden termination of Stolypin's failed attempt to revitalize the Russian autocracy signified the end of the peaceful evolution of that system, making his assassination truly consequential. Furthermore, terror was only one of several forces which rocked the Tsarist edifice to its core; the stresses of war on its creaking system were far more important.

•

In the Balkans, national liberation struggles occurred from the early nineteenth to the twentieth centuries and increasingly involved Great Power rivalry. The main players were Ottoman Turkey, which after capturing Constantinople in 1453 had assumed the regional role of the Byzantine Empire, and the Habsburgs and Romanovs, who wished to introduce Christian imperial rule. Neither had much time for the locals, who one Austrian Foreign Minister compared to 'wild Indians who could only be treated like unbroken horses, to whom corn is offered with one hand while they are threatened with the whip by the other'.[36]

The rivalry of Habsburg Austria-Hungary and Tsarist Russia was muted by Bismarck's Germany, and a three-way imperial alliance prevented a handful of independent Balkan states from wagging the tails of the big dogs. When Russia briefly engineered an independent Bulgaria through the Treaty of San Stefano, the other powers swiftly gathered at the Congress of Berlin in 1878 quickly diminished it.

While as late as 1897 Austria-Hungary and Russia could

agree to mute their Balkan rivalries, this changed after 1905. A number of fragile states ruled by rent-a-monarchs from Germany had come into existence, many with irredentist claims against their neighbours. The external catalyst for the first of two Balkan Wars was Italy's 1911 invasion of Ottoman Libya, a faraway conflict that gave anyone seeking to liquidate the centuries-long Ottoman presence in the Balkans an opportunity. It did not take long for the victors to fall out over the local spoils.[37]

The ambitions of Serbia reminded Austria-Hungary of Piedmont and Prussia, the states that had extruded the Habsburgs from Italy and Germany. More so after 1912 when it doubled its size and added a further 1.5 million people to its 2.9 million inhabitants. On the surface, Serbia looked respectable enough, with civilized ministers, civil servants, elections and a parliament called the Skrupstina. A press with 124 newspapers was relatively free, which would be a problem since the gutter end of it was rabidly nationalist. Serbia was effectively a state with dual controllers: a regular civilian government and a parallel military with some of it connected to irregular and terrorist forces via its military intelligence outfit.

The national mind is worth considering too. The remote past and present were fused into a timeless continuum as they were in many countries at the time. In the early fourteenth century Serbia had become a potent state under Emperor Stefan Dušan. Its decline and eventual extinction began with the Battle of Kosovo on 28 June 1389 against the advancing Ottoman Turks. After massive commemorations of the battle on its five hundredth anniversary in 1889, Serbia instituted an annual Vidovdan festival, which happened, in 1914, to coincide with Franz Ferdinand's visit to Sarajevo.

One mitigating occurrence during the original defeat would pass into Serb national legend. At the height of the Battle of Kosovo a knightly Serb defector, Miloš Obilić, gained access to Sultan Murad I and killed him with a dagger, only to be hacked to pieces by the Sultan's guards. Serbs have long memories and their assassins became national heroes.

After centuries of Ottoman rule, a semi-independent Serbian principality emerged in the early 1800s. Its independence was recognized by the great powers at the 1878 Congress of Berlin, long before they divided into exclusive alliance blocs. The same conference also allowed Austria-Hungary to occupy Bosnia-Herzegovina, home to many ethnic Serbs, without formally annexing it to the Habsburg empire. It was placed under the joint finance ministry in Vienna.

In 1882 Serbia became an independent kingdom, ruled by the Obrenović dynasty. Their brief span was terminated in May 1903, when nationalist officers led by a charismatic staff officer, Captain Dragutin Dimitrijević – nicknamed 'Apis' – took exception to King Alexander's marriage to Queen Draga, an older divorcee whose physical charms were well known to many in Belgrade.

Apis recruited about a hundred officers to the coup, binding them together with an oath. On 3 May, twenty-eight of them plunged the royal palace into darkness and made their way past guards to the royal bedroom. It was empty, but the beds were warm. In the confusion, Apis was shot three times in a basement tunnel. After several hours, a royal aide was forced to reveal the King and Queen's hiding place, a seamstress's cubbyhole off their bedroom. The King was shot thirty-five times, while the queen was hit with eighteen bullets. Their corpses were stripped, mutilated with sabres and defenestrated. Beyond installing the exiled Peter Karadjordjević on the vacant throne, these simple soldiers had few political ideas. It said something about Serbia that one of the assassins went about for many years with one of the desiccated breasts of the queen as a souvenir in his wallet.[38]

Regardless of the official postures of the Serbian government, nationalism represented a threat both to the remaining Ottoman presence in the Balkans and to the Austro-Hungarian monarchy. The formal annexation of Bosnia-Herzegovina by Austria-Hungary in 1908 saw a further escalation of Serb nationalist clamour, while support for Vienna from Germany meant a loss of face for Russia. Serbia may have eventually accepted the fait accompli, but nationalists were incensed. Narodna Obdrana or 'National Defence' had attracted many youthful recruits, as did Mlada Bosna or 'Young Bosnia' in the annexed province.

While Serbian army intelligence took to despatching guerrilla bands into Turkish-controlled Macedonia, with a Bosnian Serb Lieutenant Vojislav Tanković training them in irregular military tactics, Apis returned to a desk job, but this did not moderate a man described as being 'without compass or control'. He helped create a secret organization called 'Unification or Death', known colloquially as the 'Black Hand' or Crna Ruka, that was responsible for Serb external subversion. Apis drew up the organization's oath, and a symbol consisting of a skull, bomb, knife and poison. Its members and supporters reached into the heights of the army and Serbian polite society. The heir to the throne of King Peter, Crown Prince Alexander, subsidized the Black Hand journal *Pijemont*, another clear sign that Serb nationalists were bent on their own Balkan Risorgimento, for modern and industrial Piedmont had been the driving force behind Italian unification.[39]

Austria-Hungary regarded Serbia as a regional menace that represented an existential threat to the Dual Monarchy. In the space of a few years and two defeats in war, the empire had lost Germany to dynamic and warlike Prussia and most of Italy to Piedmont. When Austria annexed Bosnia-Herzegovina, it left absentee Muslim feudal lords to exact a range of pre-modern levies. In addition to peasant revolts, the rapid growth of industrial towns saw the first stirrings of socialist protests, which were ruthlessly repressed.

The variety of these Balkan peoples suggested one possible solution to some Austrians. Reformers suggested converting two ruling centres (Vienna and Budapest) into three, with a South Slav kingdom based on Croatian Catholic Zagreb. While something so bold did not appeal to the octogenarian Austrian emperor Franz Josef, it captured the imagination of the emperor's nephew and newly designated heir Franz Ferdinand, before his dilettante enthusiasm temporarily turned to the idea of a federated United States of Austria.

Franz Ferdinand was a hot-tempered anti-Semite and a fervent Catholic. Like many royals he had no real job, beyond a swift succession of military titles that took him from lieutenant to field marshal. His main passion was game shooting, with 274,889 meticulously recorded kills, though he was genuinely fond of his wife Sophie and children too. He had a foul temper, on one occasion nearly strangling a disobedient servant. In 1913 he was appointed Inspector General of the Armed Forces.

Since the Austrian occupation, the physical appearance of Bosnia's towns had rapidly changed, notably in the modest capital Sarajevo, with imperial barracks, official buildings and multiplying Catholic churches amidst the minarets and Orthodox onion domes. Religion was one way of exacerbating divisions. Even when Bosnia got its own parliament in 1910, means were found to minimize the electoral weight of the majority Serb population. The Austrian German population rose from 16,275 in 1886 to 108,000 by 1910. Bosnian Serb nationalists hated these people, and in particular the gruff military governors sent to rule over them, none of whom were known for their tact.[40]

Russia had a better class of educated revolutionary than Bosnia, where the revolutionaries were peasants. Hatred burned among the demi-educated in a society that was 80 per cent illiterate. Teenage schoolboys had one foot in the world of books and ill-digested ideas in the small towns where they attended primary and secondary schools but were only a short hop from modest village hovels, to which they returned when the harvest was due.

Every nationalist movement needs martyrs. In June 1910, one of these Serb youths, a law-school dropout called Bogdan Žerajić, fired five times at Governor Marijan Varešanin as his coach travelled across Emperor's Bridge in Sarajevo. Žerajić was a terrible shot, so five bullets cracked past the general. With his last bullet the assassin shot himself in the head to avoid capture. A couple of weeks before his death, Žerajić had cried off shooting the elderly Emperor Franz Josef, who was visiting Bosnia.

Žerajić's example – and his maxim, 'He who wants to live, let him die. He who wants to die, let him live' – motivated three youths who paid a visit to his grave on the evening of 27 June 1914. One of them was Gavrilo Princip, who the following morning would shoot dead Archduke Franz Ferdinand and his wife Sophie, Duchess of Hohenberg.[41]

Since that event would indirectly trigger the escalation from a local war between Austria-Hungary and Serbia to one involving

France, Russia, Germany and the British Empire, one could argue that these assassinations caused one of the greatest cataclysms in modern history. We do not need to explain the wider causes of these interlocking conflicts here, but we do need to look closely at the assassination.

In 1913 Apis was appointed head of Serbian military intelligence, inside the General Staff's headquarters in the Kalemegdan Fortress on the Danubian frontier. He gradually turned to fat, beneath his huge 'Mongolian' shaved head. Franz Ferdinand and Sophie were due in Bosnia to inspect Austrian troops stationed there. Since the Serbs regarded him as head of a putative war party, Apis's agents in Bosnia reported that the ensuing Eastern Manoeuvres might develop into a first strike, but they were wrong; Franz Ferdinand had vehemently opposed the annexation of Bosnia, and by then his thoughts had evolved from a South Slav pillar of the empire to a more grandiose Austrian-dominated federation.[42]

The royal inspection tour was a long one since the new Governor of Bosnia-Herzegovina, Oskar Potiorek, wanted maximum 'face time' with the archduke to engineer his promotion to commander-in-chief of the army. The royal visit was announced in the press in March 1914, one of the first things to doom the royal couple, but neither the military nor the municipal police decided who was in charge of security arrangements. The trip to Bosnia was a stately affair, by car, rail and warship to Dalmatia. En route, Franz Ferdinand added one final creature to his grim lifetime tally when a cat he spied in a woodland meadow fell victim to this crack shot. The drive into Sarajevo after the military inspections was to show the flag, with tours of a carpet works and an orphanage laid on for Sophie. They were such eager shoppers that they visited the city at night before their official entrance. It was the anniversary of the Battle of Kosovo, though few had noticed in Vienna, which might have been why Franz Ferdinand wore seven amulets on a chain beneath his shirt, while Sophie had a scapular and holy relics under her dress. There is some speculation that he might have possessed the latest silk-based body armour, but it would have been uncomfortable under a thick uniform on a summer's

day. Besides, it had a crew neck and would not have stopped a
bullet at collar height.[43]

The royal couple's formal entrance into Sarajevo had been
poorly planned as well as well-publicized – there were 170 police
on duty but no detectives offering close protection. They were
very visible in a black open-topped military touring car that
drove along the Appel Quay running along the Miljacka River,
past thin crowds and in bright sunshine. Franz Ferdinand wore
the turquoise uniform of a cavalry general, with ostrich plumes
on his hat. His wife sat next to him in white. The cars moved
too fast for the first killer stationed along this 'avenue of assassins', a twenty-seven-year-old Serbian Muslim carpenter named
Mehmed Mehmedbašić, who had a policeman standing next to
him.

As the Archduke took in the buildings, river and crowd, he
spotted a bomb flying towards the Graef und Stift touring car's
folded roof behind his head and bouncing off. The car continued
moving while the bomb exploded under the front of the following
vehicle, injuring two lieutenant colonels. A shrapnel fragment
also grazed Sophie's neck. The would-be assassin Nedeljko
Čabrinović ran from the embankment and emptied a dose of
cyanide into his mouth, before being caught limping along the
river shore.

After inspecting the wounded, Franz Ferdinand insisted on
continuing the official tour. As the lord mayor began his welcome
address, Franz Ferdinand exploded, 'What is the good of your
speeches? I come to Sarajevo on a friendly visit and someone
throws a bomb at me. This is outrageous!' The notes for his
reply were eventually found splashed with the wet blood of the
two colonels. He bravely gave his speech and decided to continue
the tour, with the minor precaution of changing the route.
Unfortunately, this was not communicated to the drivers, with
the result that the first two cars stalled as they turned.

The stalled cars presented a clear shot to the repositioned
Gavrilo Princip, standing about six feet from the royal pair with
his Browning 9mm automatic. Neither victim seemed to notice
they had been shot – Sophie in her abdomen, and Franz
Ferdinand through the right jugular vein, with the bullet lodging

in his spine. With Sophie's head slumped into his knees, Franz Ferdinand kept muttering, 'It is nothing,' as his mouth filled with blood. They were both dead by the time the car had raced back to the governor's residence.

Two of the killers, Princip and Čabrinović, were arrested on the spot, appearing before the investigating magistrate Leo Pfeffer almost immediately, and even as angry Austrians began to loot Serb businesses. Pfeffer was an expert in press censorship rather than murder, which is how the young assassins managed to obfuscate a deeper conspiracy that reached back to Serbia.

Princip was a slight youth from a peasant clan in the mountains, born on 13 July 1894. His father combined subsistence farming with the job of postman. Destined for a military school in Sarajevo, the shopkeeper from whom he was bought his first underpants and shirt suggested the Merchant School instead. Princip developed a distaste for commercial studies, trying and failing to be admitted to a grammar school in Belgrade. He moved between temporary lodgings, before being caught up in the ferment before the Balkan War against the Turks in 1912.

Like other Serb nationalists, Princip's adolescent mind wrestled with the question of whether patient, cultural gradualism would be more effective in achieving national liberation than spectacular acts of violence. Would it be best to unite all South Slavs, regardless of ethnicity or religion, into a 'Yugoslavia' rather than to incorporate them into a greater Serbia? By 1912 Princip was actively taking part in student demonstrations. A school friend recalled him using a knuckleduster to persuade contemporaries to take part.[44]

The idea of killing Franz Ferdinand came first to Princip, who then met Nedeljko Čabrinović, a nineteen-year-old typesetter, in a Belgrade cafe and invited him to join his plot. Princip then added Trifko Grabež, the nineteen-year-old son of an Orthodox priest, who had been a roommate. A fourth Bosnian Serb youth, twenty-six-year-old Milan Ciganović, came to mind as arms supplier – when Princip lodged with him in 1912, he was shown a box containing bombs. Princip did not realize that Ciganović, who worked for the state railways, was a double agent.

Another friend of Ciganović was Dujro Sarac, founder of a secret society called 'Death or Life' in April 1914. Ciganović and Princip joined too, partly because Unification or Death did not admit minors. Though Tanković was sceptical when Ciganović asked him, he agreed to supply them with weapons from the small arsenal he used to arm his guerrillas in Bosnia and Macedonia. He gave Ciganović four Browning FN automatic pistols, each with a magazine clip of six bullets, and six throwable bombs which look like tin cans in the museum. Meanwhile, Princip wrote in code to his old friend Danilo Ilić, a young schoolteacher, inducting him into the plot. Ilić would recruit a second team of assassins in Sarajevo itself.

Equipped with a budget of 130 dinars, the Belgrade team practised shooting in Kosutnak Park, using an oak tree as target. The Browning automatics had a short 3.5-inch barrel and were gas self-sealed, which meant that they could shoot faster than a revolver. Reloading meant replacing the ammunition clip in the butt, rather than fumbling with trembling fingers to insert individual bullets into separate chambers.

Having despatched arms, guerrillas and spies into Bosnia, Tanković was well placed to suggest a route for the 200-mile journey from Belgrade to Sarajevo. It helped that Major Ljubomir Vulović, commander of the entire Serbian frontier guards, was a member of Unification or Death – a chain of Serb intelligence officers within the border guard enabled the party to cross the border. While these Serbs were undoubtedly engaged in sponsoring subversion, it is unlikely that they knew that these youths were about to shoot the archduke.

The assassins reached Tuzla, where they secreted their bombs and guns with a rich businessman, who agreed to relay them to a stranger after he had been shown a particular brand of cigarette. The trio took the train to Sarajevo on 4 June. Princip lodged with Danilo Ilić and his mother, dutifully registering with the local police.

Ilić had also recruited his second team of killers: Mehmed Mehmedbašić, a seventeen-year-old, Vaso Čubrilović, and sixteen-year-old Cvetko Popović. Ilić retrieved the bombs and guns from the businessman in Tuzla before joining the two teams of three youths, so there were seven assassins placed at intervals along the Appel Quay on 28 June 1914. Helpfully, the *Bosnische Post* had published the exact route that the Archduke would take in and out of Sarajevo two days earlier.

The assassins spent the weeks before the assassination in a daze, as they arranged their final dispositions. One way or another they were going to die, since they each had small packages containing cyanide. They picked up their weapons in a cake shop or in Ilić's home, and then spent nearly two hours pacing the Appel Quay.

That was a basic flaw in the plot: the royal vehicles sped past before Mehmedbašić, the oldest assassin, could react. Čubrilović did not shoot either, allegedly because he felt sorry for Duchess Sophie. Popović was too near-sighted to see which car contained the target. Only Čubrilović hurled his bomb. Princip was too slow to shoot Franz Ferdinand on the first pass, but he knew the route the royal party would take when it left the town hall so changed his position.

Initially Princip and Čubrilović maintained to Pfeffer that they had acted alone and without mutual knowledge of each other, which was untrue. Pressure to tell the truth was added when the police rounded up two hundred Bosnian Serbs and left them in the hot sun of the prison courtyard where gallows were being hammered together to hang the peasant confederates. Pfeffer found Danilo Ilić's address in Princip's registration papers and he was arrested by the afternoon. Within a few days, all the assassins were captured, apart from one; Mehmedbašić escaped to Montenegro, probably because a mature Muslim man in a fez was not who the police were seeking.

The trial lasted from 12 October to 23 October, long after Austria-Hungary had invaded Serbia, only to suffer a crushing defeat. Grabež's lawyer uttered just fifty-six words throughout the proceedings; most of the exchanges in the transcripts involved establishing the modus operandi and the rights and wrongs of tyrannicide and the South Slav cause. Though there was evidence of the involvement of Serb army intelligence, the prosecution preferred to blame a more nebulous Serb nationalism. In his final address, Princip was keen to emphasize his own agency:

'As far as suggestions are concerned that somebody talked us into committing the assassination, that is not true. The idea for the assassination grew among us, and we realized it. We loved our people. In my own defence I have nothing to say.'

Of the twenty-four accused, nine were acquitted. Being underage, Princip, Cabrinović and Grabež were sentenced to twenty years' hard labour, with a day in a darkened cell every 28 June, the anniversary of the assassination. Princip was lucky to escape the noose after his actual birthdate was discovered by his lawyer, which corrected an official one that made him twenty and within the parameters for hanging. Five of the older assassins were sentenced to die, including Ilić and Čubrilović. Several of the peasant helpers and the Tuzla businessman were hanged, too. Princip would die of tuberculosis in the military jail at Theresienstadt in April 1918.

There was a strange coda. In 1917, Apis, Major Ljubomir Vulović and their intelligence agent Rade Malobabić were arrested and tried by the exiled Serbian regime over bogus charges concerning a plot to murder Prince Regent Alexander and the veteran Prime Minister, Pasić. The three were sentenced to death by firing squad, which was carried out before dawn in a remote quarry. However, the proscribed formalities were so protracted that the chain-smoking Apis stood surrounded by hundreds of cigarette butts by the time he was blindfolded and tied to a post in his grave.

Organized Serbian nationalism took many shapes, which all shared the same goals but differed over tactics. But there was also an uneasy relationship between the civilian government and praetorian patriots like Colonel Apis, who effectively controlled the frontiers with Austria. When the assassins struck, Serbia had multiple distractions. On 24 June the old king had stepped down in favour of Alexander. Serbia was also holding parliamentary elections, which meant that the Prime Minister was out campaigning. The state was also busy assimilating new peoples and territory, after doubling its size in the wake of the Balkan Wars. Eighty per cent of its armed forces were stationed in the south and not around Belgrade, which was where any Austro-Hungarian retaliatory strike would occur.

Pasić had got wind of a plot by May or early June. He knew that armed men were being slipped across the border, and that this would bring dangers to Serbia. However, when he told the civilian officials to prevent these 'crossings', they were ignored by military personnel answerable to Apis, Vulović and Tanković. He also sent a telegram warning of dangers awaiting the Archduke in Sarajevo to Serbia's mission in Vienna, but it never reached the ears of Austria's Foreign Minister, Count Berchtold.

Apis seems to have developed doubts after the central committee of Unification or Death resoundingly rejected his plan to arm a group of young Bosnians to assassinate Franz Ferdinand. If he belatedly tried to call off the dogs, it did not work. Maybe he thought they were too inexperienced to succeed, or perhaps he decided to replace them with more experienced former guerrillas? We will never know the definitive answer, since at his trial for treason, his chief line of defence was to exaggerate his own role in the assassination of Franz Ferdinand to underline his Serbian patriotic credentials.[45]

When Emperor Franz Joseph learned of the killing of his heir, he allegedly said he was relieved that the stain on his dynasty, meaning his nephew's bad marriage to Sophie, had been removed. Their burial was a private affair, with no European royals invited. Many Austrians were also relieved at the demise of 'a short-tempered and basically cruel pair of people'. But the Austro-Hungarians wanted vengeance and the Emperor was resolved on war against Serbia. For these reasons the two key demands that the Serbs could never accept in Austria-Hungary's ultimatum of 23 July 1914 (clauses 5 and 6) were to allow the Austrians to investigate the murder of the Archduke and Duchess and to 'collaborate in suppressing this subversive movement'. Berchtold spent a sleepless night redrafting the ultimatum so that the Serbs could never accept it.[46]

A Belgrade government which had practised subversion in Austria-Hungary and the Ottoman Empire strenuously insisted on its sovereignty, even as Pasić sought to offer concessions that he hoped would buy time to enable the great powers to persuade Vienna not to go to war. But he could not concede on clauses

5 and 6 because of the self-righteousness in Serbia's tabloid press and from the political opposition.[47]

Though Austria-Hungary was right to go through the motions so as to establish moral superiority, Vienna had long resolved to crush the Serbs and Berlin was right behind them, even if this was to risk a general European war with France and Russia. The Austrian ultimatum also gave France and Russia time to establish that they would jointly attack Germany as well as Austria in the event of war. In reality, Austria-Hungary might have immediately invaded Serbia, whose capital was a mere two miles over the border, with a general abhorrence of regicide and their claims to victimhood giving Vienna the necessary cover.

At first, news of the assassination was accepted with indifference or relief. In the event, though Princip did not trigger the First World War, the assassinations in Sarajevo were a moral convenience that lit a general conflagration which some of those involved did not sleepwalk into. The lapse of time was diminishing their perceived range of alternatives to risking everything on one giant gamble. If Germany did not strike now, its enemies would. Had Franz Ferdinand survived, he was expected to introduce reforms that would probably have brought about a war too. Next we will pass on to the assassinations of the age of dictators following the Great War, considering the assassinations they commissioned as well as attempts to kill them. These were not terrorists but rather secret policemen deliberately unleashed.

4

The Artist, the Carpenter and the Costa Rican: Assassination in the Age of Mussolini, Hitler and Stalin

The localized carnage of the Balkan Wars in 1912 and 1913 prefigured many aspects of the Great War that followed the assassination of Archduke Franz Ferdinand. On a smaller scale than the Great War which followed, total war was waged between nations, societies and 'civilizations', whose minor differences were deliberately accentuated.

When animals fight, they are said to have a 'braking mechanism' to ensure the survival of the species. After 1918, many countries did not return to pre-war peace, but saw vicious civil wars in which it was a fight to the death. Unhitched from any residual restraints and exacerbated by more local tribal animosities, this would entail another four million dead (on top of 10 million war dead in 1914–18) alongside the victims of the global flu pandemic which ravaged societies after the war was over.[1]

If the power of the state had curbed such violence before 1914, afterwards the failure or weakness of many states allowed forces to be unleashed in guises transformed by war – uniformed paramilitaries using grenades and machine guns, for example. Societies failed to psychologically demobilize, and veterans passed from wartime service into paramilitary formations that reproduced the camaraderie of the trenches. Worse, young boys who had missed serving at the front sought to catch up with their older brothers, fathers and uncles who had. In some countries, and especially where national independence and revolution coincided, civil strife involved a murderous frenzy akin to the early modern wars of religion or the violence used to subdue insurgent or unbiddable peoples in Europe's colonies.[2]

Across Europe, the vast majority of civilians turned conscript combatants returned to lead quiet uneventful lives. But others returned to independence struggles or revolutions which reanimated the furies of wartime. Assassins thrived in these conditions. One example was Ireland, struggling to realize the promise of Home Rule suspended for the duration, and even as large numbers of Irishmen had fought Germans or Turks in the British army.

The great irregular warfare tactician Michael Collins founded a special Squad within the Irish Republican Army, whose job was to assassinate the policemen, spies and thugs whom the British Crown Forces deployed against them. Their main targets were the British ruling class and the G-men of Dublin's G division of political detectives. Collins was influenced by the Finnish revolutionaries whose victims included Nikolaii Borbrikoff the Governor of Finland who was shot dead in June 1904. Collins' men began at the top, taking note of the 1912 Indian revolutionary attempt to bomb the Viceroy Lord Hardinge as he and his wife sat atop of an elephant. Both Hardinges survived though the rider and the elephant didn't. In 1920 the Squad ambushed but failed to kill the Viceroy Field Marshal Lord French at a Dublin railway station, French being the architect of a hard-line military response to Irish insurgency. Thereafter he spent most of his time as a quasi-prisoner in his Phoenix Park lodging, only venturing out escorted by an armoured car and with a gun on his lap.

Known after September 1920 as the 'Twelve Apostles' – there would soon be twenty-one of them – the carefully recruited members of the Squad lived as humdrum tradesmen by day, often in phoney builders' yards, and then went out in pairs armed with .45s to shoot their victims in both head and heart at night – when there would be fewer risks of collateral casualties. The majority of Squad members were bachelors in their late teens or twenties who were not given to deep reflection on what they were doing, which was just as well since they would have been hanged if caught. Each team had a five-man armed support unit to deal with such unforeseen problems as have-a-go hero policemen. On 21 November 1920 the Squad conducted a lethal reckoning at separate Dublin locations with fourteen members of the Cairo Gang, the nom de guerre of a counter-force of MI5 spies and assassins. Life in Dublin became so fraught for the British occupiers that when they sat down at formal dinners, they often found a revolver as part of the *placement*.[3]

The compromises which led to the establishment in 1922 of a semi-independent Irish Free State as a Crown Dominion akin to Canada viciously split the republican movement in ways which still resonate in contemporary Ireland's idiosyncratic political system. Ironically, it was Collins's relatively pragmatic stance, in seeking to consolidate the bird in the bush that was the newly founded Free State, denuded of northerly Ulster, that led to his assassination on 22 August 1922, while on a motoring tour of West Cork, by anti-Treaty fighters who ambushed his convoy near Béal na Bláth. During a firefight he was shot in the head by an anti-Treaty fighter who had been a sniper in the British army.[4]

•

The civil wars which erupted in the 1930s were especially sanguinary. The one in Spain between 1936 and 1939 resulted in a half a million fatalities. Between 1937 and 1945 (for the Japanese war in China started two years before the one in Europe, or six years by other Chinese accounts) the civilian death toll vastly exceeded that of armed combatants.

Post-war Japan witnessed a striking number of assassinations by Rightist army officers against the nation's democratic politicians, mainly for being weak in naval diplomacy with the West. Though on the winning side in 1918, like Italy, Japan lost the peace, and the Japanese were treated as second-class persons by the world's powerbrokers.

In November 1930, Prime Minister Hamaguchi Osachi was wounded by a right-wing fanatic, dying a year later. In February and March 1932 the former Finance Minister Inoue Jun'nosuke and the leading industrialist Dan Takuma were victims of the League of Blood. In May 1932, eleven naval officers killed Inukai Tsuyoshi, the seventy-six-year-old Prime Minister. His last words were: 'If I could speak, you would understand,' to which his assassins replied, 'Dialogue is useless.' The killers had also hoped to kill Charlie Chaplin, Inukai's guest, in order to trigger war with the West, but the actor was watching sumo wrestling with Inukai's son. These assassinations effectively ended civilian rule in Japan, in favour of government by senior military officers. Emperor, army and people were to be one, with internal political discord resolved by overseas empire.[5]

Violence was integral to the revolutionary movements in Russia, Italy and Germany, for killing people was regarded as purgative and transformative. Lenin may have dismissed the regicidal terrorism that claimed the life of his elder brother Aleksandr Ulyanov, but as early as 1905 he recognized the value of mass terror in revolutionary strategy. After the October Revolution, the Bolsheviks institutionalized state terror, when the party newspaper *Izvestia* made the following cryptic announcement:

> By decree of the Soviet People's Commissars is created on 7 December 1917 the all-Russian Extraordinary Commission to Combat Counter-Revolution and Sabotage (the Cheka for short). Cheka Headquarters are at 2 Gorokhovaya Street, open to inquiries every day from noon to 5 p.m.

So was born the self-styled 'shield and sword of the Party'. It included many former Socialist Revolutionary terrorists, like Yakov Blumkin, who in July 1918 walked into the German Embassy in Moscow and shot dead the ambassador, derailing the Treaty of Brest-Litovsk. Blumkin would become one of the Soviets' most successful agents, leading the illegal *rezidentura* in Constantinople, until his superiors realized that instead of watching Trotsky, he was holding secret meetings with him; he was tortured and shot in the Lubyanka prison. ·

Following the killing of a top Chekist in Petrograd and Fanny Kaplan's assassination attempt on Lenin in August 1918, 'Red Terror' became the order of the day. Kaplan was a veteran Socialist Revolutionary terrorist who had served eleven years' hard labour in Tsarist Siberian camps that had left her half-blind. The Bolsheviks reintroduced the death penalty and Kaplan was shot in the back of the neck and burned in a barrel, and the

Red Terror intensified. Hostages were seized, while anarchists, Socialist Revolutionaries and Mensheviks were scythed down, along with striking workers and soldiers. The Russian Civil War itself resulted in the deaths of 2.5 to 3.3 million people.[6]

Other European societies were convulsed by political violence in the interwar years. Pugilistic violence was integral to the '*squadrismo*' practised by Mussolini's Fascists as they waged civil war on the militant Italian left, a reflex that did not disappear after Mussolini came to power in 1922.

On the afternoon of 10 June 1924, the young reformist socialist lawyer and deputy Giacomo Matteotti was bundled into a waiting car outside his home in Rome by five agents of the newly founded Fascist 'Ceka' – the far-right found things to admire about the Bolsheviks. They had been brought from Milan on 22 May to do a job ordered by Mussolini's press secretary Cesare Rossi and funded by the Fascist party.

The initial plan to murder Matteotti on a train journey to Vienna was abandoned when he postponed the trip to deliver an important speech in the Chamber of Deputies on 11 June. A visit to London had revealed the corrupt dealings of the US company Sinclair Oil in securing a monopoly of petrol stations in Italy, on behalf of its hidden partner Standard Oil of Ohio; the Duce's corrupt brother Arnaldo was handling these negotiations with the Americans, in return for kickbacks.

While the aim was to abduct Matteotti so as to steal the contents of his briefcase, something went wrong and he was driven away, before being stabbed to death on a remote country road outside Rome and buried in a country grave.

Matteotti's murder coincided with a crisis within the Fascist regime, between hard-liners who wanted to push through a social revolution and moderates who sought to collaborate with more established forces. Opposition fury at the murder panicked Mussolini. Sensing a threat to his regime, he told supporters, 'If I get away with this we will all survive, otherwise we shall all sink together.' He was saved by the decision of the opposition to withdraw from parliament in protest and the passivity of the armed forces, the Church and the monarch. He dared his opponents to get rid of him, and in January 1926 he banned all opposition parties and clamped down on the press. A new Public Security Law gave the police dictatorial powers, while new tribunals dispensed a version of martial law.[7] Matteotti's assassins were tried and convicted, but served a mere two years in comfortable prison conditions funded by the Fascist party. The chief killer, Amerigo Dumini, had presented Mussolini with a square of the car's bloodstained upholstery and insisted in letters passed to the Duce that he had been promised 'in the most absolute terms complete criminal immunity'.

While domestic opponents were generally harassed or imprisoned, the regime reached out to those in exile abroad. It should also be pointed out that some forty-five affiliated foreign Fascists were killed by left-wing opponents between 1921 and 1932, with a further 283 wounded.[8]

The most notorious case became the basis of a great novel and film called *The Conformist*. The Rosselli brothers were Italian Jews who fought for their country in World War One and were implacable opponents of Mussolini. The economist Carlo managed to escape from a prison on Lipari and to fight against Fascism on the Republican side in Spain. In early 1937 he visited the spa town of Bagnoles-de-l'Orne in Normandy, where he was joined by his younger brother Nello.[9]

Both men were under surveillance by the Italian secret police. On 9 June they were driving from the station to their hotel, taking a circuitous country route. They stopped to help what appeared to be a broken-down car; Carlo was stabbed to death by its driver, while Nello was stabbed and shot by other men in the car. Their bodies were dumped in the undergrowth and the car was found abandoned, with a bomb inside it that had failed to explode.

Although their assassination was ordered by the Italian Foreign Minister Count Galeazzo Ciano, Mussolini's son-in-law, it had been subcontracted to a French Fascist group called La Cagoule, as part of a deal that involved the Italians supplying a hundred Beretta semi-automatic rifles. Although the French government investigated the crime and detained seven of the assassins, attempts to follow the trail to Italy were soon abandoned. The assassins were tried in late 1948 and received long jail sentences. A trial of the Italians who ordered the murders appeared to result in draconian penalties, but of the three who were under arrest, the chief suspect General Mario Roatta, head of the Italian SIM secret police, simply walked out of a military hospital and fled to Franco's Spain.

High politics ensured that Mussolini got away with another murder, though this time the victims were even more illustrious. On 9 October 1934, King Alexander I of Yugoslavia and the French Foreign Minister Louis Barthou, who was probably not a target, were shot by a Bulgarian gunman while driving through Marseille. Vlado Chernozemski was acting on behalf of the exiled Croatian fascist Ante Pavelić, though Mussolini may also have been involved. This was one of the first high-level assassinations to be caught live on film.

German nationalist fanatics never accepted the humiliations heaped on Germany after Versailles. The genial Catholic politician Matthias Erzberger was one of the civilians made to sign the armistice by the army at Compiègne in 1918. While walking in the forest at Bad Griesbach on 26 August 1921 he was assassinated by two former navy officers, Heinrich Tillessen and Heinrich Schulz, who had joined the Freikorps unit Marinebrigade Ehrhardt, a group of former sailors and marines. Myriad Freikorps brought savagery to German streets in Berlin, Bremen, Hamburg and Munich in 1919 and the Ruhr industrial region in 1920, and several socialist politicians were slain. The killers of Erzberger also belonged to Organisation Consul, the ultra-nationalist death squad of Manfred Freiherr von Killinger.

A vicious sadist, Killinger would go on to become premier of Saxony under the Nazis, before embarking on a diplomatic career. The two gunmen fled to Hungary, and returned to Germany when Hitler was in power. A year later, Organisation Consul killed the banker Walther Rathenau, Germany's first Jewish Foreign Minister, and the architect of the Treaty of Rapallo with the Soviet Union. As he was being driven from his villa in Grunewald to the Foreign Ministry, his car was passed by a Mercedes touring car, from which a gunman opened fire with a submachine gun. A grenade was lobbed into Rathenau's vehicle to finish him off. After a two-week-long manhunt that led to a castle in Thuringia, one assassin was shot dead by detectives, while another shot himself.[10]

Since violence was essential to the Bolshevik regime in Russia, it was also intrinsic to the international Comintern and the national Communist parties subordinated to it. The OGPU and NKVD operated within them, with all the prestige of revolutionaries who had triumphed in the Soviet Union. Lenin believed that Germany was ripe for revolution, envisaging a western Soviet Union clustered around that country. He advocated an alliance of far left and nationalist far-right to restore Germany's autonomy, before the final confrontation between them.[11] While German Communists construed their fight as a 'defensive' struggle, much of the violence was directed not at 'Fascists' but at policemen representing the legitimate republic. To claim, as some historians still do, that Communist violence was a case of 'rhetoric' is to ignore the reality.[12]

German Communists were trained in strategy and tactics at Moscow's Lenin School from 1926 onwards. The OGPU had a section within the Soviet embassy on Berlin's Unter den Linden, which maintained covert links with the KPD, the Communist Party of Germany. It was also responsible for a secret military apparatus of German Communists trained in the Soviet Union, who were to be found up a hidden staircase in the attic of the KPD's Karl-Liebknecht headquarters in Berlin. This was effectively a German Cheka or OGPU, linked to the various public fighting formations of the German Communist Party.

The most reliable members of the paramilitary Red Front Fighters League were recruited to act as five-man assassination squads. Their main task was to intimidate policemen, up to and including murdering them.[13] On 9 August 1931 three policemen, including Captain Paul Anlauf, were on patrol near the KPD headquarters. They had doubtless noticed posters on lampposts warning them that 'their hour had come [and that] the RFB was alive and would revenge itself'. As they passed the Babylon Cinema, Anlauf and another officer were shot dead, while a third was wounded. The order to kill them had come from the KPD Politburo the previous day. Six teams of shooters were brought in to secure the area, including Communists from

Dresden. The fatal shots came from the fifth group, which included Erich Ziemer and Erich Mielke, who both fled to the Soviet Union. Ziemer would be killed in Spain in 1937; Mielke became head of East Germany's Stasi.[14]

Endemic political violence in Germany had the effect of enhancing the appeal of any politician vowing to restore law and order. Murderous violence against Communists and Jews occurred before and after the Nazis were put into office in early 1933 by a conservative elite that could not command widespread popular support. Although the Nazis would become one of the most murderous regimes in modern history, their record of assassination was modest. There was an initial reckoning with Hitler's critics and political opponents in 1934, the year in which Austrian Nazis assassinated the Austrian Chancellor Engelbert Dollfuss, but it did not remotely resemble the social violence of the early Bolshevik period or Stalin's purges in the later 1930s.[15]

Between 30 June and 2 July 1934 Hitler eliminated the leadership of the brown-shirted SA that threatened Germany's ruling elite with social revolution. The armed forces (limited to 100,000 men by Versailles) felt menaced by a three-million-strong rowdy political army, especially when SA leaders talked of creating a 'People's Army'. When these tensions threatened Hitler's own precarious grip on power, he flew to Munich to take charge of the murders.

Himmler's 'elite' SS were the chosen instrument used on 30 June to detain the SA leadership at the Hotel Lederer at Bad Wiessee. The operation, codenamed 'Hummingbird', was conducted by the Theodore Eicke, commandant of Dachau concentration camp, and Josef 'Sepp' Dietrich, head of Hitler's SS bodyguards, a unit that fused the ethos of the SS with that of Prussian Guardsmen from an earlier era. A veteran of the trenches in Flanders and of tank warfare, Dietrich passed from the Freikorps Oberland into the SS. He enjoyed close proximity to Hitler, sharing his meals and appointing his chauffeur and pilot. Over ensuing days, the SA detainees, including their leader Ernst Röhm, were shot by Dietrich's men in Munich's Stadelheim Prison. Dietrich was not comfortable shooting men he knew as comrades and friends, but the SS carried out orders blindly. In

Berlin, Göring took charge of the purge. A police official watched as he strutted about, shouting: 'Shoot them down . . . Shoot!'[16]

Hitler also took the opportunity to reckon with assorted political foes, real and imagined. The former Chancellor and Reichswehr General Kurt von Schleicher was shot by men in trench coats, who also murdered his wife when she got in the way. Major-General Kurt von Bredow was also assassinated. Former Chancellor Franz von Papen was lucky to escape alive, though two of his key aides were among between 150 and 200 victims, as were the Bavarian politician who crushed the 1923 beer hall putsch in Munich and the leader of Catholic Action. A propaganda campaign depicted the SA leaders as traitors and sexual deviants, for Röhm was a promiscuous homosexual. The conservative elite, whose army was complicit, acquiesced in cold-blooded extra-judicial murder, with the SS established as the 'go-to' formation for executing brutal orders. On 3 July the cabinet retroactively legalized these murders, with the new Defence Minister General Werner von Blomberg thanking the Führer for 'saving the German people from civil war'.

Hitler was not responsible for assassinating Austria's plucky chancellor, an act that temporarily stiffened European opposition to his strategies. In July 1934, Austrian SS men disguised as members of the army invaded the Ballhausplatz chancellery building and shot dead the forty-one-year-old Engelbert Dollfuss in a putsch that had the support of an external SA legion in Bavaria. The Christian Socialist Dollfuss had tried to stop Socialists, Communists and Nazis from destroying the independent Alpine republic; his assassination delayed the disintegration of a sovereign Austria, with an outraged Mussolini moving troops to a threatening posture on the Brenner Pass. Realizing the Austrian Nazis had gone too far, Hitler handed back those putschists who had fled to Germany. Otto Planetta, who killed Dollfuss, was hanged, along with thirteen other rebels.[17]

Aside from the murders of Dollfuss and the SA leadership, there were no purges comparable to events in Russia. This was because the Nazi Party, rather than the embodiment of a scientific ideology that was absolute in its orthodoxy, was a group of sycophantic followers of a single living ideologue. The ideology was also fungible, except when race was involved. Nazis were, however, victims of assassination, a case in point being in 1936, when an exiled Croatian Jewish dental student put five bullets into Wilhelm Gustloff, the proselytizing head of the Nazi Party in Switzerland. Hitler let this pass because the Berlin Olympic Games were imminent. But on 9 November 1938, Ernst vom Rath, the twenty-nine-year-old third secretary in the German embassy in Paris, was shot by seventeen-year-old Herschel Grynszpan. The assassin was avenging the expected deportation of his parents to Poland along with other 'Eastern Jews'. Even as Rath expired, Hitler launched Kristallnacht, on which much more than shop windows were broken. It was his opening shot in a war on the Jews of Europe.

.

The gulf between the heroic Soviet realist art of the 1930s and the lives of ordinary comrades was stark. The assassination of Sergei Kirov in 1934 vividly shows what a grim place the Soviet Union had become and the perils of being regarded as a charismatic replacement for Stalin. It was also the beginning of the first big wave of purges, as the Communist Party cleansed itself of ideological deviants. As so often in this book, the actions of a nobody came to have dramatic consequences as those with power exploited the event for their own wider purposes.

Leonid Vasil'evich Nikolaev was born in St Petersburg in 1904. His father died of alcoholism when he was four, so he and his three siblings depended on the wages of their mother, a tram-car cleaner. He attended primary school for six years before becoming a metalworker and joined the Communist Party in 1924; despite his lack of education, he progressed to low-level clerical jobs, as the Party tried to give itself a more proletarian image. He was a difficult man, and in 1934 he was thrown out of the Party for three months before being readmitted with a black mark on his record. By this time he had a Latvian wife, Milda Draule, and two infant children, one of whom he named Karl Marx.

Nikolaev repeatedly complained about the injustice of his treatment by the Party, while in his diary and letters his thoughts inclined from bitterness to murder. In November 1934 he wrote twice to Leningrad Party Secretary Sergei Kirov asking for help. In October, the NKVD had detained him for loitering outside Kirov's apartment block. Had they searched him, they would have found a gun, and Nikolaev's firearms licence had expired in April 1931. The deputy NKVD chief Ivan Zaporozhets allegedly let him go. In November 1934, Nikolaev went to the Leningrad railway station intending to shoot Kirov as he alighted from the Moscow train, however was prevented from attempting an attack by Kirov's NKVD bodyguards.[18]

On 1 December at 1.30 p.m. Nikolaev gained access to the Leningrad Party headquarters in the Smolnyi Institute, where Kirov's office was on the third floor. He wanted a ticket for Kirov's speech at the Tauride Palace at 6 p.m. that day. Nikolaev had a Party membership card so entering the Smolnyi was easy, but a guard was posted at the top of the stairs on the third floor, and anyone seeking entrance needed to prove they worked there.

It remains unknown whether Nikolaev hid on the third floor or moved around the building until Kirov arrived at 4.30 p.m., dressed in a dark overcoat and peaked cap. He had spent the day working at home on a speech that would announce the end of bread rationing in 1935, tricky since workers in Leningrad were increasingly restive about their miserable standard of living.

Kirov's four plainclothes NKVD guards handed charge of him to his long-time bodyguard, Mikhail Borisov. Kirov went up to the third floor, moving much quicker than the fifty-three-year-old Borisov, who was too old and unfit for the job. It later transpired that his holstered gun was not even loaded. Kirov's office had recently been moved from the wide L-shaped corridor into a narrower section around a corner. Many of the Party workers were at a meeting, so this corridor felt deserted.

As Kirov turned a corner towards his office, Nikolaev stepped out and shot him once in the forehead with a Nagan pistol. Instead of running, he fired a second shot at himself, though the bullet ricocheted off the ceiling and he sank down unharmed, until Borisov and others beat him unconscious. Doctors went through the motions of trying to resuscitate Kirov as he lay on a desk, but he probably died instantly.[19]

Even before anyone told Kirov's wife that her husband was dead, a call was made to inform Stalin of the bad news; late that night he boarded a train to Leningrad, with colleagues including Genrikh Yagoda, the Jewish head of the new NKVD, chief prosecutor Andrei Vishinskii, Molotov and Khrushchev.

More significantly, Stalin's party included Nikolai Yezhov, a fast-rising expert on Party personnel and a Stalin loyalist. He was a small, thin man, as well as an alcoholic bisexual debauchee, though the full truth of his personality was masked by lies about his solid proletarian background. Two experienced NKVD officers, deputy commissar Yakov Agranov and Leonid Zakovsky, came on the train too.

These three would take over the Kirov investigation from the Leningrad NKVD. Yezhov and his men reported directly to Stalin, since discovering who killed Kirov was only part of their mission; Yezhov's arrival on the Politburo had been followed by its decision to abolish the OGPU in favour of the NKVD. The appointment of Yezhov as the lead investigator of Kirov's murder was a sign that things might change at the top of the secret police.

Before Stalin left Moscow he altered Soviet criminal procedure with what became known as the Kirov Law. In cases of terrorism, the investigation was to be completed within ten days, with the accused informed twenty-four hours before being charged. Trials would be held in secret, and would not involve the defendant or defence lawyers. Appeals were inadmissible and death sentences would be carried out immediately.[20]

Arriving in the Smolnyi, Stalin took over Kirov's office and conducted interviews, though Yezhov had already been instructed to 'look for the murderers among the Zinovievites'. Grigory Zinoviev, having connived with Stalin in ousting Trotsky, then combined with Trotsky and Kamenev against Stalin, only to recant and make their peace. His adherents were progressively sidelined and forced into a humiliating admission of defeat at the Seventeenth Party Congress in January 1934.

Borisov the bodyguard was a key witness to Kirov's assassination, but he fell from the back of the truck taking him from NKVD headquarters to the Smolnyi, sustaining massive head injuries that killed him, though the guard in the back with him was unhurt. Stalin interviewed Nikolaev himself, a weeping wreck of a man who refused to believe this was Stalin until shown a picture on the wall. Apparently Nikolaev said afterwards: 'He promised me my life if I named my accomplices, but I had no accomplices.' Stalin also interviewed Nikolaev's wife Milda, aware of rumours in Leningrad that her jealous husband had shot the womanizing Kirov, whose underwear revealed traces of recent sexual activity.

On 3 December Stalin discovered something he could work with. In 1934 a servant of one of the secretaries in the Smolnyi who was also an NKVD informer had reported the existence of a conspiracy to kill Kirov that she alleged had 700 members. At the time, Mariia Volkova was diagnosed as a schizophrenic and held in a mental institution; on 3 December she stood in front of Stalin, identified a photo of Nikolaev and volunteered fifty names of his co-conspirators. The NKVD provided her with an apartment, money and paid holidays, and she provided other names.[21]

After paying his respects to Kirov inside the Tauride Palace, Stalin escorted the gun carriage which returned him to Moscow. He wrote to the NKVD officers interrogating Nikolaev: 'Nourish Nikolaev well, buy him a chicken and other things, so that he will be strong, and then he will tell who was leading him. And if he doesn't talk, we will give it to him and he will tell and show everything.' Kirov was replaced as Party Secretary by Andreii Zhdanov, and the NKVD was purged of those officers who had failed to protect Kirov or who had pursued the evidence trail back to Nikolaev.

The NKVD rounded up many suspected conspirators. In addition to thirteen Zinovievites, thousands of other Leningraders filled the city's jails. At Yezhov's and Agranov's prompting, the NKVD rewrote their initial appraisal of Nikolaev as the impoverished and embittered cuckold who had killed Kirov out of desperation. Instead they reported that Nikolaev had a spacious apartment and plenty of money. Within an hour of being sentenced to death, he and his thirteen co-accused were shot. His wife Milda, her sister and her husband were shot too, along with Nikolaev's brother and sister. The NKVD driver and guard who had been responsible for escorting Borisov were shot in 1937 and eleven Leningrad NKVD officers disappeared into the camps, charged with dereliction of duty. But this was just the start of things. Entirely innocent hostages were executed in prisons across the Soviet Union, while in Leningrad the NKVD expelled over eleven thousand members of the former upper classes and deported them to remote locations.

Sergei Kirov was forty-eight at the time of his assassination. In a party with more than its fair share of bespectacled intellectuals, he was robustly proletarian. Born into humble circumstances in Urzhum in 1886, he grew up in an orphanage, before becoming a revolutionary and a notable journalist. Seeing the name of the Persian warrior king Kir on a calendar of saints' names, he adopted Kirov as his revolutionary moniker, just as Iosef Besarion dze Jugahsvvili had progressed from 'Koba' in 1912 to 'Stalin'.

Kirov became a Bolshevik hero, though he was no ideological sectarian; he tried to win others round rather than to cast them into darkness, and that pragmatic latitudinarianism would count against him. Short, blond and pockmarked, Kirov was a powerful orator and energetic organizer. But he was also a dedicated Leninist and did not lack the killer instinct.

That was clear when he became chairman of the Revolutionary War Committee in Astrakhan, where in 1919 he had 4,000 striking workers shot by the Cheka's Special Department. He also displayed considerable brutality with Azeri nationalists when it was invaded by the Soviets in 1920. After a stint as an envoy to Georgia, in 1921 he became Party Secretary in Azerbaijan; two years later he was made a full member of the Central Committee, with Stalin as his proposer.

While Stalin was becoming the object of a cult, men like Kirov orbited around his sun. Although he was not keen to leave Azerbaijan, in 1926 he was appointed Leningrad Party Secretary. These were the years 1926–28, in which Stalin successively moved to neutralize the 'left opposition' of Trotsky, Zinoviev and Kamenev, before turning on the 'Rightists' represented by Nikolai Bukharin, Mikhail Tomskii and Aleksei Rykov.

Although personality clashes were involved, at stake was the balance of state and private elements in the economy, and the collectivization of agriculture to enable industrialization. Kirov could see what that might lead to in a highly industrial city surrounded by forest rather than farmland. He was in a very delicate position. On the one hand he did not believe that every ideological opponent needed to be crushed into dust. But on the other, there he was with Stalin as they cruised along the new Baltic–White Sea Canal in 1933, a project on which 100,000 convicts perished out of a total workforce of 280,000, merely so as to finish this 227-kilometre-long feat in a year and a half. Matvei Berman, the Jewish head of the Gulag camp system, and Yagoda were on that cruise too.

Overwork and the nightmare of having Stalin on a telephone hotline at all hours led to a decline in Kirov's health. Since Stalin took a close interest in the health of key Party figures, the better to exploit weakness, this meant that in addition to enervating Central Committee meetings in Moscow, he would be summoned to steamy Sochi for rest and recuperation with the *Vozhd*. He developed insomnia and heart trouble, becoming irritable and ill-tempered.

However publicly indulgent Stalin may have been, Kirov gave him grounds for suspicion. He was a fluent orator, whereas Stalin read from a script. Audiences clapped Kirov enthusiastically; applause for Stalin was precautionary. Rather than mindlessly obeying Stalin, Kirov seemed to circumvent or deflect his orders.

Worse, Kirov's enemies were not above combing through those youthful articles in liberal newspapers, or the indulgence he showed to political opponents of Stalin who repented of their ways. Although Kirov lavished praise on Stalin, in 1929 he omitted a passage from a speech on Stalin's fiftieth birthday in which he explicitly mentioned 'the minus' of Lenin's testament in which the departed leader criticized Stalin's rudeness. Someone placed that missing passage on file.

Around the time of the Seventeenth Party Congress in January 1934, some Old Bolsheviks were muttering about Kirov replacing Stalin. The fact that Kirov sat not on the presidium alongside

Stalin but amidst the 132-strong Leningrad delegation underlined where the threat might come from, as did the rapturous applause that greeted Kirov's speech.

Stalin's toying with Kirov intensified with a plan to move him to Moscow as Secretary of the Central Committee, which Kirov had postponed. A less playful way of describing Stalin's reaction was that he was weighing up how to dispose of Kirov, while appearing the calm and steady face of moderation.

We may never learn whether Stalin and the NKVD murdered Kirov, using either the embittered Nikolaev or a second man who vanished from the third floor of the Smolnyi. On the surface, Kirov was elevated to the Soviet equivalent of Valhalla. The semi-religious cult was used to distract from dire economic conditions and to mask the fact that Kirov's assassination was the pretext to purges in which over 650,000 people were shot and millions more were consigned to the netherworld of camps. In Leningrad, 90,000 people were arrested by the NKVD between 1935 and 1938, after Yezhov had completed lists of names of Zinovievites, running to 2,000 pages. He also went through the files of 2,747 Leningrad NKVD officers to remove 'clutter', in a bid to replace Yagoda as head of the NKVD by constantly pointing to deficiencies in the organization.[22]

In 1935 Grigory Zinoviev and Lev Kamenev received long jail sentences for their 'moral complicity' in Kirov's murder, as part of what was dubbed the 'Moscow Centre' conspiracy. At a fresh trial in August 1936, their crimes were upgraded to active conspiracy to murder Kirov; sentenced to death, they were shot in the underground cells of the Lubyanka. The exiled Trotsky was temporarily beyond the NKVD's reach.

Yezhov's men were connecting Trotskyites, Zinovievites and Rightists with the threats from German Fascism and Japan. Yagoda and Zaporozhets were identified as the link between these conspirators and the murder of Kirov, since Zaporozhets had allegedly armed Nikolaev and cleared the way for him to act. They were charged with conspiracy to kill Lenin and Stalin and the murder of the writer Maxim Gorky. Yagoda was charged with attempting to murder Yezhov in 1936 by having his office carpet and curtains sprayed with mercury; a former pharmacist,

Yagoda had founded the NKVD's poisons unit. A search of his home revealed a vast cache of pornographic photos and films – a sprinkling of moral condemnation was always useful among these murderous puritans. At the trial Yagoda initially resembled an alerted rat, ready to controvert the prosecutors, but by the end he mumbled in a monotone. After the great show trial, leading Rightists were condemned and shot. Yagoda met the same fate, along with his wife, sister and her husband. Zaporozhets and Medved were also shot, along with the latter's thirteen-year-old son Misha.

Yezhov himself was arrested in April 1939 and sentenced to death in camera in February 1940. He was shot by Ivan Serov, a future Chairman of the KGB (the NKVD's last Soviet-era iteration) in a chamber with a sloping floor that Yezhov had designed to ease mopping down after multiple executions.

•

During the 1930s and 1940s, the NKVD reached out to Trotskyites and other Leftist heretics wherever they found them. Following the second attempt to overthrow a democratically elected Spanish government in August 1936, Stalin decided to give military aid to the beleaguered Spanish Republic.

The most well-known aspect of this was the Comintern's recruitment of international fighters, but below the surface, the NKVD established a liaison office in Spain. It worked with the Dirección General de Seguridad and hundreds of *checas*, which ran kangaroo tribunals and murder squads to deal with dissidents, spies and Fascists. The NKVD presence also helped organize a separate secret police within the Spanish Communist Party.

Being in wartime Spain was a relief for many NKVD officers, since the alternatives at home in Russia were grim. They lived in the moment, conducting affairs with the female NKVD interpreters and wireless operators who accompanied them, with enthusiastic local women and with the Russian women they took along as their wives to add legitimacy to their diplomatic cover stories.

There were usually ten or so NKVD officers in Republican

Spain, many of them Jews from the former Tsarist Pale. Their Jewishness would be useful when they ventured further afield to the US, where they could blend in with distant Yiddish-speaking cousins and construct Soviet espionage networks. In Spain their primary tasks were to monitor the International Brigades for Trotskyite deviants, to recruit some of their volunteers as deep penetration agents once the war in Spain was over and to carry out 'active measures' on behalf of the new NKVD 'Special Tasks' department.

That explains why the NKVD in Spain included many practised assassins. They included Naum Isaakovich Eitingon aka Leonid Alexandrovich Kotov, who would recruit Caridad Mercader and her son Ramon, who killed Trotsky. A Byelorussian called Stanislav Vaupshasov aka Stanislav Alexeyevich Dubovsky was a decorated Cheka assassin who built and operated the secret crematorium in which Spanish victims of the NKVD disappeared. Another killer was the Lithuanian Karaite Jew known as 'Grig', Iosif Romualdovich Grigulevich, who had the code names ARTUR, MAKS, and FELIPE. He formed a Special Brigade made up of some of the Spanish policemen who guarded the Soviet embassy. This was one of the units which secretly murdered 8,000 Nationalist captives, after they had been forcibly prised out of the sanctuary of foreign embassies. Grig's unit was also despatched to Barcelona to annihilate the POUM-Trotskyites.[23] In 1937 he was recalled to Moscow, not to be shot himself, but to train with Pavel Sudaplatov's NKVD Special Tasks unit. The main mission was to assassinate Trotsky.

Grig's successor as NKVD chief in Spain was Alexander Orlov, a specialist in organizing the deaths of 'those to be liquidated'. Even before his departure from Spain, Orlov supervised assassinations in the rest of Europe. Anyone connected to Trotsky disappeared, like his young former secretary Erwin Wolf, who was abducted in Barcelona and probably ended up in Vaupshasov's crematorium.

In May 1938 the Ukrainian nationalist leader Yevhen Konovalets – masquerading as a German called Josef Novak from Berlin – left the bar of Rotterdam's Atlanta Hotel. A Ukrainian courier had handed him a small parcel that allegedly contained secret messages from inside the Soviet Union. A few days before, the same man had given him cigarettes, chocolates and a song book; NKVD psychologists were keen to discover if he was in the habit of taking unsolicited presents. A middle-aged Dutchman watched him carrying the package along the street, until it erupted with a flash and blew Konovalets to pieces which flew across the street. The Dutchman put the stray leg next to the body which had mostly landed around a waste bin. The assassin made calls to Berlin and Vienna at the main post office, making sure he was noticed, before fleeing to France and then to Spain, where he rested with Sudaplatov, Eitingon and Orlov.

There was a strange coda. Orlov had noticed that the NKVD officers summoned back to Moscow duly vanished. Having embezzled $68,000 from NKVD operational funds, Orlov and his wife slipped away for a ship bound for Canada.

Before he left, he asked a friend to deliver a letter addressed to Nikolai Yezhov via the Soviet embassy in Paris. An appendix listed many of the murderous operations he had been involved in, and there was also a pointed reference to deep cover agents codenamed 'SÖHNSCHEN' and 'WAISE' – Kim Philby and Donald Maclean, the key Soviet spies inside British intelligence. Orlov told Yezhov to issue orders that his seventy-year-old mother should be unharmed. 'All this will never see the light of day,' he vowed. Orlov was as good as his word; after moving to the US, it was fifteen years before he surfaced as the entirely bogus 'General' Alexander Orlov of the NKVD.[24]

•

Even a decade after his enforced exile, Leon Trotsky was revered as the founder of the Red Army, his reputation still animating thousands of supporters in Europe and both Americas.

In March 1939 Pavel Sudaplatov was summoned by the new NKVD chief Lavrentii Beria, the Georgian psychopath who replaced Yezhov. This was invariably ominous, but Beria took him for a drive that ended inside Stalin's inner sanctum at Spassky Palace. Stalin acquiesced in Beria's plan to promote Sudaplatov as Deputy Director of the NKVD's Foreign Operations department. He emphasized that if a war came, the main danger to his friendships with foreign governments and Communist parties would be subversion by Trotskyites. He continued that 'Trotsky should be eliminated within a year, before war breaks out'. Sudaplatov would lead a team 'to implement the action against Trotsky'. Confessing that he did not speak Spanish, Sudaplatov said he would use NKVD operatives who had recently served in the conflict there.

The next day Sudaplatov called Eitingon, who was resting under NKVD surveillance. Together with Pavel Fitin, head of foreign intelligence, they elaborated Operation Utka, or 'Duck', for which they needed agents in Mexico whence in 1937 Trotsky had fled. A long-time admirer of Trotsky, the Mexican painter Diego Rivera persuaded President Lázaro Cardenas to offer him asylum. Rivera allowed Trotsky to lodge in his 'Blue House' on the fringes of Mexico City, which became the seat of the anti-Stalinist Fourth International. Not everyone was happy about this Russian revolutionary celebrity, notably members of the Mexican Communist Party.

The NKVD had earlier managed to get a veteran agent onto Trotsky's staff as a secretary, but Orlov's defection meant her cover was blown. Sudaplatov's plans involved two separate networks, both ultimately commanded by Eitingon. One network was codenamed 'The Horse', the other 'The Mother'. Both teams were trained by Eitingon in Paris, where he hid as a mentally ill Syrian Jew in a psychiatric clinic run by a Russian émigré who worked for Soviet intelligence. Grig was despatched to Mexico City, where he rented a fine house in Acacias, near to Trotsky's home on Avenida Viena in the suburb of Coyoacan. In addition to his future wife Laura Araujo Aguilar, he paid two pretty Communist girls to rent an apartment opposite Trotsky's home to watch any movements and to suborn his police detail with drink and sex.

Sudaplatov's first network of assassins – 'The Horse' – revolved around David Alfaro Siqueiros, an artist who had fled his wealthy family. Even though he was forty, he had gone to Spain with 533 other Mexican volunteers, of whom fifty-two would survive the civil war. As a former captain in the

Constitutionalist Army of Mexico, Siqueiros clearly had guts since he undertook solo raids and undercover missions to Fascist Italy. After a brief sojourn in Paris, in January 1939 Siqueiros resumed his artistic career in Mexico, where he was one of the founders of the country's Communist Party.[25]

The second network – 'The Mother' – involved Eitingon's old flame Eustacia Maria Caridad del Rio Hernández-Mercader, a wealthy Cuban-Spanish aristocrat whose ancestors included a governor of Cuba and Spain's ambassador to Tsarist Russia. In 1911 Caridad married a dour businessman, Pablo Mercader Marina, whom she deserted in 1925 for the lights of Paris, taking her four children with her. Caridad attempted to kill herself twice and managed to have affairs with most of the leaders of the French Communist Party.

Caridad and the children surfaced in Barcelona, the epicentre of Catalan revolutionism, where she was wounded leading a counterattack on heavily armed Francoist positions in the city. During the civil war, her eldest son Pablo died throwing himself under a tank to detonate grenades, while the middle son Ramón was a lieutenant and political commissar in the 27th Division on the Aragon front. The two youngest children were sent to Moscow in 1939, along with other fleeing Republicans.

In the summer of 1938, Ramón was moved from Barcelona to Paris to assume the identity of a louche Belgian diplomat's son-cum-playboy, 'Jacques Mornard van den Dresched'. Both Caridad and Ramón were NKVD agents.

In the US, the NKVD ordered Louis Budenz, former manager of the Trotskyite *Daily Worker*, to make the acquaintance of Ruby Weil, childhood friend of three sisters called Ageloff. Only one of them interested Budenz and his handlers, a slight and myopic twenty-eight-year-old social worker called Sylvie; Ruby cultivated her in New York and agreed to accompany her to Paris for a meeting of the Fourth International, where she and another agent propelled Sylvie into the path of the man of her dreams. Jacques Mornard was immaculately dressed, had a lot of money and claimed to be a sports reporter. Love blossomed. When Sylvie ran out of money, Mornard offered her a small fortune to write articles on psychology for a syndicated magazine called *Argus* that did not exist. However in February 1939 Sylvie went back to New York. Mornard suddenly turned up there, giving Sylvie tours of the city, though she would recall him saying he had never previously visited. But there were two attacks on Trotsky; first we should go back to Team A.

Those who could read Communist politics could sense that something big was afoot. In March 1940 the leadership of the Mexican Communist Party was purged of any residual Trotskyites, and on May Day 20,000 Communists marched, demanding that the party 'Throw out the most ominous and dangerous traitor Trotsky'.

On 23 May 1940, the gates to Trotsky's house were opened by a volunteer guard, a twenty-three-year-old American youth called Robert Sheldon Harte. Trotsky's five police guards were groggy after spending the night at a party with Anita Lopez and Julia Barrados de Serrano. Two of them were waylaid by men wearing police officer's uniforms, while the other three were overpowered in their guard box.

About twenty men, led by Grig and Siqueiros, shot up the front of the house, then entered and poured bullets into Trotsky's bedroom and a smaller side room where his fourteen-year-old grandson slept. The assassins left after firing more than 300 rounds and throwing a bomb into the house that failed to explode. Siqueiros would falsely claim they merely intended to raid Trotsky's archives and used the constant gunfire as a distraction, but that was not what Grig was there for. None of Trotsky's bodyguards fired a single shot that night. Two houseguests, a French couple called Rosmer, were unscathed by the attack.

Grig fled to Chile with the aid of the poet Pablo Neruda. Most of the Mexican hit team were detained, but Siqueiros fled, only to be caught by Mexican police four months later, after a drunken tram conductor boasted in a bar that a policeman friend had loaned three police uniforms for a tidy payment, unaware that the head of Mexico's Secret Service was sitting on the next stool. At his trial for attempted murder, he dominated proceedings with hate-filled attacks on the dead Trotsky who had been murdered by Ramon Mercader. Before the judgement he was summoned to see President Manuel Ávila Camacho, who recalled that Siqueiros had once sheltered him during a storm in Mexico's Battle of Guadalajara and promptly offered him freedom in exile. He left for Chile on 28 April 1941.

Robert Sheldon Harte, who had seen Grig's face, was taken to the group's base camp at a remote adobe farm and shot twice. His corpse was buried with lime under the kitchen's earthen floor. Meanwhile, Trotsky took the opportunity to improve his alarm system and to link it to a police station. Various tripwires were installed around the building. An admirer sent him a bulletproof vest and a loud siren. Some windows were bricked up and the bedroom door was reinforced with a device that would shoot any assailant.[26]

After the failure of the Siqueiros network, the second team swung into action. Sudaplatov had gone to Paris to assess both the Mercader and Siqueiros groups, while Caridad and Ramón were both in Mexico City. In New York, Eitingon established an import–export company in Brooklyn to funnel money to the Mercaders, and then decamped to Mexico City himself. He and Caridad conducted an affair. Ramón Mercader had become the Canadian Frank Jacson, allegedly to avoid Belgian conscription. Sylvie Ageloff accepted his explanation of his change of identity and eagerly followed him to Mexico, where they lived together in a little love nest. At Jacson's prompting, Sylvie secured a job as a secretary working for Trotsky, who in addition to his flurry of letters and pamphlets was writing a biography of Stalin.[27]

Having failed once with 'The Horse', Eitingon could not afford to fail a second time. He crossed the Atlantic in October and rented offices for his fake business in Brooklyn. He held regular clandestine meetings with Mercader, to get the assassin in the frame of mind to kill one of the great leaders of the Russian revolution. Mexico did not have the death penalty, and the Soviets would rescue him. Experienced operators like Eitingon knew the drill: cajole, flatter and threaten. Mercader also revisited his old interest in mountaineering, boasting that he had once scaled Mont Blanc. That is where he acquired a long-handled ice axe.

It proved relatively easy for Mercader to infiltrate Trotsky's household. He drove Sylvie to work in his flashy Buick, getting to know the policemen outside. In addition to courting Sylvie, he frequently volunteered to give other inmates lifts, on one occasion carrying shopping into the house, where he inspected the layout and security arrangements. The guards began to regard him as part of the wider entourage, with Trotsky's wife Natalya taking an interest in the young couple. On 23 May, four days after this gun attack, he met Trotsky briefly when he offered to drive the Rosmers and Natalya to Veracruz, a city he said he visited frequently on business.

In June 1940 Mercader flew to New York to see Sylvie, who was visiting there, but in reality he was meeting the NKVD station chief, returning to Mexico with $890 and a visa for Canada for his getaway. He taped these to his forearms on the evening of the murder.

On 17 August Mercader returned to Trotsky's house and asked him if he would look at an article he had written about French economic statistics. The NKVD knew he would not be able to resist drawing the casual socialist into his own sect. His home had become a fortress. On one occasion he asked the young man what he thought. 'In the next attack the OGPU will use other methods,' Trotsky said. 'A single agent of the OGPU who could pass himself off as my friend could assassinate me in my own home.'

Mercader appeared wearing a dark suit and hat, and carrying a raincoat, on a hot summer day. He had seemed ill and nervy for several weeks. Three days later he returned with the article he wanted Trotsky to read. The great Russian revolutionary began to read the piece, not noticing as Mercader took his shortened ice axe from the raincoat he had laid on a table. He also had a dagger sewn into a concealed pocket in the lining and a .45 Star automatic stuck down his trousers at the back. Outside, his mother Caridad waited in one car, with Eitingon parked further away in another. A private plane was at the airport.[28]

A powerfully built man, five feet ten inches tall, Mercader struck Trotsky on the head as he turned to face him. The blow did not kill Trotsky and he sank his teeth into Mercader's hand, before stumbling to Natalya in the adjacent room, his face covered with blood. Three security men overpowered Mercader, in whose pocket was found a typed letter, which claimed he had attacked Trotsky because the latter was planning to 'liquidate' Stalin, a nice touch by Eitingon. The guards smashed up Mercader with their gun butts. Trotsky died twenty-six hours later of brain injury, telling a bodyguard, 'This time . . . they've . . . succeeded.' His death was noted at 7.25p.m. on 21 August 1940. He was sixty-one years old.

The hysterical Sylvie would scream 'Kill! Kill him!' when she was told that Mercader was not who he claimed to be and that he had murdered Trotsky. Eitingon's chauffeur drove him to a rendezvous with a Soviet freighter anchored off Acapulco. Caridad followed to Moscow, where Stalin gave her two Order of the Hero medals – one for Ramón. Eitingon's next assignment was to liquidate Polish and Ukrainian opponents of the Soviets. In 1951 he was sent to prison as a suspected Zionist; briefly released by his patron Beria in 1953, he was jailed again for murdering Soviet citizens with poisons and eventually released in 1964, following the fall of Khrushchev.[29]

Jacson's cover as Jacques Mornard was easily exposed, but that first identity was as far as they got until the early 1950s, well into his twenty-year prison term. In 1940 the Mexican authorities commissioned two criminal psychologists to interview him – six hours a day, six days a week, for six months – inside Lecumberri Federal Penitentiary. Their report may not have penetrated Mornard's cover, but it reveals much about Ramón Mercader beneath his two pseudonyms. He regarded the shrinks as fools, but they got to the essence of him despite this.

Mornard was fluent in several languages, though it took expert linguists to identify his slight Catalan accent. He could pass as a gentleman, was highly attractive to women and a skilled athlete. He had extremely quick reactions and a photographic memory. He could touch tiny objects and then draw them, with the exactitude of a watchmaker. He could disassemble and reassemble a rifle in a dark room in under three minutes. In some senses he was like a human robot. The psychological sessions concluded that a hatred for his father resulted in unbounded aggression, while total love for his domineering mother resulted in deep-seated passivity.

In 1950 one of the Mexican criminologists went to a conference in Paris, taking a detour via Barcelona. He matched Mornard's Mexican police prints and mugshots with those of Ramón Mercader and it became clear who he really was. Miserable in Moscow, Caridad was allowed to leave for Mexico, where she failed to see Ramón, before spending her declining years in Paris. Upon his release in 1960, Ramón went to Cuba and then to Moscow. A chain-smoker like his mother, he died of lung cancer in Havana in 1978 and is interred in Moscow's Kuntsevo Cemetery. His final words were: 'I hear it always. I hear the scream. I know he's waiting for me on the other side.' That was self-delusory on the part of this *hombre enigmatico*.[30]

•

Hitler and Stalin both lived in fear of assassination, with security arrangements in place to ensure their survival. Stalin had his chief bodyguard Nikolai Vlasik, a crude and tough Chekist turned NKVD general and an oppressive presence. When Stalin took a train, such as when he attended the Potsdam summit in 1945, NKVD guards were stationed every hundred yards of the journey. Both men took a keen interest in assassins, with Hitler wisely deciding that he should keep his movements as irregular as possible to confound them.

Hitler was surrounded by black-uniformed toughs in a special SS-Begleitkommando des Führers, though after 1938 they exchanged the uniforms for grey ones, to placate the army leadership. About forty men provided close personal protection, with another hundred or so SS-Reichssicherheitsdienst officers patrolling whichever building Hitler visited. Security was tightened in 1936, when a decree ordered local Gestapo offices to carefully inspect any buildings that Hitler was going to stay in or visit. One particular assassination attempt led to a massive increase in Hitler's security arrangements, with 450 men guarding him and elaborate precautionary measures wherever he went, from monitoring foreign visitors to watchmakers listening for ticking bombs. From 1938 onwards he used armoured limousines, while his plane had parachutes for all on board, and a hatch under the Führer's seat should he have to drop out. All that is an indirect tribute to George Elser.[31]

There was one fateful loophole in Hitler's security arrangements: when he was among his most dedicated original Party followers, the Gestapo and police were not entrusted with security.

The annual commemoration of the abortive 1923 Munich Putsch every 9 November was the most sacred day in the Nazi calendar. Hitler would meet his surviving 'old fighters', looking them in the eye and touching the 'blood banner' of the movement in an intense bonding ritual. But in 1939 he almost missed the event, only deciding on 7 November to go by special train to Munich rather than sending Rudolf Hess. This last-minute decision was because the army high command was cutting up rough about an imminent Western offensive, postponing the day of their decision to green-light the invasion of France until 12 November.[32]

Customarily, Hitler would make a speech to his 'old fighters' and then linger afterwards to go down memory lane. This time he arrived with the usual flurry of dictatorial self-importance at 8 p.m .and spoke until 9.17. He left abruptly and at 9.31 boarded his special train back to Berlin.

At twenty past nine, a powerful bomb collapsed the column behind Hitler's podium and the steel supports on which a gallery and the ceiling rested. The rubble was more than a metre deep and six old fighters were killed, as well as a waitress. Sixty-three people were wounded, sixteen of them critically. Hitler only learned of the assassination attempt when his train stopped at Nuremberg. At 10.20 p.m. he arrived back in Berlin, dark with suspicion and fury.

Flurries of phone calls set an investigation in motion. The crime scene was to be handled by the Criminal Police chief Arthur Nebe, aided by the Criminal Counsellor and SS Obersturmbannführer Georg Huber, who was summoned from the Gestapo HQ in Vienna. While Huber got to work interviewing frightened waitresses and dazed old fighters, customs officers in Konstanz filed a routine report to the Gestapo HQ in Karlsruhe on an arrest two of them had made at 8.45 p.m. Looking out of their vantage point at a garden next to the frontier with Switzerland while listening to Hitler on the radio, they saw a man sneaking towards the frontier. Brandishing their rifles they stopped a small and unremarkable thirty-six-year-old man, in whose pockets they found wire cutters, machine parts, a Red Front Fighters' badge, some small change, flyers for an armaments company and a blank picture postcard of the Bürgerbräukeller. The suspect, a carpenter called Georg Elser, was transported to the Munich Gestapo HQ in the Wittelsbach Palace.

Back in Munich, Nebe's forensic investigators used a square-grid method to comb through the dust and rubble for parts of the bomb. They were looking for wires to a remote ignition system, but instead found the brass plates on which two clock mechanisms had been mounted and cork soundproofing board used to muffle the sound of ticking. Both had manufacturers' names stamped on them. Huber and his team continued to interview witnesses; Himmler was also around, and in a foul mood since his security men had failed to protect the Führer even though it was he who dispensed with them on these anniversaries. He and his closest colleagues were more than prepared to indulge Hitler's belief that any attack on his life must be a ramified conspiracy.

Seizing control of the investigation, their line of inquiry benefited from the coincidental abduction on 9 November of two highly experienced British SIS officers, Captain Sigismund Payne Best and Major Richard Stevens, from the Dutch border town of Venlo by SD agents. They were running an incompetent Anglo-Dutch operation to persuade German generals to move against Hitler, without realizing that their interlocutors were double agents from the SD. Arriving in an apparently sleepy Venlo in Best's ostentatious Lincoln Zephyr car, they were overpowered by sub-machinegun-toting SD agents and driven across the German frontier 150 yards away.[33]

These two captives were imaginatively connected to the exiled Otto Strasser, whose brother Gregor had perished during the Night of the Long Knives in 1934. The leader of a putative

Nazi Left, Otto Strasser had been ejected from asylum in Switzerland and was living in France. These lines were connected to the taciturn little man in a cell in Munich. Waiters who had paid no attention to his regular sojourns in the beer hall recalled his distinctive Swabian accent and the fact that he drank hardly anything with his sixty-pfennig meal.

Himmler arrived to participate in 'enhanced interrogations' of Elser. He is often depicted as a reluctant man of violence, but he spent hours kicking Elser, who was bound on the floor, before the suspect was dragged into a washroom where he was beaten senseless, before being dragged back to Himmler. His teeth were knocked out, his face bruised and bloodied, and his feet swollen from being crushed. This continued until the night of 13 November, when he cracked.

Meanwhile, Gestapo agents descended on a tiny village called Königsbronn to detain a hundred people, including Elser's entire family and many acquaintances, including members of a choir and his workmates at a quarry. A sixteen-year-old girl called Maria Schmauder with whose family Elser had lodged was plucked from sleepy Schnaitheim and put under house arrest in the home of a Gestapo officer. Elser's only true love interest, Elsa Härlen, a married woman with whom he had had a long affair, was scooped up too. The Elsers were taken to Gestapo HQ in Stuttgart before being moved to Berlin on a night train. After a stint in Moabit Prison, they were detained on a separate floor of the luxury Kaiserhof Hotel, in the government quarter. This was handy for the SS-Reichssicherheitshauptamt, the nerve centre of SS operations, as well as for Hitler's Reich Chancellery. Härlen and the Elsers were confronted with the broken man to shock them into filling out a story he had volunteered.

The Nazi leaders were keen to know who sleeps with a monster. Himmler personally questioned Härlen in the dead of night. She was also escorted through the marble corridors of the Chancellery to Hitler, who spent eight hours aggressively querying every answer. Once Elser's captors were satisfied that his own family, friends and workmates regarded him as an oddball, they were returned to their everyday lives, though with black spots on their records. Others, like the owner of a quarry where Elser stole explosives, were sent to the camps.

On 18 November, Elser was moved to the RSHA in Berlin and reinterrogated until the 23rd. He was locked up in one of the fifty overcrowded subterranean cells where the heating and the lights were always on full blast. His diet solely consisted of salted herrings with no water. When physical torture failed, Hitler ordered that Elser be injected with the truth serum Pervertin, and then subjected to the best efforts of four hypnotists, to no effect.

Georg Elser was born in 1903 in the Swabian Jura. His father was a violent drunk who mismanaged his timber business, while his abused mother looked after their small agricultural holding. As the oldest child, Georg had to go to school, help his parents and look after younger siblings. He completed seven years of primary school before an apprenticeship in carpentry. Attempts to work for others failed since he regarded himself as an artiste, so he became a jobbing carpenter. He lived in cheap rented rooms, spending months on the dole when firms went bankrupt. In 1925 he left the Black Forest for Lake Constance and discovered that he could easily find work in Switzerland with clockmakers.

Back in Germany by 1932 Elser had no profound interest in politics, though he always voted for the Communists. He did join the Red Front Fighters League but again was inactive, and a trade union only because it was what workers did to get a job. He rarely read books and only occasionally glanced through newspapers, but he took a keen interest in the gulf between the Nazi regime's ostentatious 'workerism' and the realities of declining hourly wages and exorbitant welfare deductions. He resented restrictions on labour mobility in Germany as the economy was geared up for war, and the Hitler Youth's usurpation of parental responsibilities and the cult represented by the German Christians. After the Sudeten crisis and Munich, he sensed Hitler's drive to war.[34]

He visited Munich on 8 November 1938, ironically the same day as a Swiss theology student called Maurice Bavaud, who had come to Munich with a view to shooting Hitler. Bavaud had been a Fascist sympathizer and anti-Semite, who thought Hitler soft on Communism. This belief grew in the wake of the Molotov–Ribbentrop Pact. After criss-crossing Germany with a pistol in his jacket and failing to get within firing distance of Hitler in Munich, Bavaud was arrested on the train back to France, tried and beheaded in 1941.[35]

Elser carefully inspected the Bürgerbräukeller, noting that it was less risky to put a bomb halfway up the column behind the speaker's stage. He left Munich before the Nazis went on the Jew-hunting rampage known as Kristallnacht. There is no mention of Jews in the interrogation records of Elser, though that was probably an omission by the Gestapo rather than their prisoner.[36]

Of the many places where Elser worked, two stand out, apart from the arms firm where he stole small batches of compressed explosive charges and detonators. He learned how to make the wooden cases in which clocks are housed, which enabled him to study their mechanisms. He also worked as a stock-keeper at the Steinbruch Vollmer quarry, whose lax security gave him access to detonators and explosives.

The Gestapo encouraged Elser to reconstruct his device, which they kept for teaching new recruits. The main technical problem was how to connect the clocks to the bomb without requiring a fuse and remote ignition; he cracked it with a small box that would fire bullet cartridges that drove three nails into explosives. He worked for hours drawing his device, while altering the clock mechanisms so that the bomb could be primed to explode six days later. He built a special wooden chest to house the clocks, the detonators and the explosives, with a secret drawer for the technical drawings, and dragged it wherever he lodged.[37]

Once in Munich, Elser had to work out how to get the bomb into a column. The Bürgerbräukeller stood between two busy streets that people used as short cut, which enabled him to come and go at leisure. After visiting for a couple of nights, he slipped up to the gallery where he had found a hidey-hole. As the hall emptied for the night, he emerged and worked on the column until 2 a.m. or 3 a.m. Then he concealed himself again until he could merge with the mid-morning boozers and leave. Realizing that chisels and hammer made too much noise, he excavated his hole using hand drills with masonry bits. Elser was only once surprised by the landlord, who told him off. He befriended the nightwatchman's dog by feeding him pieces of meat from his plate, so that it did not bark. Excavating the hole in the column took between thirty and thirty-five nights, leaving Elser with badly bruised knees that required medical attention.

Since the bomb could be set six days in advance to within a fifteen-minute window, it became clear to Elser's interrogators that only he could have devised and built this 'hellish machine'. He primed the timer on Sunday 5 November in a marathon work session that ended at 6 a.m., before drinking a celebratory coffee at a local kiosk. By 8 p.m. on 8 November he was in Konstanz, waiting for the two frontier guards to be replaced, the moment he was going through the fence with his cutters.

The investigators and interrogators who chronicled all this did a thorough job, though Himmler was not pleased with the results, scribbling 'Which idiot wrote this report?' in his reserved green ink. Elser manifestly had nothing to do with Best, Stevens or Strasser, so it was impossible to claim he was the sharp end of a conspiracy. To the question 'Who is behind this?', the answer was 'nobody'. Elser was a genuine 'lone wolf', which is what made him so lethal.

Elser was never tried, but was sent to a special cell block in Sachsenhausen concentration camp north of Berlin. His quarters were three cells knocked into one at the end of the special pris-oners' block. He was given carpentry equipment, with which he made knick-knacks for the two SS guards who slept in the third cell of his 'suite'. He was near Best and Stevens, but never spoke to them. From time to time he may have amused himself by telling the guards that the SS had organized his bid to kill Hitler, but none of the evidence bears that out.

The regime's reserved role for Elser was to conduct a massive show trial, where he would be the star witness against the defunct British state personified by Best and Stevens. This never happened, and Elser was relocated in February 1945 to Dachau near Munich. The younger SS guards had gone to die on the

Russian front and were replaced by old lags, many missing a limb. Elser was a wreck, smoking the full ration of forty cigarettes daily with shaking hands. No wonder, since he once asked a guard whether cyanide gas, the guillotine or a bullet was his fate.

On Hitler's orders, Elser was shot dead at around 11 p.m. on 9 April 1945 near the isolated crematorium complex where 200–250 corpses were incinerated per day. Hitler shot himself a few weeks later, having tidied up these final dispositions of celebrity prisoners. Artur Nebe had been executed in March 1945 for his part in the earlier 1944 bomb plot in which his role was to kill Himmler, despite Nebe's having commanded Einsatzgruppe B, killing Jews and deploying mobile gassing vans. He has been airbrushed out of the 1944 bomb plot too.

Elser's killer was a drunken, brutal SS NCO called Theodore Bongartz, who quietly came up behind Elser and shot him in the neck. He was cremated before the four ovens were blown up by the SS. The three SS officers who monitored such covert executions were hanged by the Americans; Bongartz died of cirrhosis on 15 May 1945 in a POW camp before he could be hanged.

The German historian Joachim Fest claimed that many millions of lives would have been spared had the conservative plotters killed Hitler that June day in his Rastenburg HQ. Sticking with German fatalities, 2.8 million soldiers died between 1 September 1939 and 20 July 1944, but another 4.8 million died by early May 1945. The 1944 bomb plotters had considerably more post-war political utility to the class of person who reads broadsheet German newspapers than a humble Swabian Communist carpenter.[38]

Elser was a more implacable assassin, regretful that his attack did not succeed and not exactly remorseful about the eight collateral fatalities his bomb caused. At the conclusion of his formal interrogation, he said, 'I certainly believe that my plan would have succeeded if my views were the right ones. After [it] did not succeed, I am convinced that it was not meant to succeed and that my outlook was wrong.' Had Elser killed Hitler in Munich in November 1939 there might not have been a lengthy war at all; none of Hitler's peers possessed his charisma or oratorical skills, and the army high command might have swept them aside in favour of an authoritarian puppet of their choosing. There were worse fates for Germany than a military dictatorship of limited duration, as was also evident to some in 1932–33. The extreme 'scientific' racism of the Nazis had one major echo following their defeat in 1945 – in South Africa where similar racial prejudice was institutionalized in law and life.[39]

5

Momentous Killings: Verwoerd, Lumumba and Habyarimana: South Africa, Congo and Rwanda, 1960–94

South African history certainly involves the long march to freedom of the Black majority, but it also revolved around a conflict between two white tribes. Like the ancient Israelites, Afrikaner history had a founding flight, in their case away from the British-dominated Cape. From 1834 onwards, Afrikaners or Boers trekked northwards in their ox wagons, clashing with the African kingdoms that blocked their path. It was an ever-moving frontier, somewhat similar to the American West.[1]

Tensions between the two white tribes intensified once diamonds and gold were discovered in Afrikaner areas, requiring an influx of white skilled workers and cheap Black labour. Johannesburg became a gold-rush town, populated by a polyglot army of chancers, dismissed as Uitlanders (outsiders) by the more puritanically solid country Boers.

Eventually, the Afrikaners declared two Boer Republics: the South African Republic in 1852, and the Orange Free State two years later, in the north of what remained a British colony subject to the Crown. They fought two wars to maintain their autonomy and self-rule against perpetual British incursions, one in 1880–81 and the second in 1899–1901. The Boers fought bravely against vastly superior forces, with 75,000 irregulars pitted against 450,000 British soldiers with £120 million behind them.[2]

Like the Irish in their contemporaneous struggle, the insurgent Boers became the darlings of liberal and socialist opinion. There were two Transvaal Irish Brigades, while at home the Irish Transvaal Committee included W. B. Yeats, Maud Gonne,

James Connolly and Arthur Griffith. The future IRA leader Michael Collins also corresponded admiringly with veteran Boer leader Christiaan de Wet.[3]

Extreme resentment against the British became part of Afrikaner identity, which combined a sense of victimhood with racialist superiority towards the surrounding Black African majority. After a negotiated peace settlement, the two Boer republics were abolished, albeit with the promise of self-determination, which came five years later. In 1910 these Afrikaner republics joined two other provinces in the newly founded Union of South Africa, a self-governed dominion of the British Crown.

These events were the backdrop to Hendrik Verwoerd's life. He was born in 1901 in Amsterdam to Dutch parents, who emigrated to Cape Town when he was a toddler. His father, Wilhelm Johannes, was a carpenter and a lay preacher for the Calvinist Dutch Reformed Church. Perhaps fed up with being called a foreigner, Verwoerd senior moved his young family to Bulawayo in what was then white Rhodesia.

The Verwoerd family's adoptive Afrikaner identity calcified in a settler society where loyalty to Britain was intense, especially on the eve of the First World War. In 1917 the Verwoerds returned to the Orange Free State. Hendrik did exceptionally well at every school, and at Stellenbosch University, where he switched from theology to applied psychology, which he taught there from 1927 onwards. He married and would have seven children. Five years later he became the university's first professor of sociology, training social workers to deal with the problems of poor whites.

By the early 1930s, a quarter of the white population were classed as poor. Verwoerd felt that if they fell further they would blend with poor Blacks, bringing the nightmare of 'miscegenation'. The 1930s also brought another 'horror' in an influx of European Jews; Verwoerd was a convinced anti-Semite who would campaign to prevent the recognition of Yiddish as a European language.

Verwoerd led a delegation of Stellenbosch professors lobbying to prevent more Jews from entering South Africa. The United Party government of General Hertzog and Jan Smuts obliged

with a ban effective from 1 January 1936, but not before the
SS *Stuttgart* was en route with 500 Jewish refugees from
Germany. A campaign to turn it back was mounted by the
pro-Nazi Greyshirts and the Afrikaner-dominated Nationalist
Party. Verwoerd would later stop another rescue ship.[4]

Verwoerd progressed from academia to journalism, becoming
editor of the new Afrikaans daily *Die Transvaler*. The peasant
provincialism of Afrikaner culture made it easy for a relatively
well-educated young man to do very well, though he was hardly
in the same league as Smuts, who would go on to a bigger stage,
as a member of Churchill's war cabinet and then as a founder
of the UN. Verwoerd's career was more provincial.

As an adoptive Afrikaner, he gravitated to the most extreme
expression of that identity, joining the 'Purified' National Party
founded in 1914, whose leader was Dr Daniel Malan. These
new Nationalists viewed the political union under British
auspices forged between Smuts and Hertzog's old Nationalists
as a betrayal.

Afrikanerdom was as much cultural as economic and political, and it mimicked the organizational forms that nationalist
movements assumed in nineteenth-century Europe. There was a
'Young South Africa' to propagate language and culture;
modelled on Mazzini's 'Young Italy', it evolved into the
Broederbund or Brotherhood, a secret society to rival the
Freemasons. It had about 2,800 members drawn from the professional classes. Verwoerd joined in 1937 and became a member
of the 'BB' Executive Council three years later.

In 1929 the Broederbund created the Federation of Afrikaans
Cultural Associations to bolster cultural identity, though the
Dutch Reformed Church was active in this too. The leading
Dutch Calvinist theologian turned Prime Minister Abraham
Kuyper had coined the concept of *verzuiling*, meaning that Dutch
people were born into political and sectarian 'pillars' in which
they remained throughout their lives. The idea was easily trans-
ferable to race.

A leading Afrikaans poet, J. D. du Toit, described God as
the Great Divider, who had used the Tower of Babel to condemn
the effects of racial mixing, but it was academic sociology that

really hardened these beliefs. The sociologist Geoffrey Cronjé's anxieties were focused on Indians, whose entrepreneurship threatened white economic dominance, and the larger set of mixed-race or 'Coloured' *sluwe insluiper* (sly stealers-in), who personified the evils of race-mixing in the past. These ideas appealed at a time of heightened Afrikaner self-awareness, and scientistic racism was all the rage in Europe and the US in the late 1930s.[5]

The 1938 centenary of the Great Trek provided tremendous emotional focus. Meanwhile, the Broederbund developed banking, insurance, trade unions and welfare arms to help poor Afrikaners and to foster a thriving middle class. The decision to aid Britain in the Second World War passed by only thirteen votes in the South African parliament – many Afrikaners were aggressively neutral, while some joined overtly fascist organizations.

These entities included the Ossewabrandwag (Ox-wagon sentinel), with its paramilitary wing the Stormjaers or Storm Riders, and a new party called New Order. The OB membership included future Prime Minister John Vorster and Hendrik Van Den Bergh, the future head of the South African security police. The group's chairman Piet Meyer was a fanatic who christened his son 'Izan', Nazi spelled backwards. Verwoerd would appoint him head of the SABC, the country's broadcasting service. The fortunes of these Nazis rose and fell with those of German divisions on Russian and North African battlefields, even as other South Africans fought alongside the Allies in the skies over Britain. When Verwoerd sued a rival English paper which had accused him of supporting Hitler's Germany, the judge found in favour of the defendants.

While Verwoerd raged against what he called 'England's wars' and the 'British–Jewish system' that ruled South Africa, he was too wedded to his own religious and nationalist roots to become a full-blown Nazi. With the war turning against Germany by 1943, South Africa returned to the polls. Though Verwoerd narrowly failed to be elected to the House of Assembly, he was appointed to the Senate, which enabled him to become a government minister.

A tour by King George VI, Queen Mary and Princesses Elizabeth and Margaret in 1947 backfired on Smuts, who hoped it would win him the 1948 election. In his *Die Transvaler* the republican Verwoerd reported only on the traffic congestion it caused. Worse, another 60,000 British immigrants arrived in 1947–48, exported by their grey, bankrupt country. The new United Nations General Assembly gave a respectful audience to a newly emboldened African National Congress (ANC), which seemed to Afrikaners to be riddled with both white and Black Communists, many of the latter Jewish. The solution to this and the related problem of the advancing 'Black peril' was the doctrine of 'separate development' or apartheid.

Apartheid was nakedly racist, but at its heart lay a contradiction. A booming economy, with manufacturing eclipsing agriculture and mining, meant that Blacks moved into white areas, so that by 1946 Johannesburg was a predominantly Black city. Apartheid was designed to reimpose a more stringent rules- and science-based segregation than had existed for decades. Smuts' own achievements included the 1913 Native Land Act, which had constricted Black land-ownership. The 1920 Native Affairs Act established parallel administrative systems and three years later the Native (Urban Areas) Act separated white and Black urban areas. But demography and economics subverted the forms of segregation that apartheid was designed to reinforce.

Verwoerd was a leading exponent of these views, and in 1950 he became Minister of Native Affairs in Malan's government. After eight years he replaced Malan's successor Johannes Strijdom as Prime Minister, a post he occupied until his assassination in 1966.

An aloof and domineering personality with an incredible capacity for hard work, he was responsible for ensuring territorial separation of the races. Blacks were gradually corralled on native reservations, except in towns where economic necessity dictated otherwise, in which case they were deemed transient visitors without civic rights.

The 1949 Population Registration Act sought to racially classify the entire population in line with visual criteria, such as broad noses and curly hair. In the same year, the Prohibition of Mixed Marriages Act did exactly what it promised, while the Immorality Act criminalized interracial sexual relations. The 1952 Abolition of Passes and Consolidation of Documents Act obliged all Blacks to carry a reference booklet giving the bare details of their entire lives, from criminal records to employment. The same year, the Native Laws Amendment Act pinned Blacks to a single domicile, with the Group Areas Act of 1950 making it possible to 'repatriate' Coloureds and Indians convicted of crimes to designated areas. This resulted in the removal of such people from an entire district of Cape Town. Starting with Transkei in 1963, Blacks were granted ten homelands, six of these in Transvaal.

In 1953 the Bantu Education Act restricted Black education to levels commensurate with their lowly status, while the Reservation of Separate Amenities Act was responsible for the *blankes alleen* (whites only) notices on beaches, counters, elevators, lavatories and park benches. The Bantu Authorities Act imposed chiefs as the rulers of the native reservations.[6] This system was so implacably enforced that when in 1955 the US carrier *Midway* stopped in Cape Town, the eighty-six Blacks and 3,000 Filipinos among the huge crew were only allowed on shore if they agreed to stick with segregated entertainment facilities. The US embassy in Pretoria, which failed to protest, did not have a single African-American member of staff, as apartheid was internalized too.[7]

Finally, in May 1961 Verwoerd realized his life's dream of declaring South Africa a republic, thereby terminating the suspect dual loyalties of the Anglophone white population. Fifty-two per cent of South Africans voted for the republic in a referendum held in October 1960, not least after British Prime Minister Harold Macmillan's 'winds of change' speech in the Assembly favouring African nationhood went down very badly. A year later the new South African Republic would be shown the door by the Commonwealth.

The first attempt on Verwoerd's life happened after African protests against the pass laws resulted in the Sharpeville Massacre on 21 March 1960, in which 150 panicked white

policemen shot indiscriminately into a crowd of several thousand Black protestors. The protest, organized by the newly
established Pan African Congress, involved Blacks leaving their
passes at home and inundating police stations, so that the jails
would be clogged with prisoners. At Sharpeville, a township
outside Vereeniging in the Transvaal, the police killed sixty-nine
protestors and wounded 186 others. Verwoerd's cold response
in the Assembly was to claim that such protests came in cyclical
waves, though this was belied by a new Unlawful Organisations
Act rushed through in late March, under which 18,000 ANC
and PAC supporters were detained in pre-dawn arrests. The
South African police and the Bureau of State Security, founded
in 1969, quickly acquired international notoriety for brutality,
torture and murder.

One person who deplored apartheid was a millionaire
farmer of British descent called David Pratt. On 9 April,
Verwoerd went to Johannesburg to open the Rand Easter
Agricultural Show. After delivering his speech, Verwoerd sat
down, glancing up when a small white man advanced on him
shouting his name.

Pratt shot Verwoerd twice in the cheek at point-blank range,
but the small-calibre .22 revolver did little damage and the two
bullets were removed a month later. On one level, Pratt was an
improbable assassin. A prosperous gentleman farmer, he had
volunteered for the wartime RAF, employed eleven servants at
home and was driven to the Rand Show by his Black chauffeur.

But Pratt was also a depressive with two failed marriages
behind him. Although he kept up a respectable exterior, he was
in a worsening state of turmoil, once pursuing his second Dutch
ex-wife to Amsterdam with a gun and cartridges in his pocket.
He had tried to kill himself at least once.

After the shooting, Pratt's lawyers argued insanity as a
defence, though his final peroration to the court was entirely
reasoned. He claimed that following a four-month sojourn in
Europe, he had seen policemen manhandling Black South
Africans into a police van on trumped-up charges of loitering
and regarded Verwoerd as the architect of apartheid. He planned
to argue that he was sane at an appeal, but he did not get the

chance; within a year of being committed to Bloemfontein Fort mental asylum, he allegedly strangled himself with bed sheets, dying on his fifty-third birthday.[8]

Verwoerd dismissed this experience, remarking, 'If someone really wants to kill you, it's not a very hard job. One thing is certain, there's no point going around worrying about it.' The events at Sharpeville played into his argument that a republic would unify all white South Africans amidst Black chaos.[9]

On the day of his death, the Verwoerds flew to Cape Town from their coastal home in the Transvaal for the opening of parliament. In the afternoon he took his seat next to the Speaker of the House of Assembly.

That morning, a heavy-set Greek man had visited a gun store, but realizing he would need a licence, bought a sheath knife and scabbard instead. Moving on to a hardware store, he purchased a kitchen knife with a six-inch double-edged blade. Then he went to work as a uniformed parliamentary messenger, hiding both knives inside his trouser waistband. He knew that Verwoerd would sit alone next to the Speaker, temporarily without his two bodyguards.

As the House filled with MPs, Verwoerd failed to notice a messenger hurrying towards the opposition benches and suddenly swerving towards him. The man seemed to stumble, falling on Verwoerd, before stabbing him four times, twice in the chest and twice in the neck. One wound went through a lung and punctured Verwoerd's left ventricle. Blood spread across his white shirt.

The assassin was dragged off by another MP, a former Springbok rugby player who took the opportunity to break the assailant's nose. It took many politicians and policemen to pacify the man, who even when pinned to the floor, kept shouting, 'Where's that bastard? I'll get that bastard.' As for Verwoerd, six MPs who were physicians tried CPR, but his heart gave out. He was just two days short of his sixty-fifth birthday. While Black Africa from Lagos to Nairobi celebrated, about a quarter of a million South Africans attended Verwoerd's burial in Heroes' Acre in Pretoria, a hallowed resting place for South Africa's greatest. His successor was Baltazar John Vorster, the hard-line Minister of Justice, who vowed to 'walk further along the road set by Hendrik Verwoerd'.

Meanwhile, after receiving multiple beatings on the way to the cells, Verwoerd's killer was made to relate his life story, first to Major-General Hendrik van den Bergh, the best interrogator in the South African security police and future head of South Africa's fearsome Bureau of State Security.

Verwoerd's assassin's story can be told in at least two ways, both of which might be true, but which show the evolution of his state of mind. Forty-eight-year-old Demetri Tsafendas had been born in Mozambique in 1918, to a Cretan anarchist father turned businessman and a Portuguese-African maid who died young. As a child, Tsafendas had once been ill with a tapeworm.

For a time Tsafendas lived in Alexandria in Egypt with his Greek grandmother; after his father married a younger Greek woman, he returned to Mozambique to join his new family, though he was sent to school in Transvaal. He had warm relations with his father, an anarchist who encouraged his son to read Dickens and to listen to the stirring recordings of the American Communist singer Paul Robeson. The father had a secret library with books and periodicals by Italian anarchists, and even a bomb-making manual that his teenage son read and used to accidentally blow up half the house. Tsafendas Junior was a happy youth who ate and talked too much. He liked singing, especially an Italian Communist song, 'Bella Ciao'. He took a keen interest in his Cretan rebel ancestors, in Simón Bolívar and the Spanish Republicans, working for a Communist bookshop owner before training as a welder. Very occasionally some malicious person in the tight-lipped Greek community would remind him that his features were not entirely European, and that his mother had vanished mysteriously.

The Salazar dictatorship's secret police determined that Tsafendas was a Communist 'half-caste' in the file they opened on him in 1934. In 1936 he slipped across the frontier to Johannesburg, where he worked for a few months as a waiter and joined the South African Communist Party. Three years later he found he was barred from entering South Africa again; he entered illegally and worked welding armoured cars in the thriving wartime economy.

Facing deportation, the twenty-four-year-old Tsafendas went to sea in June 1942, on a Greek cargo vessel bound for Canada. Having illegally entered the US he found himself in detention again, but was soon transferred to a mental hospital. He befriended a young Irish patient, who entertained doctors and nurses with tales of an insatiable, talkative tapeworm in his stomach, which thus guaranteed him extra food and relief from serving on murderous wartime North Atlantic convoys. Tsafendas had been torpedoed once on such a voyage, and he was never going to repeat the experience. After the war he sailed to Greece, where he spent some months in the Communist army that was fighting Greek Royalists.

For over twenty years Tsafendas hitched berths on merchant ships, dabbling with Communism and a non-churched brand of Christianity. Everything he owned was in a pair of suitcases, which he humped between hostels. The happiest six months of his life were spent teaching English in Turkey, where he was loved and respected by his students. Any human contact he had usually came through the tiny Greek diaspora enclaves he alighted on in most places.

Many of Tsafendas's longer sojourns ashore were punctuated by spells in psychiatric institutions; whether he was in Canada, Germany, Portugal, Britain or the US, the talkative tapeworm story worked every time, even securing transfers from bad to de luxe asylums. Terms like 'schizophrenic' and 'psychopath' were jotted down, and then, when his mania stabilized, he would be released with some pills. From 1959 onwards his visa applications to South Africa were serially rejected, but no one could stop him returning to Mozambique, the country of his birth.[10]

Tsafendas arrived home in Mozambique in 1963, but bribed a South African consular official into giving him a temporary visa. He surfaced in South Africa later that year but was back in Mozambique a year later, his suitcase filled with books by or about Castro, Frantz Fanon and Patrice Lumumba. He was arrested by the Portuguese secret police, but pretended to be

St Peter and was sent to a Beira hospital. On his release, Tsafendas resumed his career as a waiter, though he clashed with right-wing customers in any cafe foolish enough to employ him. In March 1965 he entered Durban by ship, resuming his life of temporary jobs and political arguments. These included occasional threats to kill Verwoerd, which in his eyes would be no crime at all.

Tsafendas moved to Cape Town, where he applied for a job as a parliamentary messenger, while scouting the building in order to kidnap or murder the Prime Minister. As yet he was undecided about using a bomb, which he was qualified to make, having undergone a refresher course in Greece in the late 1940s. He confided his intentions to a sympathetic landlord, Patrick O'Ryan, telling him, 'If I ever got hold of Dr Verwoerd, I would bash his skull in.'

•

Jobs in parliament were reserved for whites, but a lack of applicants meant that the mixed-race Tsafendas was acceptable as a messenger, even though at the time he was an illegal alien. That summer he also befriended Greek sailors on the SS *Eleni*, a tanker in Cape Town for over forty days of repairs. He vainly tried to buy a gun from one of them – they tricked him into paying for a replica Beretta – while scouting the ship's engine room for somewhere he could hide after the assassination. Before the tanker departed, Tsafendas attended a final dinner, discussing politics with the oldest crewman. While the other sailors drank and sang, Tsafendas spoke learnedly about what Aquinas and Benjamin Franklin had said about killing tyrants. The ancient Greeks would have killed Verwoerd, he said.[11]

Listening to Tsafendas's life story, an aghast Major-General van den Bergh realized he had a major problem. Normally he solved problems by quietly bumping the person off, but Tsafendas was the most notorious man in South Africa. The immigration authorities had messed up by allowing Tsafendas into the country, and they were led by van den Bergh's patron Vorster. The corrupt consular official in Mozambique was arrested and tortured. However, the South African security police had not taken advantage of abundant evidence that Tsafendas was a dangerous Communist. Worse still, like the failed assassin David Pratt, he was white.

Van den Bergh's solution was to authorize twenty days of torture, in order to convince a sane man that he was being controlled by a tapeworm inside him. Tsafendas was electrocuted every day, usually on his genitals, and taken up a few floors and dangled from a window by his feet. He was also bound and hooded and subjected to a mock-hanging. This was all interspersed with ferocious attacks with baton blows and kicks, sometimes with him hung upside down inside a strait-jacket. And if he vomited, he was forced to lick the vomit from the floor.

This treatment convinced Tsafendas to revisit the tapeworm story. His hospital records were hurriedly retrieved from four countries, and several psychiatrists were brought in to manufacture a diagnosis of schizophrenia.

As in Pratt's case, Tsafendas was ruled guilty by virtue of insanity, which avoided the embarrassment of trying a white man for killing the architect of apartheid. Of course, Tsafendas probably did suffer from mental illness – he had been in and out of eight mental hospitals in four countries. He now claimed, or so van den Bergh ensured, that a huge 'dragon-tapeworm' inside his stomach had urged him to kill Verwoerd. In fact, at no point did Tsafendas say that. During his initial police interview, he was all too lucid as to why he killed Verwoerd:

> Every day, you see a man you know committing a very serious crime for which millions of people suffer. You cannot take him to court or report him to the police because he is the law in the country. Would you remain silent and let him continue with his crime or would you do something to stop him? You are guilty not only when you commit a crime, but also when you do nothing to prevent it when you have the chance.

The judge in Tsafendas's case ordered he be sent to Robben Island, four miles off Cape Town, and home to the likes of Nelson Mandela and Walter Sisulu, who were political prisoners.

He was kept in the darkened isolation cells and was beaten several times a day by guards who pissed or spat in his food. He saw no one else for seven months.

He was then transferred to a cell next to the execution chamber on death row in Pretoria Central Prison. Every day he heard the sounds of gallows being tested with weights, and was subjected to serious violence by the guards. In 1989 he was transferred to a lower-security prison at Zonderwater, outside Pretoria. Five years later, as a frail old man, he was transferred to the asylum at Sterkfontein in the countryside outside Pretoria.

Although he had been feted by the international Left in 1966, by the time of his death in 1999, Tsafendas was a neglected figure. The ANC government refused to provide him with a hearing aid and claimed that it would be too divisive to free him, even at a time when they were ostentatiously removing Verwoerd's name from every building and street. In total, Tsafendas spent thirty-three years incarcerated for what he did one afternoon. In his will, Tsafendas insisted that after his death, doctors should perform an autopsy in search of the tapeworm inside him. Maybe he was joking, or maybe he was actually mad all along.

•

For Verwoerd and many Westerners, the Congo was a byword for a unique kind of horror, its literary rendering long patented by Joseph Conrad's 1899 novella *Heart of Darkness*. Until 1908 it was the personal fiefdom of Belgium's King Leopold II, who made a fortune from ivory and wild rubber, but then he was compelled to relinquish Congo to the Belgian state. The Belgians split the huge country and its approximately 250 individual tribes into six giant provinces. The colonial regime was one of the worst, in a competitive field; if Congolese workers failed to meet their rubber quotas, the Belgians would hack off a daughter's hand and foot.[12]

Our story involves a martyred legend of the African national liberation struggle during the Cold War in the 1960s. He was independent Congo's Prime Minister for just sixty-seven days, before his murder at the age of thirty-five in January 1961. Within a year he had assumed such mythic status that the Peoples' Friendship University in Moscow was renamed in his honour.

'Patrice Lumumba' was born Isaie Tasumbu Tawosa in July 1925 in a small Congolese village, soon adopting the nickname Lumumba, which meant 'in-crowd'. He belonged to the Batetla people, most of whom worked harvesting rubber under onerous conditions. After four years of formal education, he could read, write, and had a smattering of French. In 1944 he set out for Stanleyville, Congo's second largest city. With a population of 14 million people, the country had undergone a boom during the Second World War, with Belgium conglomerates making enormous profits from rubber, cotton, industrial diamonds, copper, cobalt and uranium. The big corporate players were the joint Belgian and British owned Union Minière du Haut-Katanga, Société Générale and Forminière. Behind them were Belgian courtiers and ministers, and faceless stockholders in London, New York and Paris.

Lumumba secured a job as a post office clerk on a modest salary; no Congolese person could occupy any post above clerical grade. He completed a nine-month course at the Post Office School in the capital Léopoldville, a thoroughly modern city.[13] Bright and personable, he was eligible for the 'Register of the Civilised Indigenous Population' in what was a starkly segregated society. Inclusion depended on dressing like a European in collar and tie, while white home visitors checked on use of bathrooms, knives and forks and so on. Once classified as an 'evolved person', men like Lumumba could enter whites-only shops, but they were still called '*Tu*' by even the lowliest white interlocutor and when dealing with officials they had to stand to attention. To see how things might be different, Lumumba only needed to cross the Congo River to French Brazzaville, where white and Black people could drink or dance together, with the Blacks also represented in the metropolitan National Assembly. It was there that de Gaulle proclaimed the end of French empire in Africa and its replacement by a Commonwealth-style Union.[14]

Outside of his official duties, Lumumba wrote for the colony's French-language Belgian newspapers. Some of his articles were full of praise for Léopold and his cipher Henry Morton

Stanley. He was also indignant about the daily humiliations inflicted on *évolués* such as himself, but not so much that he turned down being President of Stanleyville's Association of *Évolués*, an elite group of 116 Africans who were subject to European civil law.

The fluently plausible Lumumba soon found himself gaining the ear of the Belgian provincial governor, and even of King Baudouin when he visited Congo in 1955. Pride was followed by a fall when in 1956 he was jailed for taking money from one lot of postal accounts and replenishing the shortfall from others, a scam he had employed for several years. He claimed he committed fraud so as to send his three children to European schools.

Although he received European treatment in jail, Lumumba used the time to develop his critique of colonial rule. He wrote a book, *Congo, My Country*, in which his grievances about the tribulations of his own privileged class widened to the economic injustices of the Congo as a whole.

Despite his conviction for fraud, on his release in autumn 1957 Lumumba joined the accounts department of Brancongo brewery, quickly moving to promote its Polar brand beer. His salary was 25,000 Belgian francs, five times what he had earned with the post office.

This was a time of very rapid growth of political parties, as Congolese reacted to Belgian talk of granting the colony independence. One early entrant was Joseph Kasa-Vubu, a civil servant who would become the country's first President. Lumumba used his automatic entrée to bars in African neighbourhoods to build clubs for aficionados of the Polar brand; these would mutate into cells of the Mouvement National Congolais (MNC), whose President Lumumba became in October 1958. In that capacity he was invited to the Sixth Pan-African Congress in Ghana. Though he would be caricatured as a Communist by the Americans, the Chinese and Russians seem to have made little impression on a man who was opportunistic in his foreign friendships.[15] He was far more taken with the heady creed of Pan-Africanism, but not to the exclusion of the nation state.

In early 1959 Lumumba became the first founder of the MNC to give up his day job for a full-time political career. In a country with only thirty African university graduates and three Congolese in management posts in a civil service elite of 5,000, a man with modest education could do surprisingly well. By then, rioting had broken out in Léopoldville, which resulted in the Force Publique, an African army officered by Belgians, shooting dead 500 people. Throughout the following year people in remoter villages went on a tax strike, boycotting not only the colonial administration but European doctors. With King Baudouin the first to panic, Lumumba thrust himself into the Round Table dialogues which commenced in Brussels to parlay Congolese independence on Belgian terms.[16]

Lumumba was inadvertently helped by the fact that after riots in Stanleyville, he was briefly detained and roughed up by the colonial authorities, which made it all the more sensational when he dramatically emerged from a plane in Brussels, bloodied and bruised from his experiences. International celebrity beckoned.

A Belgian government that had hoped to drag out the transition to independence for thirty years agreed in January 1960 to grant it on 30 June. This was to deliberately invite chaos, since the Congolese lacked the capabilities to run a huge country riven with tribal and regional animosities. In fact, within the Belgian deep state it was secretly hoped that while an *évolué* elite swanned around in big cars and occupied grand villas, Belgians would endure in the army, bureaucracy and mining, because there were insufficient Congolese to usurp them.

Four months before independence, a group of Belgian civil servants resolved to 'eliminate' the newly designated Prime Minister, Lumumba, and to build an opposition to the MNC in provinces that mattered economically. At that stage, 'eliminate' probably meant depose rather than murder. It was not a happy transfer of power. On 30 June the new President, Joseph Kasa-Vubu, acknowledged the 'wisdom' of an ill-considered and patronizing speech by King Baudouin, who claimed his rapacious ancestor Léopold was a civilizing genius. Although he had not been invited to the ceremony, Prime Minister Lumumba launched into an excoriating attack on the departing colonial masters:

We have known ironies, insults, blows that we endured morning, noon, and night, because we are negroes. Who will forget that to a Black one said '*tu*', certainly not as to a friend, but because the more honourable '*vous*' was reserved for whites alone? We have seen our lands seized in the name of allegedly legal laws which in fact recognized only that might is right. We have seen that the law was not the same for a white and for a Black, accommodating for the first, cruel and inhuman for the other.

His final flourish was to jibe at Baudouin: 'We are your monkeys no more.' It was two hours before a furious Baudouin could be persuaded to attend the official lunch, and then he flew home abruptly.

Within a few days, the 25,000-strong Force Publique mutinied over conditions and pay, not surprising since the Congo's first crop of parliamentarians had increased their own salaries five-fold, to the equivalent of $10,000 a year in a country where the average annual income was below $50.[17] Imagining that independence would bring better pay and promotions, African troops were incensed when their commander-in-chief General Émile Janssens scrawled 'Before independence = After independence' on a blackboard. Lumumba dismissed Janssens, replacing him with his own uncle Victor Lundula, with Joseph Désiré Mobutu, a twenty-nine-year-old regimental sergeant major who had become a colonel, as his deputy. These two got a grip on the mutiny in what was rechristened the Armée Nationale Congolaise.

At the time of independence, there were 112,000 Europeans in the Congo, including 89,000 Belgian nationals. During the mutiny, 38,000 of them fled to avoid death, brutality and rape by marauding soldiers. Belgian troops landed at four or five towns on 10 July to augment those already based in-country. At the time, Lumumba and Kasa-Vubu were trying and failing to fly into Katanga, which declared independence on 11 July. Even as they were in the air, other ministers asked for help from the US and UN. The US said no, but the UN said yes.

Katanga was a huge province abutting British Northern

Rhodesia which is now independent Zambia. It may have represented only 12 per cent of the population, but it had 60 per cent of the country's enormous mineral reserves. Katanga's self-appointed saviour, a wealthy entrepreneur called Moïse Tshombe, received a Belgian knighthood as a royal seal of approval for declaring independence. Belgian troops took over security there, in line with the wishes of Belgian court functionaries who had deep connections to major banking, mining, industrial and trading interests. These corporations now paid their sterling equivalent revenues of £15 million a year directly to Tshombe's regime rather than to Congo's central government. Major Guy Weber, who reported directly to King Baudouin's chief of staff René Lefebure, was never far from Tshombe's side. In Brussels, the Minister of African Affairs, Count Harold d'Aspremont Lynden, played a sinister role throughout.[18]

Married into an African royal dynasty, the forty-three-year-old Tshombe acted the part allotted by his foreign masters. He occupied the palatial Hotel Léopold II in Élisabethville, surrounded by presidential guards in preposterous uniforms. French cheese and wine were flown in twice a week.

Tshombe gradually replaced Belgian troops with hired mercenaries. The officers were paid £4,000 a year, a small fortune in the early 1960s. These men were from Britain, Belgium, Rhodesia and South Africa, but with a highly professional core of French right-wing former paratroopers who had fought in Indochina and Algeria. These thugs took out their fury on the Baluba people, who remained loyal to the central government. By their own account, they had no qualms about spraying men, women and children with machine-gun fire.

Lumumba reluctantly accepted UN help to stabilize the Congo, provided it forced the Belgian army out. These decisions passed to Secretary-General Dag Hammarskjöld – he despatched the first of what would become 20,000 peacekeeping troops, but caution meant that they did not act with the resolution required to crush the rebel Republic of Katanga.

Lumumba turned to the Soviets for help instead. His appeal to Khrushchev rang alarm bells in the Eisenhower administration, with CIA chief Allen Dulles calling him 'a Castro or worse'.

When Lumumba visited Washington in July 1960, Eisenhower was in Newport. The CIA reported that Lumumba had behaved like a madman, raving semi-coherently while demanding '*une blonde blanche*' in his suite. This was very much the Lumumba they wanted – a crazy African sex fiend.

With no sympathy in Washington, Lumumba doubled down on demands that the UN crush the separatist regime in Katanga, fearing that diamond-rich South Kasai might jump next. Hammarskjöld began to fear that the UN itself might disintegrate with the Congo, as factional, regional and tribal rivalries tore it apart. More immediately, Lumumba's wild imprecations jeopardized the lives of UN peacekeeping troops, while his uncle Lundula's forces massacred Baluba civilians as they advanced towards Katanga.[19]

On 15 August 1960, Lumumba issued a formal request for Soviet military assistance.

The Americans feared that the Soviets would exploit Congo as a base to spread Communism into nine adjacent countries, though this massively exaggerated Russia's ability to project power in Africa. Ten Ilyushin Il-14 aircraft loaded with Soviet 'advisers' and their equipment landed in the Congo, including trucks to move Lumumba's forces around. Each fresh arrival was carefully counted by African eyes put in place by the CIA Congo station chief Larry Devlin.

Devlin had served in Brussels, where he fully ingested the colonialist view of the Congo. So too did the US ambassador to Belgium, William Burden, who in a 'diptel' sowed the idea in Washington that Lumumba was a Communist. US policy was also influenced by the NATO Secretary-General Paul-Henri Spaak, who used threats of collapsing the alliance to ensure Eisenhower backed Belgium.[20]

By this time, the seventy-year-old Eisenhower was in the lame-duck year of his presidency, and suffering from various health issues. When not playing golf with his rich cronies, he would give vent to the crotchety side of his nature, while the CIA chief Allen Dulles indulged his fascination with cloak-and-dagger paramilitary operations. A committee chaired by retired Air Force General James Doolittle reassured the President that anything was OK in the struggle with Communism: 'There are no rules in such a game. Hitherto acceptable norms of human conduct do not apply.'[21]

Like Mafia bosses, political leaders do not say, 'Go and kill x, y or z.' On 18 August Eisenhower authorized the CIA to kill Lumumba at an NSC meeting where 'We will have to do whatever is necessary to get rid of him' was interpreted as an instruction to kill the Congolese politician. Fears that the US was losing a country were potent after the 'loss' of China to the Communists in 1949. Eisenhower's heir apparent Richard Nixon had Senator John F. Kennedy accusing the Republicans of letting Castro's Communists take Cuba, with Congo to follow under Lumumba.[22] The message to kill Lumumba was confirmed to the CIA by Gordon Gray, Eisenhower's NSA special adviser who worked on covert operations. The job devolved on Larry Devlin who dubbed it 'Project Wizard'.

Devlin's cover was as agricultural attaché in the embassy. Having grown up in California, he served as a wartime army captain, before being tapped by a professor at Harvard for the newly founded CIA. He was married to a Corsican woman who had fought for the Free French and won the Croix de Guerre.

Devlin worked for Bronson Tweedy, the head of the CIA's new Africa section, who had once numbered among OSS spies in World War Two. Tweedy reported to Deputy Director of Plans Richard Bissell, who was answerable to Allen Dulles.

On the ground, Devlin had the support of several officers who recruited local agents. The Americans were aided by Devlin's British SIS equivalent, Daphne Park, masquerading as another 'diplomat' in Léopoldville – ministers Alec Douglas Home and Edward Heath fully shared the negative view of Lumumba. A year before her death in 2010, Park would claim to have played a commanding role in the plot to kill Lumumba, but the evidence points to Devlin and his superiors as the more serious operators.

The order to kill Lumumba came from Bissell in a cable with the codeword 'PROP', which ordered Devlin to meet a 'Joe from Paris' after he landed at Léopoldville airport. A fat man with a club foot, a Bronx accent and a stutter, 'Joe' sat in Devlin's car and explained that the assassination order had come from

Eisenhower. 'Joe' was Dr Sidney Gottlieb, a CIA chemist known as 'Dr Death' around Langley. He handed Devlin a package with a range of lethal poisons from Army Chemical Corps stores at Fort Detrick in Maryland. One toxin to be mixed in toothpaste would replicate the symptoms of polio, which was rampant in Congo. Gottlieb also brought such 'accessories' as hypodermic needles, rubber gloves and gauze masks, since the toxin was tricky to handle. As Gottlieb left, Devlin dumped the poison kit in the Congo River – he would later claim that local assassins lacked sufficient access to Lumumba's home to get such substances into his body. A scrupulous man, Devlin allegedly baulked at what he described as murder. Killing a tyrant like Hitler was one thing, but a Congolese politician? Here Devlin's ex post facto reservations jar with the triumphalism fellow agents heard at the time of Lumumba's death, for then he thought Lumumba was dreaming of a very Hitlerian march across central Africa.[23]

Despite his 'reservations', Devlin dutifully reported the progress of his preparations, while requesting that a specialist be sent, along with a rifle with telescopic sight as an alternative murder weapon. The gun never arrived, but in November a real 'snake eater' called Justin O'Donnell flew in to re-energize the team, followed by two Europeans: WI/ROGUE, 'essentially a stateless soldier of fortune, a forger and former bank robber', and QJ/WIN, another man with a criminal background.[24]

The Americans like to gild their activities with spurious moralizing concerns. Tweedy wrote a kind of character reference for 'ROGUE': 'He is indeed aware of the precepts of right and wrong, but if he is given an assignment which may be morally wrong in the eyes of the world, but necessary because his case officer ordered him to carry it out, then it is right, and he will dutifully undertake appropriate action for its execution without pangs of conscience. In a word, he can rationalize all actions.' Devlin's observations were less Jesuitical: 'WI/ROGUE is a man with a rather unsavoury reputation, who would try anything once, at least.'[25]

Devlin's mind was turning to the more deniable solution of deliberately putting Lumumba in harm's way at the hands of his many local African enemies.[26] While he fomented disorder in the streets, the Belgians and the UN persuaded President Kasa-Vubu to dismiss Lumumba. Kasa-Vubu was ejected in turn by Mobutu, whose soldiers sought to replace civilian politicians with a technocratic government 'Commission' run by the Congo's modest cohort of graduates. Ousted from office but not silenced, Lumumba remained dangerous to the Belgians, especially as the parliament was backing him against Mobutu's soldiers. To that end, d'Aspremont Lynden activated Operation Barracuda, which involved a commando officer called Major Noël Dedeken, aided by two intelligence officers and African soldiers, kidnapping and killing Lumumba.[27]

The UN envoy on the ground, Andrew Cordier, literally silenced Lumumba by ordering the crystal to be removed from the state radio transmitter, while Ghanaian troops obstructed him as he entered the station building. Despite all the new independent African nations represented in the General Assembly, the UN was more susceptible to the influence of the great Western powers, and both Britain and the US were openly hostile to Lumumba. Cordier's successor, Rajeshwar Dayal, then put Lumumba under house arrest, with UN troops and Mobutu's soldiers preventing him leaving Léopoldville. Devlin's spies kept watch on the house, anticipating a breakout.

One night during a thunderstorm, Lumumba hid himself in the back of a car and set off on an 800-mile journey to Stanleyville, his power base. Before leaving he remarked to a friend: 'Don't worry about me . . . if I die, *tant pis*, the Congo needs martyrs.' Devlin despatched QJ/WIN to catch up with him; Mobutu sent the Sûreté police and a low-flying spotter plane. Once he had made it as far as Kasai, Lumumba felt sufficiently secure to stop and deliver the odd village speech and then bigger ad hoc rallies, rather than travelling straight to Stanleyville.

Lumumba was soon intercepted by Mobutu's men. He tried to persuade them to disobey orders to kill him: 'If you kill me, I will not die. If you throw me in the river, the fish will eat my flesh. The Congolese will eat the fish, and then I will be in the bellies of the people and will never be far from my people. I will be in the belly of each Congolese.' However, generous rations of cannabis to the troops ensured they obeyed their commander and not Lumumba.[28]

The fugitive was returned to Léopoldville, where the UN failed to stop him being beaten with rifle butts. The US ambassador tried in vain to suppress the footage of these public beatings. Then Lumumba was taken to a military barracks at Thysville, hundreds of miles away. There he wrote to his wife, knowing that time was limited. 'My faith will stay unbreakable. I know and I feel to the depth of my being that sooner or later my people will get rid of all their internal and external enemies, that they will rise up like a single person to say no to a degrading and shameful colonialism and to reassume their dignity under a pure sun.'[29]

At Belgian urging, Lumumba was moved to a remote airfield on the Atlantic coast and then flown in a Douglas DC-4 to Élisabethville. He and two fellow captives were tied to their seats, with tape over their eyes and mouths. They were so savagely assaulted by drunk African guards during the flight that the Belgian crew locked themselves in the cabin.

Belgian officers were present among the grim reception party on the runway at Élisabethville. Two Flemish gendarmerie officers, Colonel Frans Verscheure and Captain Julien Gat, helped escort Lumumba a few miles to a bungalow on a poultry farm, where he and the other men were detained in a bathroom. Dirty and having worn the same clothes for the last thirty-five days, he was intermittently tortured, with wood splinters rammed under his fingernails. On one occasion, Tshombe showed up, leaving the bungalow with his suit covered in blood.[30]

On the night of 17 January, Lumumba's captors drove all three prisoners towards Jadotville, where Katanga's main prison lay. After thirty miles the small convoy stopped on a dirt track, where graves had already been dug. Four-man firing squads used rifles and sub-machine guns to shoot all three men under vehicle headlights, before burying them so hastily that one arm was left sticking out of the dirt. Verscheure noted '9–43 L dead' in Flemish in his notebook entry for 17 January to record the precise time.

Fearing that Lumumba's body had been too hastily buried, Verscheure despatched a Belgian police commissioner called Gerard Soete to disinter Lumumba, for reburial 150 miles away. However, such was the international clamour regarding Lumumba's disappearance that on 27 January Soete was sent out again, this time to saw up the body and dissolve it in sulphuric acid. Bizarrely, Gat and a police escort drove out of Élisabethville with three African soldiers in civilian garb, posing as the three dead captives en route to jail. A few weeks later, Katanga's government reported that the men had escaped but been killed in the bush by angry villagers. There were death certificates signed by Belgian doctors, but no bodies. The eight soldiers and nine policemen involved in the murder and cover-up received generous bonuses, while King Baudouin awarded honours to their superiors in Belgium. Mobutu ruled Congo, or Zaire as it became from 1971, from 1965 until he was overthrown in 1997, due to events in neighbouring Rwanda. The Belgian authorities only began investigating Lumumba's murder in 2012; in July 2020 prosecutors announced plans to prosecute two elderly men suspected of the 'war crime' of killing Lumumba, after one of his teeth was found in the home of a relative of one of the suspects.[31]

•

A tiny central African neighbour of the Democratic Republic of the Congo, Burundi is one of the few African states to retain its pre-colonial territory, which derived from a Tutsi kingdom dating back to the sixteenth century. A Rwandan kingdom was consolidated later. In the European 'Scramble for Africa', Burundi successively became an imperial German colony and then Ruanda-Urundi a Belgian-administered League of Nations mandate that after 1945 was held in trust for the UN until the two states achieved independence in 1962 as Rwanda and Burundi.

In the 1920s Belgian officials adopted German ethnographical classification of the minority Tutsis and the majority Hutus, formalizing them in mandatory identity cards.

The Germans believed that the tall, slim and tawny Tutsis

were descended from migrant 'Hamitic' peoples, while Hutus were shorter, broad-faced, ebony-skinned and 'primitive'. In effect, an historic feudal order, with the Tutsis in charge, was codified as an indelible racial fact – despite any blurring of these distinctions through intermarriage. The Roman Catholic Church, which controlled schools, cemented these distinctions, feeding Tutsis into every administrative niche, other than when they were overseers for Hutu labourers.

Hutu resentment meant that in 1959–60, on the eve of independence, explosive violence led to the killing of hundreds of Tutsis, with 130,000 fleeing to neighbouring states like Burundi, Congo and Uganda. From 1963, some of these refugees fought back with raids into Rwanda. It is worth stressing that at the time of the events described, Burundi and Rwanda's populations were each around 3 million, though they rose to 6 and 7 million by the mid-1990s.[32]

Burundi and Rwanda gained their independence in 1962, the former as an independent constitutional monarchy and the latter a republic. In Rwanda, President Grégoire Kayibanda, a Hutu, boosted his flagging popularity by encouraging Hutu self-defence groups to massacre Tutsis. About 100,000 were killed, with many more fleeing the country. In Burundi, a Tutsi army officer named Michel Micombero advanced himself from Prime Minister to President in 1966. In 1972, following an attempted Hutu coup in which a thousand Tutsis were killed, Micombero's troops and some Tutsi civilians slaughtered 200,000 Hutus, causing tens of thousands more to flee north into Rwanda or to Tanzania. As in Rwanda, these exiles were used to prop-agate the idea of sinister external conspiracies, which licensed strikes at the remaining enemy within. Events in Tutsi-dominated Burundi had an impact in Rwanda, from which a million Tutsis had fled. Tutsis made up a third of Uganda's army, and played a role in Yoweri Museveni's toppling of the autocratic Milton Obote there. One recruit was a young officer called Paul Kagame, who as a four-year-old child had seen Hutus burn down Tutsi houses, including his own.

In Rwanda, President Kayibanda had imposed strict quotas limiting Tutsis to 9 per cent of all jobs in education, the civil service, private business and the armed forces, regardless of their representation in the population. It was his preference for his own southern Rwandan Hutu that led to a coup led by General Juvénal Habyarimana in 1973.

Habyarimana was a northerner from Gisenyi and inserted his own people into every major position, from the army and bureaucracy to foreign scholarships for students. He routinely dealt with journalist critics and political opponents through such methods as faked fatal traffic accidents. He established a one-party state in which all citizens, including babies, were obliged to join his Mouvement Révolutionnaire National pour le Développement (MRND) and Tutsis were excluded from power. External donors began to worry about Rwanda once coffee and tea prices plummeted in the late 1980s. In 1990, armed Rwandan Tutsi exiles from the Rwandese Patriotic Front (RPF) launched more serious cross-border raids into Rwanda from Uganda.

Habyarimana solved his problems by eliding the alleged external and internal Tutsi threat. In fact, he organized his own gunfire in Kigali so as to arrest entirely innocent Tutsis. In one northern village, 350 Tutsis were slaughtered by their Hutu neighbours to the sound of rhythmic drumming. Worse, elements in the regime were not above mounting false-flag operations so that the RPF would be blamed for strangling a group of village children.[33]

The hatred was articulated through modern media. Habyarimana's wife Agathe had alighted on a sleazy Muslim newspaper humourist, Hassan Ngeze, who was encouraged to establish a paper called *Wake It Up!*. It was a sensation in a society where only 30 per cent of people were literate, but evil words spread like wildfire. It was Ngeze who published the Hutu Ten Commandments:

1. Every Hutu male should know that Tutsi women, wherever they may be, are working in the pay of their Tutsi ethnic group. Consequently, shall be deemed a traitor:

    – Any Hutu male who marries a Tutsi woman;
    – Any Hutu male who keeps a Tutsi concubine;

- Any Hutu male who makes a Tutsi woman his secretary or protégée.

2. Every Hutu male must know that our Hutu daughters are more dignified and conscientious in their role of woman, wife and mother. Are they not pretty, good secretaries and more honest!

3. Hutu women, be vigilant and bring your husbands, brothers and sons back to their senses.

4. Every Hutu male must know that all Tutsis are dishonest in their business dealings. They are only seeking ethnic supremacy. Shall be consequently considered a traitor, any Hutu male:

   - who enters into a business partnership with Tutsis;
   - who invests his money or State money in a Tutsi company;
   - who lends to, or borrows from, a Tutsi;
   - who grants business favours to Tutsis.

5. Strategic positions in the political, administrative, economic, military and security domain should, to a large extent, be entrusted to Hutus.

6. In the education sector, pupils, students, teachers must be in the majority Hutu.

7. The Rwandan Armed Forces should be exclusively Hutu. That is the lesson we learned from the October 1990 war. No soldier must marry a Tutsi woman.

8. Hutus must cease having any pity for the Tutsis.

9. The Hutu male, wherever he may be, should be united, in solidarity and be concerned about the fate of his Hutu brothers.

   - The Hutus at home and abroad must constantly seek friends and allies for the Hutu Cause, beginning with their Bantu brothers.
   - They must constantly counteract Tutsi propaganda.

- The Hutu must be firm and vigilant towards their common Tutsi enemy.

10. The 1959 social revolution, the 1961 referendum and the Hutu ideology must be taught to Hutus at all levels. Every Hutu must propagate the present ideology widely. Any Hutu who persecutes his brother for having read, disseminated and taught this ideology shall be deemed a traitor.[34]

Behind the scenes, Agathe Habyarimana and her coterie established a shadowy 'zero network' throughout the army, security services, media and universities to promote Hutu Power. Within the army, secret cells called the *amasusu* formed, which trained and armed Hutu youth militias called the Interahamwe. Influential university professors warned the Hutus that the Tutsis were planning to slaughter them to reimpose their feudal dominance. Better to kill them all and float their corpses downriver, back to their ancient Ethiopian homelands. One historian concluded such a speech with the warning: 'Know that the person whose throat you do not cut now will be the one who will cut yours.'[35]

In a 1992 report, the Belgian ambassador to Kigali told Brussels: 'This secret group is planning the extermination of the Tutsi of Rwanda to resolve once and for all, in their own way, the ethnic problem and to crush internal Hutu opposition.' Two years later the Belgian Foreign Ministry telexed the ambassador, Paul Noeterdaeme 'Political assassinations and deterioration in security could lead to a new bloodbath. In case of deterioration . . . it would be unacceptable for public opinion if Belgium blue helmets [UN troops] found themselves as passive witness to *genocide*'.[36] Although in classified documents the Clinton administration would refer to 'a final solution' being enacted in Rwanda, when they belatedly and reluctantly publicly used the 'g' word, it was as the more feeble 'acts of genocide' and by that time (May 1994) the killings were in high gear.[37]

Habyarimana's immediate military problem was alleviated by French troops supplied after a failed journalist turned businessman called Jean-Christophe Mitterrand intervened. Though

France had let go its colonies in the 1960s, this was a case of *partir pour le mieux rester*, with dreams of a Françafrique to sustain the glory of France. In practice that meant conditional or limited sovereignty for the new rulers, an anodyne way of saying they could be removed by fair means or foul.

Jean-Christophe ran an Africa Cell inside the presidential office of his father François. He urged his father to despatch troops to save Habyarimana's regime from the RPF. But with the emergence of democratic parties opposed to the dictator, other external donor powers forced Habyarimana to negotiate a peace with the RPF. The IMF were also beginning to wonder how a country dependent on its structural loans could spend $100 million on imported small arms.[38]

Under these 1994 Arusha Accords, named after the town in Tanzania where the talks took place, Habyarimana would include Hutu opposition parties and the RPF in a new government, until elections produced a new order. UN peacekeepers would help integrate RPF units into the army on a 40:60 basis, and an RPF force would move into Kigali under UN auspices. Though he never attended the talks, Habyarimana claimed that the Hutu delegates had been hoodwinked by the crafty Tutsis. During one break in the talks, the most extreme Hutu present, Colonel Théoneste Bagosora, responded to the Vice-President of the RPF by saying he was leaving to prepare '*apocalypse deux*' back in Rwanda, before asking, 'How did your people's blood get mixed up with ours?'[39]

Almost immediately, a new 'private' radio station, Radio-Television Libres des Mille Collines, began broadcasting a programme of Afro-rock and phone-ins including instructions to Hutu Power cells. Never has talk radio had such monstrous effects. School teachers also began dividing classes of children along ethnic lines, and carefully recording the names of Tutsi pupils.[40]

An army colonel provided the 'self-defence militias' with guns and grenades, as well as half a million Chinese-manufactured machetes. The Rwandan embassy in Paris bought small arms in huge quantities. After much haggling by the Americans and British over the cost of a UN peace mission, the French Canadian

Major-General Roméo Dallaire was chosen to lead 2,548 troops rather than the 4,500 he had requested. Their mission was scaled back from contributing to nationwide security to securing Kigali, while clauses instructing them to deter armed gangs and seize illegal weapons caches were deleted. Dallaire was also denied intelligence support, notably the kind of intercept capabilities that would have been vital, since neither the Rwandan government nor the RPF used encrypted communications.[41]

In January 1994 a CIA report concluded that the Arusha Accords would fail and that half a million Rwandans would die in ensuing hostilities. Dallaire learned that the Interahamwe had the capacity to kill a thousand people inside twenty minutes. The barrage of Hutu Power propaganda was incessant, and some of it was directed at Habyarimana for caving in to the Tutsis and the 'international community'. On 3 April, Radio Mille Collines warned that 'a little something' was about to happen.

The final act in this drama involved neighbouring Burundi. Things had seemed to improve there after years of misrule by Micombero and his Tutsi successors. The election in 1993 of a returned Hutu exile, Melchior Ndadaye, as President boded well, and he appointed a Tutsi as Prime Minister and Tutsis to a third of cabinet posts. But in October he was bayonetted to death by Tutsi army putschists, compounding Rwandan Hutu fears of what the RPF might do once in power. Fifty thousand Hutus were slain in the ensuing Tutsi crackdown in Burundi, and thousands more fled into Rwanda. After a brief hiatus, in February 1993 the Minister of Agriculture, a moderate Hutu called Cyprien Ntaryamira, was elected President.

On Wednesday 6 April 1994, President Ntaryamira was travelling home from Dar-es-Salaam with the Rwandan Habyarimana in the latter's Dassault Falcon 50 executive jet, a gift from Mitterrand. Both Presidents and their entourages had been attending a conference. As the jet descended below 1000 feet to land at Kigali's Gregoire Kayibanda International Airport at around 8.20 p.m., eyewitnesses saw two bright lines of light streak up to the wing and tail. Two explosions sent the plane down in flames, killing its three crew and nine passengers. The missiles were most likely SA-7s, a Soviet infra-red heat-seeking missile, with a range of about 3,500 feet.

While Rwandan troops and militias denied the UN access to the airport and palace, Radio Mille Collines reported the double slaying. With the most senior government ministers and the head of the armed forces now dead, army colonels took charge, though they were careful to claim it was not a coup, initially blaming 'the Belgians' for shooting the plane down as part of a campaign to get the UN contingent withdrawn.

Before dawn broke on Thursday, units of the Presidential Guard para-commandos were combing Kigali, killing senior politicians. The first victims included ten Belgian UN troops who had been sent to protect the interim Hutu Prime Minister, who was herself butchered with her husband. After senior officers like Bagosora issued orders, anyone identified with an ID card as a Tutsi was fair game, and the killing quickly spread to other parts of Rwanda.

On the streets, there were so many corpses scattered around Hutu army and militia checkpoints that they had to be collected in dumper trucks.

Belgian, French and then UN peacekeeping troops were withdrawn after evacuating foreign nationals. The killing continued for a hundred days, during which time between 800,000 and 1,000,000 Tutsis were hacked or shot to death. It is estimated that 100,000 Hutus took part in the killing, with written instructions and lists of victims underpinning a frenzy that the killers' regarded as their 'work'. After the RPF took over the country, the mass-murderers slipped away among columns of Hutu refugees, finding succour in UN-protected camps over the border in Zaire. These camps were dominated by Hutu Power murderers, and were so well-appointed that Congolese went there to shop.[42]

Few assassinations have had such fateful consequences. We can rule out that Belgian UN troops were responsible, not least because ten of them were also killed. Witnesses gave three conflicting locations for where the two SA-7 missiles were launched from. One of the most specific testimonies came from a retired Belgian called Paul Henrion, who claimed to have noticed a military vehicle with an artillery piece behind it, with a dozen or so Rwandan soldiers. Among them, he said, were two with newer uniforms, their black berets cocked to the left. Rwandan soldiers were shabbily attired and their berets slanted to the right. Some suspect that these two better-clothed soldiers were French volunteers from Cameroon or Guadalupe, attached to a French base commanded by Major de Saint-Quentin, an adviser to Rwandan paratroops. A later French report would claim that the missiles were fired from within the presidential guard base at Kanobe, directly below the aircraft's flight path.[43]

The alleged involvement of foreigners should not distract from two rival claims of ultimate responsibility. Both Rwandan factions had these missiles, and it requires no special skill to use them. The most plausible explanation is that extreme Hutu elements decided to kill Habyarimana, both to sabotage the Arusha Accords and to initiate a genocide they had carefully planned years in advance. That was the view of a report by Belgian intelligence, which pointed the finger at Colonel Bagosora, who was close to people who had benefited most from the regime Habyarimana was trying to dissolve. Others implicated a breakaway party from Habyarimana's MRND, which refused to sign the Arusha Accords. Founded in 1993, the Coalition pour la Défense de la République was an even more implacable advocate of Hutu power. Its militia song was called 'Tubatsembasembe', meaning 'we shall exterminate them'.[44]

The French preferred to blame the anglophone RPF. A French judicial enquiry was established in 1998, but it was wound up in 2018 after concluding that there was no evidence to implicate the RPF.

Claims that the RPF killed the two Presidents rely on patterns of behaviour. One effect of the crash was to eliminate the Rwandan chief of staff, throwing the army into confusion. The French were convinced that the invading RPF carried out the attack, killing Habyarimana so as to install Prime Minister Agathe Uwilingiymana in power. This version of events is vehemently denied by Rwanda's current President, Paul Kagame, who was a major-general in the RPF invasion force at the time.

He claims the French were trying to obscure their aggressive support for Habyarimana in order to defend their sphere of influence. In 2009 Rwanda followed Mozambique as the second African country without historic UK ties to join the Commonwealth. Kagame wants to turn it into Singapore or South Korea.[45]

The assassinations of Habyarimana and Ntaryamira unleashed a spiral of violence that did not end with the genocide in Rwanda. The Hutu in Zaire built a 30–50,000-strong army, which launched attacks into Rwanda. The debilitation of Zaire's American- and French-backed dictator Mobutu led Angola, Burundi, Rwanda, Uganda and Zimbabwe to invade Zaire, deposing Mobutu and installing Laurent Kabila in power over what would in 1997 become the Democratic Republic of the Congo. If the invading countries had been motivated by the need to stop Congo acting as a safe haven for rebels against their own regimes, they fell out over their desire to capture Congo's rich mineral resources. Between 3 and 4 million more people perished in the Congo and Great Lakes wars, as countries fell out and sub-divided. Kabila was assassinated in his office in January 2001; his son Joseph finally stepped down from office in January 2019. Paul Kagame has been repeatedly accused of assassinating exiled political opponents who were previously officers in the RPF, most recently in South Africa.[46]

6

The Assassins go to War: Vietnam and Laos in the 1960s

The CIA conspiracy to murder Patrice Lumumba in the Congo was part of the US government's strenuous efforts in the 1950s and 1960s to prevent Asian, African and Latin American 'dominos' falling to Communism. In 1953–54 the CIA had two successes. One coup brought down Iran's popular nationalist Prime Minister Mohammad Mossadeq to protect Anglo-American oil interests, while another saw off reforming Guatemalan President Jacobo Árbenz Guzmán after he made an enemy of the United Fruit Company. That operation was preceded by an anonymous 1953 CIA handbook entitled *A Study of Assassination*.

The paper includes such thoughts as 'Assassination can seldom be employed with a clear conscience. Persons who are morally squeamish should not attempt it.' Those planning assassinations have to weigh up whether the assassin is expendable or not, with those motivated by 'politics, religion and revenge' most suitable for a suicidal role.

Most of the paper is dedicated to techniques. Few people know how to kill someone with their bare hands, but many can use a hammer or lampstand, provided they know that it is best to hit a victim on the temple or the back of the head, where the skull is weakest. A contrived accident, with the subject falling at least seventy-five feet onto a hard surface, was recommended, though it may mean grabbing him by the ankles first. Car accidents were not favoured. Drugs and poisons were viewed as 'very effective'. Manufacturers' estimates of ranges for firearms need to be halved, and the advertised power of a gun underestimated the need to choose a lethal one, as the first attempt on the life of Verwoerd proved. Sub-machine guns were only to be used to spray several targets at once, preferably in the course of 'indoor work'.[1]

As we have seen, the CIA tried to kill Patrice Lumumba. It made eighteen attempts to assassinate the Cuban revolutionary leaders Fidel and Raul Castro and Ernesto 'Che' Guevara, in the first case with assistance from the Mafia. The desire to quarantine the Cuban Revolution also led to the CIA arming the killers of President Rafael Trujillo in the Dominican Republic, despite the Kennedy administration ruling out his assassination.[2]

In Vietnam, the Kennedy administration was complicit in the slaughter of President Ngo Dinh Diem and his younger brother Nhu, who were supposed to be America's allies; but there was also the secret CIA war in Laos and a darker campaign of militarized assassination. This Phoenix Program ran out of control, half a dozen years after Kennedy's own death in November 1963.

Despite American moralism, the CIA was also as ruthless as its Soviet counterpart. While the CIA had some notable successes in rigging Italian elections and suborning British trade unions, its attempts to spy in the Soviet Bloc were unimpressive, a few starry defectors notwithstanding. The Agency eagerly grabbed at opportunities to operate in the new 'peripheral' theatres of the Cold War because there were fewer legal restraints there and more bribeable clients. New recruits learned less about codes, counter-surveillance and dead drops, and more about HALO parachuting and demolition. This was a kind of failure.[3]

Subject to light Congressional oversight, the CIA was able to muscle into paramilitary operations to the point of running its own private armies backed up by all the firepower the Pentagon could loan them. This came at a cost to what was supposed to be an intelligence service, and it also involved administration officials and diplomats actively lying to Congress, the media and the American people. In 1971 William Colby, the CIA's executive director, told the House Committee on Government Operations: 'The Phoenix Program is not a program of assassination.' That was contradicted when President Nixon himself angrily rejected cuts to the program, on the grounds that 'we've got to do more of this. Assassinations. That's what they [the VC] are doing'.[4]

The White House chose to attach such significance to a region where the US would expend much blood and money for so little gain. This was not just a matter of checking the spread of Communism, but of transforming post-colonial societies into approximations of modern nation states. This was the fig leaf which distinguished 'US jeans, shades and bomber jackets' imperialism from the 'European pith helmet colonial' versions. In some respects, the varieties of imperialism *were* different. The spirit of sociologist Talcott Parsons lurked behind America's spooks and gunmen. A generation of men tantalized by organizational structures and statistical data was on the loose, for if WW1 was a chemists war, and WW2 one for physicists, Vietnam was the high tide of sociologists crunching endless data designed to 'explain' what was going on in Vietnamese villages. If a problem could not be reduced to a flowchart or could not be expressed in a glib slogan, it did not really exist. Effectively the worst aspects of US academic, corporate and advertorial culture went to war in an old and complex society about which most Americans knew nothing.[5]

We must first revert to the point at which the French colonial war in Indochina became America's war in Vietnam. Following the defeat of the French at the Battle of Dien Bien Phu, the 1954 Geneva Accords established a demilitarized line at the 17th parallel between the Communist Democratic Republic of Vietnam in the north and the French-backed state of Vietnam in the south. Huge population transfers occurred, with 1.5 million northerners being moved southwards, while some 30,000 Communist sympathizers went north. CIA psy-ops experts were on hand to spin this 'Passage to Freedom'.

The Geneva Accords also made provision for an independent Laos, on Vietnam's western border, though power there was almost instantly contested by the Communist Pathet Lao, allied to Hanoi and backed by China, and the royalist government in the Laotian capital Vientiane. Laos initially seemed far more strategically important to the US than Vietnam. If it fell to the Pathet Lao, Communism might creep west into Thailand, Burma,

Malaysia and ultimately India. That belief explains why the country would acquire a huge CIA presence to enable the Agency to direct its own $500 million a year war: Operation Momentum.

This secret war was effectively directed by the US ambassador to Laos, William Sullivan, who reported directly to the White House. The more maverick 'practitioners' included CIA contractor 'Tony Poe' (Anthony Poshepny) who dwelt in a remote jungle hut with Pathet Lao heads stuck on spikes. The side war's aim was to divert as many North Vietnamese troops from Vietnam to Laos as possible, and to disrupt the Vietcong's traffic along the Ho Chi Minh Trail. Sullivan and the CIA also directed the bombing strikes on Laos that, when averaged out, involved one bomb every eight minutes for ten years. Even when there was a bombing pause on North Vietnam, the bombers continued to strike Laos – as it was deemed better not to have these planes rusting on the tarmac.[6]

The Americans also alighted upon a winner in South Vietnam. Although the exiled Emperor Bao Dai was notionally head of state in the south, power was skilfully accrued by his Prime Minister, Ngo Dinh Diem. He was the son of a Mandarin-literate civil servant, who espoused the obscurantist Catholic philosophy of personalism and neo-Confucianism. Invariably dressed in white suits, he was a humourless bore who could talk about frothy metaphysics for hours at a time.[7] Vice-President Lyndon Johnson paid a flying visit to weigh up the Diem regime in May 1961, remaining on the ground for all of thirty-six hours.

Hostile to French colonialism, Diem had, like other nationalists in Indonesia, India and China, collaborated with the Japanese overlords of Vichy Indochina, but was briefly tantalized by the revolutionary leader Ho Chi Minh after the Communists captured him. He cultivated Catholic contacts during protracted spells in the US, including Cardinal Joseph Spellman, and Senators Mike Mansfield and John F. Kennedy. Indeed, one could argue that Communist persecution of Catholics was the one theme that gripped Americans about Vietnam. Interest in this distant country only really peaked when a naval medical officer called Tom Dooley published a lurid account of Operation Passage to Freedom called *Deliver Us From Evil*.[8]

Diem had five siblings who were integral to his regime.[9] His eldest brother, a provincial governor called Khoi, was assassinated by the Vietminh in 1945. A younger brother, Ngo Dinh Nhu, and his glamorous wife Tran Le Xuan, aka Madame Nhu, regarded themselves as master conspirators, and created a secret party called Can Lao to support Diem. A third brother, Pierre Martin Ngo Dinh Thuc, would become the Catholic Archbishop of Hué, Vietnam's traditional royal capital. The bias shown to minority Catholics in a country that was 80 per cent culturally Buddhist would dog the Diem regime; out of a hundred southern Army of the Republic of Vietnam (ARVN) generals, only four were Buddhists. The more thuggish face of the family was that of the 'baby' brother Ngo Dinh Can, who combined running the secret police with trafficking opium. In 1955, after Diem had eliminated criminal-cum-political sects, he became President and promptly postponed the elections.

American influence in South Vietnam was exerted through a 685-strong Military Assistance Command, led by General Paul Harkins. The CIA had been a presence in Indochina since 1950, with the usual Agency station lurking within the US embassy; two years later this was augmented by a Saigon Military Mission based in private houses rented around the capital.

This was the domain of Colonel Edward Lansdale, a former Californian advertising executive turned Asian political fixer and psy-ops counter-terrorism guru. His nickname, Colonel Landslide, accurately described his chief talent: rigging elections. He was on loan to the CIA from the US Air Force, but army commanders and ambassadors did not like this opinionated maverick, as he did not conform to any defined hierarchies. Lansdale had his own handpicked staff of buccaneering tough guys, interspersed with younger Agency idealists. He focused on boosting Diem as an Asian George Washington, while the main CIA station and the State Department cultivated the more sinister Nhus.

In essence, any US attempt to turn Vietnam into a rough simulacrum of a Western democracy had to work with the warped timbers of the Diem family clan, and within the endemic rivalries of various US bureaucracies. It was a tall order, but the 'best and brightest' Kennedy team thought nothing was beyond their capabilities.[10]

•

This was also a nation at war. Three days before Christmas 1961, a radio-detection truck lumbered along a highway in South Vietnam. On board were nine ARVN soldiers and an American army specialist, twenty-five-year-old James 'Tom' Davis from Tennessee. A mine hurled the truck thirty yards into a ditch. As the dazed occupants climbed back onto the road, hidden Vietcong gunmen arose from the adjacent paddy fields and killed them all, including Davis. He is often referred to as the first US soldier to die in Vietnam at the hands of the Vietcong. A major and a master sergeant had been killed two years earlier, but Davis was the first fatality of President John F. Kennedy's choice to authorize Operation Beef-Up.

Months of tortuous discussions in the Kennedy White House had concluded that the best way to reduce US involvement in South Vietnam was to increase it. This seemed a sensible alternative to despatching 200,000 US troops and bombing North Vietnam, options which some of Kennedy's civilian and military advisors favoured. By contrast, American doves warned of a jungle quagmire that might suck in as many as 300,000 troops without clear outcome, in order to prop up a corrupt, discredited and failing regime in Saigon.

Vietnam was one of several Cold War flash points where successive US administrations decided to halt the global spread of Communism. The goal was to avoid 'losing' another country as China had been 'lost' to Mao Zedong in 1949 and to give the US's colonial allies in the region a fighting chance by bolstering trade. That on coming to power the Kennedy administration had almost immediately botched a poorly conceived sea invasion of Cuba at the Bay of Pigs added pressure that Kennedy be seen to succeed in Vietnam and Laos.

Before 1961 ended, Kennedy had 'merely' doubled the number of military 'advisors' in Vietnam, though tellingly, the existing MAAG was now subordinated to a new Military Assistance Command, Vietnam. The number of American 'advisors' would rise to 9,000 by the end of 1962 and to 32,000 by the end of 1963. Kennedy approved the strategic hamlets programme whereby corralled villagers had to pay for their huts and the barbed wire enclosing them. American 'Jungle Jim' planes flew tactical ground-support operations alongside South Vietnamese Air Force pilots, sometimes flying into Laos to bomb enemy staging posts. Operation Ranch Hand used chemical defoliants to destroy vegetation and rice paddies, to deny the Vietcong cover and food. Napalm was used to create 'shock and awe', with huge vivid explosions. And naval patrols illegally ventured into the seas north of the 17th parallel to wage war on the Vietcong's maritime supply routes to the south.

In April 1961, Kennedy had violated the Geneva Accords by adding a hundred extra 'advisors' to the 685 authorized in the agreement. Prior to the reinforcements, the President's legal advisors also established that taking part in combat in South Vietnam was illegal under United Nations law, but they went ahead regardless. As a devotee of Ian Fleming's Bond thrillers, Kennedy was tantalized by acts of derring-do, as were many of the 'action intellectuals' around him. In men like Lansdale, the President had people from wartime Office of Strategic Services backgrounds. That would prove catastrophic for the CIA, as gung-ho paramilitary operations eclipsed the business of recruiting agents and analysing intelligence.

In contrast to Britain, where the Secret Intelligence Service pre-dated the wartime Special Operations Executive, in the United States the Office of Strategic Services evolved *into* the new CIA. Under the direction of Allen Dulles, himself a wartime OSS agent in Switzerland, paramilitary acts of derring-do were celebrated by an agency that was often East Coast 'liberal' in its outlook. The OSS legacy led the US into the murky business of murder. In later life, Truman would profoundly regret having created this Frankenstein's monster, describing the Agency as 'a cloudy organism of uncertain purpose and appalling power'.[11]

Diem's regime came under sustained assault from a guerrilla army, mainly consisting of southerners who had fled north in 1954. One of them was Le Duan, the main advocate of a southern revolutionary strategy in the Politburo. From late 1957 onwards, there was a discernible uptick in Communist activity. That year the visiting war correspondent Bernard Fall noticed a large number of obituaries of village chiefs in South Vietnamese newspapers. After realizing that 452 of them had died within a year, Fall correlated these deaths with maps where guerrillas were especially active and realized that Saigon was ringed by hostile forces. In 1959, Le Duan and his comrades decided to infiltrate forces on what became known as the Ho Chi Minh Trail, a 1,500-mile-long track that darted in and out of Cambodia and Laos into Vietnam. In February 1961, these well-trained repatriates merged with local supporters to become the People's Liberation Armed Forces. Diem gave them the derisive nickname 'Vietcong', short for Vietnamese Communists.[12]

The main Vietcong units were heavily armed and mobile, and they were increasingly supplemented by North Vietnamese regular troops. Guerrilla units came in two varieties. Some operated as full-time fighters, while others fought at night and farmed during the day. Unfortunately for the Americans, these were some of the toughest fighters on the planet.

The VC retained a permanent grip on the countryside – where roughly 85 per cent of Vietnamese lived – through a shadow government. This was the Vietcong Infrastructure (the VCI), who were not fighters but professional political cadres, perhaps 80–100,000 strong. They were either covert agents with legal South Vietnamese identity documents or 'illegals' who moved around with squads of Vietcong guards between well-defended compounds. A parallel urban operation focused on mobilizing a broad political front, combined with sporadic acts of terrorism. There was a sharp increase in VC violence, as they drew up blacklists of people involved in administration, government programmes (like 'Chieu Hoi' or 'open arms for defectors') and reactionary political movements.

Coercion was carried out by specialized VC Security Sections. In 1957 some 472 government officials were assassinated, but between 1958 and 1965, the VC assassinated 9,700 people and kidnapped a further 36,800. A notice would be pinned to the victim's corpse, stating: 'This man was a lackey of the US–Diem clique, has been warned . . . twice by us, but continues to work for the traitor Duong Van Minh . . . we, the Liberation Forces, have punished him, as we punish anyone who continues, after having been warned and re-educated.' In areas not controlled by the VC, victims would simply be killed; in areas under their control, a more graduated system of threats ensued, with warnings followed up with confinement, or sometimes execution following some sort of rigged public trial.[13]

Vietcong strategy was intended to nullify the role of the Saigon government through a combination of precisely targeted terror and political work at the grassroots. Since the Saigon government often worked against the grain of peasant sentiment, the Vietcong could pose as the peasants' protectors. After all, the main supporters of the Saigon regime were city dwellers, who included large numbers of Catholics, and such non-ethnic Vietnamese as the Chams and Khmers. Unlike many of Diem's corrupted officials, Vietcong cadres were articulate, puritanical and ruthless.[14]

Diem's primary strategy for defeating the Vietcong was to secure territory by establishing fortified hamlets into which unwilling peasants would be herded, breaking family ties to where their ancestors were buried. Once there were enough of these hamlets, a province could be declared cleansed of VC. Imprisoning between a third and a half of the population seems a dubious way to build a nation, but reality rarely impinges on this kind of warfare.

In theory, small static self-defence forces would protect these hamlets against the Vietcong, while more mobile ARVN ranger units would prevent enemy movement across frontiers, or kill them in the free-fire zones established around the hamlets. The problem was that Diem insisted on keeping the ARVN on a tight leash, while regarding high casualty rates as a black mark against any commander. Since this led to a reluctance to fight, it impelled the Americans to take a larger role, for example by increasing ARVN mobility through deployment of US helicopters. High American visibility in turn increased the Vietnamese perception that Diem was merely their puppet, a line hammered home in relentless Communist propaganda.

The Americans were confident they could help Diem win this

war. They knew that in the late 1940s Greek royalists had defeated Communist partisans, failing to note that the former were suffi- ciently strong to drive the enemy into barren mountainous terrain that disadvantaged them. British counter-insurgency know-alls advertised their successes against a Communist enemy in Malaya. The differences were that the British ruled Malaya rather than having to work through touchy clients like the Diems, and the 'Chi-Comms' they fought were a distinct Chinese ethnic minority in a sea of more biddable Malays.

However, neither Greece nor Malaya had neighbouring states like Cambodia and Laos into which the enemy could duck and dive, nor the equivalent of North Vietnam that bordered the People's Republic of China. Mao's regime could supply arms in vast quantities to North Vietnam without even breaking into a sweat, and the Soviets might also lend a hand. Being wholly ignorant of Vietnam's deeper history, the Americans did not grasp that they had picked a fight with a people who had spent centuries resisting imperial Chinese dictation, while imposing their own mini-empire over their less warlike neighbours. They had their own idea of a Chinese-style heavenly mandate to rule, and could sense which way the wind was blowing.

By 1961 there were about 16,000 Vietcong fighters in the South. They were responsible for abductions, assassinations and sabotage, all designed to advertise the nullity of Diem's authority. In the first half of the year they assassinated more than 500 government officials, kidnapped a further 1,000 and killed 1,500 of the ARVN troops that were vainly engaged in hunting them down. They could also mount much larger assaults, just to make their point.

On 18 September 1961, a thousand Vietcong fighters attacked the provincial capital of Phuoc Vinh, less than sixty miles north of Saigon. The civil guards defending the city were overwhelmed, while two ARVN ranger companies fled. The Vietcong held the city for about six hours, freeing 250 Communists from its jail. They also tried and publicly beheaded the provincial governor and his assistant, and then left. Even when the ARVN thought it had the Vietcong in an ambush, the results proved disastrous. At Ap Bac in early 1963, the Vietcong decimated a superior

ARVN force and shot down five of the fifteen US helicopters that flew in reinforcements. Critical US officers could see that something was very wrong.

A lack of progress in the ground war, despite the steadily rising number of strategic hamlets, was one problem, but then the Diems contrived to cause a bigger one. In May 1963 rioting erupted in Hué, after a deputy provincial security chief invoked the Decree Number 10 to prohibit the flying of flags to celebrate the Buddha's 2,527th birthday. A week before, the same man, a Catholic, had raised no objections when white and gold papal emblems were displayed to celebrate the twenty-fifth anniversary of Diem's brother Ngo Dinh Thuc becoming the city's archbishop. Although actively committed Buddhists were a large minority in Vietnam, this was also how the majority defined itself in a cultural sense. Worse, a minority of Buddhist monks had become aggressively militant, with a firebrand leader called Thich Tri Quang. Inept and overly aggressive policing of Buddhist demonstrations led to disturbing pictures filling the world's eager media. It did not help that those arrested were herded onto trucks bearing the clasped hands logo used to depict US–Vietnamese amity.

These grim scenes led the US embassy in Saigon to investigate alternative leaders to Diem. Matters went from bad to worse when on 11 June 1963 an elderly monk called Quang Duc sat down at a Saigon intersection, whereupon colleagues poured a mixture of gasoline and diesel over his head. Quang Duc calmly lit a match and burned to death while chanting 'return to eternal Buddha'. As images of Quang Duc's immolation were beamed around the world, Kennedy exploded: 'How could this have happened? Who are these people? Why didn't we know about them before?'[15]

Diem refused to make concessions to the protestors, while Nhu sent heavily armed special forces troops into Buddhist pagodas in Hue and Saigon, killing dozens of people and arresting 1,400. Diem's abrasive sister-in-law Madame Nhu contrived to worsen matters when she offered to supply gasoline and matches for the next 'spectacle'.

The images of the burning monk explain why Kennedy

decided to replace his ambassador in Saigon, the Diem apologist Frederick Nolting, with Henry Cabot Lodge Jr., who became the President's 'personal representative'. His appointment was a key response to reports that coups against Diem were being plotted, although it transpired that the ARVN conspirators were too fearful to make their move without a green light from Washington as to how such a step might be received by the Kennedy administration.

The plotters could not devise a workable plan, which gave the Kennedy team a dilemma. It resulted in such sophistries as the US Chief of Staff ordering General Harkins to establish contacts with plotters to 'review' any plan these generals might show him, without 'engaging directly in joint coup planning'. The decision to approve the ouster of Diem and Nhu was also related to suspicion that Nhu was in clandestine talks with the North Vietnamese, covertly brokered by the French ambassador, whose President, de Gaulle, had grandiose ideas of restoring French influence in the region once it had been unified. At best, Nhu was trying to gain leverage with the Americans.

The green light for the coup took the form of Telegram 243, sent from the White House to Lodge on 24 August 1963. Those on Kennedy's team who most opposed the Diems circulated it or relayed its gist, for most of the wider presidential team were enjoying their Saturday afternoon's recreations. In essence, the pro-coup element in the administration pulled a fast one on a lazy weekend afternoon.

The telegram instructed Lodge to 'urgently examine all possible alternative leadership and make detailed plans as to how we might bring about Diem's replacement if this should become necessary'. With consensus apparently secured, Kennedy ordered that it be sent. Several senior figures in the administration would later claim they were tricked into approving the telegram by a militantly anti-Diem minority. Even though Kennedy had said, 'This shit has to stop,' he did not revoke the orders to Lodge.

The Buddhist crisis showed no signs of abating; when an eighth monk burned himself to death, he did so in front of cameras. Incredibly, the US government's response to the plot relied on one low-level CIA agent. Lou Conein was the only direct point of contact with the conspirators. He met them in his dentist's surgery, joking that he visited so often that his teeth were an orthodontic miracle. He gave General Khiem of the ARVN details of the US ordnance supplied to its special forces. When Conein met Generals Don and Minh on 2 and 5 October, they told him that members of the Ngo family were going to be assassinated. They needed assurances that the US would not thwart what they planned to do.

On 5 October Kennedy approved cuts to the aid package for the Diem government, including assistance that went to ARVN special forces. On 9 October, Lodge was told by the White House: 'While we do not wish to stimulate a coup, we also do not wish to leave the impression that the US would thwart a change of government or deny economic and military assistance to a new regime if it appeared capable of increasing the effectiveness of the ARVN military effort.'[16]

The coup was launched on the afternoon of 1 November 1963 with a siege of Gia Long, Diem's presidential palace. The head of ARVN special forces had been executed the previous day by Captain Nguyen Van Nhung, who was to play a key role in the following days. The plotters controlled units in or close to Saigon, while frustrating the movement of any loyalist troops further afield.

Protected by their presidential guard behind heavy fortifications, the Diem brothers were relaxed about the gunfire outside. They imagined it was from an operation of the kind that Nhu had set in motion from time to time, to draw any plotters from their cover. The moment the coup started, Conein attached himself to General Duong 'Big' Van Minh at rebel headquarters, with $42,000 in Vietnamese piasters scooped from the CIA station safe. The battle at the palace raged for seventeen hours. The rebels selected a young colonel, Nguyen Van Thieu, to lead the final assault on the palace.

Realizing that the game was up, Diem and Nhu appeared to negotiate a ceasefire and safe passage, before fleeing in a Citroën DV into Saigon's Chinese quarter, much to the fury of their generals, who thought they were still inside the palace.

They were tracked down to a small Catholic church called St Francis Xavier, where they were extracted, bound and shoved into an M113 armoured personnel carrier. As they were driven away, the Diems shouted furiously at Captain Nguyen Van Nhung, who rode inside the vehicle. Threatening him with a firing squad was a mistake, since Nhung was a professional killer with forty notches on his revolver, the latest added the previous day. He used a bayonet to stab Nhu fifteen to twenty times, before shooting them both in the head.

As news of this development reached Washington, it was presented as 'suicide', though how the Diems could have wounded themselves to this extent then killed themselves while their hands were bound was not explained. A photo of their corpses appeared in a Saigon newspaper with the caption '"Suicide" with no hands'. The story then shifted to them 'self-destructing' by grabbing a gun or grenade from their captors.

Although the Kennedy team knew enough about the Diems to realize that killing the 'bad' brother would invite vengeance by the survivor, they affected shock that both men had been murdered. Kennedy jumped from his chair and left the Oval Office with the blood drained from his face, appalled by acts that he later called 'particularly abhorrent'. His shock may have been related to the fact that his government was up to its neck in the coup and the assassinations.

When the worst Diem brother, Ngo Dinh Can, was apprehended on his rural estate, Lou Conein was waiting at Saigon Airport to hand him over to the coup generals. He was tried for murder and torture in the spring of 1964 and sentenced to death by firing squad. Madame Nhu, who was in Beverly Hills at the time of the coup, moved to Rome and then to France. She died in Rome in 2011.[17]

The assassination of the Diem brothers plunged Saigon into political confusion; the rebel generals were soon at war with themselves, providing Hanoi with an excuse to escalate Vietcong operations. Attacks rose from 400 to 1,000 a week, including systematic terror strikes on cinemas and bars where American troops gathered. In January 1964, thirty-six-year-old General Nguyen Khanh, who had not benefited from the earlier coup, carried out his own. One of his first victims was Captain Nhung, slayer of the Diems, who was found hanged in his cell.

Following Kennedy's assassination in Dallas, President Lyndon Johnson – who had opposed supporting the anti-Diem coup – explained why he was so conflicted to Senator Richard Russell:

> I'm confronted (sic). I don't believe the American people ever want me to run [quit Vietnam]. If I lose it, I think they'll say I've lost it . . . At the same time, I don't want to commit us to a war. And I'm in a hell of a shape.[18]

Russell prophesied that half a million men would be bogged down for a decade in this quagmire.

But Johnson (and the advisers he inherited from JFK) also construed the war as a test of American resolve, and as a Texan he was not going to be the man who lost the Alamo. He wanted a quick victory and then to leave with honour but this was not to be. In a typically homely simile, LBJ compared himself to a fisherman eagerly grabbing a fat worm, only to discover it contained a sharp hook. Operation Plan 34A initiated a covert war in North Vietnam, which resulted in the Gulf of Tonkin incident in August 1964, when misread radar signals were imagined to be an attack on US warships, and LBJ's decisions to bomb North Vietnam and commit what ultimately became half a million more US combat troops. At the same time he stepped up a local version of his Great Society: ploughing billions into civic aid programmes, whose only effect was to distort the economy to serve US forces with drugs, drink and prostitutes in cities in which corruption was endemic. Some cynics wondered aloud that it might be better to just buy off the Viet Cong with grants of $500. In fact, the US military chiefs had costed that, arriving at $2,500 per head as a more realistic sum. They also claimed that the cost of killing a single VC was estimated at $60,000, though in fact it was more like $337,500. These numbers were insane.[19]

•

In 1968 as the bombing campaign Operation Rolling Thunder reached a crescendo, US warplanes dropped a million tons of bombs on South Vietnam and a hundred thousand GIs were despatched to destroy Vietcong guerrillas in the provinces around Saigon. Then came the Tet Offensive on the Lunar New Year 1968, which gave a powerful shock to US popular opinion, even if it failed to spark a general uprising throughout South Vietnam. Most alarmingly, the Communist offensive brought an underground Vietcong apparatus into plain sight.[20]

Tet galvanized a renewed and coordinated push for peace, though many Americans simply wanted to avenge themselves on a VCI that had conducted wholesale massacres of collaborators in cities like Hué, which briefly fell into VC hands in 1968.

The CIA's Robert 'Blowtorch' Komer had been appointed in 1967 to lead a new Civil Operations and Rural Development Support agency. In effect, the US intended to conduct two parallel wars within one, although the CIA had previously been engaged in desultory military actions, as it sought to 'mirror' the VC's own efforts. The US and South Vietnamese military provided large numbers of search-and-destroy troops, helicopters and trucks to bolster the CIA's limited armed resources.

Komer was also responsible for Intelligence Coordination and Exploitation (ICEX), a programme that was the brainchild of a CIA analyst called Nelson Brickham, who arrived in Vietnam in 1965. He steeped himself in French counter-insurgency literature while trying to apply the organizational structures of the Ford Motor Company to an intelligence-driven war on the Vietcong Infrastructure. His chief realization was that a bewildering variety of US and South Vietnamese intelligence units found it easier to receive than share information about the same subjects.[21]

ICEX was intended to harvest and coordinate intelligence on VCI personnel from multiple agencies, so that they could be captured or eliminated. In 1968 it was renamed 'Phoenix'. There was also a technical intelligence programme based on electronic ground sensors placed along the Ho Chi Minh Trail, which beamed information about enemy movements to circling aircraft, helping US and South Vietnamese special forces kill VC raiding parties.[22]

The first person Komer approached to be the military deputy to the Phoenix Program, Colonel Robert Gard, turned down the offer: 'I didn't know a lot about it, except that it was an assassination program, subject to killing innocents,' he said. Komer quickly moved on to become US Ambassador to Turkey. His successor was the CIA's director of the Far East division, William Colby.[23]

A Minnesotan former wartime OSS operator, Colby had been deputy and then station chief in Saigon between 1959 and 1962 and knew Vietnam well. On his return to Saigon he was the first CIA officer in the Agency's history to be given ambassadorial rank. He was a Columbia-schooled lawyer and a dedicated Roman Catholic. Colby would fall victim to a gulf that opened up between serving his President and having to account for questionable deeds to an increasingly assertive Congress, especially when a crooked President in Nixon was succeeded by an unelected weak one in Ford.

Phoenix was supposed to deliver the equivalent of a rifle shot rather than a shotgun blast at the VCI, at both provincial and district levels. So as not to be seen to surrender the counter-insurgency campaign to the Americans, the South Vietnamese established their own parallel programme, its name derived from a legendary bird in Vietnamese mythology. From 1968 to 1972 Phung Hoang did its share of the heavy lifting in the struggle to shatter the VCI. Both combined intelligence collation with kinetic operations. The Vietnamese ones consisted of up to 5,000 volunteers from the National Police Force, National Police Field Force and Special Police Branch. There were five eighteen-man PRU teams in each province – they were directly controlled by the CIA, which had its own shadow army of Agency contractors, Green Berets and Navy SEALS.

Phoenix had an army major in each district, with younger lieutenants and captains as local advisors. The job involved what amounted to social work, combined with going out to kill the enemy. Moving around the hot and humid country with heavy packs and weapons quickly became uncomfortable, while the backpack straps cut into shoulders. Apart from biting insects and reptiles, the ground could conceal mines or sharp spiked traps.

All Phoenix operations were based on a monthly Hamlet Evaluation Report in each district. This involved establishing the frequency of VC attacks, whether there was a school, a village chief, a market place, sanitation and so forth. This information was then interpreted by a computer in Saigon that graded each hamlet by letter. D, E and V suggested that the VC were in charge at night.[24]

Phoenix advisors were involved in civic amelioration and the elimination of Vietcong agents at the village and hamlet level. Since every act of amelioration, from providing medical help to children with club feet to supplying pigs, was regarded as a provocation by the Vietcong, the Americans knew that each good deed was liable to be repaid with a bad one.

America did not want to publicly admit that they murdered people, so Phoenix invented the fiction that they were attempting to capture senior VC personnel. In reality, the South Vietnamese criminal justice system was so corrupt that an estimated 70 per cent of captured VCI were able to bribe their way back to freedom. That was one spurious justification for simply murdering any suspects. The word 'elimination' was quickly replaced by the more anodyne 'neutralization' in US military and CIA jargon, though its meaning was just as clear. In practice, routine exposure to the corpses of innocent villagers who had not paid Vietcong taxes, or who were killed for purely tokenistic purposes, meant that the VC were often slain either in the course of ambushes or within the tunnels where they laid up by day.[25]

Phoenix's image was not helped by the 1969 prosecution of Green Berets who murdered a Vietnamese agent they suspected of spying, nor by the My Lai massacre. Those sections of the American public who believed their government was running a covert assassination campaign were right. In February 1969 a SEAL team led by Bob Kerrey, the future Nebraska senator and governor, disembarked near the hamlet of Thanh Phong. After knifing the occupants of the first hut, Kerrey's team ended up in a gunfight, where thirteen of the twenty-four people they killed were women and children.[26]

It is hard to feel sentimental about the Vietcong victims of

Phoenix, since many of them were professional assassins who terrified simple farmers and made examples of government collaborators. When on 5 December 1967 a Vietcong team descended on the village of Dak Son, a government-controlled hamlet in the Central Highlands, they used flame-throwers and grenades to massacre about two hundred people, most of them women and children. Across South Vietnam, villagers who were merely paying taxes to the VC incurred imprisonment of up to two years, and South Vietnam's prisons were notoriously brutal and overcrowded.[27]

Since senior VCI personnel had armed bodyguards, Phoenix ambushes could be reasonably construed as regular military engagements, in which it was a case of 'kill or be killed' in conditions of almost zero visibility in the lush foliage. The success of Phoenix depended on serial betrayals by informants or VC defectors, as well as information extracted by torture from prisoners. One obvious danger was that informers might regard their power as an income stream, threatening wealthier people with delation so as to extract money. Some of the most effective killers in the PRUs were former VC who were eager to advertise their new loyalties. It was not a hard choice to make when VC rations consisted of twenty kilograms of rice a month, supplemented with dog, elephant or monkey meat, or the jungle moths that flew around kerosene lamps. By contrast, America's South Vietnamese allies lived in a land of endless commissary plenty.[28]

Most VC captured by South Vietnamese forces could expect to be tortured with electricity, water or truncheons, especially if the situation was tactically critical. A proportion of such captives were also summarily executed, *pour encourager les autres*.[29] But torture was also routine in special centres where tactical intelligence was out of date. A CIA front company called Pacific Architects & Engineers built all the Provincial Interrogation Centers to a standard format and CIA instructors taught Vietnamese policemen interrogation methods. Senior VC captives were detained in solitary confinement at the CIA's National Interrogation Center in a naval compound on the Saigon River.[30]

Judging from an account by a Phoenix advisor, few of the VCI personnel surrendered when they were tracked down to their hideouts. The District Party Secretary in Di An, To Van Phoung, was betrayed by a pregnant older girlfriend after he swapped her for a younger woman. She collected what the US did not advertise as a bounty of $1,000 on his head, though that was made clear to each village after more senior Phoenix officers vetoed a simple 'Dead or Alive' poster as being in breach of the Geneva Conventions.

Phoung was trapped in a tunnel near some rusty drainpipes. After failing to surrender, smoke grenades were lobbed into his hiding place. A South Vietnamese policeman who volunteered to go in was shot in the shoulder, so a grenade was tossed in and Phoung was killed. His corpse was transported back to base lashed to the bonnet of a jeep so that villagers could see that he was dead.

While those who participated in Phoenix often argue that it was effective, its emphasis on statistical targets meant that some results were better in appearance than in reality. After Accelerated Pacification was introduced, monthly quotas of five kills were imposed on each district. This did not matter much if that district was averaging ten VCI dead a month, but if it wasn't it was tempting to record conventional guerrilla deaths as a VCI, pretending that some unrecognizably mangled corpse was a senior VCI official. Reports and charts took on their own reality, at variance with what the VC were doing on the ground.[31] A young Japanese-American officer called Vincent Okamoto, assigned to Phoenix for a couple of months but later a Los Angeles Supreme Court judge, described the modus operandi:

I had never heard of it until they told me I was part of it. I did it for two months and didn't like it at all . . . the CIA and the boys in Saigon would feed information into computers and would come up with a blacklist of Vietnamese who were aiding the enemy. The problem was, how do you find the people on the blacklist? It's not like you had their address and telephone number. The normal procedure would be to go into a village and just grab someone and say, 'Where's

Nguyen so-and-so?' Half the time, the people were so afraid they would say anything. Then a Phoenix team would take the informant, put a sandbag over his head, poke out two holes so he could see, put commo wire around his neck like a long leash, and walk him through the village and say, 'When we go by Nguyen's house, scratch your head.' Then that night Phoenix would come back, knock on the door and say, 'April Fool, motherfucker.' Whoever answered the door would get wasted.[32]

On paper, the results of Phoenix looked impressive: between 1968 and 1972 some 80,000 VCI personnel were 'neutralized'. Between 20,000 and 40,000 people were killed, some of them innocent victims of a grudge by their informant neighbours or where the kill rate had been set at 50 or 80 per cent a month. However, most statistics become less impressive when one looks deeper into them. Many of the victims were low- rather than high-ranking VCI cadres, and it is unclear whether they were killed in the course of Tet or by strategic hamlet self-defence forces rather than by a small army of professional killers.

The fact that the North Vietnamese and Vietcong acknowledged the harm Phoenix had done to their political infrastructure pales beside the longer-term reputational damage it did to the US, and to the CIA in particular. How could the US make a moral case against Communist tyranny when its own agencies were waging a murderous campaign that relied on widespread torture? Any lawyer could have written Colby's thin claim that Phoenix was reconcilable with the Geneva Conventions.[33] Indeed, after he became CIA director in 1973, Colby had the unenviable task of explaining what the CIA had done in the last two decades to an incredulous Congress. Many felt that he revealed more about Agency activities than he should have. He became a liberal lawyer, and drowned in a canoeing accident in 1996.

Instead of focusing on the difficult business of gathering intelligence, a powerful caucus within the CIA would continue to believe in such paramilitary operations, not least in the context of the global war on terrorism after 9/11. It did not help that this war would be mainly waged in a region where intelligence agencies were already used to acting like cowboys – the Greater Middle East. But we must first look at the most notorious assassinations in contemporary history, which themselves impacted on future US covert operations. The subject had become so toxic that in 1975 President Gerald Ford banned assassinations by agents of the US government, though creative ways of getting round this obstacle were soon found. Before we get to the Kennedys and King, we must examine what a real conspiracy to assassinate another global leader feels like.

7

Democracy, Death and the Dynasts:
France, the US and India, 1961–91

Some conspiracies to assassinate world leaders have really existed. We can follow one in detail before contrasting it with other better-known examples where conspiracies have merely been alleged. It is time to revisit the times fictionalised in *Day of the Jackal* by an English journalist down on his luck at the time.

French President Charles de Gaulle (1890–1970) was the target of thirty assassination attempts by the Secret Army Organization (OAS), a right-wing terrorist group dedicated to keeping Algeria part of metropolitan France. It was founded by three fugitives in a Madrid hotel room in December 1960. They had fled to Franco's Spain after the failure of a settler insurrection in Algiers that was supposed to presage a military coup in mainland France.

One of these men was sixty-one-year-old General Raoul Salan. As a thrusting colonel he had helped liberate Toulon from the Germans in 1944 before becoming army commander in Indochina, where France was involved in a deadly colonial small war. He was joined by Jean-Jacques Susini, a lanky twenty-seven-year-old, and Pierre Lagaillarde, a handsome twenty-eight-year-old lawyer turned reserve parachute officer who considered himself a fascist rather than a reactionary.

Susini was the most dangerous of this trio. After an Arab egg seller was blown up with a bomb, Susini commented: 'Well, are we going to use FLN [National Liberation Front] tactics, yes or no? The egg seller was first to go. Now they'll understand.'[1] Over time, the leadership of the OAS would mutate in the wake of arrests. One new face was the former Governor-General of Algeria, Jacques Soustelle, and another was the Gaullist wartime resistance leader and two-time Prime Minister Georges Bidault. Under the sympathetic and watchful eyes of the Spanish or Italian intelligence services, such men plotted de Gaulle's murder in hotel dining rooms, or during agreeable strolls through Europe's great cities.

The OAS felt betrayed by de Gaulle's abandonment of the French, Corsican, Italian, Maltese and Spanish settlers in Algeria even as the army was fighting a counter-insurgency against the secular nationalist – but majority Muslim – National Liberation Front. This 'betrayal' followed defeat in Indochina by the Viet Minh six years earlier at Dien Bien Phu. The war in Algeria allowed French soldiers to correct the mistakes that had led to this earlier defeat, even if it meant using torture and terrorism as part of their campaign.

General de Gaulle believed that an era of organized continents was supplanting one of disparate colonies and that an independent French nuclear bomb mattered more than massed paratroopers. He despised the parochial vision of the white settlers in Algeria and the 'romantic' military renegades who supported them. The latter increasingly subscribed to belief in a clash between Christian and Muslim civilizations, in which they imagined themselves as latter-day saints or crusaders. Such paranoid fantasies are widely held today on the far-right.

Ironically, de Gaulle himself feared for the future of France as a culturally Christian country, if the alternative to Algerian independence was the integration of nine million Algerian Muslims in the metropolitan mainland. His critics despised him as a glorified accountant calculating the costs and benefits of Algeria; de Gaulle took a broad strategic view of the costs of war in Algeria and decided to agree majority self-determination, despite having said 'Long live French Algeria' a couple of years before.

Over-confident of metropolitan support, the OAS graduated from murdering Muslim charwomen and French policemen in Algeria to serial plots to kill the man whose ascendancy to the presidency of the new Fifth Republic they had initially supported. The mass exodus of a million Europeans from independent Algeria and an accompanying wave of FLN terror fuelled the mindless murderousness of the OAS, which had no difficulties in recruiting civilian and soldierly thugs to do its dirty work.

The OAS had a command structure, led by Colonel Yves Godard; Soustelle took care of the finances, and there was a deep pool of active sympathizers, from bombmakers and spotters to men and women who rented cars and safehouses. A few of the more spectacular attacks convey the depth of planning.

On 8 September 1961 de Gaulle and his wife Yvonne set off from the Élysée towards their home at Colombey-les-deux-Églises. Almost immediately a phone call was made – presumably from an OAS spy inside the Élysée – to the first of two people waiting in cafes along the probable route: 'Monsieur Paul here. I have found you an apartment. It is on the first floor but you will have to pay 801,000 francs cash for it.' When decoded, that meant that de Gaulle would be in the first vehicle, whose number plate included 912.[2]

The device had been buried in a large pile of sand used to counter ice in winter, and connected to a firing mechanism operated by a man hiding in a thicket. When the fifteen litres of napalm exploded, rather than the separately housed main charge of 100 pounds of plastique, de Gaulle's quick-thinking driver Francis Marroux saved his life by accelerating as the DS was engulfed by a fireball.

After this attack, de Gaulle agreed to shorten his journeys to and from the Élysée Palace. He would be driven the forty miles from his home to Saint-Dizier before being flown by helicopter or plane to Villacoublay and then driven the final eight miles into central Paris.

On the evening of 22 August 1962, de Gaulle was returning home after a long cabinet session devoted to the violence in Algeria. He and his wife Yvonne sat in the rear of a Citroën DS 19, with his military aide de camp and son-in-law Alain de Boissieu and an army driver in front of them. A second DS 19 containing a doctor and two bodyguards travelled behind them, followed by two police motorcycle escorts.

An OAS spotter made a phone call when the convoy left the palace, and a second noted that the convoy had taken one of two possible routes to Villacoublay. More calls went to a third man, who was waiting in a cafe in the suburb of Meudon. He used a rolled-up newspaper to alert a team of shooters in a yellow Estafette van, parked on the road de Gaulle was travelling along.

The attack had been rehearsed seventeen times, which may explain why reactions were dulled rather than sharp. In failing light and driving rain, the killers were not quick enough to leap out and shoot, though they ran round to the front of the yellow van and fired at the speeding convoy as it went past. The main gunman was Serge Bernier, a veteran of the Korean War, accompanied by a couple of Hungarian refugees who thought de Gaulle was a Communist.

A second vehicle, a stolen car, managed to race out of a sideroad and get between the two presidential vehicles. Its driver was Alain de Bougrenet de la Tocnaye, a thirty-five-year-old aristocratic Breton army lieutenant. In the front passenger seat was Georges Watin, Algeria's largest landowner. He fired his sub-machine gun at de Gaulle's car, shattering the rear windscreen. Inside, Alain de Boissieu ordered de Gaulle and Yvonne to duck down in the footwell, as one round came within inches of the General's head.

De Gaulle's driver accelerated away from the underpowered pursuit vehicle. At Villacoublay police counted six bullet holes, one just above where de Gaulle's head would have been. Forensic experts established that 150 rounds had been fired during the entire attack, which had been codenamed Operation Charlotte Corday, after the Catholic assassin who in 1793 stabbed the Jacobin journalist Marat in the bath.[3] As his plane took off, de Gaulle reflected on the assassination attempt. 'Their operation was badly organized. Their shooting was hopeless. They were no experts. But I congratulate you; in moments of crisis there is a ring of command in your voice.' He kissed his son-in-law and ordered a whisky, with a beer for Yvonne.[4]

By early September, all but three of the dozen assassins were in police custody, with the others having fled to Franco's Spain.

One of the first to be picked up, a young army deserter, was persuaded to identify the ringleaders as Lieutenant Colonel Jean-Marie Bastien-Thiry and de la Tocnaye. The former imagined himself to be a French Claus von Stauffenberg, the Wehrmacht colonel who had nearly killed Hitler at Rastenburg in 1944.

Having volunteered for service in restive Algeria in 1958, Tocnaye was appalled as de Gaulle appeared to sell out the European colonists. He joined the OAS, writing to de Gaulle: 'Now that you have betrayed the army and the French people and given away Algeria, the only solution I see left is to kill you, and that is what I propose to do. You call yourself the Guide of the French people, but you are a bad Guide, and in any case it does not take a man of great morality to be the head of such people'. With OAS funding, Bastien-Thiry and Tocnaye recruited the team of killers.[5]

The trial of the main accused in early 1963 resulted in death sentences for Bastien-Thiry, Tocnaye and Jacques Prevost, a former Parachute Regiment sergeant who had served in Indochina. Thiry was shot by firing squad at the Ivry fortress on 11 March. Tocnaye's sentence was commuted to life imprisonment, though he was released in 1968 and would later run a road-haulage business, with no regrets about his actions. Georges Watin was never caught and ended his days in Paraguay.

The Petit Clamart attack was followed by several others. One involved a camera adapted to fire poisoned bullets during a visit by de Gaulle to Athens; another involved a long-range rifle during the 14 July celebrations in Paris. Plans to assassinate de Gaulle while he attended John F. Kennedy's funeral in Washington were abandoned after the FBI got wind of what was afoot.

Susini's mind turned to remote-controlled explosions. In August 1964, plotters installed a remotely detonated bomb in a large flowerpot at the base of a memorial at Mont-Faron near Toulon commemorating wartime Franco-American landings in Provence. De Gaulle stood a few feet from the flowerpot on 15 August, safe because agents had removed the explosives after gaining intelligence of the plan. In May 1965, a plan was made to hide a similar device in the base of a monument to Georges Clemenceau at Sainte-Hermine in the Vendée. The plot to detonate it when de Gaulle inaugurated the monument was betrayed and a heavy police presence guarded the site night and day before a bomb could be placed. There are reports that in 1965 the OAS approached the CIA about getting hold of a ring with a curare-laced pin concealed within it. An old soldier would clasp de Gaulle's outstretched hand at a veterans' day parade, killing him with the poison.[6]

The OAS was systematically smashed by coercive diplomacy, police infiltration and a vicious terror campaign using undercover operatives. What these serial attacks show is that conspiracies of like-minded fanatics do exist, sometimes straddling several countries and involving elite figures from bankers to generals. They are relatively easy to penetrate – crazy right-wingers are usually unrestrained in advertising their hatreds after a drink or two when they imagine they are among the likeminded. They are often betrayed by the cowardly, greedy or disillusioned in their own ranks. Detectives apply pressure to captives, before prosecutors unravel conspiracies in overwhelming detail.

Unsurprisingly, de Gaulle himself was sure that his American counterpart John F. Kennedy was killed as a result of a conspiracy. He told his Minister of Information Alain Peyrefitte: 'What happened to Kennedy is what nearly happened to me. His story is the same as mine.' De Gaulle firmly believed that Lee Harvey Oswald was set up and then killed to prevent a public trial, that 'The security forces were in cahoots with the extremists'.[7]

Since Kennedy favoured Algerian independence, we need not linger over claims that the CIA had some role in OAS plots to kill de Gaulle. As in many other countries where it operated, the Agency had connections throughout the French security services, and it would be unsurprising that some of the latter were sympathetic towards the OAS, but this does not mean the CIA was involved in trying to assassinate the French President, or that de Gaulle was right to transpose his own experiences onto the ill-fated Kennedy.[8]

•

President Kennedy arrived in Dallas on Friday 22 November 1963 for a forty-eight-hour visit to Texas, following a similarly brief tour of Florida. Both states were important to counter any electoral shift to the Republicans in the South in the 1964 national election. Texas could also be a source of big campaign money for Kennedy, though it was home to many virulent extremists. One, retired general Edwin Walker, a secretly homosexual enthusiast for the anti-communist John Birch Society, had denounced Kennedy as 'a liability to the free world' and compared him and his brother Bobby to Fidel and Raul Castro. His latest venture was 'Operation Midnight Ride', a speaking tour in tandem with Billy James 'Balloon' Hargis, an Evangelical who had tried to drop Bibles into Eastern Europe with balloons.

Walker came onto Oswald's radar and when he failed to kill the general, it would prove ominous for Kennedy. Oswald acquired both a mail-order revolver and an Italian Mannlicher-Carcano rifle with a screw-on telescopic sight. He took typing classes at night after days working in a printing works, the only job he had ever liked, but which he soon lost as his attention wandered to higher things. His wife Marina was not sure what he was doing either in his little private room or on his mystery night-time outings. In fact, Oswald was building up a dossier on Walker's home which he observed through a telescope he had brought from Russia. That included studying the change of buses he would need to take to get to his victim, for Oswald turned his inability to drive into a positive that would throw the police off his trail. What assassin goes to work by bus? He also wrote a manifesto called 'The Atheian System', which sought to transcend Communism and capitalism.

On 31 March, after their neighbours had set off for Sunday church, Oswald persuaded Marina to photograph him in the garden. He was dressed in black and held his rifle in one hand and copies of *The Worker* and *The Militant* in the other, with his revolver strapped to his waist. Having paid the rent and power bills he left Marina a key to a safe deposit box with a cheque for $60 and various instructions. He assumed he would be killed by the police or if not, then he left Marina instructions on how to find the city jail.[9]

On the evening of Wednesday 10 April 1963, Walker had settled down to do his income tax return in his large house on the secluded Turtle Creek Boulevard. At around 9 p.m. a bullet fired from the picket fence ninety feet away passed through his hair before embedding itself in the wall. Because of the bright interior light, Lee Harvey Oswald presumably could not see the narrow horizontal window frame that slightly deflected his bullet. When he arrived home at midnight, Oswald was so agitated that he told Marina that he had attempted to shoot Walker, who by morning Oswald knew had survived his attack. Oswald waited until Sunday before retrieving his rifle from where he had buried it.

The John Birch Society placed a black-bordered advert in the *Dallas Morning News* on 22 November to greet Kennedy, while others distributed 'Wanted for Treason' handbills. It was so striking that the President showed it to his wife Jackie, commenting: 'We're heading into nut country today. But if somebody wants to shoot me from a window with a rifle, nobody can stop it, so why worry about it?' Threats against a US President are a federal offence. The psychiatrists who examined the men who committed such crimes and were jailed in federal prisons concluded that the threat itself was cathartic and that none of these patients was a realistic threat to any President.[10]

Oswald did not hate Kennedy in the same way as he hated the fascist Walker. Instead he needed Kennedy's fame to increase his own. On the coffee table in the sparely furnished Fort Worth apartment he shared with Marina and their children, the student Paul Gregory, one of Oswald's few friends, always noticed the 5 January edition of *Time* magazine, with Kennedy as the Man of the Year on the cover. The President was young, handsome, had a beautiful wife and was backed by an Irish-American clan which functioned like a machine in support of its most favoured member whose father provided a Black personal valet when JFK studied at Harvard. He was everything Oswald was not. Oswald would become an equivalent somebody by killing the President.[11]

The White House had announced the Texas trip on 26 September. For three days beforehand, Dallas newspapers publicized the ten-mile route of the presidential motorcade through the downtown area of a city Kennedy had lost in the 1960 election. The convoy of vehicles would leave Main Street and progress along the intersection of Elm and Houston Streets towards the Dallas Trade Mart for an official lunch. Then Kennedy would fly to Austin for a fundraising dinner, before spending a day on Lyndon Johnson's ranch.

It promised to be a fine day, so the bubbletop rain cover was removed from the Presidential limousine. Kennedy sat upright, with a back brace under his shirt to keep him out of chronic pain. Two members of the Secret Service were in the front of his Lincoln Continental limousine with eight agents in the follow-up vehicle, including two men on the running boards scanning the crowds and high buildings. A car with Johnson and Lady Bird took up the rear.

The atmosphere was sufficiently relaxed for Kennedy to twice halt the convoy and greet well-wishers. As the vehicles slowed to 11 miles per hour and turned onto Elm Street, a rapid succession of shots – which caused pigeons to fly upward from the Texas School Book Depository – made Kennedy move involuntarily and unnaturally, as did Governor John Connally on the seat in front of him. Both men had been shot. The last of three rounds blew away part of Kennedy's head, spraying bits of skull and brain onto the rear of the car. Jackie Kennedy, in a pink Chanel suit, had to be pulled down as she clambered to reunite it with her husband's head. She kept a small piece of Jack in her white gloved hand, only reluctantly surrendering it during the autopsy. It was 12.30 p.m. Half an hour later Kennedy was pronounced dead in Parkland Memorial Hospital.

Attention focused on the Book Depository; 85 per cent of the hundreds of witnesses would maintain the shots had come from that building, though the acoustics around Dealey Plaza were confusing. But at least two workers on the fifth floor of the depository, having heard shots above and ejected empty cartridges hitting the temporary floor, were so certain that they poked their heads out of the window and looked up. There on the sixth floor Oswald had used boxes to form a shooting platform and others to conceal this from anyone working on that floor.

A police patrolman entered the building and asked anyone he encountered, including Lee Harvey Oswald, to identify themselves, by this time at gunpoint. Oswald had worked there since 16 October so was familiar to his manager. After the shooting, Oswald took his time leaving the building, first boarding a bus which got stuck in traffic and then taking a taxi to the rooming house where he lodged in order to collect his handgun. At about 1.15 p.m. he was stopped by a police patrol car driven by J. D. Tippit. Physically, he roughly corresponded to a description being circulated of a white male aged about thirty, five feet ten inches tall and around 165 pounds. As Tibbit got out to question Oswald, the suspect drew his .38 and shot Tibbit dead with the casualness with which one might swat a fly.

Oswald next hurried along Jefferson Street before entering the Texas Theatre cinema without paying for a ticket. Police converged on the building after descriptions of Tibbit's killer circulated and corresponded with those of the President's alleged assassin. When Patrolman M. N. Macdonald approached Oswald in the audience of *War Is Hell*, he rose and punched the policeman while drawing his gun but was overpowered before he could shoot. By 2 p.m. he was in custody in Dallas police headquarters, a little worse for wear having been given a black eye by the policemen who subdued him in the cinema. He would have forty-eight hours to live, though he cockily imagined that arrest was but the prelude to his grand finale of a trial.

Dallas homicide detectives had found the shooter's hide plus three spent shell cases next to a half-open window on the sixth floor of the Depository. After a further search they found an Italian Mannlicher-Carcano rifle with a telescopic sight still attached, wedged between two rows of boxes and next to paper wrapping taped into a carry bag. A colleague who occasionally gave Oswald lifts would recall him placing such wrapping in the back of his car saying it contained curtain rods.

Though the Dallas detectives who interviewed Oswald were scrupulous, they had no means of recording the interviews and did not transcribe what he said. That was probably not accidental since tapes would lead to defence objections based on faulty police procedure. Oswald was questioned inside the Dallas police HQ for twelve hours, amidst chaotic scenes outside where a mess of television and radio cables sprawled over the floor, all under blinding TV lights and camera flashbulbs. In other words this was a media circus of the kind that has become normative the world over. At one point Jack Ruby, a Dallas nightclub owner who regularly socialized with the police and knew about a hundred members of the Dallas PD alone, tried to enter through the interview-room door.

The Dallas police obliged the media with regular updates, including parading Oswald at a midnight press conference. Ruby was present at that gathering, too. Born Jacob Rubinstein in Chicago in 1911, Ruby was notoriously quick-tempered and violent but he was not a Mafia gangster, as is often claimed – the Chicago Mob did not include Jews. Rather Ruby was a serial failure, whether in Chicago or after he moved to Dallas in 1947. There he ran two heavily indebted strip joints, the Carousel and Vegas, that were frequented by criminals and policemen alike. Ruby took a hands-on approach to drunks and troublemakers, throwing them down the stairs after pulverizing them with blackjacks and knuckledusters. An inveterate hanger-on, he was attracted to the slightest glimmer of celebrity or money that entered his dingy world. Now he appointed himself local fixer-in-chief to the out-of-town reporters in the police station. Reportedly deeply affected by the murder of the youthful President and the public distress of Jackie, Ruby resolved to punch Oswald after seeing him smirking during the late-night press session. As he brooded, wept and prayed at his synagogue he imagined how intolerable it would be for Jackie to have to return to Dallas when and if Oswald went on trial. There is no evidence that he was a Mob hit-man sent to close Oswald down; the Mob had many more professional killers than Ruby on its books, though they would have lacked his access.[12]

At 7.10 a.m. Oswald was charged with murdering Officer Tibbit; by 1.30 a.m. the next day, the charges had escalated to the assassination of President John F. Kennedy. Detectives had established that the rifle had been bought from a New York gun distributor, via a mail-order firm in Chicago. The purchaser was one A. Hidell, who paid by mail order and also bought a .38 revolver, identical to the one used to kill Tibbit. In Oswald's wallet was a forged Selective Service card in the name of Alek J. Hidell. Alek was what his Russian friends used to call him. The rifle had been delivered to a Dallas post office box rented by Oswald, and his palm print was lifted from the rifle's stock and from the boxes of books which had been used to form the hide in the Book Depository.

On the morning of Sunday 24 November, Oswald was to be moved to Dallas County jail. He was handcuffed to a huge detective, Jim Leavelle, who joked, 'Lee, I hope if anybody shoots at you, they're as good a shot as you are.' Oswald replied, 'Oh, you're just being melodramatic.' The media were advised of the move and crammed into the basement though which Oswald would pass, but Leavelle noticed someone standing in front of the reporters. Jack Ruby rushed at Oswald and shot him in the stomach with a Colt Cobra .38 revolver. This highly emotional man – who half an hour before wired $30 to a financially distressed stripper known as Little Lynn – had shown his fellow American patriots what 'tough Jews' like him could do.[13]

Oswald died at Parkland Memorial Hospital at 1.07 p.m. He was twenty-four. Ruby was arrested, claiming he had killed Oswald in a fit of depression and rage at Kennedy's slaying. Sentenced to death, he was kept in the Dallas County Criminal Courts Building on Dealey Plaza, next to where Kennedy was shot, and he died in Parkland Memorial Hospital in 1967 as Kennedy and Oswald had done, convinced that Jews were being burned en masse on the floor below his cell.

That much is certain. The rest also involves facts and motives, but they can be so elaborated that one loses sight of Oswald, the one person who can be plausibly connected with the death of President Kennedy just as he alone had tried to shoot Walker.

Hyping Kennedy beyond what the historical figure can bear, while viewing Oswald as an incidental detail bobbing above more powerful and sinister forces helps too.

Oswald was born in New Orleans in 1939. His father died a couple of months before his birth, and he was brought up by his overbearing single mother Marguerite, mainly in Louisiana and Texas but with a stint in a basement in New York's Bronx. Even after Oswald's arrest, it was all about Marguerite: 'My boy couldn't have killed the President. I know him. Nobody else knows him. He's been persecuted for so long. I've been persecuted, he's been persecuted.'[14]

Instability was a constant; mother and son moved home twenty times and his attendance at twelve different schools was fitful. Oswald was a slightly built and prickly loner. Rather than wandering the streets making mischief, he was so reluctant to leave the house that he spent a brief spell in youth custody for truancy, where psychiatric social workers examined him. 'I dislike everybody' was a memorable line from this fourteen-year-old who spoke of a veil that separated him from other people. Since he thought school had little to teach him, Oswald read widely, alighting upon Marxism in his early teens and developing a fascination with Soviet Russia. He was dyslexic and spelled poorly in adulthood, but like many autodidacts he was skilled in argument.

When he was seventeen, Oswald followed his admired older brother Robert into the US Marines. During basic training, bullies targeted this weedy figure as 'Ozzie Rabbit' and 'Mrs Oswald' or more often 'shit-bird'. Posted to a naval airbase in Japan, he tried and failed to learn Russian, but did save $1,500 from his modest salary. A minor promotion to corporal was nullified by disciplinary infractions, in one of which he shot himself with an illegal gun. After his discharge, Oswald claimed he wanted to study in Finland, where on arrival he visited the Soviet consulate.

In October 1959 he was given a six-day Soviet tourist visa and entered a tightly monitored world. Emboldened, he visited the US embassy in Moscow and tried to renounce his citizenship, but left after being told this was not a simple affair. With just hours remaining on his tourist visa, Oswald slit his wrist, resulting in three days in a Russian psychiatric hospital. It was too embarrassing for the Russians to arrest him or put him on a ship home. Why not give him leave to remain without conferring citizenship? At no point did Oswald pass information on military secrets, and the Russians had no interest in recruiting him as an agent. Instead, the KGB despatched him to provincial Minsk and a job in a radio electronics plant. His workmates were routinely questioned by the KGB, which tracked his every movement and also bugged the apartment it arranged for him. Any celebrity as the only American in town wore off, though he did meet another damaged soul, Marina, who probably saw him as a reliable meal ticket. They married in April 1961 and both soon wanted to leave a society that was grey, dull and conformist.[15]

Oswald was sufficiently inconsequential for the US embassy to return his passport with permission to take Marina to the US if the Soviets agreed and loaned them the money for their sea passage. The KGB had no interest in either of them. 'A useless man,' scribbled the KGB chief on the files the sub-office in Minsk had dutifully maintained on Oswald. The US authorities hardly bestirred themselves to take an interest in this odd returnee from Russia, though he probably acquired a routine CIA 201 file. Oswald was disappointed that no reporters showed up when he, Marina and their daughter June landed at Love Field on 14 June 1962. He had high hopes of a book he began to sketch out while at sea, based on his notes about life in the Soviet Union, but no one was interested. He would found a new political movement to synthesize the best of the two rival systems. Though he deplored Hitler, he regarded himself as a similar ordinary man with a transformative message. In other words he was a delusional autodidact.

Oswald resumed drifting, initially in Fort Worth, but with a Russian wife and baby June in tow. During the marriage Oswald refused to teach Marina the language of their elective home, presumably so that he could better control her. Crammed into a one-bedroom apartment, the couple often rowed, and Oswald would routinely slap and then punch his wife when the mood took him. She frequently appeared at social gatherings with black eyes. Marina constantly nagged Oswald about his inadequacies, sometimes alluding in company to his lack of sex drive; he retaliated by getting her to write to the Soviet embassy requesting repatriation while simultaneously refusing to give her a divorce. They scraped along in a way which must have been wearing. Whenever Oswald tried to make something of himself, he was reminded of his inadequacy.[16]

A small circle of Russian emigres afforded the couple charity and a social life, in which Marina could take part in conversations. Most of these Russians deplored Oswald's apologias for the Soviet regime and his coolness towards a country which had given them refuge. One bullshitting 'aristocratic' Russian entrepreneur called George de Mohrenschildt had connections with the CIA, since he travelled overseas a lot and the Agency debriefed 25,000 such travellers each year. There is no evidence that he was trying to recruit Oswald; he just liked the young man he described as 'a semi-educated hillbilly' with interesting contrarian views.[17]

Moving to New Orleans in late April 1963, Oswald, Marina and June lived in the kind of slums where the cockroaches teemed on the kitchen floors at night. Oswald transferred his naive political enthusiasms from Soviet Russia to Cuba. There is no evidence that Oswald ever had contact with Guy Bannister, a thuggish former FBI agent turned private eye, or the prominent gay businessman Clay Shaw. As a teenager, however, Oswald had been in the local Air Cadet unit commanded by the peculiar-looking David Ferrie, a notorious homosexual predator who wore a wig and false eyebrows made of mohair. One of the few conspiracy theories that remain underexplored is that Kennedy was a victim of a gay fascist plot, though it would have no more plausibility than many others.

When the New Orleans District Attorney Jim Garrison first aired a JFK conspiracy theory, he said: 'It was a homosexual thrill-killing, plus the excitement of getting away with a perfect crime. John Kennedy was everything that Dave Ferrie was not – a successful, handsome, popular, wealthy, virile man. You can

just picture the charge Ferrie got out of plotting his death . . .
Look at the people involved. Dave Ferrie, homosexual. Clay
Shaw, homosexual, Jack Ruby, homosexual . . . And then there's
Lee Harvey Oswald. A switch-hitter who couldn't satisfy his
wife.'[18]

Oswald founded a branch of the Fair Play For Cuba movement, printing leaflets and provoking clashes with the anti-Castro
sub-culture that was a fixture of a city with many angry Cuban
exiles. He also sought to infiltrate a group of militantly anti-
Castroite exiled Cuban students called the Cuban Student
Directorate, but they thought he was an FBI plant. Both the
pro- and anti-Castro groups were under FBI surveillance. These
activities led to Oswald appearing on TV and radio, in debates
which were designed to discredit him as a Communist. The FBI
helpfully shared background information on his Russian sojourn
with his interlocutors. His enthusiasm for the Castro regime led
him to try to co-opt Marina into hijacking a plane to Cuba. He
tried to show her how to shout 'stick 'em up' but she could not
pronounce it properly and he settled for 'hands up' though she
was still incapable of pointing a gun. At the time she was eight
months pregnant.

Talk of Cuba brings us to the very murky world of espionage. At the highest level, the CIA were aware that it would
not be easy to topple Castro, whose Soviet-trained secret service
had an iron grip on Cuba. The Cubans had also penetrated
many of the exile circles in Florida. But as careerist bureaucrats,
those at the highest levels in the Agency were also obliged to
indulge the Kennedys' love of cloak and dagger, elaborating the
lines of command so as to try to bring down Castro. Despite
their bosses, many of the agents at the sharp end despised the
Kennedys and bitterly resented how they had left 'their' people
to be killed or captured at the Bay of Pigs. And they regarded
the peaceful resolution of the 1962 missile crisis as an example
of 'appeasement'.

AMSPELL was part of Bobby Kennedy's larger plan codenamed AMWORLD, which was briefed to all CIA stations in
the sub-continent. While the President seemed keen on cooling
things with Castro after the missile crisis, his brother Bobby

and many in the CIA were still endeavouring to sabotage the Castro regime and replace it with handpicked exiles, while also curtailing Cuban influence throughout Central and South America.

Apart from Miami, another nodal point in these operations was Mexico City, through which Cuban officials could move at will. As a result, the CIA station in the Mexico City embassy was a large one and led by another star performer, Winston Scott. One of Scott's roles, apart from becoming close to the Mexican President, Adolfo López Mateos, was to tap telephones in the Cuban, Czech and Soviet embassies and install cameras that photographed people entering or leaving these buildings. These materials were sent either to Washington to enhance general intelligence or to a more select CIA audience if the material triggered alarms about US security.[19]

Back in Texas, Oswald's recreations included the spy thrillers of Ian Fleming and familiarizing himself with his rifle's bolt action and lovingly polishing its stock and cleaning the barrel. In September 1963, Marina and June went to lodge with a divorced family friend called Ruth Paine in nearby Irvine, while Oswald remained in Dallas, living under an assumed name in a boarding house. He soon set off by bus to Mexico City.

Once there, Oswald visited both the Cuban and Soviet embassies, immediately tripping the alarms that the CIA had laid. He found himself in a difficult situation: he needed a Soviet visa to get a transit visa to Havana, but the Russians said they needed to refer the case to their mission in Washington and it would take four months. The KGB men who were among his interviewers were dressed for a forthcoming volleyball match and wanted him out of the embassy as soon as they could, especially after he produced a handgun which they unloaded. Oswald became furious, and took a bus back to Texas after a week. Transcripts of phone intercepts were sent back to the CIA at Langley, where information about Oswald's visit seems to have circulated at a high level. Although he entered and left both hostile embassies and consulates, no photos of him doing so have emerged. It could be that somebody inside the CIA regarded him as a possible intelligence asset, though it is a big leap to then claim that the CIA was part of a conspiracy to kill Kennedy.

Oswald's job opportunities in Texas were limited by the fact that he had never learned to drive. The kindness of strangers resulted in him obtaining a $1.25-an-hour job in mid-October, fetching books at the Texas School Book Depository, a huge publishers' warehouse in Dallas. He lived alone during the week and took a bus to visit Marina and June in Irvine at weekends. The night before the assassination he turned up unexpectedly and played with June in Ruth Paine's garden. He seemed unusually calm, and may have been in a kind of mental mist for the mission he was preparing himself for. Heavily pregnant, Marina slept next to him, though he did not sleep and left early without saying goodbye.

Conspiracy theorists are good at insinuating motives for Kennedy's assassination, overlooking the lone attempt to shoot General Edwin Walker, where no conspiracy has been proved, and the facile way in which Oswald murdered Tibbit, but tying them to how Oswald came to be employed in the Dallas Book Depository is another matter. Those who imagine that Oswald was an innocent dupe of a darker conspiracy must explain how several local employers declined to give Oswald a job, so that he would eventually secure one in a building overlooking Kennedy's route, where the physical evidence pointing to his role as the assassin would be found. And what about Marina's friend Ruth Paine, who casually asked a friend about any vacancies in the Book Depository? At any rate, Oswald got a job in the Book Depository and from there shot Kennedy. When he was arrested he was en route to a bus which would have taken him back to Mexico. But he was also prepared to be killed, or better yet, to be captured and grandstand at his trial where he could expound his political philosophy at leisure. Once he had murdered Tibbit, the likelihood of him enjoying any limited public sympathy evaporated.

Oswald had left $170 and his wedding ring for Marina to discover when the FBI came pounding on Paine's door. Killing Kennedy was his last desperate attempt to show Marina that he was 'an outstanding man'. His frustration with being a loser burst out in two acts of violence. One in April against Edwin Walker failed; the other spectacularly succeeded, immortalizing both Oswald and his victim.[20]

•

Kennedy's assassination accelerated the pace of civil-rights reform under his successor Lyndon Johnson. Had he lived, there is scant likelihood that he would have de-escalated US involvement in Vietnam; he had Americanized the war, and a marginal second-term victory would have further constrained his choices. But his death seemed to require a grander explanation than an aggrieved loner getting lucky one day in Dallas with a 265-foot shot against a moving target.

There were two successive inquiries into the killing of Kennedy, with another on US involvement in foreign assassinations. The Minsk KGB were also told to bring their long-dormant files on Oswald to an anxious headquarters in Moscow. In 1963 President Lyndon Johnson established the Warren Commission four weeks after the assassination; urgency stemmed from the need to quash suspicions of Cuban or Soviet involvement, as well as to prove that Oswald was a lone gunman. A conspiracy might have divided America, as it had been divided in the McCarthy era under Eisenhower. To make sure Warren took the poisoned chalice, Johnson conjured up images of mushroom clouds vaporizing 40 million Americans if Cuban or Soviet involvement in Kennedy's death were proved. The question had become urgent after a Nicaraguan man named Gilberto Alvarado walked into the Mexico City CIA station and claimed to have seen Oswald accept $6,500 from a red-haired Black man in the Cuban consulate. It turned out to be disinformation on the part of the Nicaraguan regime, keen for the US to attack Cuba. Alvarado was distantly on the CIA payroll, too.[21]

In Havana, Fidel Castro spoke at length about a conspiracy to kill Kennedy, but it was ultimately directed against himself. Referring to the murky activities of the Student Revolutionary Directorate, Castro said: 'from these incidents there could be a new trap, an ambush, a Machiavellian plot against our country; that on the very blood of the assassinated President there might be unscrupulous people who would begin to work out immediately an aggressive policy against Cuba . . . But there is no doubt that this policy is being built on the still warm blood and unburied body of their tragically assassinated President.'[22] Fears that this might be so underlay attempts to prove that neither the Cubans nor the Soviets were involved in killing Kennedy.

Most of the Commission members, including Supreme Court Justice Earl Warren, had demanding day jobs, which was handy for the only retiree appointed – Allen Dulles, who Kennedy had eased out as Director of the CIA.[23] One of his initial contributions was a CIA paper on seven historical attempts on the lives of US Presidents, which 'proved' there were no such conspiracies. When another commissioner objected with the names Lincoln and Booth, Dulles said, 'Yes, but one man [Booth] was so dominant, it almost wasn't a plot.'

Dulles's role was to keep the CIA out of the picture, and to ensure that when the Commission asked the Agency questions, it had the right answers.[24] Most of the information regarding Oswald's visit to Mexico City was withheld on the grounds that the Agency needed to protect its sources; as it would transpire, Winston Scott, the station chief, had a poor grasp of what his deputy David Phillips had been doing, and the ambassador was so clueless that he initially demanded all the relevant materials be released.

Suspicions that the CIA or the Mafia were involved in killing Kennedy came later. The Agency's role in assassinating foreign leaders like Castro or Lumumba was revealed by Senator Frank Church's Senate Intelligence Committee on Foreign Assassinations in 1975, which in 1976 passed the baton to the House Select Committee on Assassinations. Reporting in 1979, it reviewed the killing of Kennedy in great detail and claimed that more than one shooter had been involved, following a misreading of audio evidence from a police motorcyclist's equipment.

The belief that Kennedy had been killed as a result of a conspiracy gained traction in the 1960s with the idiosyncratic investigations of District Attorney Garrison and the proliferation of JFK assassination buffs, some of whom had worked on

Garrison's team. Garrison had close connections to the New Orleans Mafia, routinely intimidated witnesses and suffered from persecution mania. This worsened as he styled himself as a lone crusader against monstrous plots against Kennedy that reached the highest levels of the government. Garrison also thought nothing of bribing, coercing, drugging or hypnotizing witnesses to shape their testimony. And when a man calling himself Julius Caesar appeared wearing a toga and sandals, claiming that he had seen Oswald, Ferrie and Shaw together, Garrison entertained the idea, until the gentleman was exposed as a former mental patient.[25]

What of claims that the Mafia or the CIA killed Kennedy? The Church Committee exposed Mafia involvement in serial plots to kill Fidel Castro; American Mobsters had thrived in entertainment, gaming and prostitution under the Cuban Batista regime which Castro ousted; the Mafia turned the island into a moral sewer.[26]

The CIA had initially limited its plots on Castro to releasing LSD into a broadcast studio to make him sound crazy, or to dusting his boots with a depilatory powder and making his beard fall out. But these plots soon escalated to thoughts of murder, and two CIA officers were authorized to talk with leading Mafia figures.

The intermediary was former FBI man Robert Maheu, whose investigations business the CIA rescued from bankruptcy with a contract to conduct their dirty work. Maheu put the CIA men in touch with 'Handsome' Johnny Rosselli, a former associate of Al Capone who had ended up running the Mob's extensive gambling interests in Las Vegas. Rosselli in turn connected the CIA with 'Sam Gold', the alias of Chicago Mob boss Sam Giancana, and his sidekick 'Joe', his Miami counterpart Santo Trafficante Jr. These men turned down the CIA's offer of $150,000 to have Castro murdered, having advised against a Mob-style gun attack in favour of poisoning.

This conspiracy was then presented for approval to Allen Dulles and his deputy. The plot involved delivering poisoned pills into something Castro would drink. They found an insider in Juan Orta, chief of Castro's office; Trafficante had paid him enormous kickbacks and he was in debt. The poison pills were manufactured by the CIA's technical experts and successfully tested on monkeys. But Orta was sacked, and the chance never presented itself.

After the failure of the Bay of Pigs invasion, reckoning with Castro became personal to both Jack and Bobby Kennedy, his Attorney-General. They turned to a familiar figure, ignoring the fact that his experience in 'nation-building' concerned a one-off success in the Philippines rather than Cuba. Brigadier-General Edward Lansdale devised and took charge of a campaign of sabotage and subversion codenamed Operation Mongoose that would draw on the combined skills of various government departments. From the start, the CIA hated 'servicing' a man they did not regard as a professional spook.

The CIA were obliged to make available the enormous JM/WAVE station with about 600 staff at Miami University, 200 more at the new Langley headquarters and an annual budget of $50 million. The Agency assigned former FBI man William Harvey as liaison with Lansdale under the new rubric Task Force W. Harvey was coarse and rude, drank too much and concealed guns all over his person. He was a legend for having suspected that Kim Philby was a Soviet spy, and had used a tunnel to plug an intercept into Soviet cable traffic in Berlin, though it transpired that the KGB used it to transmit disinformation. Harvey despised Lansdale, whose uniform reminded him of a Christmas tree, while words like 'fag' and 'fucker' summed up his view of Kennedy.

Harvey was also chosen to lead a new Executive Action group, codenamed ZR/RIFLE, whose main business was killing people. It had a budget, its own agents and a full-time contract employee codenamed QJ/WIN, who we encountered in the Congo in Chapter 5. All these arrangements were approved by Richard Helms, who had replaced Richard Bissell, another Agency fall guy for the Bay of Pigs fiasco.[27]

Although Harvey's first rule of thumb was never to put anything compromising in writing, he did make notes outlining how ZR/RIFLE was organized. In one section the paper observed: 'Exclude organized criminals, e.g. Sicilians, criminals, those w/ records of arrests, those w/ instability of purpose as criminals . . . planning should include provision for blaming Sovs or Czechs in case of blow . . . organization criminals, those with records of arrests, those who have engaged in several types of crime. Corsicans recommended. Sicilians could lead to Mafia.'[28]

Robert Kennedy was the most implacable law officer in US history in his pursuit of the Mafia, even as he and the CIA conspired to kill Fidel Castro with its assistance. The Mafia had reorganized itself under a national commission, a change that coincided with law-enforcement agencies resorting to electronic surveillance. While top-level gangsters were careful about what they said on the phone, they were more expansive when they imagined they were among their own. In Buffalo, the Mobster Stefano Maggadino once said of the Kennedys: 'They should kill the whole family, the mother and father too. When he [JFK] talks, he talks like a mad dog.'[29]

But verbal malice against the Kennedys was not the same as involvement in killing them. The two Mob bosses most often mentioned in connection with the assassination of Kennedy were the New Orleans overlord Carlos Marcello and Miami's Santo Trafficante; not only was Trafficante the Mobster most closely involved in CIA plots to kill Castro, but he also said to Marcello, 'Carlos, the next thing you know they will be blaming the President's assassination on us' – hard to reconcile with either man having originated it.

There was also a matter of Mob culture and ethics. Murder was part of the Mafia business model, but killing lawyers, judges, policemen or journalists would attract too much adverse attention. Furthermore, most gangsters are conventionally patriotic – killing the US President was not part of that worldview and would have required approval by the national commission, for its consequences would affect them all. There is no proof that they killed Kennedy to oblige their trades union friend Jimmy Hoffa in order to get his corrupt Teamster union funding for their casino ventures in Nevada either.[30]

As the Mobsters withdrew back into the shadows, the CIA took over attempts to kill Castro, this time using local assets

identified by Cuban defectors. One plot involved contaminating
Castro's wetsuit with Madura foot disease and his breathing
apparatus with tubercle bacilli. Another envisaged a tiny submarine dropping a striking conch shell on the seabed that would
explode when Castro touched it. One other plot that involved
a pen containing a syringe of the toxin Blackleaf 40 was being
handed over to a Cuban agent in Paris at exactly the time
Kennedy was assassinated.[31]

Lansdale devised such fanciful stunts as using biological
weapons to incapacitate Cuban sugar workers, and the administration's enthusiasm for him quickly waned. Ironically, the sole
result of these attempts to kill Castro was to increase Fidel's
paranoia so that he urged Nikita Khrushchev to place tactical
nuclear missiles on the island. Kennedy may deserve credit for
avoiding the all-out nuclear exchange sought by some of his
advisors, but by authorizing clandestine activity against Castro
he helped bring about the 1962 Cuban missile crisis.[32]

If it seems unlikely that the Mafia was involved in killing
Kennedy, what about the CIA itself? In the immediate aftermath
of the assassination, President Eisenhower wondered how the
US had become a banana republic like Haiti, while his predecessor Harry Truman wrote in the *Washington Post* of his regret
that the CIA, which he had founded in 1947, had degenerated
from an intelligence-gathering agency into a gung-ho paramilitary organization.

Kennedy was the President who deliberately converted US
military advisors into military partners of the Diem regime in
Saigon, whose subventions he also increased. Claims that the
CIA wanted to thwart his alleged peace efforts partly depend
on conjecture as to what policies he would have pursued in
Vietnam or towards the Soviet Union had he been re-elected for
a second term in 1964.[33]

So modest were JFK's domestic policy achievements that he
had to seek glory in foreign affairs, already his special subject
as a Senator. Though there is no doubt that he was glamorous
and telegenic, his liberality was more a matter of image rather
than reality. Aged forty-six, he represented the promise of youth
destroyed, with the starry Camelot legend concealing the more

sordid aspects of his presidency. Though people around the world were right to be shocked by the sudden manner of Kennedy's departure, the asymmetry between his stature and the obscure little man who shot him does not have to result in a search for commensurately large causes.[34]

At the root of claims that Kennedy fell victim to a high-level conspiracy is the idea that a shadowy 'deep state' military-industrial complex feared an end to their global imperium of arms and men so much that they would kill the President. It is impossible to connect something so superficially compelling with the events in Dallas, not least because the deep state was not of one mind about foreign policy, and it consisted of competitive bureaucracies, not to mention an independent private sector, with its own agendas and clashes of purpose.

Kennedy was entirely of his time in believing that Communism had to be checked, and that appeasement was a bad idea though his father had been a leading exponent of it. So did half of the American population, who even at the height of the anti-war movement in 1968 thought assistance to South Vietnam should be increased.

Kennedy was cautious after the Bay of Pigs fiasco, and his senior policy makers were divided on how to proceed in Vietnam, even as they agreed on the need to halt Communist aggression. It was hard to get an accurate picture of the war's progress, let alone the domestic politics of South Vietnam, and the advisers coming in and out of the Oval Office had such conflicting views that when Kennedy heard reports about the state of play he wondered whether two men had visited the same country. That is how some historians reach the view that Kennedy would have withdrawn troops from Vietnam had he been re-elected in 1964.

With an election looming, Kennedy ducked and dived along a middle course between advocating an increase in US forces and a controlled draw-down. Having increased troops in country to 16,000, in October 1963 he ordered the withdrawal of a 1,000-man battalion. Kennedy hoped that with the Diems gone he could hand the conflict over to a more popular South Vietnamese regime and scale back the numbers of US advisors.

But chaos and instability ensued; there was a second coup against the original plotters, and the Vietcong went on the offensive at Tet.

We are being asked to believe that a small reduction of US troops so incensed the 'military-industrial complex' that 'they' resolved that JFK had to be killed. Such a plot would have required a controlling intelligence to focus grumbling in smoke-filled DC gentlemen's clubs, and to connect it with embittered CIA agents and their client groups in the field. It presumes that 'they' not only set up Oswald, but used Cuban exiles to carry out the killing. However, the problems commence when one tries to put faces to 'they'. Enter a pipe-smoking stage villain. Despite being put out to grass by Kennedy, the embittered Allen Dulles retained a huge contacts book, as well as the loyalty of CIA agents.

While plenty of vested interests disliked Kennedy, there is not a shred of evidence connecting any of them to Oswald in Dallas. That is not to claim that the CIA and FBI did not have prior involvements with Oswald, nor that a less than perfect police investigation left plenty of cracks through which elaborate conspiracies have entered. On the day of the assassination, Dulles was not at home as usual as was his wont 'at the outset of major operations'. He was on a book tour touting *The Craft of Intelligence*. Along with the incompetent Secret Service, both the CIA and FBI can be justifiably criticized for failing to ensure that Oswald, whose zig-zag odyssey should have triggered more alarm bells, did not get anywhere near Kennedy in Dallas. They then covered up the information they should have shared and acted on, but they were bureaucracies first and foremost, whose primary business was covering their own backs. Nothing connects them to Oswald's finger on the trigger in Dallas; the fractured and alienated background of the assassin contrasted all too vividly with his victim, who had a silver spoon in his mouth from the day he was born.

•

We return now to the unresolved legacies of the American Civil War. Race was and remains at the heart of a country whose military and moralizing stridency overseas and mindless consumerism masked the decayed civic fabric at home. In 1967–68 America lost its mind as its chronic racial tensions and hubris overseas exploded in spectacular fashion, despite the decade being one of considerable prosperity and advances in domestic civil rights. As we can see these pathologies are resurgent in the perfect storm that saw Trump become President.

It began with the shock of the Tet Offensive in Vietnam, in which Vietcong guerrillas and North Vietnamese regulars launched an all-out assault on most of the South's provincial capitals, as well as on Saigon. Although the offensive failed, the abiding image was of Saigon police chief Nguyen Ngoc Loan casually firing a pistol into the head of Vietcong captive Nguyen Van Lem at point-blank range. Domestically, African-Americans' fury at the failure to improve their economic lot led to explosions of urban rioting. In 1967 there were 164 riots in Baltimore, Boston, Chicago, Kansas, Pittsburgh and Washington DC; state police were deployed on thirty-three occasions, the National Guard on eight. After a week of rioting, Detroit reminded its mayor of Berlin in 1945.[35]

In Memphis, Tennessee, a strike by poorly paid and Black garbage collectors after two men were crushed in the back of a sanitation truck led to the deployment of the National Guard when riots destroyed parts of the downtown area. The civil rights leader Dr Martin Luther King supported the striking Memphis workers, partly to neutralize Black radicals who had grown frustrated with his campaigns of non-violent civil disobedience.

King was from a family of Baptist ministers and had studied Gandhi as well as the American theologian Reinhold Niebuhr. Like his father, Dr King originally supported the Republican Nixon against Kennedy, but then changed his mind despite not being invited to Kennedy's inauguration. The fact that Kennedy had reluctantly helped free King from a short jail sentence probably helped.[36] He believed that it was crucial to maintain the moral high ground against white policemen who conformed to thuggish stereotypes. But he had more radical competitors, such as the Nation of Islam and the Organization of African Unity, vying for the allegiances of younger African-Americans in the northern cities, even as he retained his hold on the Christian Blacks of the Deep South.

Aged thirty-nine and already a Nobel laureate, Dr King made one of the greatest speeches of his life in Memphis's Mason Temple on 3 April. He was not scheduled to speak, and the crowd was a modest two thousand because of the inclement weather. The main thrust of the speech was to advocate a Black economic boycott of such white products as Coca-Cola and Wonder Bread, using the power of African-American consumers to impel Lyndon Johnson to enforce the civil rights that he had legislated in 1964. Johnson had one eye on the alarming rise of Alabama Democrat Governor George Wallace, a bantam-weight boxing champion turned populist racist, or as LBJ himself had it, 'a runty little bastard and just about the most dangerous person around'.[37]

Mortality was clearly on King's mind as he spoke. He mentioned a deranged African-American woman called Izola Curry who had attempted to kill him with a steel letter opener at a book launch in Harlem in 1958. The day before, his plane to Memphis had been delayed by a bomb threat. After waiting for the bags to be unloaded, checked and reloaded, King had joked, 'Well it looks like they won't kill me this flight.' He returned to the subject of death in a speech where the printed word fails to capture the rising cadences of the brief snippet of audio:

> What would happen to me from some of our sick white brothers? Well I don't know what will happen now. We've got some difficult days ahead. But it does not really matter with me now. Because I've been to the mountaintop. And I don't mind. Like anybody I would like to live a long life – longevity has its place. But I'm not concerned about that now. I just want to do God's will. And He's allowed me to go up to the mountain. And I've looked over. And I've seen the Promised Land. I may not get there with you. But I want you to know tonight, that we as a people will get to the Promised Land. And I'm happy tonight. I'm not worried about anything. I'm not fearing any man. Mine eyes have seen the glory of the coming of the Lord.[38]

With storms raging and lightning crackling across Memphis, a lone middle-aged man in an off-white Mustang pulled into the darkening city. He checked into the New Rebel Motel under the name Eric S. Galt, though his real name was James Earl Ray. The following day, Ray sought out the Lorraine Motel where King and his entourage were staying. It was a nondescript place, which King preferred to more expensive establishments. Ray looked briefly at the adjacent fire station from where, unbeknown to him, Memphis police detectives, FBI agents and military intelligence personnel had King under observation with binoculars. They had accumulated piles of dirt about his alleged serial womanizing, though they had not used it to publicly smear him.

The Bureau had been watching King for three years, under a secret programme called COINTELPRO. Originally created in 1956 to subvert American Communists, J. Edgar Hoover extended its scope across the entire dissident spectrum, from animal-rights activists to Islamists. King was one of the main targets for its smear operations after he publicly noted the Bureau's reluctance to investigate white supremacist terrorists.

Ray opted for a rooming house on South Main Street, after establishing that its rear bathroom window had a clear view of the Lorraine Motel's inner courtyard. He knew the drill, having spent most of his life in dingy rooming houses or in jail. Realizing that a room with a fridge and stove did not overlook the Lorraine, he insisted on one without, and paid the $8.50 weekly rent in advance. His room was vacant since the previous occupant had died, and the lodgers were almost all alcoholics or invalids.

Ray ventured out to buy binoculars with which to watch the Lorraine's balcony. That afternoon he sat in his Mustang until the street emptied and he could take a package to his room. The other boarders noticed that he kept visiting a bathroom about thirteen paces from his room, occupying it for long periods.

In Room 306 of the Lorraine, King and his entourage were engaged in a combination of horseplay and what they dubbed 'preacher talk', mainly involving whether they were going to get

proper 'soul food' that night or something fancier. At 6 p.m.
King went onto the balcony to shoot the breeze with a small
gathering of staff, including musicians who he insisted were to
sing 'Precious Lord' at a dinner in his honour. He was happy
and relaxed.

One minute later, a single bullet smashed through King's
jaw, severing his jugular vein and spinal cord. The shot threw
King off his feet and he landed beside the balcony's rear wall,
bleeding profusely. At 7 p.m. he was pronounced dead in nearby
St Joseph's Hospital. As news of the assassination spread, riots
erupted across the country. Forty-six people died, all but five of
them African-American.

Ray had hurried back to his room from the bathroom, where
he had rammed up the window and levered aside some wire
mesh to give him a clear shot at King. The distance was 207
feet, but the seven times magnification on his telescopic sight
made King's face seem much closer.

Calling himself Harvey Lowmeyer, Ray had toured several
gun stores in Birmingham, Alabama, asking staff how far bullets
dropped in flight and opting for a Remington Gamemaster .243
and a Redfield 2x7 scope. The next day he exchanged that
weapon for a more powerful Remington 760, .30-06. This was
the gun Ray used to shoot Dr King.

Perhaps surprised by the commotion and with King's aides
pointing in the direction of the boarding house, Ray swept up
the gun and various bits and pieces into a blanket and raced
out of the building. Spotting police cars between himself and
the parked Mustang, he discarded the wrapped-up rifle and
walked to his car. Although the FBI were on the scene in minutes,
and 3,500 agents were assigned to the hunt for King's assassin,
Memphis was convenient to any fugitive, since Alabama,
Arkansas, Georgia and Mississippi were within driving distance.

The police and FBI did a fine job in identifying the assassin.
Ray's abandoned Mustang was found in Atlanta, and agents
determine it that had been in Memphis at the time of the shooting
as it stood out in the city's flophouse landscape. And Ray's shorts
and vest yielded laundry marks that were traceable to Los
Angeles.

There, neighbours recalled that 'Galt' had taken dance classes, as well as enrolling at the School of Bartending on Sunset Boulevard. There was a graduation photo of him, his eyes shut at the crucial moment. Twelve hours later, staff at the Aeromarine Supply Company gun store in Birmingham identified him as 'Lowmeyer'. Hair and handwriting samples enabled the FBI to reach the conclusion that Galt and Lowmeyer were one and the same person, while the rifle and scope yielded fingerprints. By checking all the money orders issued in Los Angeles, the FBI traced an address in LA that he had used for a locksmithing correspondence course. On entering the apartment, they found John Birch Society pamphlets and a map of Atlanta with four sites ringed, all of which were connected to King. The map also yielded a clear left thumb print.

In this pre-computer era, FBI fingerprint experts began the laborious task of matching these prints with card records of 55,000 white males aged between thirty and fifty. On 17 April, after only 700 cards had been checked, a technician matched them with the record of James Earl Ray.

Ray had spent twelve of the last sixteen years behind bars for burglary and armed robbery. He was supposed to be serving a twenty-year sentence in Missouri State Penitentiary, but had escaped in April 1967. The FBI sought out Ray's siblings, who were also criminals. 'What's all the excitement about? He only killed a nigger. If he'd killed a white man, you wouldn't be here. King should've been killed ten years ago,' opined his brother John.

The Ray clan were like a modern eugenicist's fantasy of white trash. James Earl Ray was born in Alton, Illinois in March 1928. His idle father was known as 'Speedy' because he spoke so slowly, while his mother was a chaotic alcoholic. Having moved to Ewing, Missouri, as the 'Raynes', to avoid the comeback from Speedy's botched attempts at forgery, the family lived in a draughty house with no electricity or sanitation. Nine children became eight after a six-year-old sister set fire to her dress while playing with matches and died a day later.

Ewing was a rough riverboat town of the kind Ray would

always favour. As a boy, he reluctantly tramped to a three-class school, often barefoot and wearing one of his father's oil-stained jackets. The sole teacher disliked this persistent truant and wrote 'Repulsive' on the 'Appearance' section of his report card. Although Ray would later write extensively, he hardly grasped grammar and words like 'might' became 'mite' in his spelling. Ray regarded his father as a wastrel and hero-worshipped his uncle Earl, a violent carnival boxer who once threw carbolic acid in his wife's face. Though he spent more time inside prisons than out, Earl encouraged his nephews into a life of crime, acting as a fence for goods the brothers stole.[39]

After learning about Adolf Hitler from an ethnic German workmate, Ray joined the US Army at seventeen to visit Germany. He immersed himself in Bremerhaven's black market and vice scene, until a drunken episode resulted in a spell in a military prison and dishonourable discharge. After returning to the squalor that had engulfed the lives of his parents, he turned to life as a career criminal.

Ray's first conviction was in 1949. In 1952 he received a two-year sentence for a botched robbery of a taxi driver in Illinois. In 1955 he was sentenced to four years in Leavenworth Federal Penitentiary after cashing a batch of stolen postal money orders. A probation officer's pre-sentence report said about him that he 'shows absolutely no remorse at this time . . . he is a confirmed criminal and a menace to society when in the free world.'

Prisons were a more hierarchical and orderly alternative to the chaotic life Ray lived on the outside. The one notable blemish on his Leavenworth record was when in 1957 he refused a transfer to the Honor Farm for well-behaved inmates, on the grounds that its dormitories were desegregated.

Following Ray's release from custody, he returned to a life of crime, blowing his modest returns on cars and whores. Having graduated to armed robberies of supermarkets, in 1959 he was sentenced to twenty years in Missouri State Penitentiary. By 1966 he had decided to break out, managing to traverse the prison when most of the guards were off duty, but failing when a section of guttering collapsed as he tried to vault the high outer wall. He avoided solitary confinement by faking insanity, though he was soon transferred back to MSP.

At some point Ray secured a job pushing the food cart in the infirmary, an ideal role to obtain amphetamines to sell in the prison. This is also where he may have learned that John Sutherland, a rich St Louis lawyer with strident Confederate views on race, had offered a $50,000 bounty to anyone who would kill Martin Luther King. After being transferred to work in the prison bakery, he hid himself in a special compartment built within a case of bread on Sunday 23 April 1967, leaping out when the truck stopped.

After a precautionary interval of six weeks, Ray met up with his brothers John and Jerry in Chicago, where he had sought refuge. After discussing various lucrative kidnappings, Ray announced, 'I'm going to kill that nigger King,' though his brothers would later deny any such meeting.

As they travelled through several riverboat towns, Ray held up a bank in Alton, possibly with his brothers, stealing $27,230 in what was Ray's biggest haul to date. While waiting to cross into Canada, he adopted the identity 'Eric Stavro Galt', one of twenty aliases he would subsequently adopt. Once ensconced in Montreal's seedy waterfront area, Ray set about obtaining a Canadian passport, with a view to moving to Europe, Latin America or Africa.

It was also around this time that Ray invented a fictitious acquaintance called Raoul, a man of mystery who apparently tried to recruit him into a cross-border smuggling operation. If he could easily invent multiple identities for himself, why not invent a fictitious person to provide alibis for his ventures?

Ray re-entered the US in the summer of 1967 with his sights on Birmingham, Alabama, where Governor George Wallace was thinking of mounting a bid for the Democratic presidential nomination on a segregationist ticket. Since King was a regular visitor to this racially troubled state, Ray conceived the idea of 'helping' Wallace by killing him. At the back of his mind was Sutherland's $50,000 bounty.

First, however, he drove his new Mustang down to Nuevo Laredo in Mexico for a vacation. He spent most of his time in whorehouses or smoking dope and pretending to be a visiting writer, for he had also bought a portable typewriter. In November he crossed from Tijuana into the States, arriving in Los Angeles on 19 November. After celebrating his first free Christmas in eight years – though still a fugitive – Ray spent his time seeking contact with societies sympathetic to the Rhodesian and South African settler regimes, and attended ballroom-dance classes. In mid-January he enrolled in the bartending school, perhaps with a view to joining his brother John in his newly purchased Grapevine Tavern in St Louis, a haunt of enthusiastic racists.

In March Ray underwent rhinoplastic surgery to flatten his pointy nose and to alter the shape of his ears. This was not done to get a Canadian passport for travel to Africa, but to confuse anyone searching for him after he had killed King. A hired assassin would have commanded a healthy advance fee, but Ray began exchanging his depleted stock of Canadian dollars to cover what was a speculative enterprise to collect a rumoured bounty.

On 19 March he began the long drive from Los Angeles; five days later he rented the room in Atlanta. By the end of the month he was touring gun stores to buy equipment for the kill, pestering the assistants with technical questions. Though he claimed he never revisited Atlanta, a 198-page inventory from Piedmont Cleaners in the city placed him dropping off clothes on 1 April 1968 and collecting them on 5 April, the day after King's assassination. This undermined his claim that he had meandered through Mississippi and delivered the gun to Raoul, who he said wanted the gun as a sample for criminal buyers in Mexico.

On 1 April the Southern Christian Leadership Conference announced that King would head a march in Memphis on Friday 5 April. On 3 April Ray set off for the city in his white Mustang. He claimed he handed over the Remington rifle to Raoul in the New Rebel Hotel, and never saw him or the gun again.

After murdering King, Ray drove eleven hours back to Atlanta before wiping the Mustang clean of prints, collecting his laundry and setting off for Canada on a bus. Forty hours after the shooting he was in Toronto, renting a room with a Polish couple who spoke almost no English. He destroyed all trace of Eric Stavro Galt, who was by now sought by the FBI.

Ray spent his time identifying Canadian men in his demographic whose identity he might use to apply for a Canadian passport. He alighted on a young policeman called Ramon George Sneyd, phoning him to establish that he did not have a passport. A travel agency informed Ray that he could apply for one after he bought a return ticket to London. By this time he had relocated to another boarding house with a Chinese landlady who spoke even less English than the Poles. On his sole excursion, Ray watched a TV crime show in a bar; when the Feds announced that they were looking for an escaped convict called James Earl Ray, fellow drinkers failed to connect the mugshots shown with the man sitting next to them.

Equipped with his new Canadian passport, Ray/Sneyd flew to London on 7 May, before leaving for Lisbon on a night flight. He was planning to go to Angola and then on to 'white' South Africa but running low on money, he returned to London and rented a room in Earl's Court.

With no money to pay his modest rent, he held up the Trustee Savings Bank in Fulham, stealing £105 at gunpoint, but leaving a small bag with his right thumbprint. On 27 May an attempt to rob a jewellery store in Paddington was thwarted by the owners. He was still in London on 5 June, when the twenty-four-year-old Jordanian-Palestinian Christian assassin Sirhan Sirhan shot Robert Kennedy in LA's Ambassador Hotel. Kennedy died of a head wound a day later.

On 8 June Ray presented the Sneyd passport at Heathrow's Terminal 2's exit desk, but an officer noticed that as he returned the passport to his wallet, he accidentally revealed another. He next spotted that this cancelled document was in the name of Ramon George Sneya rather than Sneyd. The officer looked through a 'Watch for and Detain' booklet and discovered that Scotland Yard wanted Ramon George Sneyd for 'serious offences' – the Canadian Royal Mounted Police had combed through 264,000 passport applications made since Ray had escaped from the Missouri prison in 1967. FBI handwriting experts had matched his writing with the signature of Eric S. Galt. Ray was escorted to a side room, where a search revealed a loaded .38 revolver in his jacket pocket. Scotland Yard detectives escorted him to Cannon Row Police Station on charges of unlawful possession of a firearm, where he gave evasive answers. When the detectives returned to his cell at 5 p.m. they told him that they believed he was James Earl Ray. Once he calmed down, his chief concern was his coverage in the UK press.

Ray was speedily extradited to the US. The main interest of the British and US lawyers clamouring to represent him was in cutting deals for a book and film, which explains why the role of the imaginary Raoul grew in the telling. The co-option of District Attorney Jim Garrison to Ray's 'cause' helped his lawyers and demented enthusiasts to elaborate wild conspiracy theories, aided by publicity-seeking 'witnesses'.

By 19 July, Ray was back in a Memphis jail. There was no trial, since he pleaded guilty to killing King so as to avoid the electric chair. He was sentenced to ninety-nine years in jail, serving his sentence in Brushy Mountain State Penitentiary in East Tennessee. In 1971, after his second appeal for a fresh trial was rejected, Ray excavated a hole in his cell wall, leaving a dummy on his cot while he crawled along an air vent. Plans to leave the jail via a steam vent under the perimeter wall failed, and he was recaptured hiding in the yard.

Nine months later, Ray tried to cut a hole in the roof of the prison gym. And in 1977, he and four comrades used a ladder made with pipes to clamber over the outer prison wall. After fifty-four hours on the run, two bloodhounds detected him hiding under a pile of leaves and his sentence was increased by a year, to a century.

Despite persistent claims that Ray was part of a bigger conspiracy, he seems not to have been paid an advance, and afterwards none of the putative conspirators seem to have thought of liquidating him. He eventually died aged seventy, of kidney and liver disease caused by hepatitis C, in a Nashville hospital on 23 April 1998. The family had his ashes scattered in the Rays' ancestral Irish homeland.

What did King's murder achieve? The victim became one of

the most admired figures in modern American history, with his 15 January birthday added to the official calendar of federal holidays in 1983. His slaying gave impetus to those African-American radicals who believed in efficacious violence; the ensuing urban riots prompted the Johnson administration to improve housing rights for African Americans. But the breakdown of law and order in over a hundred US cities during the Holy Week Riots in April 1968 also swelled support for the law and order lobby that swept Richard Nixon to victory. The Republican conquest of the South was almost complete, as Democrats there switched allegiances. James Earl Ray's assassination of King was an example of a strain of racist violence that had persisted since the time of John Wilkes Booth. His political hero George Wallace was shot by a young fantasist called Arthur Bremer at a campaign appearance in Maryland in May 1972. Wallace survived, but was paralysed from the waist down.[40]

•

We will end this chapter in India and another privileged dynasty. On the last morning of his life, Mahatma Gandhi woke at his customary 3.30 a.m. Birla House in New Delhi had been built for the Birla tycoons in 1928, and became Gandhi's home for his last days.

Six months earlier, on 15 August 1947, the former capital of the British Raj had witnessed the birth of independent India. Seventy-eight at the time of his death, Gandhi weighed a mere fifty kilograms after a series of protracted fasts, intended to halt the communal violence that accompanied Britain's botched partition of India and Pakistan. Fifteen million people were forcibly displaced and a million were killed. Delhi swarmed with Hindu and Sikh refugees; some in camps, others in the vacated properties of Muslims who had fled to Pakistan. Sensing that his influence was waning, Gandhi's latest fast was an attempt to persuade India's government to honour its financial commitments to Pakistan as the cash balances of the Reserve Bank were divided, a stance which infuriated Hindu nationalists in the Mahasabha party. Worse, Gandhi had vowed to visit Pakistan itself.[41]

With the aid of his two human 'walking sticks' – his grand-nieces Abhabehn and Manubehn – Gandhi spent his final day receiving visitors. The last was the deputy Prime Minister and Home Minister Vallabhbhai Patel, who was engaged in a long-standing conflict with Prime Minister Jawaharlal Nehru, who was also scheduled to meet Gandhi that evening. Another of Gandhi's roles was that of peacemaker within a Congress Party riddled with factionalism and personal rivalries.[42]

The meeting with Patel delayed a nightly prayer session for which about a hundred people had gathered. Gandhi walked into the garden at 5.10 p.m., propped up by his grandnieces. As he crossed the grass to a small raised terrace, a young man in a khaki shirt moved to the front of the crowd. He seemed to be attempting to kiss Gandhi's feet, but he had a Beretta automatic in his hand.

The assassin was thirty-seven-year-old Nathuram Godse, editor of the nationalist *Hindu Rashtra* newspaper in Bombay. After his three brothers died in infancy, he was brought up initially as a girl. A high-caste Brahmin, he drifted between lowly jobs until he became a columnist specializing in moral outrage. After initially being a devotee of Gandhi, Nathuram had joined the extremist Rashtriya Swayamsevak Singh organization in 1932. Its leader, Veer 'the Brave' Savakar, who wished to treat Muslims as Nazism treated Jews, had personally sanctioned Gandhi's assassination in mid-January when he received Nathuram Godse. The manager of the newspaper, Narayan Apte, said: 'Be successful . . . and come back.' Three years younger than Nathuram, Apte was a more worldly figure than his friend. At this time, he was incensed about the mass rapes that accompanied partition.[43]

These two were the principals in a conspiracy to kill Gandhi; the plot also involved five others. Some of their names were known to the police, who had been secretly monitoring their meetings. These were amateur killers, but they benefited from the incompetence of India's police and intelligence services, which might have identified the conspirators after their first attempt failed.

Their first attempt on Gandhi's life on 20 January 1948

consisted of a bomb attack designed to panic those attending a garden prayer session, during which the main target would be killed with guns and a grenade. Although the bomb went off as planned, the thrower was too short to push the grenade through a high window and the gunman fled.

The attack's failure left the original bomber, Madanlal Pahwa, in the hands of the police. Although he gave precise descriptions of the remaining conspirators and their location to a Hindu newspaper in Pune, the policemen contrived not to find them. And when detectives flew to Bombay to help the local police identify the conspirators, they forgot to take the pertinent files. Nor did the Delhi police consult a list of newspapers in the Bombay area, despite Madanlal having said that the assassins edited one. And even when a hooded Madanlal was escorted through Delhi's main station to identify his co-conspirators who were loitering in its cafe, they managed to get back to Bombay to plan another attempt on Gandhi's life.

Gandhi himself refused to have uniformed police bodyguards, though thirty-six plain-clothes officers were added to the perimeter guards positioned around Birla House. Fortunately for the assassins, Gandhi's usual Sikh attendant-cum-bodyguard was called away on 30 January and a policeman who volunteered to protect him went down with flu. As Gandhi walked across the grass, the omens were not propitious.

Nathuram Godse and Narayan Apte flew from Bombay to New Delhi, meeting Vishnu Karkare in a lodging house while they attempted to buy a gun. They had decided that the best chance of killing Gandhi would be assassination by one man, with Nathuram volunteering to pull the trigger. The three set off for Birla House the following afternoon.

Rather than risk a long-range shot at a seated Gandhi, Nathuram Godse fired three shots at point-blank range; two went through Gandhi's abdomen, while the third punctured a lung. Gandhi fell to the grass crying to Rama, his favourite Hindu god, while Godse was overpowered by an American consular worker and led away. In his jail cell he explained: 'For the present I only want to say that I am not sorry for what I have done. The rest I will explain in court.' In the presence of

Gandhi's body, Nehru wept while laying his head in his deputy Patel's lap. The Governor-General, Louis Mountbatten, busied himself with arranging the funerary rites; Gandhi was cremated in front of a vast crowd, and his ashes were scattered in the Ganges.

Following a year-long trial, Nathuram Godse and Narayan Apte were hanged at Ambala Jail on 15 November 1949, with Nehru and Patel ignoring the wishes of the Gandhi family and rejecting pleas for clemency. While the other conspirators were jailed, the chief instigator Veer Savarkar was acquitted on the grounds that the testimony of Digambar Badge, the criminal who supplied explosives for the plot, was tainted. The apotheosis of Gandhi was one result of his violent demise, but the assassins did not achieve their main goal of an exclusively Hindu nationalist India. The former British Raj was partitioned into two states, India and Pakistan, leaving a 14 per cent Muslim minority in India, but over 560 independent princely states were absorbed into the new Indian Republic and in 1952 the country conducted the largest democratic elections in world history. As for Mahatma Gandhi, his example would inspire such giants as Martin Luther King and Nelson Mandela, as well as a uniquely Indian non-aligned approach to international affairs.[44]

Indira Gandhi was Nehru's daughter. She had married Feroze Gandhi (no relation) in 1942, despite her father seeking Mahatma's intervention to prevent a union of which Nehru disapproved. She became India's first female leader and its third Prime Minister, from 1966 to 1977, and in 1980 returned to power in a landslide election after three years in opposition.

In her first period of office Indira became progressively autocratic, imposing both mass sterilization – mainly on Muslims – and then emergency powers from 1975 to 1977 which resulted in 36,000 people being imprisoned. The connections between big business and the political class also multiplied. When her second son Sanjay fatally crashed his aircraft near his mother's house, the dynastic succession devolved on his older brother Rajiv, until then a commercial airline pilot. Although India was a secular state as well as a democracy, in the 1980s politics began to fragment along sectarian lines, not least with the ultra-Hindu BJP, founded in 1980. This would eventually be matched by violent Islamist groups, especially in disputed Kashmir.

On 31 October 1984, Indira Gandhi breakfasted at her residence on 1 Safdarjang Road in New Delhi. She had a busy day ahead; she was to be interviewed by the actor Peter Ustinov, whose TV crew were setting up on the lawn of the adjacent bungalow.

Seven minutes late, Gandhi walked along the concrete path between the two bungalows, as she did every day; it was her favourite spot, flanked by bougainvillea. She was escorted by Narain Singh, Head Constable, as well as her special assistant and a male servant. As they approached the gate, Gandhi smiled at her two Sikh bodyguards – Sub-Inspector Beant Singh and Constable Satwant Singh. Beant Singh suddenly drew his .38 revolver, as Indira uttered her last words: 'What are you doing?'

Beant fired three shots into Indira Gandhi's abdomen. Satwant hesitated before turning his gun on Gandhi and firing thirty more rounds into her body. Gandhi's entourage were paralysed. Sub-Inspector Rameshwar Dayal, patrolling the gardens with the television crew, rushed at the attackers but was gunned down. Narain struggled with Beant, before Indo-Tibetan Border Police commandos arrested both attackers. Being led away, Beant stated, 'We have done what we wanted to. Now you can do what you want to.'

Indira was bundled into a white Ambassador car – the on-call ambulance driver was on a tea break – with her head in the lap of her daughter Sonia. At the All-India Institutes of Medical Sciences, she was in surgery for four hours though she was clinically dead on arrival. Ustinov later noted that the assassination was uncannily quiet. 'There was nothing very dramatic about it,' he said. 'In fact, hardly anybody saw it.'

Indira Gandhi had acquired the reputation of a modern-day Ahmad Shah Admali, the eighteenth-century Afghan invader of the Punjab. On 2 June 1984, she had ordered the storming of the Golden Temple in Amritsar, where Jarnail Singh Bhindranwale

was holed up with armed supporters. Bhindranwale was a radical
Sikh theologian and militant, leading the cause for an independent Sikh state called Khalistan. The first assault on the
Temple by the Indian army was easily repulsed by the Sikh
defenders. After sending in tanks, the siege ended with heavy
damage to the temple's minarets and holy books, with the library
and archives gutted by fire, and as many as three thousand
pilgrims slain. Gandhi alienated 12 million Sikhs worldwide,
especially when the army immediately raided Sikh peasant
villages searching for terrorists. The backlash caused a constitutional crisis, with Sikh soldiers deserting and mutinying.

Dr Jagjit Singh, the self-declared President of Khalistan,
predicted that Gandhi would be assassinated. In a similar vein
to Mahatma, Indira repeatedly spoke of her own death; the day
before her murder, she shouted at a rally, 'I am here today, I
may not be here tomorrow.'

However, the lack of vigilance in Gandhi's security was
shocking. The Intelligence Bureau warned of Sikhs in her personal
bodyguard, but no proper security and intelligence procedures
existed around her. 'Aren't we secular?' she expostulated when
asked to replace her Sikh protectors.[45] Bhindranwale had previously met a short-tempered Sikh police officer, Simranjeet Singh
Mann, who had been transferred out of the Punjab to Bombay,
but had written an angry telegram to Gandhi as tensions in
Amritsar increased. Both Mann and Bhindranwale advocated
revenge for the Golden Temple siege. Along with two professors
from Bombay, they conspired with Atinder Pal Singh, head of
the banned All-India Sikh Student Federation. Atinder knew of
some Sikh security guards within Gandhi's inner circle, stationed
at her residence. Speaking thirty years later, Indira's grandson
Rahul said that Beant Singh had taught him badminton growing
up, but had then started to ask questions about his grandmother's sleeping habits and security, as well as telling him to
lie down if someone threw a grenade.

Thirty minutes after murdering Indira, Beant was beaten and
shot by the ITBP commandos in a police station nearby. Satwant
was later tried and hanged. Meanwhile, Rajiv Gandhi, who had
been campaigning in West Bengal, was rushed home by plane.

Congress immediately appointed him as his mother's successor, while murderous pogroms in Delhi and elsewhere killed thousands of Sikhs. Even as Indira was being laid out inside Teen Murti House – her father's old residence – crowds outside were screaming, 'Blood will be avenged by blood.'

In late 1990 the Hindu nationalist BJP withdrew their support for a national government headed by Janata Dal, thereby forcing fresh elections. Because of the size of the country, Indian elections are staggered across multiple rounds, with the final tally not revealed until the end. After the first round, in which 206 constituencies had voted, the Congress Party had secured 33 per cent of the vote and won only 26 per cent of the constituencies. That was how things stood as Rajiv Gandhi, son and grandson of Prime Ministers, arrived on the evening of 21 May 1991 at a Congress Party rally in Sriperumbudur, in the southern state of Tamil Nadu. On the journey from Madras, he had stopped to pay his respects at a statue of his murdered mother, unaware that he was about to be assassinated himself.

For all her many flaws, Indira Gandhi had been a successful leader in war, giving Pakistan a bloody nose in the late-1971 clash when East Pakistan broke away to become Bangladesh. Her son ended up rashly intervening in someone else's civil war, putting himself in the sights of one of the most deadly terrorist organizations in history, the Liberation Tigers of Tamil Eelam (LTTE).

Representing about 15 per cent of the total population, the Tamils were a privileged minority in the former British colony of Ceylon and as such they were long the object of resentment by the majority Buddhist Sinhalese of independent Sri Lanka. This became a vicious armed conflict, with India providing covert military support to the Tigers and other armed groups. Rajiv Gandhi's female assassin was one of the LTTE fighters who were trained in secret Indian military camps for Tamil guerrillas.

In mid-1987 the Sri Lankan government of J. R. Jayewardene launched an offensive against LTTE bases in the Jaffna Peninsula. India decided to intervene with a so-called 'peace-keeping force', effectively occupying northern and eastern districts of the tear-drop-shaped island.

Under the ensuing Indo-Lanka Accord of 27 July 1987, all Tamil militant groups were supposed to demobilize, in return for regional autonomy. While this might have been welcomed by many Tamils, the LTTE regarded it as an Indian stab in the back. Its cultic leader Velupillai Prabhakaran was forced to accept the accord while under de facto house arrest in New Delhi, though he had no intention of maintaining it. The son of a lowly civil servant, his violent career commenced in 1975 when he shot Alfred Duraiappah, the Tamil Mayor of Jaffna, in the head at point-blank range in a Hindu temple in Colombo. His terrorist group enjoyed much sympathy throughout the Tamil diaspora, notably in Australia, Canada and the UK.

By 10 October 1987 the Indian peacekeepers and LTTE were at war, much to the secret delight of Jayewardene. Despite deploying 48,000 troops, India lost 945 dead to the Tigers' 754 before India withdrew its forces. Prabhakaran's hatred of Rajiv Gandhi was evident in a manual called *The Satanic Force* that chronicled Indian massacres and rapes in northerly Sri Lanka. When the National Front government of V. P. Singh collapsed in 1990, it seemed likely that Rajiv Gandhi would return to power at the next elections in 1991. The LTTE leader was convinced that Gandhi would sell out an independent Tamil Eelam and that he would send Indian troops back to Sri Lanka. Better he should die before the election, he thought.

The Tigers did not invent suicide bombing, but they used it as a force multiplier perhaps better than any terrorists before ISIS. The so-called 'Black Tigers' included many women, since they found it easier to gain access to their targets. All Black Tigers carried glass vials of cyanide around their necks in case they were caught alive.

Planning for the attack on Gandhi began in November or December 1990, even as Prabhakaran despatched emissaries to consult him, an outward show of reconciliation designed to make him drop his guard. The operation was planned by the Tigers' Intelligence Wing, whose commander Pottu Amman co-ordinated operations, using an agent called Sivarasan on the ground. Across the water, the LTTE chief in Tamil Nadu, 'Baby' Subramaniam – compiler of *The Satanic Force* – recruited a team of assassins and acquired safehouses for them. Funding for the operation took the form of smuggled gold tablets. A Tiger team was smuggled into India among Tamil refugees, where they joined locally recruited personnel. Although India's Intelligence Bureau did a good job of monitoring Tiger activity in Tamil Nadu, the assassination team were hidden in safehouses that were not known to the authorities.[46]

Two women called Dhanu and Subha were chosen for suicide bombing. In April 1991 Dhanu bought the saffron and green salwar kameez she would wear in the attack. On 21 May, Subha helped rig the suicide belt, a simple affair of grenades filled with explosives surrounded by ball bearings, underneath it. They and two others, including a cameraman, took a bus to Sriperumbudur, where the press had revealed that Gandhi was due to speak. They were met by a photographer called Hari Babu, who may have been one of the so-called 'Truth Tigers' routinely used to record such murderous events. Hari Babu gave Dhanu a garland of beads perfumed with sandalwood to wear around her neck.[47]

At the rally, Dhanu and the photographer deftly attached themselves to two female Congress Party activists who were waiting to greet Gandhi with a poem. Amidst the usual chaos, Sivarasan loitered in the background, a revolver hidden under his shirt. Dhanu slipped through a relaxed security cordon and came face to face with Rajiv Gandhi. At 10.20 p.m., the bomb tore off his face as he bent to accept the garland proffered by the small bespectacled girl in front of him. As for Dhanu, the bomb ripped through her midriff and decapitated her. Fifteen people were killed that night, including the photographer Hari Babu, though his intact camera gave the most immediate evidence of who had been involved in the attack, as did a cache of letters that a Tiger courier hid when getting to Sri Lanka proved impossible. The Indian police quickly established that over forty people had been in the plot. Twelve of them committed suicide when capture was imminent, including Sivarasan and Subha, who shot themselves in a hideout after being cornered by Indian commandos three months later.

Rajiv Gandhi's death gave a boost to the electoral fortunes

of the Congress Party, with P. V. Narasimha Rao becoming Prime Minister. None of the three assassinations made much of an impact on the longer-term political culture of India; the Nehru–Gandhi political dynasty continued with Rajiv's Italian-born widow Sonia and her son Rahul.

As for Prabhakaran and the Tigers, their forces acquired a naval arm and submarines, as well as the 'Baby Tiger' child soldiers. In 1991 they placed a sleeper agent, disguised as a general store owner, in a shop directly opposite the presidential residence in Colombo. On 1 May 1993, President Ranasinghe Premadasa came out to review a workers' parade. The familiar young store owner was allowed through to greet him, before blowing himself up, killing the President and seventeen others. It would take a full-blown military assault in 2009 to eliminate the threat from the Tigers which had rocked Sri Lanka for a quarter of a century.[48]

8

'Too Many to Kill – Even for Us': Putin's Russia

Under the Bolsheviks, state murder was a means to rapidly reorder society while also eradicating the ideologically deviant.[1] There was a bureaucratization of murderous violence in the modern period, which removed human passions and dissolved such crimes into compartmentalized and limited culpabilities. A 2021 Russian novel by Sergei Lebedev points to the clandestine chemical warfare experiments which the Bolsheviks conducted with the forces of the Weimar Republic in the 1920s as a precursor of later poisonings involving weapons of war. But what of Stalin's Communist successors or the present Russian President Vladimir Putin, who rules a highly capitalist successor to the Soviet Union? The continuities are there, but they are far from straightforward.

Following Stalin's death in 1953, assassination became less central to foreign policy, with the conspicuous exception of anti-Soviet émigré nationalist groups, many of them Ukrainian. Comparative restraint under Khrushchev and Brezhnev also reflected a few well-publicized failures of nerve by their trained killers.

One such killer was Nikolai Kholkov, a blond, blue-eyed actor who had worked as an undercover NKVD agent in wartime Minsk, scene of terrible Nazi atrocities. One SS victim died after getting into bed with a mine hidden in the mattress by a servant. After the war, Pavel Sudaplatov, the head of Special Tasks and the organizer of Trotsky's murder, carefully regroomed Kholkov. He went to Moscow University 'without passing any entrance exams' and then travelled back and forth to Austria, Germany and Switzerland.[2]

Kholkov was instructed to kill Georgi Okolovich, a Ukrainian exile in West Germany. His weapon was an electrically charged gun inside a cigarette packet, which fired cyanide-laced darts. But when Kholkov appeared on the victim's doorstep in February 1954, he announced: 'Georgi Sergeyevich, I've come to you from Moscow. The Central Committee of the Communist Party of the Soviet Union has ordered your assassination.' He defected to the CIA and in April displayed his lethal cigarette box at a press conference.

Two years later, the KGB tried to kill Kholkov with radio-active thallium, but with no success; hiring a German contract killer to murder another Ukrainian exile in 1955 was another embarrassing flop.[3] They had better luck in 1957, when a young KGB assassin of Ukrainian origin, Bohdan Stashynsky, used a cyanide spray gun against a Ukrainian nationalist ideologue, before using the same device against the wartime Ukrainian nationalist leader Stepan Bandera in the stairwell of a Munich apartment block. Unfortunately, the young assassin then fell in love with an East German girl and fled with her to West Berlin in 1961. After serving a prison sentence for murder, the couple disappeared, perhaps to South Africa.[4]

Killing Trotsky or Ukrainian nationalists was one thing, but murdering the head of another state and a wartime Allied legend was quite another. Yet in February 1953 Sudaplatov had an audience with an ailing Stalin, who handed him the draft outline of a plan to kill Yugoslavia's President Tito.[5]

The plan involved one of the NKVD's most experienced organizers of murder abroad: Iosif Romualdovich Grigulevich, or 'Grig', who had been involved in the first failed attempt on Trotsky's life. While stationed in Chile, he assumed the identity of Teodoro Castro, the illegitimate son of a wealthy deceased Costa Rican. This was sufficiently plausible for the Costa Rican consul to Chile to supply letters of recommendation to go with the fake ID documents. This led to a bogus business operation in Rome, where 'Castro' befriended further Costa Ricans, who introduced him to José Figueres Ferrer, the former and future President of Costa Rica. From there, it was a short jump to becoming an honorary member of the Costa Rican legation in Italy. On a trip to the UN, his delegation even voted against the Soviet delegation on one matter.[6]

In 1952, Castro was twice sent to Yugoslavia, representing Costa Rica as a non-residential envoy. It was he who conveyed plans to kill Tito to the MVD station in Vienna. One option involved an audience with Tito in which Castro would spray him with pneumonic plague, having already taken an antidote himself. Or he would use a silenced gun to shoot Tito at a diplomatic reception in London or Belgrade, with smoke grenades enabling him to flee. Or finally, once MVD psychologists had determined how Tito received impromptu gifts, a box containing jewellery would release a deadly gas once opened.

Sudaplatov knew that Grig was not a practised killer, and that the Soviets only sent agents on suicide missions in wartime. However, despite his objections to the 'bad tradecraft', he was overruled. Grig got as far as writing a farewell letter to his Mexican wife, but Stalin died on 5 March, so the operation was called off.

This mixed record explains why the KGB and the military intelligence GRU only rarely resorted to assassinations in the ensuing couple of decades. They did extend their technical expertise to fraternal services in the Communist bloc from time to time. On 7 September 1978, the exiled Bulgarian dissident playwright Georgi Markov was injected in the calf with a tiny ricin-filled pellet as he waited for a bus on Waterloo Bridge in London. He imagined that he had been stung by an insect, but died four days later, as British experts worked out that the coating over the pellet disintegrated at body temperature and that it had been fired from an adapted umbrella. Another Bulgarian had been attacked in the same fashion in Paris ten days earlier and survived. KGB defectors claim that their former agency supplied the device and the poison pellets to their Bulgarian colleagues; Markov's broadcasts against Todor Zhivkov's regime had become too personal. He is buried in a Dorset graveyard.

Heightened tensions during the Cold War explain why the GRU and KGB returned to 'wetwork' in 1979. In April 1978, the People's Democratic Party of Afghanistan seized power in Kabul. However, not only were there very few Afghan Communists, perhaps 50,000 in a country of 13.31 million, but they were split into two rival factions. The first was called

Parcham, who realized that this backward country lacked a vanguard proletariat and thought the Communists would have to work with other parties. The second faction, called Khalq, believed in the revolutionary potency of the peasantry, despite them being socially conservative and devout in Muslim Afghanistan.

The PDPA used the usual mixture of enforced enlightenment and brutal repression to consolidate its minority rule. Its leader, President Nur Muhammad Taraki, quickly alienated majority Muslim opinion by torturing and murdering religious leaders and confiscating their lands. Attempts to improve the lot of Afghan women sparked a powerful backlash from fighters who called themselves Mujahedeen, first in western Herat in March 1979, where 5,000 government troops and some Soviet advisors were slaughtered before Russian bombers intervened.

The Afghan Communists appealed to the Soviet Union for military support in crushing the insurgency. The elderly Politburo leadership under the ailing Leonid Brezhnev were exasperated by the murderous rivalries and dogmatic obtuseness of their Afghan 'clients', but anxious that their own influence not be displaced. Over the summer, they declined to send large-scale military assistance but did reinforce the protective troops inside the Soviet embassy in Kabul and increased the number of troops stationed across the Afghan border in Tajikistan. Meanwhile, the GRU formed a 500-strong unit of Central Asian troops who could pass as non-Pashtun Afghans, while the KGB rotated two successive teams of Alfa group special forces in the Kabul embassy. An air assault battalion landed at Bagram airbase, seventy miles outside Kabul, allegedly to supervise the evacuation of the many Soviet 'advisors' and embassy staff in the country.[7]

The Soviets urged the Afghan Communists to broaden the base of their regime, a line also pushed by the Soviet ambassador, Aleksandr Puzanov. Moscow's reluctant decision to invade was closely connected to the murderous feuding between President Taraki and his Prime Minister and Defence Minister, Hafizullah Amin; Moscow decided that the hot-headed Amin was the problem and wanted him gone. Despite patching up their relationship to appease the Russians, on 14 September Taraki's men tried to shoot Amin on a 'reconciliatory' visit to the Arg Palace. Worse, the Soviet ambassador happened to be hanging around when the gunfire erupted. Amin escaped, and then ordered the army to depose Taraki.

Brezhnev had not reckoned on how murderous the Afghans could be and was adamant that no one should touch the deposed Taraki. In early October 1979 he was taken from his comfortable place of detention, bound and then smothered with a pillow by a lieutenant acting on orders from Amin. On learning of Taraki's death from 'a brief and serious illness', Brezhnev exploded: 'What a bastard, Amin, to murder the man with whom he made the revolution . . . Who will now believe my promises, if my promises of protection are shown to be no more than empty words?'

Even while donning traditional garb and invoking 'Allah', Amin had no more success in pacifying the religious insurgents. Despite keeping a photo of Stalin on his desk as a reminder of how to develop a country, Amin also explored hedging the Communist country's orientation to the Soviets. Superpower tensions were in an acute phase, and the Soviets worried that having lost Iran, the Americans might move NSA radars used to monitor Soviet ballistic missile tests from Iran to Afghanistan. Worse for Amin, KGB chief Yuri Andropov recalled that the new Afghan leader had studied in the US in the 1960s and may have been influenced by the CIA. Some in the KGB claimed Amin was about 'to do a Sadat' and abandon the Soviet camp by wholeheartedly embracing the US.[8]

The inner Politburo Committee on Afghanistan decided what would happen. In November, the KGB brought Babrak Karmal, a Parcham supporter and the Afghan ambassador to Prague, back to Moscow; he was told to prepare an alternative government to Amin's. On 10 December Nikolai Ogarkov, the Chief of the General Staff, was ordered to ready an 'assistance force' of 75–80,000 men. Two days later, the Politburo took the decision to send in its troops on Christmas Day. As the Defence Minister Ustinov reminded Brezhnev: 'The Americans have done it over and over in Latin America. What are we, worse than they are?'⁹ From Christmas Day onwards, 500 sorties of Soviet troop transporters landed at Bagram, every four minutes, while columns of tanks, trucks and APCs crossed the frontier from the west and east.

Within the invasion, the KGB was responsible for Operation AGAT to kill Amin. This involved deploying forces allegedly to protect him, while in reality plotting to oust him while taking over key sites in the capital. Russian special forces commanders quietly went about noting the defences of Amin's Tajbeg Palace, about ten miles outside Kabul. The Soviet advisers inside reported that the palace had rings of defences manned by 2,500 troops, with tanks and anti-aircraft guns at ground level. The Soviet assault force was 700 strong.

In these circumstances Plan B was also activated. The KGB had tried and failed to kill Amin with a sniper, and on 13 December they tried to poison him with toxified Coca-Cola, but that also failed. On the day the Russian assault was planned for, Amin held a lunch for his new Politburo and government ministers with their wives and families. During the meal Amin fell unconscious, as did many of his guests. The cook was apparently a KGB agent, sent to put them to sleep rather than kill them. Soviet doctors from the embassy spent several hours waking Amin, even as his Soviet advisers slipped away to attend a birthday party.

Shortly after six that evening, the forty-five-minute assault commenced, with KGB special forces and the Muslim Battalion racing up to the palace in armoured personnel carriers. When commandos burst into the building, its defenders retreated to the higher floors. Amin, wearing shorts and a T-shirt, groggily limped through the ballroom accompanied by his five-year-old son; he was shot dead and the son was fatally wounded. The Soviet military doctor who had treated him after the poisoning was also slain, as was the Russian commander of the operation. In all, ten of the assault troops were killed, not counting the thirty-five paratroopers who died when their plane crashed into a mountain while landing at Bagram.

The captured Radio and Television Centre began broadcasting a taped address by Karmal to the Afghan people, exhorting them to rejoice in the defeat of 'primitive executioners, usurpers and murderers of tens of thousands'. The Soviets embarked on a war that would become as attritional as the Americans' war in Vietnam.

•

Few of Brezhnev's successors lasted long enough for a discernible policy on assassination to be established. KGB chief Yuri Andropov presided for fourteen months between 1982 and 1984, and the similarly ailing Konstantin Chernenko expired after thirteen months. He was followed by Mikhail Gorbachev. Under these three leaders, the KGB and GRU would never have killed without explicit authorization from their masters in the Politburo.

Since the millennium, which saw the replacement of President Boris Yeltsin by Vladimir Putin, matters have become more complicated, though the opacity surrounding the workings of the ruling group remains just as striking. To complicate matters, between 2008 and 2012 Putin swapped roles with his Prime Minister, Dmitri Medvedev, though it is pretty clear who is the dominant partner in the relationship.

Moreover, Putin is far from the authoritarian of Western imagining – indeed, some have described 'his' regime as 'authoritarianism without authority'. How efficient can the regime be when the Chief Military Prosecutor reported in 2011 that 20 per cent of the defence budget was 'stolen', or when Medvedev, noting an annual 65 per cent rise in the implementation of presidential instructions, added that this brought the total delivered on time to a modest 20 per cent? Whether involving nuclear power plant explosions, lost submarines, endemic forest fires or terrorist attacks at airports, too often Russia's rulers realize that preventative measures they had decreed were never implemented by a bureaucracy that lied that it had.

The old pastime of Kremlinology – meaning more or less informed speculation about rank among the Soviet ruling Politburo – has been supplanted by 'Putinology'. A particularly crass example of this was a 2008 Pentagon study which concluded that the Russian leader suffered from Asperger's syndrome. The evidence for Putin ordering assassinations is in reality much more ambiguous than his regular tough-guy pronouncements may suggest. Despite nearly twenty years in power, he has scarcely managed to diversify an economy as dependent on oil and gas exports as any petrodollar autocracy in the Middle East. Indeed the economy is roughly on a par with that of Italy's.[10]

•

At lunchtime on 27 February 2015, Anna Duritskaya, a twenty-three-year-old Ukrainian model, landed in Moscow to rendezvous with her Russian lover, the fifty-five-year-old Russian opposition politician Boris Nemtsov. He had divorced his wife to focus on his relationship with Anna. Meanwhile, Russia had been supporting armed separatists in eastern Ukraine for a year.

Nemtsov's chauffeur drove the couple to Nemtsov's home, where they planned to spend the afternoon watching a movie. In the evening, Anna visited a beauty salon, while Nemtsov went to a radio station for an interview to publicize a major opposition demonstration. The lovers reunited at Café Bosco in the GUM department store, where Nemtsov paid 12,000 roubles for a very good meal.

To the chippy and sour, the handsome Nemtsov's louche character and the 'aristocratic' nature of the democratic opposition to the Putin regime would be salient. Nemtsov had been a minister, vice-premier, deputy speaker of the Duma and co-founder of successive opposition parties and movements. There had been arrests and short spells in jail. He issued regular reports criticizing the regime, including one about to appear on covert Russian involvement in the civil war in Ukraine. He had also actively lobbied the US Congress to expand the reach of sanctions under the 2012 Magnitsky Act, introduced after a Russian lawyer was murdered in jail to cover up a financial raid by corrupt Russian policemen on a US hedge fund. Worse, Nemtsov remarked that 'Putin is really fucked up' during a public Q&A in Kiev.[11] Three weeks before his death, he told an interviewer, 'If I was afraid of Putin, I would not be in this line of work.'[12]

At 11.15 p.m. the couple left Café Bosco and began to walk back to Nemtsov's house. They decided to cross the Bolshoi Moskvoretskii Bridge, which starts directly below the walls of the Kremlin. There may have been eight other people on the opposite path over the bridge, while one young man, Evgenii Molodych, walked some way behind them, apparently absorbed by hard rock music. As if from nowhere, a man appeared and shot Nemtsov twice in the back. While the first assassin leaped into a passing car, another man, presumed by some to be Molodych, knelt to shoot Nemtsov twice as he lay on the ground.

Conspicuous in a white fur coat, Anna had hailed a garbage truck which had slowly moved past her after the first shots. The driver used her mobile phone to call 112, Russia's emergency services number. About five minutes later the police showed up, though the garbage truck had gone. Russia's leading opposition politician had been assassinated.

The Kremlin is guarded by a 3,000-strong Federal Protection Service, some of them on extramural foot patrols. In addition, 300 sites around the complex, including the Moskvoretskii Bridge, are covered by CCTV. But that night these cameras were all either being repaired or facing inside the Kremlin walls. Never mind, because like most capital cities, Moscow also bristles with a municipal traffic-monitoring CCTV system, called Potok or 'Flow', to relieve congestion as well as to identify vehicles and licence plates. There were eighteen of these attached to lanterns on the bridge, but they recorded nothing untoward either – or if they did, it will never be seen.

Like many motorists nowadays, drivers in Russia have dash-cams to record accidents. At 11.35 p.m., a motorist in a passing Audi caught a second shooter kneeling over Nemtsov, presumably to finish him off. The motorist's footage was ruled inadmissible in court, because he had neglected to seasonally adjust the camera's timer. The FSO and Potok footage was never produced at all, along with any from a parked municipal bus, whose four cameras covered most of the murder vista.[13]

A TV weather camera outside TVT's centre on the south bank caught a glimpse of a man jumping into a car on the bridge, although the camera's view was blocked by the garbage truck for a few seconds. The kneeling Molodych was allegedly a Russian 'clean-up man', trained to ensure the victim was dead. However he was never investigated as such, nor involved in the prosecution other than as an eye-witness.

While much footage was available, none of it appeared at the trial of five Chechen men accused of killing Nemtsov. One reason was that Nemtsov had been under FSB surveillance for a long time. A team of plainclothes experts were trailing him on foot, especially in the days before a major demonstration against Russia's role in the war raging in eastern Ukraine.

Quite why these agents never collided with a small team of Chechen assassins who had been shadowing Nemtsov since October 2014 remained a mystery, especially since two of these Chechens were members of the Sever Battalion of Russian Federation (MVD) Interior Ministry Troops based in Chechnya, a small region of 1.4 million people with a very troubled history.

Only one of this pair, the thirty-three-year-old MVD Lieutenant Zaur Dadaev, went on trial, since Beslan Shavonov – who was probably the initial shooter – had allegedly blown himself up with a grenade during his arrest in Grozny. The four other accused were allegedly arrested by federal narcotics agents as they were engaged in a drugs deal in Ingushetia, a smaller republic neighbouring Chechnya. They were actually arrested by masked spetsnaz of the FSB.

The five Chechen accused were tortured before they stood trial in a military court, which was an elaborate piece of theatre choreographed by the judge and prosecution that lasted nine months. The accused sat in a cage, and were sometimes removed for disturbing the proceedings. Lawyers representing the Nemtsov family had to intervene to protect the rights of the accused, since the defence lawyers did not unduly exert themselves.

The trial also took place against a backdrop of deliberate misinformation in the Russian press. Juicy titbits were laid to interest readers in Anna Duritskaya, the insinuation being that she was a high-class escort. There was also an entirely imaginative trail of 'evidence' leading not just to Ukraine's secret service but the CIA. The aim was to depict Russia rather than Nemtsov as the victim, in this case of sinister foreign machinations.

Similar-sounding names had the Chechen Dadaev serving in the Dudaev battalion of Islamists, volunteering with 'fascist' Ukrainians against Russophone insurgents. Another clincher was that the murder weapon was alleged to be made from stray parts of Ukrainian provenance. So although the assassins were connected to Chechen strongman Ramzan Kadyrov, the evidence pointed to Ukraine, and in particular to one Adam Osmaev, who in 2012 had served three years in jail for allegedly plotting to assassinate Putin.

The trial highlighted visits paid to Dadaev's apartment by fellow Chechens Ruslan Mukhutdinov, a driver who worked for Interior Ministry, and Colonel Ruslan Geremeev, deputy commander of the Sever Battalion in Chechnya. Geremeev rented the Moscow apartment in which the assassins lived. The day after the assassination, Geremeev and Dadaev were caught by airport surveillance cameras flying from Moscow to Grozny.[14]

When the trial concluded, all five Chechens were found guilty of Nemtsov's murder. They were allegedly to be paid fifteen million rubles or US $234,000, though since Mukhutdinov and Geremeev fled to 'the UAE', following the money trail proved impossible. Neither man has ever been interviewed by the Russian authorities, though they are believed to be in Chechnya, which is part of Russia. Dadaev was jailed for twenty years, and his four associates for between eleven and nineteen years. The search for who commissioned Nemtsov's murder petered out. The Russian authorities refused to consider the assassination in terms of Article 277 of the Criminal Code regarding 'encroachment on the life of a statesman or a public figure' but rather under Article 105 that deals with common murder, even though at the time of his death Nemtsov was a member of the Yaroslavl regional assembly.[15]

All roads seemed to point to Chechen leader Ramzan Kadyrov – many of those named were close to him and his security forces obey his every whim. Many ethnic Russians would have found this plausible, since Chechens are widely associated with Islamist fanatics and organized crime. It was insinuated that the killers had been enraged by Nemtsov's defence of the controversial French *Charlie Hebdo* cartoonists, but things may have been less straightforward.

First, Kadyrov would not have launched an assassination of such a prominent figure as Nemtsov outside the Kremlin's Spassky Gate without someone close to Putin giving him the go-ahead, before or after. An aide to Putin reported that the Russian strongman was 'stunned' by the killing, commenting, 'If you can do something outside the Spassky Gate, then maybe you could do this inside Spassky Gate as well.' So who might have given the orders to kill Nemtsov, if not Putin himself? That someone is believed to be General Victor Zolotov, the head of the MVD troops, to whom the Sever Battalion in Chechnya were subordinate. The FSB wanted to reassert Russian control of Kadyrov's fiefdom.

The assassination of Nemtsov interrupted the FSB's own surveillance operation on him. Embarrassed, they rapidly rounded up the Chechen likely lads – though the presumed first shooter Dadaev had an alibi, having been caught on CCTV at his home at the time of the shooting, footage that was never shown to the court. The witness who identified him was Evgenii Molodykh, who was probably the second shooter himself.

It may be that Zolotov was working towards Putin's expressed loathing of Nemtsov but not in tandem with the FSB, which saw a chance to exert leverage over Putin while curbing the power of his 'Chechen dragon'. An SVR defector alleged in 2000 that Zolotov had drawn up a list of influential people to kill with the head of the Federal Protection Service, Evgenii Morov, before exclaiming: 'There are too many. It's too many to kill – even for us.'[16]

Putin allegedly vanished for ten days after the assassination, as if to consider how to resolve a rift between powerful elements of his security establishment. The fact that Zolotov was appointed chief of the newly founded National Guard a year later suggests that Putin went with his man, while also retaining the services of Ramzan Kadyrov – having invested so much in him to keep a lid on Chechnya, he could not simply drop him.

Kadyrov is like a ferocious pet that licks its master's hand while remaining extremely dangerous. But this leaves unresolved Putin's own role in assassinations. Some argue he has established a climate but cannot be blamed for every instance of bad weather. Others claim that nothing happens without his more or less explicit authorization.

•

Days before his death, Nemtsov told a *Financial Times* journalist in a basement Irish pub in Moscow that Putin 'Is a totally amoral human being. Totally amoral. He is a Leviathan. Putin is very dangerous. He is more dangerous than the Soviets were. In the Soviet Union, there was at least a system, and decisions were taken in the Politburo. Decisions about war, decisions to kill people, were not taken by Brezhnev alone, or by Andropov either, but that's how it works now.'[17] That is certainly true; moreover, in Soviet times the secret services were not only subordinate to the ruling Politburo, but were riddled with Communist Party informers who ensured they toed the Party line.

We know much about Putin the former spy, though that conjures up a life of daring that is far from the dull realities of Putin's humdrum KGB career. His grandfather cooked for Lenin and Stalin, and his father fought in wartime Leningrad as a member of an NKVD military unit. As a child and adolescent, Putin devoured books and films about the secret agencies, which had a certain glamour in grey post-war Russia. In 1975 he joined the KGB's Fifth Chief Directorate as a trainee after taking the law degree the KGB recommended, which meant that he avoided military conscription. He was eventually transferred to the First Chief Directorate, which was responsible for external espionage.

Major Putin's first overseas posting in 1985 was to Dresden rather than to the KGB headquarters in East Berlin or Bonn, London or Paris. Four years later he would experience the existential shock of the fall of Communism. Crowds of emboldened

East Germans mobbed the headquarters of the Stasi opposite Putin's own headquarters, as he and his colleagues frenziedly burned their files. The structures he and his colleagues had put in place to earn foreign currency by exporting raw materials at ruble prices would prove useful when they went into 'business'.[18]

But what about the boy before the man? Putin's elder brother died in the siege of Leningrad, which also severely impaired the health of his parents. Physically small at five feet six and a half inches, his major enthusiasm was (and is) judo. Many of his intimates are men he has hurled onto mats; he learned this martial art after getting into fights as a boy in a rough district of post-war Leningrad. He was bullied by local toughs, and though he had the ability to make others like him, he pretended to be a tearaway himself. 'I was a hooligan, not a Pioneer,' he explained, referring to the junior Communist Party organization he did not join.[19]

Though Putin is a proud servant of the elite 'Sword and Shield' of the Party, he has a delinquent teenager lurking within him. Although he normally speaks with the '*Sachlichkeit*' of technocrats, his use of crude gangland slang reveals another side to his character. He is not a scion of the fabled Russian intelligentsia, and he was a provincial outsider to the men of power in the Kremlin. But he is also clever enough to adopt ideas that others in his circle present to him; as a trainee in the KGB, his contemporaries noted his gift for convincing superiors that everything he did was the result of profound insight and careful deliberation.[20]

In addition, there is also Putin the operator, weighing up his interlocutors, knowing when to speak or remain silent. He is a lawyer, after all. Returned to Moscow in early 1990, within a decade he became Russia's Prime Minister. And at New Year 2000, as the sun stole across Russia's eleven time zones, Putin became President. He moved so fast during this decade that his main recollection was of temporary apartments crowded with packing cases and of time snatched with his family.

After leaving East Germany, Putin's prospects looked as bleak as those of Russia itself. As he explained to Russia's Federal Assembly in 2018: 'Soviet Russia lost 23.8 per cent of its national territory, 48.5 per cent of its population, 41 per cent of the GDP, 39.4 per cent of its industrial potential . . . as well as 44.6 per cent of its military capability due to the division of the Soviet armed forces among the former Soviet republics.' As Russia emerged like a moth from a chrysalis, 25 million ethnic Russians were marooned in the new abroad.[21]

Putin discovered that the KGB could not pay him for three months or provide his young family with an apartment. He accepted a post as an in-house spy at Leningrad University, where his parents had an apartment going spare. He reacquainted himself with a former law professor, St Petersburg's Mayor, Anatoly Sobchak, becoming his liaison to the security agencies, and he was rapidly promoted to lead the mayor's new committee on foreign economic affairs. Sure of his footing in this political stream, Putin resigned from the KGB to focus on public administration. This was timely, since Russia's new President, Boris Yeltsin, banned the Communist Party and dismantled the KGB's vast apparatus, creating the FSB and SVR to handle domestic and foreign intelligence. The GRU continued under Russia's Chief of the General Staff.

Putin's opportunity came when Sobchak decided to stimulate Leningrad's ruined industrial economy with casinos. He was appointed to license two dozen such ventures and to lease them premises, while retaining a 51 per cent municipal share in each establishment via layered holding companies. The contracts were devised by a clever young lawyer called Dmitri Medvedev, Putin's future alternate as Prime Minister and President, but these all-cash operations reported losses as their profits disappeared elsewhere. As in further scandals, Putin was temporarily embarrassed, but his low profile meant they never halted his ascent.

Putin was next deputed to sell $120 million worth of cotton, scrap metal, oil and timber, in exchange for the food which Leningraders desperately needed. How the contractors were chosen remained opaque. The huge commissions the city charged vanished, and no food was ever imported in return for the exports, which were deliberately undervalued. Many of the contractors were hidden by multiple shell companies, which declared bankruptcy after their profits had disappeared into overseas bank accounts. The scandal did Putin no personal harm; he also made friends with some of these contractors and advanced to deputy mayor, with special responsibility for attracting foreign investment. He also negotiated the arrival of Dresdner Bank in St Petersburg with a former Stasi officer he knew from his previous career. More foreign corporations followed: Otis Elevators, Proctor & Gamble, Coca-Cola, Ford, Heineken and Wrigley.[22]

But there were shadier associates in Russia's most violent city. In 1998–9 there were seven hundred actual or attempted assassinations, and some of the new companies Putin registered were fronts for organized crime groups. Behind the Petersburg Fuel Company lurked such Mafiosi as Vladimir Kumarin, head of the notorious Tambovskaya Gang. A private security firm, the gang provided bodyguards for city officials like Sobchak and Putin. Kumarin coveted St Petersburg's seaport, and he got his hands on it through Sobchak's head of anti-smuggling operations, another former KGB mediocrity called Viktor Ivanov. The entire Baltic merchant fleet followed into their clutches.[23]

Though Putin showed few signs of having made any real money, he joined some of his new business associates in a gated dacha cooperative called Ozero outside St Petersburg. This spawned a joint business enterprise, while two of Ozero's partners acquired Bank Rossiya. When his dacha burned down, he rescued just a briefcase containing $5,000, his life's savings, and his personal crucifix, but it seems improbable that anyone involved in casino licensing would not have benefited financially.

The electoral defeat and flight of Sobchak in 1996 indicated it was time for Putin to leave his home city. Having wagered on Boris Yeltsin as well as Sobchak, Putin moved to Moscow, and a new job in the Presidential Property Management Directorate. This agency oversaw not just the presidential patrimony in Russia but the vast properties of the former Soviet Union, plus embassies and the like in seventy-eight countries. In 1997 Putin was promoted to run the Main Control Directorate, which inspected Russia's regional administrations, and in July

1998 Yeltsin appointed him head of the FSB. At this point, devious and meddling oligarchs like Boris Berezovsky, by now controlling Channel One and other slices of the Russian media, began to notice this new man, who had the major merit that he was not a major financial player. He was also loyally ruthless on behalf of Yeltsin and his daughter Tatyana Dymachenko, the key member of 'The Family'.

Three weeks before Putin was appointed head of the FSB, Lev Rokhlin was shot dead while in bed in his country dacha. A veteran of the Soviet's Afghan campaign, he was the general who took Grozny in the First Chechen War in 1995. Deeply critical of Yeltsin, he had tried to mobilize a new army party, and talked of impeaching the President. Since the couple were known to have drunken arguments, it was easy to charge his wife Tamara with her husband's murder, and her claims of three masked intruders were ignored. The fact that the burned corpses of three men were found near the scene of the crime was put down to coincidence. Her case dragged through the courts, ending with a short prison sentence.

On other occasions shooting someone was unnecessary. Kompromat would do instead. As soon as Putin became FSB director, kompromat was deployed against Yeltsin's opponents. The wife of Moscow Mayor Yuri Luzhkov was investigated by the FSB for money-laundering. When general prosecutor Yuri Skuratov pursued the Yeltsin clan for corrupt links to a Swiss construction firm, it did not take long for grainy footage of him scampering on a bed with two naked women to emerge, forcing his resignation. Aleksandr Litvinenko would maintain that similar compromising footage of Putin existed.[24]

At the FSB's Lubyanka HQ, the former KGB lieutenant colonel declined the executive suite but did put a statuette of KGB founder 'Iron Felix' on his desk. In the early 1990s Yeltsin had sought to break apart the vast organization by separating domestic and foreign intelligence into the FSB and SVR. Signals intelligence was hived off to a new agency called FRAPSI, while a new Federal Border Service took over watching the frontiers. Putin saw his task as reassembling the formidable powers 'his' old KGB had lost.[25]

He fired a third of the occupants of the FSB headquarters and brought in reliable old comrades from the St Petersburg KGB. He chose Nikolai Patrushev as his deputy, Vladimir Pronichev as the new head of counter-terrorism, and Viktor Ivanov as head of FSB internal counter-intelligence. The newly promoted Colonel Igor Sechin became Putin's executive assistant. These loyalists shared similar backgrounds and goals, except when they fell out over money. Beyond the core group are professional bureaucrats and members of regional elites, like Foreign Minister Lavrov or Sergi Shoigu, since 2012 Russia's Defence Minister and a likely successor to Putin.

Putin's technocratic management of the FSB suffered one public glitch. In November 1998 a panel of masked men in dark glasses appeared at a televised press conference. They were members of the FSB's organized crime squad who claimed that the organization had been subverted by Russian and Chechen gangsters. They also claimed that their superiors had ordered them to kill Boris Berezovsky. He and Putin had been linked in 1997 when a St Petersburg journalist who was investigating both men was attacked in his apartment foyer, so badly that he died of his injuries.

The chief spokesman for the aggrieved FSB panellists was Lieutenant Colonel Aleksandr Litvinenko. He had joined the KGB in 1988 and initially worked protecting government bullion shipments, before moving into a department tackling organized crime. The unit was as thuggish as the people it was supposed to bring to justice; he strongly believed that his bosses were involved in such crimes, too.[26]

Litvinenko had also investigated a failed assassination attempt on Berezovsky, when a remotely detonated bomb had blown off the head of the oligarch's chauffeur. This odd couple tantalized each other with conspiracy theories that Litvinenko eagerly embraced when he joined Berezovsky's payroll while still working for the FSB. Berezovsky regarded himself as the nation's king-maker. No wonder since he and his fellow oligarchs – a mere 110 people – controlled 35 per cent of Russia's wealth.

Putin's response to the FSB's bizarrely delivered 'revelations' was to summon Litvinenko for an audience. In his own TV appearance, he mocked the masked men, adding that the ex-wife of one of them had called to complain that her ex was behind with alimony payments. Putin then fired Litvinenko and the others. His relations with Berezovsky were undamaged and he advanced a further square on the chessboard, to Chairman of the nation's Security Council.

A highly disturbed external scene following the end of the Cold War and the visible physical degeneration of President Yeltsin accompanied Putin's final assault on the summit of power in Russia. After the collapse of Communism, many Russians hoped that Russia would join a 'Greater West'. Instead, they were offered a subordinate role in the 'Historic West', alongside such medium-sized US clients like France or the UK.[27] After offering Russia strategic partnership, NATO rubbed Moscow's face in the dirt with its armed intervention in Kosovo.

Yeltsin wanted to prevent dangerous political rivals succeeding him, for they might poke around in the murky business affairs of his family and associates. In August 1999 he offered Putin the post of Prime Minister. A pro-Putin claque called the Unity Party was duly conjured into existence, and Putin became Prime Minister in August 1999. His appointment was in tune with public opinion in other respects. In 1999, 37 per cent of Russians thought the state security agencies 'had too little power' and 50 per cent thought the same of the armed forces. They were regarded as honest, apolitical, patriotic professionals who did what they were told, unlike the amoral, greedy crooks produced by the era of privatization.[28]

But Berezovsky was central to getting Putin accepted as a strong new leader. By this time, Putin was paying covert visits to the oligarch's Spanish beach resort at Sotogrande, a favoured destination of Russian mobsters. Berezovsky had extensive connections to Chechen separatists and Islamists; thus it was that they raided neighbouring Dagestan, killing hundreds of Russians, but arriving and departing without hindrance by Russia's secret services. And on 9 and 13 September, two apartment blocks housing working-class Muscovites were demolished in the night by tons of explosives in their basements, killing three hundred people. The Russian authorities and media immediately blamed Arab Wahhabis among the Chechens, even detecting the remote hand of Osama bin Laden.

These mass murders sparked Russian public fury towards the Chechens, though some people wondered why an FSB unit had been caught red-handed secreting sacks of 'sugar' in an apartment block basement, in what they claimed was a counter-terrorism exercise. It is entirely plausible that the FSB blew up the apartments to justify a war in Chechnya, and to boost Putin's patriotic profile. After all, with Duma deputies calling for the use of nuclear bombs and napalm on Chechnya, the man who talked like a gangster was always going to be popular.[29]

With Putin's opinion poll ratings soaring, Yeltsin took the decision to hand over the presidency to his forty-six-year-old Prime Minister. Putin's first act was to issue a blanket immunity from future prosecution to Yeltsin and his family and to co-opt his core staff to his inner team. On 7 May he was inaugurated as President in St Andrew's Hall within the Kremlin Palace, marching along the long red carpet with his asymmetric gait.

Putin's aims as President were to restore the 'power vertical' that has kept Russia together as a state since the early modern period, and to restore the international respect once paid to the Soviet Union, though without the burdens of a vast polyglot empire. In reality, only 45–50 per cent of what Putin decrees is actually implemented, since Russia is a case of 'authoritarianism without authority'.[30]

Under Putin we have seen the destabilization of immediate neighbours, the annexation and reunification of Crimea by kidnap, murder and a referendum, and the resumption of the projection of Russian power in Africa, the Middle East and elsewhere.[31] This also reflects the mindset of the people with real power in Russia, since they are obsessed with force and 'grand strategy' rather than hospitals, school meals or pensions.

Putin increased the control Yeltsin had already established over the 'force ministries' that stood under presidential power, while talented 'civilians' continued running other areas of policy. Former security agency personnel found berths in state agencies and regional administrations, as well as going into private business. The men closest to Putin, in the Federal Security Service or FSO, have reaped the rewards of proximity; four of his bodyguards are currently regional governors, with a fifth the head of the National Guard.[32] Overmighty oligarchs were easily brought to heel, not least because their business empires had been acquired through fraudulent means at the expense of the Russian people and structured to avoid paying tax. Putin offered them a straight choice of staying out of politics or going to jail, and most took the deal.

•

While Putin is perfectly capable of ordering someone's death, we need to be careful in not attributing to him every suspicious death in what has become a murderous society ruled by a fractious security elite and their business and gangland cronies.

The path to killing people in the middle of London must first go via Chechnya, though the tally of Chechen Islamist leaders killed by Russia is modest compared with global drone strikes by the Americans. In 1996 the Chechen independence leader Dzhokhar Dudayev was killed in a Russian missile strike. The killing of his successor, Zelimkhan Yanderbiyev, was different.

Yanderbiyev was killed on 13 February 2004, when his car exploded as he was leaving a mosque in Doha. The Qataris detained the two FSB agents who were responsible at a villa near the Russian embassy, presumably after US assistance. One of them had diplomatic cover. They had arrived in Doha three weeks before, receiving explosives from the driver of a Russian vehicle with diplomatic plates and attaching the bomb to Yanderbiyev's car. After pressure from Putin and the detention of two Qatari athletes in Moscow Airport, the Russian diplomat was allowed to leave, but the two agents were put on trial. Though sentenced to life imprisonment, they were repatriated to serve their sentences in Russia after a quick change in Qatari law. Flown home on a government jet and decorated by Putin, they have never seen the inside of a Russian jail.

In 2005, FSB commandos killed the Chechen guerrilla leader Aslan Maskhadov with a grenade thrown into a bunker where he was hiding. A year later Shamil Basayev, the terror chief responsible for the ghastly Beslan school siege, was killed in Ingushetia by a mine he either mishandled, or which the FSB had rigged to explode. Accident or not, the FSB claimed it was their handiwork. None of these killings required Putin's authority and the victims were a grim crew. In June 2006 five Russian diplomats were abducted by gunmen in Baghdad. One died of wounds in a firefight and the other four were beheaded after Russia refused to release Chechen detainees. From March 2006 the Duma had sought to introduce a new law licensing killing terrorists on foreign soil; it passed within a week of the slaughter in Baghdad.

On 17 August 2007 a radical Muslim activist was shot dead in Abkhazia in northern Georgia. The victim had been involved in funnelling Turkish money to Chechen terrorists, and was machine-gunned outside a mosque by men whose vehicle had arrived from Russia days before. More assassinations of Chechen exiles then occurred in Azerbaijan, before the mystery hitmen turned their attention to Turkey. Between 2008 and 2009, three exiled Chechens were shot dead in Istanbul.[33] There are more than 100,000 Chechen exiles living in Europe. A minority are involved in gangs and organized crime. The more prominent among them seem to die violently at an alarming rate, especially if they have publicly criticized Kadyrov. Four have been murdered in Vienna alone. Another was stabbed 135 times in a hotel room in Lille. In August 2019 a former Georgian-Chechen fighter called Zelimkhan Khangoshvili was shot in the back of the head in a Berlin park by a man on a bicycle. He was wearing a wig and had a Glock 26 with a silencer. Having been witnessed ditching his gun and the wig, while also changing his clothes, the police were quick to intercept him. His Russian passport identified him as Vadim Sokolov aged forty-nine, though his name and St Petersburg address did not exist. It transpired that his real name was Vadim Nikolaevich Krasikov, born in 1965 rather than 1970. In 2013 he had used a bicycle and gun to kill a Russian businessman in Moscow. After initial police inquiries, all official documentary trace of Krasikov seems to have been erased in

Russia. The German government blamed the Russians, since how did a man without an identity (who had been wanted for murder) acquire a legitimate passport?[34]

Beyond Chechen Islamists and separatists, there was another kind of violent death involving a much more select group of Russians. As a man whose mindset was formed by the KGB, Putin divides mankind into enemies and traitors. Enemies are the West and those Russians who collude with it in trying to break up Russia, while traitors are those who violate the honour codes of agencies that KGB men like Putin regard as akin to a holy order. That includes any former security personnel who work for foreign intelligence agencies.

In 2010 he spoke about traitors as he welcomed Anna Chapman, a Russian 'sleeper' agent, home from US captivity to Moscow under the spy swap that freed Sergei Skripal from a Russian jail: 'They live by their own laws, and these laws are well known to our secret services. Things always end badly for traitors. They usually end up in the gutter, from alcohol or drugs.'[35] As we saw in Chapter 4, the old NKVD and KGB had a lengthy history of reckoning not just with defectors but with anyone categorized as 'Trotskyite' fascist deviants and would go far and wide in pursuit of them. Vladimir Putin is more cognisant of that than most; as a KGB officer he would have heard talks in the Lubyanka by the old-timers who conducted such operations.

We have already encountered Aleksandr Litvinenko. He joined the KGB in 1988 and did a further stint in intelligence during the Chechen War. But his key career move was into a department tackling organized crime, from Georgian kidnappers to gangs trafficking heroin from Afghanistan. He strongly believed that his bosses were involved in such crimes too. After confronting Putin about criminality within the FSB, he was arrested and detained for nearly a year.

Aided by Boris Berezovsky, in late 2000 Litvinenko and his wife Marina took circuitous routes out of Russia and landed in London. He was granted political asylum, naturalization, and finally British citizenship. He worked for his oligarch patron as a security advisor for $6,000 a month, while trying his hand as an author and journalist. Berezovsky soon reduced his stipend, though his obsession with toppling Putin endured.

One of Litvinenko's first products was a controversial co-authored book pointing the finger at the FSB for the 1999 bombings of the two Moscow apartment blocks. His subsequent claims bordered on the bizarre. He blamed the FSB for the Islamist bombings in London in July 2005. His charges against Putin became more indiscriminate. He claimed on a Chechen website that Putin was a paedophile, on the grounds that on encountering a group of tourists in the Kremlin, he had had lifted the shirt of a small boy and kissed his stomach. While news of this charge would have infuriated Putin, it was probably another aspect of Litvinenko's London years that got him killed.[36]

Litvinenko had never been an intelligence officer; he was the equivalent of a gang-busting detective. But given the murky overlaps between organized crime, big business and the Russian security elite, he was interesting to British intelligence – especially because they had cut back on Russian expertise in favour of experts on Islamism and the greater Middle East.

SIS allegedly paid Litvinenko's £2,000 a month for briefings on Russian organized crime. Rashly, they also began touting him out to other friendly services, notably in Spain, where the authorities were concerned about Russian involvement in drugs, prostitution and arms trafficking. Big Russian corporations were keen to do business in Spain, establishing chains of petrol stations and the like, cash enterprises that also offered fertile ground for money-laundering.

Spanish prosecutors eagerly followed up Litvinenko's leads, which took him to senior figures in the Russian government, and also to a President who earlier in his life had been in the orbit of Vladimir Kumarin's Tambovskaya Gang.

One of those of particular interest to Spanish prosecutor José Grinda Gonzalez was Gennady Petrov. He was a tall ex-boxer and member of the Tambovskaya Gang, who had spent six years in jail for extortion and fraud. He owned a chain of jewellery stores in Russia, but could also lay hands on a MiG fighter jet if the price was right. And if he sent men to intimidate an enemy, they were just as likely to be thuggish members of the FSB as of a crime syndicate.

In Spain, Petrov had a $10 million villa in Mallorca, a $4 million yacht, a Bentley, a co-leased executive jet and $50 million in various property assets, as well as eighty-nine Spanish bank accounts. Intercepts recorded him talking to a Russian deputy Prime Minister and five members of the cabinet, including the Minister of Defence. And an Interior Ministry general who provided military-grade security for Petrov on home visits called him more than seventy times.[37]

While working for MI6, Litvinenko also touted his expertise in the corporate sector, where due diligence is essential to any business venture in Russia. However, for that he needed a reliable Russian source to do the local legwork. At that point, an acquaintance from the Berezovsky circle appeared out of the blue: Andrei Luguvoi, another former KGB officer turned successful businessman. Litvinenko should have wondered why he would suddenly appear, just a few weeks after he had publicly accused Putin of responsibility for the Mafia-style assassination of investigative journalist Anna Politskaya.

On 16 October 2006, Luguvoi flew into London Gatwick with a sidekick called Dmitri Kovtun. A vaguely inquisitive detective on secondary screening duty asked the two garishly dressed men about their business in London.

In the afternoon they met Litvinenko in the boardroom of a company called Continental Petroleum on Grosvenor Street and tried to poison him with polonium-210 slipped into a pot of tea, but he did not ingest enough to be harmed beyond an upset stomach. His two would-be killers left traces of polonium in the S-bend of the sink in their hotel bathroom, in which they had presumably transferred it between containers. On 19 October Litvinenko publicly asserted that Putin had had Politskaya killed. He then claimed to have secured a hit list put together by retired KGB veterans called 'Dignity and Honour'; Politskaya was on it, along with Berezovsky and Litvinenko himself.

Luguvoi was back in London on 25 October. This time, traces of radiation were found in a car that drove him to see the oligarch Badri Patarkatsishvili in Surrey, and in the Mayfair offices of Berezovsky.

On 1 November, Kovtun and Luguvoi flew back to London separately, ostensibly to watch a football match between Arsenal and CSKA Moscow. In Hamburg, where Kovtun flew first from Moscow, German detectives found traces of polonium in his mother-in-law's home, where he had stayed overnight. While there, Kovtun tried to interest his former restaurant boss in finding an Albanian cook who he wanted to pay to poison Litvinenko in London.

The two assassins met Litvinenko in the evening at the Pine Bar of the Millennium Hotel in Mayfair. They were in a rush to get to the Arsenal match and urged Litvinenko to help himself to their pot of tea. A fresh cup was brought. Luguvoi introduced his young son Igor to his 'Uncle Sasha'. Litvinenko briefly called on Berezovsky, using his photocopier to copy the 'hit list'. Berezovsky left him to it as he was going to the Arsenal match, too.

Litvinenko spent the night vomiting, so much so that Marina called an ambulance. At first doctors suspected food poisoning, but after a few days his hair began to fall out and his immune system was failing. A toxicologist initially suspected thallium poisoning, but thallium weakens muscles and Litvinenko's hand-shake was still strong. On 23 November several toxicologists concluded that he had had ingested polonium, whose effects were akin to a nuclear bomb detonating inside the body. It was too late for Litvinenko, and he died that night, having dictated a testament that spoke of Putin's responsibility for his demise. Berezovsky's PR man, Lord (Tim) Bell, ensured that images of the dying man and his testament flew around the world. Luguvoi and Kovtun flew back to Moscow on 3 November, leaving traces of polonium across central London and in the planes they travelled on. A discarded hotel towel was so contaminated that it had to be sent to the UK's Atomic Weapons Research Establishment. Both men were allegedly also suffering from radiation sickness, though not fatally. When scanned for radiation, the tea pot and the sink trap in their bathroom lit up like Christmas trees.

Although Luguvoi and Kovtun were identified as the assassins, they were not charged until May 2006 and November 2011 respectively. A formal inquiry dragged on until 2016, before concluding that they had poisoned Litvinenko with polonium-210, in an FSB operation that had probably been authorized by its chief, Nikolai Patrushev, and with the approval of Putin.

As Professor Robert Service argued in his expert testimony to the Litvinenko Inquiry, it remained impossible to ascertain whether Putin had given the FSB chief authorization to kill men like Litvinenko, or whether Patrushev acted on his own in line with service tradition. Putin retained oversight of the security agencies, but whether this extended to operational details remains unknown. Russian opinion was divided between those who bought into their government's version, which blamed Berezovsky and British secret agencies for Litvinenko's death, and those who thought Litvinenko deserved such a fate. Issues of national pride also supervened; the killing became a question of refusing to be bossed about by the British.

To emphasize that point, Putin decorated both assassins, and ensured Luguvoi's immunity by engineering his election to the 'systemic' Liberal Democrat party in the Duma. Frequent appearances as a TV pundit were another sign of favour. After losing an epic financial battle against rival oligarch Roman Abramovich in a London courtroom, in 2013 a depressed Berezovsky hanged himself in his bathroom, though the inquest recorded an open verdict. Though it is worth noting that every controversial death generates conspiracy fantasies, it does not help that both Britain and Russia are prone to spy mania – or that the kind of shady characters who worked for the likes of Berezovsky were connected to underworld figures who might have also wished to kill them.[38]

If the FSB were responsible for killing Litvinenko, in recent years their GRU colleagues have also become notorious for a series of foreign operations. In 2015 a Bulgarian arms dealer called Emilian Gebrev was taken ill during a meal in an expensive Sofia restaurant. It is likely he had been given an organophosphate toxin. His son, who was in the same business, lapsed into a coma after being poisoned elsewhere. Some think they were targeted because they beat Russian arms salesmen to their customers in Africa and Asia. Six GRU agents were in Sofia at the time; the name of one of them, Sergei Fedotov, would recur in another more notorious GRU operation.

As part of the armed forces, the GRU tends to specialize in risky operations. One such was an attempted coup in Montenegro in 2016, designed to forestall the Balkan state's desire to become NATO's twenty-ninth member. Two GRU agents in Belgrade used a lot of money to assemble an alternative government, which was to be installed after the assassination of long-time Montenegrin Prime Minister Milo Djukanović. Western intelligence agencies helped detect the plot and two Russians, Eduard Shishmakov and Vladimir Popov, were jailed in absentia for fifteen and twelve years, along with fourteen Montenegrin accomplices.

The GRU were also held responsible for a botched operation in the UK, which resulted in several countries expelling 150 Russian agents. Although it did not succeed, it did demonstrate the 'reach' of Russia's security services, perhaps acting as a deterrent to anyone else who broke their honour code.

The attempted assassination in Salisbury, using a weapons-grade nerve agent, of former GRU Colonel Sergei Skripal and his daughter Yulia in March 2018 claimed the life of an entirely innocent British citizen called Dawn Sturgess. On 30 June she and her partner became gravely ill, after she used a discarded spray perfume dispenser her partner had given her; she died on 8 July. The Skripals recovered from near death once it was established that they had been exposed to Novichok, which had been smeared or sprayed on the door handle of Skripal's house.

A veteran of Soviet airborne troops in Afghanistan, Skripal joined the GRU in the early 1990s. He was turned by British intelligence officers in 1995 and a year later he was reassigned to the GRU's 'Aquarium' headquarters, where he was acting director of personnel until his retirement in 1999. Skripal was arrested by the FSB in 2004 and sentenced to thirteen years in prison, after his confession knocked two years off the sentence. In the summer of 2010 he was released in a spy swap for ten

Russian deep-cover illegals who had been unearthed by US agencies. Skripal lived quietly in a modest house in Wiltshire purchased by British intelligence, but like Litvinenko he was 'still in the game'. In order to supplement a modest stipend from MI6, he assisted the British in advising the agencies of the Czech Republic, Estonia and Spain on Russian espionage or organized crime. The Russians may have suspected that Skripal was helping the Czechs and Estonians recruit more agents, behaviour that put him and his daughter in harm's way.

A meticulous British intelligence and police investigation narrowed down the suspects from thousands of hours of CCTV footage. The movements in Salisbury of two forty-year-old Russian men were reassembled, and correlated with their arrival in the UK. Russian claims that they were sightseeing in Salisbury were preposterous once the investigative news service Bellingcat had established that Ruslan Boshirov and Alexander Petrov were in fact Colonels Anatoliy Chepiga and Alexander Mishkin, and both were serving GRU officers.[39]

It also emerged that Major-General Sergei Fedotov had also visited Britain twice a year before the Skripal attack, in the company of Mishkin and Sergei Pavlov, who had been involved in the attack on Gebrev in 2015. Fedotov was based in a hotel in Paddington during the Skripal attack, from where he made multiple calls to Mishkin and Chepiga, as well as meeting them at Waterloo Station on the day they set off for Salisbury by train. Bellingcat investigators have established that 'Sergei Fedotov' is the alias of a GRU officer called Denis Sergeev.[40] His boss was Major General Andrey Vladimirovich Averyanov, head of the ominous GRU Unit 20155, which specialized in assassinations.

Vladimir Putin and his secret agencies believe that fear should precede them. One could imagine them being resented by the smoother diplomatic spies of the SVR, especially as the GRU seem to botch many of the operations they are responsible for. Whether or not this is deliberate, it is certainly contemptuous of Western intelligence agencies that are supposed to protect the victims. Putin seems to have the measure of the British, noting their endless hope that relations with Russia can be 'managed' or 'reset' once he realizes the error of his ways.

As for Russia itself, a pervasive belief that 'might is right' means that powerful people feel empowered to eliminate their rivals. However, Putin is responsible for the extremely weak rule of law in Russia and the belief that powerful people can get away with anything. Under his regime, there has been an uptick in both FSB and GRU assassinations, spreading from Chechnya to neighbouring countries and then into the UK and Germany.

We should never forget that brazenly killing people can become contagious. The Russians claim the Israelis do it and the American President admits the US does it, so what prevents anyone else from going down the same route – especially in countries where the rule of law is non-existent, like the feudal autocracies of the Middle East?[41]

9

Hard Places: The Middle East

The Middle East and North Africa are the global epicentre of political assassination, and some of the responsibility for the region's dismal modern record in this area lies in its troubled post-colonial political geography. Ethnic or religious self-determination has long been frustrated by artificially contrived states, though it is important to note that there are no 'natural' borders. The Kurds have been denied statehood by Iran, Iraq, Syria and Turkey, and the Palestinians by Israel, while Syria's Assad regime refused to accept that Lebanon, with its Christians and Druze, Shia and Sunni Muslims, was a separate state at all. In most Sunni states, Shia Muslims are a downtrodden minority – notoriously in Saudi Arabia and Turkey – and Turkish officials have lived in terror of being murdered by Armenians for many decades. There was also a powerful external actor, but the US has consistently mispriced its own violence in this region, imagining that killing individuals, be they dictators or terrorists, has a greater pay off than this delivers.[1]

With one or two exceptions, the Middle East has an autocratic political culture, whether monarchical or republican. Even the region's one democracy (other than Tunisia) is 'thin', for there are many religious Jews who believe that Jewish religious law overrides that of the secular state of Israel. Add revolutionary nationalism and sectarian tensions to clannish societies where biblical or blood vengeance is habitual, and the scene is set for widespread resort to political assassination. Some of this is mindless, but mostly the carnage is the result of cool calculation, and carefully calibrated. Some of the region's states also regard 'targeted killings' as a legitimate form of statecraft, much as other states have lashed out at those who do them harm. The many terrorist organizations with which the peoples of the region are burdened behave similarly. Some of them are also proxies of powerful states that act in a calculating fashion, most notably when they have an ulterior motive for helping a foreign state to abduct or murder its enemies.

•

Three of the region's four highest-profile assassinations – Saudi Arabia's King Faisal in 1975, Egyptian President Anwar Sadat in 1981 and Israel's Premier Yitzhak Rabin in 1995 – were the work of religious zealots. The fourth, former Lebanese Prime Minister Rafik Hariri in 2005, was a more calculated affair involving high-level external state actors. It remains fully un-resolved to this day.

Crown Prince Faisal displaced his spendthrift brother King Saud as regent in 1958 before usurping him as king six years later after a bloodless palace coup. Faisal was exceptionally well-travelled and had served as a roving diplomat. He was also a noted modernizer, abolishing slavery and reforming education. Later he consolidated the Saudi alliance with the US, and used the country's burgeoning petro-dollars to turn the kingdom into a major international force. Fatefully, his decision to introduce state television in 1965 was connected to his assassination, for some of the Wahhabis, the puritanical sect that forged a crucial compact with the al-Saud dynasty, thought TV idolatrous.

One of the King's nephews so objected to showing moving images of human beings that in 1966 he stormed into the tele-vision station and tried to kill its personnel, before being shot dead by security guards. His US-educated brother, Prince Faisal bin Musaid, had easy access to the King at regular council meetings. On 25 March 1975, as the King bent to kiss his nephew, he produced a gun and shot King Faisal in the chin and ear. The Prince was felled by a guard with a heavy sword; although he was declared insane, this did not prevent his being sentenced to death. He was publicly beheaded outside Riyadh's Great Mosque for the crime of regicide.

Radical Islamists were responsible for murdering Egyptian President Anwar Sadat on 6 October 1981. Sadat was a former

radical nationalist who in 1946 had taken part in the assassination of the pro-British Finance Minister Amin Uthman. One
of the few world leaders to admit he was a former assassin,
Sadat told a *Sunday Times* journalist that he and a comrade
had tossed a five-piastre coin for the privilege of shooting Uthman
but Husayn Tawfiq won. Sadat provided the grenades which
enabled Tawfiq to make his getaway. 'It is I who make assassinations,' Sadat claimed with a proud toss of his head as he patted
reporter John Slade-Baker's knee.

When Sadat replaced Nasser in 1970, no one expected much
of the long-time deputy of Egypt's charismatic hero, but he
improved relations with the Shah's Iran and tilted Egypt away
from the Soviets and towards the Americans, while also forging
a chilly peace treaty with Israel. Even broaching peace with
Israel was like signing one's own death warrant, as the Jordanian
King Abdullah I discovered in July 1951 when a Palestinian
tailor's apprentice shot him in the head as he exited Jerusalem's
Al-Aqsa Mosque, the tip of a larger conspiracy.[2]

On the day of his death, Sadat was the guest of honour at
a military parade to celebrate Egypt's forcing of a bridgehead
across the Suez Canal into Israel eight years earlier. Any sense
of Arab pride in this event was dispelled by the Egyptian-Israeli
peace treaty of 1979, which appalled not just Arafat and the
PLO, but Egypt's Arab League. Domestically, though peace
enabled Sadat to improve Egypt's economy, his alternating liberal
and oppressive treatment of the country's radical Islamists
provided plenty of reasons for trouble. These radicals were
disciples of the assassinated Muslim Brotherhood founder
Hassan al-Banna (shot dead by the political police in 1949) and
were generously represented in the armed forces. Their leader
was Aboud al-Zamor, a military intelligence officer, who organized the plot.

Heavily medalled in a military uniform, Sadat doubtless felt
safe on a reviewing stand, as Egyptian Air Force Mirage jets
thundered overhead. He had eight bodyguards in his immediate
vicinity, and the soldiers on parade had not been issued with
ammunition. As a truck towing an M-46 artillery piece crept
past, the men inside dismounted and ran towards the reviewing

stand. They were led by a twenty-seven-year-old lieutenant, Khalid al-Islambouli, who threw three grenades that he had concealed in his helmet. Only one of them exploded, as chairs were upturned and people tried to flee. Thinking this was a prearranged military display, Sadat rose in anticipation of a salute. Al-Islambouli emptied his assault rifle into the President, who died two hours later in hospital. Ten others were killed in the attack that lasted two minutes, including an Omani general, a Coptic bishop and the Cuban ambassador. Three of the assassins, who surrendered after their ammunition ran out, were tried and shot by firing squad in April 1982. Al-Zamor was sentenced to life imprisonment, and was succeeded as head of Islamic Jihad by the surgeon Ayman al-Zawahiri, the current head of Al-Qaeda. Hosni Mubarak succeeded Sadat and ruled until forced to resign in February 2011. Killing Sadat achieved nothing; following a brief Islamist hiatus, the military-industrial deep state is currently firmly in charge of Egypt under President Abdel Fattah el-Sisi.

Ironically when Zionist terrorists murdered the British colonial official Lord Moyne in Cairo in 1944, the then Captain Nasser in Egypt commented, 'Here were men ready to die for their cause, who hold an example to us.' Mutual respect vanished once Arab nationalists and Zionists were in power themselves. Like many Israeli military men, Yitzhak Rabin (1922–95) became considerably more 'doveish' as he grew older. He was a native-born 'sabra' turned career soldier, who in 1948 had fired on the Altelena, a ship bringing arms to the Irgun leader Menachem Begin at a time when Ben Gurion was trying to absorb the Irgun into the Israel Defense Forces (IDF).

An austere man of few words, Rabin was the IDF chief of staff during the 1967 Six-Day War. Like many Israeli military figures, he moved into politics and naturally opted for Labor, the party of Israel's more cosmopolitan upper classes.[3] His first term as Prime Minister was from 1974 to 1978, after which he served as Labor leader, and then Defence Minister in successive national unity governments led by Yitzhak Shamir and Shimon Peres.

Rabin became known as the 'Bonebreaker' because of the brutal measures he authorized to supress the first Palestinian

Intifada. In 1992 he became Prime Minister for a second time in the first Labor government for fifteen years. Given his military record, he was confident enough to agree the 1993 Oslo Accords, in which Israel recognized the PLO in return for toleration of the state of Israel. Israel also agreed to pull out of some territories, an incredibly brave step in two respects. First, with the advent of Hamas and Hezbollah, the PLO no longer had a monopoly of Palestinian violence, and besides, Chairman Arafat was notoriously untrustworthy. Second, Oslo appalled the Israeli nationalist and religious Right as an act of betrayal of the Jewish people.

Benjamin Netanyahu, the leader of the largest such party, the Likud, was not above inciting his Orthodox religious allies. They held mass rallies at which placards showed Rabin dressed either in Arafat's chequered kefiyeh headdress or a Nazi officer's uniform.[4] Some of the protests seemed eccentric. On 6 October 1995, a group of extremists gathered outside Rabin's home and performed a ritual called *Pulsa di Nura*, 'blaze of fire' in Aramaic. Rabin's image was set aflame and coffins bearing his name were carried. Rabin was contemptuous of this mystically minded rabble and refused to use an armoured vehicle or a bulletproof vest, relying instead on the reputation and skill of his bodyguards.[5]

However, his security advisers should have noted that Palestinian terrorism had crept towards the settlers, many of whom were armed and responded with murderous vigilantism against Arabs. The ghastliest example of this took place on 25 February 1994 when Baruch Goldstein, a doctor and a captain in the IDF reserves, donned his military uniform, went to Hebron's Tomb of the Patriarchs and waited in its Isaac Hall, assault rifle in hand. When the worshippers bent forwards in the *sojud* facing Mecca, he opened fire, killing twenty-nine people and wounding a further hundred. When his gun jammed at the fifth reload, he was felled with a fire extinguisher and bashed to death by the survivors. Unsurprisingly, Hamas responded by escalating terrorist attacks, even as Goldstein became a martyr figure on the religious nationalist Israeli Right and the subject of adoring pirated books which circulated among the racist like-minded.

Such sentiments were also given rabbinical sanction. Three Orthodox rabbis from the West Bank called Rabin a *din moser* and *din rodef*, meaning one who gives Jewish property to Gentiles or facilitates the murder of any Jew; in the latter case, the person can be killed without a trial. This view was echoed by a few Orthodox American rabbis. Dangerous talk like this was enough to prompt individuals to contemplate assassinating Rabin.

On 4 November 1995 Rabin attended a rally in a Tel Aviv square to mark the signing of the Oslo Accords. He gruffly tried to sing along with Miri Aloni's 'Song of Peace'. As he descended the steps of City Hall, Yigal Amir, a short and skinny right-wing religious law student, who had taken a bus to the rally and loitered in the car park, slipped past Rabin's four bodyguards and shot him twice in the back with a 9mm Beretta automatic loaded with dum-dum bullets which he had concealed in the waistband of his black jeans. A third shot missed but wounded Rabin's bodyguard, Yorum Rubin. Rabin died on the operating table from punctured lungs and blood loss, after a chaotic journey to hospital by a driver who did not know where he was going, his last words being disbelief that his murderer was a fellow Jew.[6]

Born in 1970, Amir was one of eight children from a family of Yemeni Jews. His father did calligraphic transcriptions of holy books; his mother Geula ran a small nursery school. Amir's youth was spent in yeshivas, a closed world where any madnesses can be propagated by rabbinical fanatics. Amir emerged highly argumentative and with an abundance of historical examples from the Torah to justify any malign deeds. Unusually for an ultra Orthodox Jew Amir performed national service, becoming notorious while serving in the tough Golani Brigade for beating and torturing Palestinians captured in the Intifada. His comrades noted that he seemed to enjoy this. At the orthodox Bar-Ilan university he gravitated to the most extreme activists and professors, who supported the illegal West Bank settlers in their bid to create Judea and Sumeria there and viscerally opposed the Oslo Accords. Soon Amir was organising students to join the settlers in confronting the army as they tried to grab more land.[7]

Amir also suffered from depression, after the family of Nava Holtzman, the girl he wanted to marry objected because of his Mizrahi, or dark-skinned Yemeni, origins; she married his best friend five months later. At a wedding in Tel Aviv, Amir unexpectedly spotted Rabin, and was shocked how close he could get to him with a pistol tucked into his belt. He vowed never to let the chance slip by again.[8] He seems to have announced his intention to kill Rabin to another religious Jew who was an agent of Shin Bet, the Israel Security Agency; it kept a file on Amir, though it contained only a few sentences. He also talked about how to kill Rabin with his brother Heggai, a gun enthusiast who made the dum-dum bullets. Haggai also told Yigal about Forsyth's *Day of the Jackal*, for French Algeria in the early 1960s had parallels with Israel itself. Amir stalked Rabin on at least four occasions with a view to killing him, once indeed at the Yad Vashem Holocaust memorial, but the opportunity never arose. On 4 November he got lucky. He wanted to show his ex-girlfriend Nava and friends and family that he had meant what he said, but he had also convinced himself that he was following in the footsteps of Phineas, who had killed Zimri, one of those Jews who defied God, after which a plague was lifted and the male descendants of Phineas became priests of Israel.

Incurious journalists compared Rabin with John F. Kennedy, though in reality he better resembled Abraham Lincoln, who was also trying to weld a young nation together. His killer was also less like the apparently motiveless Lee Harvey Oswald than John Wilkes Booth, an ideological fanatic whose views were shared by many of his countrymen. Rabin's killer is still feted in some quarters today; having spent fifteen years of his life sentence in solitary confinement, he remains in prison, aged fifty. Though there is a vociferous campaign for his release, it is highly unlikely that any Israeli government will dare to set him free. While Lincoln's belief in emancipation ultimately won the day, the jury is very much out on whether or not Israel will pursue a just peace with the Palestinians. Mr Netanyahu is currently enjoying his fourth term as Prime Minister, despite multiple charges of corruption in public office.

Rafik Hariri's was a Lebanese rags-to-riches story on an epic scale. Born into a poor Sunni tenant-farming family in Sidon, he made his fortune working in Saudi Arabia just as it became flush with petro-dollars and as Lebanon plunged into the 1975–90 civil wars. An estimated 150,000 people were killed, with another 100,000 wounded. A quarter of the population emigrated, and it is a near-miracle that civilized society survived at all.

Blessed with charm and organizational talent, Hariri used an ailing French construction company called Oger to build a royal hotel in nine months, becoming the King's builder of choice and a billionaire, with multiple residences, private jets and luxury cars. A big man with immense black bushy eyebrows, he exuded the can-do optimism of many tycoons, but in his case there seems to have been a religious as well as a patriotic obligation to put his country back on its feet.

Hariri devoted a considerable part of his fortune, amplified by the patronage of Saudi Arabia's King Fahd, to reconstruct Beirut, much of which lay in ruins. We need not enter the bewildering complexity of the factions involved, save to note that Israel, Syria and Saudi Arabia supported rival elements, with France and the US as interested parties too. Hariri acted as Saudi Arabia's diplomatic representative, and his critics regarded him as Riyadh's stooge.[9]

After 1990, Hariri stepped into the dangerous arena of Lebanese politics. He served his first term as Prime Minister from 1992 to 1998 and a second term from 2000 to October 2004, when he suddenly resigned. His attempts to privatize whole tranches of Lebanon's economy ran into the corruption which dominated the public sector and, in particular, the grip Lebanese and Syrian security officers had on the telecommunications sector.[10]

At this point we need to explain the Israeli presence in Lebanon. Successive Israeli governments had decided on swift retaliatory strikes whenever PLO militants attacked Israel from Lebanese territory. That changed after 1977 with the election of the right-wing Likud government of Menachem Begin, who two years later added General Ariel Sharon to his team as Defence Minister. Instead of small-scale strikes, these men launched a 25,000-strong invasion of southern Lebanon in 1978. A quarter of a million refugees fled northwards, along with most of the PLO fighters.

In spring 1982, Israel launched a full-blown invasion of Lebanon called Operation Peace for Galilee. Its aims were to dislodge the PLO once and for all, and to install a biddable Christian-led government in Beirut. The invasion turned IDF troops into occupiers, which had a demoralizing effect on them. Worse, the Israelis had neglected one important element in the equation: the Lebanese Shia. While they might have welcomed the crushing of arrogant PLO fighters, they would never accept Israeli occupation, and the Iranian-backed Hezbollah gained their support. Moreover, Israel's plans to politically rearrange Lebanon came to nothing after Lebanese President-elect Bachir Gemayel was assassinated on 14 September 1982 by Syrian intelligence.

The PLO were expelled to Tunis, but now Israel had a powerful foe in Hezbollah. Worse, its own soldiers, demoralized by occupation and collaboration with murderous Christian Phalangist militias, found themselves losing a war of attrition against Hezbollah guerrillas. When Israel tried to up the ante, Hezbollah contrived to retaliate with rocket attacks on Galilee or raids on Israeli fortified positions. Support for Hezbollah flourished whenever Israel indiscriminately bombed or shelled civilian homes and infrastructure in Shia areas.[11] Having invaded Lebanon to crush one 'terrorist' organization, the Israelis had created a much more powerful one, and much of the Israeli public grew sick of this unwinnable war. But what of Lebanon itself?

Power in Lebanon is distributed along sectarian lines. After fifteen years of civil war, the 1989 Ta'if National Reconciliation Accord adjusted political representation and boosted the power of the Sunni premier and the Shiite parliamentary speaker. It also left Israeli troops ensconced in a security zone in southern Lebanon until 2000, with Syrian troops present in the east until 2005. After the civil war, Syria acted as a 'balance' between rival Lebanese factions. But Damascus's influence was also covertly exercised through close relations between Lebanese and Syrian intelligence, as well as via Hezbollah. Syria effectively supported Hezbollah to gain leverage in prising Israel off the occupied Golan Heights. Syria was itself a useful logistical junction for Iran, which armed Hezbollah so as to menace Israel.

In the year of his death, Hariri made the mistake of aligning his Sunni 'Future Movement' supporters with the Christian and Druze political blocs, in order to end the Pax Syriana administered by Damascus's cipher Émile Lahoud. Hariri's close relations with French President Jacques Chirac proved fatal, after Chirac and Bush combined behind UN Security Council Resolution 1559, which called for a Syrian evacuation of Lebanon and the disarming of both Hezbollah and Palestinian armed factions. Free and fair elections would also see off Lahoud. Syria's Bashar al-Assad suspected that the powers that had ousted the Baathist regime in Iraq were gathering against him, with Chirac taking a hard line to compensate for his earlier refusal to back America's war against Saddam Hussein.

On 26 August, Assad summoned Hariri to a meeting in Damascus. The Syrian President knew he had close contacts with an older generation of Syrian officials who doubted he had his late father Hafez's steel. In an account of the meeting by the head of Syrian intelligence in Lebanon, Assad explained that Hariri should make up his mind whether to back an extension of Lahoud's presidential term. Two other accounts have Hariri exhausted and sweating. Assad had said, 'If you think you and President Chirac are going to run Lebanon, you are mistaken. It's not going to happen. President Lahoud is me. Whatever I tell him, he follows suit. This extension is going to happen or I will break Lebanon over your head . . . so either do as you are told or we will get you and your family, wherever you are.'[12]

On 3 September, Hariri's political bloc decided to grant Lahoud his extension. Hariri was fatalistic about the dangers of crossing the Syrians, who had deep connections with the Lebanese security state and perhaps more importantly with the intelligence outfits of some of the confessional groups. On 1 October 2004 Marwan Hamadeh, the Economy Minister who also opposed Syria's influence, narrowly survived when a car bomb was detonated as his Mercedes inched around a speed bump near his home. This was the first of a series of assassination attempts on figures who were opposed to the continuing Syrian presence in Lebanon.

On 14 February 2005, Hariri left his fortified mansion in an armoured Mercedes for a series of meetings, followed at a distance by his private ambulance. At lunchtime he signalled that he wanted to return home, leaving his security team to decide which route his convoy should take. He chose to drive himself. They chose the route along the seafront Corniche in downtown Beirut, past the newly reconstructed St George Hotel.

But someone was watching through binoculars, and in contact with at least four people. A bomb was hidden inside a Mitsubishi Canter delivery truck; after crawling along at nine miles per hour, the driver parked and waited patiently for Hariri's convoy, before pressing a trigger the moment the car containing Hariri sped by. The blast was so loud that people all over Beirut looked upwards, thinking it was the sonic boom of an Israeli jet, a frequent occurrence when tensions with Hezbollah were high. The bomb probably consisted of 1,200 kilograms of TNT mixed with plastic explosives; it obliterated Hariri's convoy and left very little of 'Mr Lebanon' himself. Twenty-two people perished, and Hariri was identified by his manicured fingernails and remnants of the striped tie that an aide had chosen for him that morning.[13] Some 230 others were wounded along with 20 dead. In one case a family had to hire a sniffer dog which eventually detected the corpse, seventeen days after the blast.

Hariri's assassination sparked enormous demonstrations that escalated into mass protests against the Lebanese government and Syria's role within it. While Syria was forced to vacate its troops, it retained enough of an intelligence network inside Lebanon – the kaleidoscope of rival sectarian intelligence services – to move the balance back in its favour. Hariri's killing was followed by others that removed critical journalists and political figures, though they did not include Hariri's son Saad, who took up his political banner.

Uniquely, the UN mandated an inquiry into Hariri's assassination as an international crime, under Chapter VII of the UN

Charter. It was initially led by the German prosecutor Detlev Mehlis, whose interim report blamed Bashar al-Assad's brother and his brother-in-law for Hariri's death, as well as both Syrian and Lebanese security officials. Mehlis was replaced by a Belgian, Serge Brammertz, and then by the Canadian Daniel Bellemare. From the start, the tribunal was bogged down in disputes about its remit. The US and France, and Lebanon's coalition of Hariri supporters, wanted to finger Syria for a terrorist crime to eliminate Damascus's influence, while the rival coalition of Shiite parties, Amal and Hezbollah, insisted that this would license external interference in Lebanese affairs. The UN compromised by viewing the assassination as an affront to international peace and stability, but judged it according to Lebanese domestic law.

Although the crime scene had been completely compromised by endless people milling about, as well as a burst water main that filled the bomb crater with water, the investigation continued by other means. The key breakthrough was made when a Lebanese police captain, Wissam Eid, used new technology to painstakingly link the mobile phones of the eight-member 'red' network that had shadowed Hariri for a year with other networks that he linked to the Hezbollah heartland. Unsurprisingly, Eid was killed in a car bomb attack in January 2008, just after this crucial information was delivered to the UN. Successive reports gradually moved the finger of blame from Assad towards Hezbollah, four of whose personnel indicted for killing Hariri. Hezbollah's chief Hassan Nasrallah refused applications for questioning of Hezbollah members, claiming that those in the vicinity of Hariri that day were hunting down Israeli assassins sent to kill the former Prime Minister. A $700 million UN-backed trial in the Hague of four low-level Hizbollah suspects was as politically compromised as one might expect and it did not address myriad more political murders in Lebanon's bleak recent history. One absentee, Salim Ayyash, was found guilty of involvement and sentenced to five concurrent life sentences, while the other three were acquitted. Ayyash's whereabouts remain unknown. A fifth suspect had died fighting for Assad in Syria in 2016. This was a very meagre result for such a huge procedural effort.[14]

·

The Western media's obsession with murders committed by Israel's Mossad is slightly illusory, though with what expert Ronen Bergman estimated as 2,700 victims, it has committed more state-sponsored assassinations than any other equivalent organization excepting the CIA in its paramilitary phase. Mossad is primarily involved in intelligence collection and analysis for Israel's government. Its biggest coups included purloining Khrushchev's 1956 'secret' speech condemning Stalin and the 1965 bugging of the Moroccan hotel which provided vital intelligence for the 1967 war. Clandestine diplomacy is another large part of the agency's remit; for example, visiting North Korea to persuade the Kims not to sell ballistic missiles to Arab countries or Iran. Cultivating both Chinese and Russian contacts is another important task, for Israel has cordial relations with both. In the memoir of Efraim Halevi, Mossad chief from 1998 to 2002, there is much high-level diplomacy and hardly any mention of the sharp end of things that so tantalizes the TV industry. Indeed, having been shrouded in secrecy, Mossad now uses the US film and television industries as recruiting tools. A Mossad liaison officer is a permanent fixture of the series *NCIS* about naval criminal investigations, and Hollywood boasts the Spy Legends Agency run by a veteran ex-Mossad agent, a consultancy which provide technical advice for the many film productions in which Mossad figures.[15]

Mossad's autocratic directors impress their own characters on the people they command. Some are glorified bureaucrats, others are primarily diplomats, and others gung-ho special-forces types. The credulous rarely ask whether training people to use extreme violence can lead to some recruits becoming addicted to it along the way, a problem which has occurred too with Australian and Canadian special forces accused of heinous war crimes.[16]

Mossad is not the only game in town. Since the Jewish state's creation in 1948, two of Israel's other intelligence agencies, AMAN and Shin Bet, have probably killed far more people than Mossad, mainly Palestinian Arabs in occupied Gaza and the West Bank. Mossad's killings have mainly been abroad, by agents using assumed or stolen identities. Despite Prime Minister

Netanyahu having formally assured the UK government in the 1990s that agents would not nefariously purloin British identities, when a Hamas target, Mahmoud al-Mabhouh, was smothered in his hotel room in Dubai in 2010, half of the twenty-six-strong team of Mossad operatives were travelling on cloned British passports. This did not do down well with SIS.

Why is the Western world often indulgent towards what amounts to serial murder by one state, which otherwise aggressively asserts its democratic normalcy through paid lobbyists and a bent or credulous foreign media? Only rarely do other states give Mossad more than a slap on the wrist, the imprisonment of American traitor Jonathan Pollard who sold US secrets to Israel being a rare exception. It helps, Yotam Peri argues, that Jews regard themselves as peaceful victims of perpetual external persecution. Indeed the Jewish faith has a feast day dedicated to a *victim* of assassination, the Fast of Gedahlia bin Achikam, a Jewish governor who collaborated with the Babylonian monarch Nebuchadnezzar II and who was killed in around 586 BC by one Yishmael bin Netanya (2 Kings 25: verses 25–26). But more recent history exerts a greater influence.

One of Mossad's recent chiefs, Meir Dagan, kept a photo in his office of a Polish Jewish rabbi kneeling before a German executioner. What happened to his grandfather was never going to happen again, Dagan averred. Many Israelis were Holocaust survivors and shared that view. To its supporters, Israel is an eternal David, though for several decades it has been the regional Goliath, the only nuclear armed power in its region.

That background also explains why Mossad agents posture as moral murderers, rather than being driven by bloodlust, excitement, machismo, vengeance or realpolitik. Wherever men are trained to be professional killers it is unsurprising that some of them enjoy it. Mossad also lends out its services. Mossad cultivated close relations with the brutal King Hassan II of Morocco (1961–1999). When they were approached by the opposition Leftist Mehdi Ben Barka, they promptly betrayed his plot to overthrow the king. When in 1965 Hassan enabled Mossad to bug the hotel in Casablanca where Arab leaders were staying, the Israelis repaid the favour by planning and organising

Ben Barka's abduction and murder in Paris, though Moroccan agents actually killed him. Mossad arranged to dispose of the body. With Mossad's help, in 1998 Turkey managed to track down and kidnap in the militant Kurdish leader Abdullah Öcalan from a temporary refuge in Kenya, where Mossad had long-standing connections with Kenyan intelligence.[17]

Mossad and its sister agencies often evoke the Old Testament, linking themselves to a deep Jewish religious tradition. The Shin Bet motto – 'He who watches over Israel shall neither slumber nor sleep' – is from Psalm 121, while Mossad's motto – 'Where no counsel is, the people fall, but in the multitude of counsellors there is safety' – derives from the Book of Proverbs. The broader history of the Jews also plays a role, with the Holocaust invoked to justify killing mainly Arab or Iranian victims who had an exiguous relationship to that uniquely horrible crime, though some of them are 'deniers' too of course. In reality, Mossad and its sister agencies also drew strength from Jewish participation in Social Revolutionary terrorism in Tsarist Russia and from Zionist terrorism directed at the colonial British power in Palestine during the 1930s and 1940s though these affiliations are not advertised outside Israel.

Possibly uniquely among modern states, Israel has had at least three Prime Ministers who were professional killers. Prime Ministers Menachem Begin and Yitzhak Shamir were members of Irgun and Lehi respectively,[18] splinter groups that terrorized Arabs in the 1930s and graduated to murdering over a hundred British colonial officials, soldiers and policemen before, during and after the Second World War. Shamir's nom de guerre was 'Michael Collins', in a further snub to the British.

The victims included Prime Minister Winston Churchill's friend Lord Moyne, who was shot dead in wartime Cairo along with his military driver in 1944. The bodies of the two Zionist assassins, who were hanged, were returned to Israel in 1975 and accorded a state funeral. Both killers were commemorated on postage stamps. In July 1946, the Irgun detonated 350 kilo-grams of explosives hidden in milk churns inside Jerusalem's King David Hotel, killing ninety-one people and wounding forty-five others. British diplomatic missions abroad were also targeted

– the embassy in Rome was blown up in October 1946 by the Irgun – while letter bombs were sent to every member of the British cabinet in London. Before and after the foundation of the state of Israel in 1948, terrorists co-opted into Israel's initial fighting army attempted to assassinate Palestinian Arab leaders.

The Nazi era colours Israeli decision-making in other respects. Although the wartime Allies ruled out assassinating Hitler until late in the conflict, most people would agree that killing him in 1938-39 or 1944 might have spared mankind much bloodshed. That explains why so many attempts have been made to reconstrue minor Arab dictators as 'latter-day Hitlers', while diplomacy and sanctions against leaders such as Nasser, Galtieri, Saddam and Qaddafi are dismissed as 'appeasement' by leaders who are quick to imagine themselves as Churchill. To a certain kind of Israeli mind, Prime Minister Bibi Netanyahu being a striking example, it is forever 1938, the year of the ill-fated four-power agreement in Munich.

While assassination is still taboo in inter-state conflicts, that is not the case in asymmetric wars with insurgents and terrorists. Since attacking them might well incur civilian casualties or a major war, the obvious course of action is what is euphemistically called 'targeted killing', first by soldiers and secret agents, and more recently by remote unmanned drone strikes using GPS and facial recognition technology. The alternative of large-scale invasion and occupation, whether by Israel in southern Lebanon, the US in Afghanistan and Iraq, or Russia in Afghanistan and Chechnya, brings major costs in both blood and treasure that tend to nullify initial military superiority. Israel's incursion into Lebanon was an unmitigated disaster, allowing Hezbollah to rally many Lebanese to their yellow and green flag.

But first we need to go back to the beginning of Israel, a time of great hope after the end of the Second World War, not least for the Holocaust survivors who Israeli services exfiltrated from Europe. Israel's founding father, David Ben-Gurion, sanctioned three intelligence agencies. The Military Intelligence Directorate (AMAN) operated under the Israeli Defense Forces General Staff. The domestically focused Shin Bet was modelled on America's FBI and Britain's MI5. And the newly created

Foreign Ministry was responsible for the Political Department, which was soon renamed as the Institute for Intelligence and Special Operations and taken over by Ben-Gurion himself. Its Hebrew name is Mossad, 'The Institute'. All three agencies had access to a pool of highly trained killers from the army's Sayeret Matkal (General Staff Reconnaissance Unit) and the navy's Flotilla Thirteen commandos, while Shin Bet had undercover armed units that passed as Arabs.

Since the existence of these agencies was not public until 1960, their activities (and budgets) were shrouded in censorship and secrecy and lacked legal cover. The impression of weighty deliberation by serious men was not always matched by a reality, in which political expediency and intra-bureaucratic rivalries also played a role.

The most heavily publicized operations naturally involved former Nazis. Under Issar Harel, the Belarusian emigrant who switched from leading Shin Bet to become chief of Mossad between 1952 and 1963, the abduction of Adolf Eichmann, one of the key bureaucratic executants of the Final Solution, was a global sensation.

But that coup de théâtre masked a more pressing intelligence failure, since Mossad had not detected German engineers and scientists who helped Nasser's Egypt to develop long-range ballistic missiles. Some of these men had worked on Hitler's V1 and V2 rocket programmes. Finding themselves in a post-war Germany with reduced defence budgets, they switched to a foreign employer with deep pockets.

Dr Heinz Krug was abducted in Munich and flown to Israel, where he was subjected to torture, before being shot dead and dumped in the sea. Since this could not be repeated with every German scientist, Mossad turned to letter bombs, which might take an eye out or a hand off when opened.

Mail tends to be handled by innocent third parties, like the secretary Hannelore Wende, who lost an eye and some fingers when she opened a letter addressed to her boss. And an attempt to shoot another scientist on a German street failed due to malfunctioning weapons. As a result of these setbacks, in 1963 Ben-Gurion fired Harel, who had imagined himself indispensable, and replaced him with Meir Amit, widely regarded as the best chief of the agency. Mossad had more luck in recruiting the hulking former paratrooper Otto Skorzeny, a favourite of Hitler, to give it access via a network of old comrades to German scientists and technicians, who could then be intimidated with threatening letters and phone calls.[19]

In these early years, Meir Amit was fertile in creating specialized departments. Colossus collected intelligence, while Universe handled clandestine diplomacy. But the murderous activity devolved on a new group called Caesarea, closely associated with Michael Harari, who in 1970 moved from being deputy chief to head of this Mossad subdivision.

Born in Tel Aviv in 1927, Harari was a Zionist warrior in his teens, before being recruited by Mossad. He was responsible for the creation in 1969 of a tighter group within Caesarea called Kidon, explicitly responsible for assassinations. Harari also introduced a certain bureaucratic formality to state killings, with a 'targets committee' to discuss possible victims. This would also take place at cabinet level, where a committee chaired by the Prime Minister authorized assassinations. With every change of government, decisions would have to be reauthorized. The assassins were trained in pistol marksmanship and face make-up; being few in number, they would have to adopt multiple disguises.

We should be clear that these were never intended as 'hard arrests', in which the primary aim is to capture the target for prosecution, even though the likelihood is that they will resist. There was never any intention to capture Mossad's targets, as most were unarmed, murdered by agents in cold blood, in their own homes or on the street using car bombs.

Three-quarters of a million Palestinians were driven out or expelled from the first iteration of the State of Israel. After the Six-Day War in 1967, Israel's self-image as the regional David to several thuggish, autocratic or nationalist Arab Goliaths was complicated by the reality that its territory suddenly increased by 300 per cent, and now included millions more Palestinian Arabs.

In 1959 two rapidly rising leaders of Palestinian militancy, Khalil al-Wazir (aka Abu Jihad) and Abdel Rahman Abdel Raouf

Arafat al-Qudwa al-Husseini, established Fatah, the Arab acronym for the Palestinian Liberation Movement. The founding articles of its covenant denied the right of Jews who had not dwelled in Palestine before 1917 to be there. Ironically, Mossad's preoccupation with intimidating German scientists meant that it was only four years later that the Israelis realized they had a dangerous new enemy.

At first the Israelis did not take Fatah seriously, but the number of attacks rose through the late 1960s, with a hundred in the first six months of 1967 before the Six-Day War broke out in July. During this period Mossad played second fiddle to Shin Bet, whose remit included dealing with Fatah militants in Gaza. They decided to eliminate the key men involved, a task requiring many hardmen who were supplied by Ariel Sharon, head of the IDF's southern command. The tough Polish Holocaust survivor turned Israeli former paratrooper Meir Dagan, who would later be chief of Mossad, pioneered the use of undercover elite troops who went into Gaza to eliminate Fatah supporters. As it expanded, this commando unit became habituated to killing rather than capturing targets.

Rather than bow to such murderous pressure, the PLO responded by going international, first with a series of 'spectacular' aircraft hijackings. The campaign started with El Al Flight 426, which took off from Rome for Tel Aviv on 23 June 1968, but whose passengers found themselves held hostage in Algiers until Israel released twenty-four prisoners. Palestinian hijackers were media celebrities in European countries. Mossad's Kidon killers were the obvious people to deal with the problem.

The decision to activate Kidon was made for the Israelis by the Palestinians. The PLO had licensed the formation of a terror cell called Black September, to commemorate the thousands of Palestinian fighters killed by the Jordanian army in the last two weeks of September 1970. Black September was founded by Abu Iyad, Yasir Arafat's deputy, with Abu Daoud as his operational commander. One of its first acts was the assassination of Jordanian Prime Minister Wasfi al-Tal, outside Cairo's Sheraton Hotel on 28 November 1971.

On 5 September 1972 this cell launched an attack on Israeli athletes at the Munich Olympics that left eleven sportsmen and coaches dead. The German police comprehensively botched a belated rescue attempt, to the fury of Mossad agents watching from the sidelines. On 11 September, the Israeli Prime Minister Golda Meir authorized Mossad to kill the perpetrators and anyone who had assisted them. The surviving perpetrators were virtually inaccessible behind the Iron Curtain or in Arab states with serious security services, which meant that the hit list largely consisted of Palestinian militants who lacked any direct connection with the Black September attack in Munich. The point was to sow anxiety and fear in such circles, after the Munich attack had succeeded in bringing the Palestinians' plight to the world's attention.

That was how a Palestinian translator called Wael Zwaiter came to be shot dead in the lobby of his Rome apartment. There was nothing linking the next victim, Mahmoud Hamshiri, to the Munich attack either; he was blown to pieces by a bomb placed inside a marble phone stand on the desk in his Paris apartment, which exploded as he answered it.

The biggest prize was Ali Hassan Salameh, whose father Hassan Salameh was a veteran Palestinian guerrilla, mortally wounded at the age of thirty-seven in a gun battle with the Irgun in 1948. His charismatic son quickly rose to become head of Force 17, Arafat's bodyguard, and was a playboy murderer though he moved easily in the murky world of business fixers, diplomats and spooks.

Salameh had no connection with the Munich attack, but Mossad had other reasons to kill him. He was in regular contact with the CIA officer Robert Ames, who was more sympathetic to the Palestinians than to the Israelis, like many in the Agency's 'Arabist' Middle Eastern division. He never agreed to become a CIA agent, but he was certainly its main back channel to the PLO leadership. When Ames and Salameh overlapped in Beirut, they saw each other every evening. Since Salameh guaranteed the lives of US diplomatic personnel in Beirut, the Agency beefed up his security, and flew him and his second wife to Langley and on to a tour of Disneyland. The fact that Salameh refused to become a CIA asset proved fateful after Mossad insisted on knowing whether he was. The ambiguous response from Ames's superiors was Salameh's death warrant.

By tracking a Fatah suspect with links to Black September, Mossad observers reasoned that Salameh was hiding in the sleepy Norwegian town of Lillehammer. Surveillance experts convinced themselves that a man living with a pregnant Norwegian 'girlfriend', and whose recreations were swimming and the odd game of pool, was Salameh, but this was Ahmed Bouchiki, a young Moroccan waiter and pool attendant who had no connections with any Palestinians. He was shot eight times while alighting from a bus. His wife Torill, seven months pregnant, was left screaming beside his corpse.

The Mossad hit team, supervised in person by Harari, fled the country, leaving the chief of Mossad to dismiss the incident as a 'mistake'. Three operatives were caught before they could flee Norway, and one, a loose-lipped Dan Arbel, spilt the beans on three more comrades, who were detained in France and Italy. Five of these six were convicted of killing Bouchiki, though they were released after a short spell in a Norwegian jail.

Neither Salameh nor Waddid Haddad, another senior Palestinian figure, were safe from Mossad's attentions. A long-time KGB asset, Haddad died in an East Berlin clinic after Mossad succeeded in lacing his toothpaste with a deadly poison. Salameh was kept under close observation in Beirut by an Israeli agent, who befriended him in a hotel gym. He was killed in June 1978 when a British-born female Mossad agent called Erika Chambers triggered a car bomb as his small convoy passed by, it having been established that women had quicker reaction times in using bomb triggers against moving targets. The blast also killed his driver and two bodyguards, three innocent Lebanese civilians, a Briton and a German, who were regarded as acceptable collateral damage.

An absence of moral scruples was also evident once cross-border incursions into Lebanon to root out the PLO were superseded in June 1982 by a full-blown invasion. With Meir Dagan waging clandestine warfare before the invasion, hundreds of Lebanese were killed in terror bombings involving cars, motorbikes, bicycles and even explosives rigged to donkeys.

Dagan also developed links to Maronite Christian Phalangist groups who wanted to create a second Israel in Lebanon, while creating his own bogus Front for the Liberation of Lebanon from Foreigners, which took responsibility for Israel's own terror attacks. The aim of Defence Minister Ariel Sharon was to provoke the PLO to attack Israel or to retaliate against the Phalange, in order to justify an incursion by Israel into Lebanon. Sharon and Rafael Eitan, the IDF Chief of Staff, ordered the Phalangists to sweep through Palestinian refugee camps in West Beirut. This was in the immediate aftermath of the assassination of Lebanon's newly elected President Bashir Gemayel on 14 September 1982, in a powerful bomb blast which killed twenty-six people. The attack was not conducted by Palestinians but by a fellow Christian Lebanese, Habib Tanious Shartouni, on behalf of Syria.

Vengeance was nonetheless taken on one of the refugee camps surrounding Beirut. A Maronite militia stormed through the Sabra and Shatila refugee camp on 15 September, murdering between 700 and 2,750 civilians. Although an Israeli inquiry found Sharon, Eitan and others culpable, with the Israelis providing perimeter security and lighting up the scene of the massacre with floodlights and flares, the blame was shifted onto the Phalangists. By any measure that was a war crime, compounding the state terrorism that Israel perpetrated in Lebanon before the invasion.

A consequence of the 'Lebanonization' of Israel's security methods was an increase in brutality in other contexts. In April 1984, four young Palestinian terrorists, armed with knives, a grenade and a fake bomb, hijacked a bus that had departed Tel Aviv for Ashkalon. After a passenger managed to escape, the bus was stopped by police, special forces troops and Shin Bet agents. A Shin Bet negotiator established that the four men were amateurs, but commandos stormed the bus, killing two of the terrorists and one passenger.

The two remaining Palestinian terrorists were surrounded by an angry mob of security personnel and the Shin Bet chief Avrum Shalom hit one of the captives so hard with a pistol butt that it entered his skull. He gave the order that the men should be killed before being brought back to a Shin Bet interrogation centre. They were driven a few miles and told to lie on the ground, then their heads were smashed with rocks and iron bars. Back at the interrogation centre, a waiting operative was told the men had been killed by a civilian mob, but unfortunately for Shalom, a press photographer had snapped the two hand-cuffed men being dragged off the bus. Since the international press ran the photo, Israel had no alternative to a secret inquiry.

Shalom and the killers met secretly to concoct an alternative story. One aim of this conspiracy was to insert a friend of Shalom's into the inquiry panel; another was to set up the IDF commander Brigadier General Yitzhak Mordechai, whose troops terminated the hijacking, as a patsy.

Mordechai was accused of doing what Shalom himself had done to one terrorist with his automatic, with testimony from thirteen Shin Bet men who claimed he had beaten both men to death. Although he was facing murder charges, Mordechai did not easily buckle, and attempts to force him out of Shin Bet failed. He accused Defence Minister Rabin and Prime Minister Peres of ordering him to kill the two terrorists, but kept his trump card until last: he and two colleagues drew up a list of sixty-seven extrajudicial killings by Shin Bet and AMAN, as well as four Iranian diplomats who has been murdered by Mossad in Beirut. Since the exposure of such practices would gravely harm Israel's image, the Shin Bet personnel involved in these killings were pre-emptively exonerated in return for Shalom's resignation as head of Shin Bet.

Even more gravely, as elements in these agencies habituated themselves to murder and torture, they missed key international developments that would shake their world. Having rejected an invitation by the Shah to assassinate Ayatollah Ruhollah Khomeini in his Parisian exile, Mossad failed to notice the powerful links which revolutionary Iran was forging with downtrodden Shiites in southern Lebanon, all quietly brokered by the cleric Ali Akbar Mohtashamipur, Iran's ambassador in neighbouring Syria. The ambassador was also a member of the newly minted Revolutionary Guard Corps (IRGC), which encouraged Lebanese Shia to form a new entity. Part political party, part social welfare agency and also a terrorist group, it called itself Hezbollah.

At the top of Hezbollah was a shadowy Council influenced by the formidable Shia cleric Sheikh Mohammad Fadlallah, who was himself the target of multiple Mossad assassination attempts, including one which killed eighty innocent people outside a Beirut mosque in 1985.

His successor, Hussein Abbas al-Musawi, was killed by the Israelis in the first Apache helicopter missile strike in 1992 that involved an unmanned reconnaissance drone. His wife and five-year-old son also perished. Hezbollah responded with the heaviest barrage of rockets on Israel since the June 1982 invasion, while in March 1992 it killed thirty Israelis in a bomb attack on the Buenos Aires embassy.[20] The leadership passed to a more radical and pro-Iranian cleric, Sheikh Hassan Nasrullah, who remains Hezbollah's leader today.

One of Hezbollah's earliest recruits was a young veteran of Arafat's Force 17, an engineering student called Sayyid Imad Mughniyeh. In 1981 he left Fatah and gravitated towards explicitly Shia terror groups with ties to Iran, which he visited a year later. These links explain why a twenty-one-year-old played a crucial role in a series of devastating bombings that were allegedly organized by the IRGC commander Ali-Reza Asgari; only a state could supply such a quantity of explosives.

In April 1983 Mughniyeh's team blew up the US embassy in Beirut, killing most of its resident CIA contingent, including the visiting Robert Ames. In October, six tons of TNT were used in two vehicular attacks that killed 241 US peacekeepers and 58 French paratroopers at their Beirut barracks respectively. Mughniyeh also organized the kidnapping of over forty Western hostages, including William Francis Buckley, the new CIA station chief sent to Beirut to revive operations, who died following two years in captivity. Mughniyeh's men also killed sixty people with a suicide attack on a Shin Bet base in Tyre. He went on to become the most feared of Hezbollah's chiefs of operations, and was known as the 'father of smoke', due to his elusive nature.[21]

It was Israel that sought to encourage a parallel Islamist counterweight to the nationalist PLO in the Gaza Strip, despite evidence that the PLO's grip was weakening. In order to undermine Fatah, Israel encouraged Muslim Brotherhood trained clerics, whom Shin Bet imagined would be a stabilizing influence upon the young Palestinians engaged in the first Intifada.

One of the main beneficiaries of Israeli interest was a paraplegic called Ahmed Yassin, who in 1987 established the Islamic Resistance Movement, with the Arabic acronym Hamas. Like Hezbollah, it was responsible for a range of charitable and educational activities, but it also had a military wing. Despite being in and out of Israeli prisons, Yassin managed a terrorist organization that was responsible for kidnapping and murdering Israeli policemen and soldiers, as well as suicide-bomb attacks on regular passenger buses. He was also vehemently opposed to the expansion of Iranian influence among the Palestinians, which is why Israeli leaders hesitated to kill him. That changed in January 2004, when the Israelis linked him with the first female suicide bomber to attack an Israeli checkpoint.

By this point, assassination had been redubbed 'interceptions' or 'targeted killings', carried out as the final outcome of a bureaucratic process involving hundreds of personnel. Faced with a suicide-bombing campaign which never lacked volunteers, the Israelis escalated their campaign from individuals who posed an immediate threat to the 'ticking infrastructure' of terror. These killings became routine, with the victims rising from 24 in 2000 to 135 in 2003. One of the major considerations was that the Israeli public wanted revenge.

Operations involved sophisticated electronic surveillance, unmanned drones and fighter bombers or attack helicopters. Yassin's movements were entirely restricted to his journeys in a two-van convoy to a mosque or his sister's home. After being trapped in the mosque with drones circling overhead, he and his guards decided to make a dash for it. Two missiles fired by an Apache helicopter blew him and everyone around him to pieces.

'Mowing the grass' of Hamas's terrorist wing paid dividends; the suicide-bombing campaign abated as the infrastructure of suicide bombing was 'de-skilled', leading to declining efficiency. Persistent strikes meant that the successors of Sheikh Yassin and his replacement Abdel Aziz Ali Abdul Majid al-Rantisi, who was assassinated in 2004, lacked visibility. As a former head of Shin Bet remarked: 'Senior Hamas leaders decided they were tired of seeing the sun only in pictures.' This was not without costs and mistakes.[22]

One major mistake arose when Prime Minister Benyamin Netanyahu decided to target 'big fish' rather than minnows, after Hamas bombers killed fifteen people in a Jerusalem market in July 1997. He brought endless pressure to bear on Mossad chief Danny Yatom, who came up with the names of four Hamas leaders resident in friendly Jordan.[23]

The biggest fish, Musa Abu Marzook, head of Hamas's political bureau, was the last ranked target since he was a US citizen; attention focused instead on his forty-one-year-old deputy Khaled Mashal, whose Palestinian aid centre was located on the third floor of a shopping mall in Amman. Since Jordan was a friendly country with a peace treaty with Israel, the assassination method had to be covert. A dose of Levofentanyl – an opioid a hundred times stronger than morphine – would be administered with an ultrasound device. Two operatives would splash him with shaken-up Coca-Cola, distracting his attention from a momentary blast of damp air on the back of his neck as he tried to wipe down his suit.

An eight-person Mossad team identifying as Canadians, one of them a female anaesthesiologist with an antidote for Levofentanyl, should one of the attackers suffer exposure, flew to Amman. On the morning of the attack, 24 September, everything went wrong. The surveillance team tracking Mashal did not notice his small children on the back seat of his car, and could not communicate with the smaller hit team. Just as the two assassins were poised to strike, Mashal's daughter ran to him, chased by the driver who suspected a knife attack on his employer. Something damp hit Mashal in the ear as he turned.

A passing Hamas supporter was quick-witted enough to note the licence plate of the car bearing the fleeing assassins and followed them in another car. After the assassins decided to split up, Abu Seif tackled one of them. The other returned to strangle Abu Seif, but a passing former Fatah fighter joined the fray and restrained him. Both Israelis were taken to a police station, where the Canadian consul quickly established that they were not his compatriots. The remaining members of the Mossad team fled to the Israeli embassy, while Danny Yatom flew to Amman to plead for with King Hussein.

Meanwhile, Mashal's condition rapidly deteriorated. Since Hamas blamed the Jordanians for being complicit in what they knew was a Mossad attack, King Hussein had Mashal moved to the Royal Wing of Queen Alia Military Hospital to be treated by Jordan's best physicians. The retired former Mossad deputy chief, Efraim Halevi, was summoned from Brussels to get Netanyahu out of a hole.

The first element of the deal was that the antidote would be delivered to Mashal's doctors, in return for the four Mossad agents in the embassy being allowed to leave. The second element, which outraged many in Mossad, saw the two captured assassins exchanged for high-ranking prisoners held by the Israelis, including Sheikh Yassin. The more politically sinuous Mashal, who survived the poisoning attempt, and the other politicians were soon eclipsed by this clerical zealot. Yatom was forced out of the top job at Mossad, and Halevi replaced him.[24]

The Israelis had not forgotten about Imad Mughniyeh, head of Hezbollah operations. In 1997 they detonated a bomb outside his brother Fouad's hardware store, in the hope that Mughniyeh might be enticed to attend his funeral, where he would be killed.

While Sheikh Nasrallah was untouchable in a deep bunker under south Beirut, Mughniyeh had taken up residence in Damascus under the protection of the powerful General Mohammad Suleiman. Since Israel lacked much of an operation inside Syria, Mossad relied on the CIA to gather detailed information on their target. They did so eagerly, the fate of Buckley still in their memories – after the bombings in Beirut in the early 1980s, Mughniyeh had a $25 million American bounty on his head.

The immediate justification for assassinating him was his involvement in sophisticated IED attacks on US forces in occupied Iraq. This enabled US lawyers to circumvent Executive Order 12333, while President George W. Bush and Prime Minister Ehud Olmert agreed to cooperate in killing Mughniyeh.

The CIA Director Michael Hayden authorized a bomb attack on him and the CIA's Technical Services carried out twenty-five test blasts, before deciding on one that was lethal within a limited range. The Agency's Near Eastern Division helped smuggle the device into Syria, where agents inserted it into the rear spare tyre of a silver Mitsubishi SUV.

The Americans and Israelis established that Mughniyeh was careful in his security arrangements, frequently swapping mobile phones and moving between several abodes. His guards looked inside and under his car before every journey. His only predictable movements were to the apartment of a woman friend and another in the plush Kfar Sousa district. The Mitsubishi was parked outside the entrance to the latter, where Mughniyeh was likely to alight, and surveillance experts took up position.

After more than thirty attempts, on the evening of 12 February 2008 Mughniyeh's car pulled up outside the Kfar Sousa apartment. But so did two more vehicles with VIP passengers: General Suleiman and Qassem Soleimani, Iran's roving coordinator of its external proxies. The three men greeted each other like old friends. Although Mossad thought it had a once-in-a-lifetime chance to kill all three of them, they did not have authorization from either the Americans or Prime Minister Olmert. Two spotters – one from the CIA and one from Mossad – watched from an apartment opposite as Suleiman and Soleimani drove away. After ten minutes Mughniyeh exited. The Mossad man identified him while the CIA pressed a remote-control device. Mughniyeh was dismembered in mid-stride, his torso flying through a window fifty feet away. Only later did Mossad learn that both Olmert and Bush would have authorized killing all three men.[25]

In high summer General Suleiman repaired to his villa on the coast near Tartus, unaware that his movements were being tracked and that cameras were monitoring the villa. On 1 August an Israeli submarine surfaced off Syria, with six snipers disembarking into a smaller semi-submersible and coming ashore. Suleiman was sat at the head of a table on his large terrace, surrounded by dinner guests, when his body suddenly jerked around as six bullets cracked into his head, heart, neck and back. This was the first time Israel had killed a major foreign political figure. Whereas Mughniyeh was buried with full fanfare in Beirut, Suleiman was put in a body bag and quietly buried outside Tartus. Neither Assad nor Israel made anything of his demise and made no comment on his death, though there is a museum dedicated to his memory in South Beirut.[26]

While Mossad continued to use human assassins in countries where any other approach would amount to a declaration of war, increasingly technology came to dominate Israeli operations. Paradoxically, the development of drones came about because of the lacklustre performance of the Israeli Air Force in the Yom Kippur War; despite its absorbing half of the defence budget, Israel lost a quarter of its combat planes. One of their first attacks using this new method was in 1992, killing Hezbollah leader Abbas al-Musawi, his wife and young son. This paved the way for his much more charismatic successor.

•

The history of Israeli assassinations gradually coalesced with that of Iran. After the 1979 Revolution, Iran went from being a crucial ally, under the Shah, to the Jewish state's most implacable opponent, under its Shia clerical rulers. While the Islamic Republic has its own dismal record of political killings, history shows it has often been the victim of campaigns of assassinations. That story is often underplayed in the West, which has uncritically bought into Israel's version of hostilities. Influential American politicians are active supporters of a cultic terrorist organization that has for decades sought to violently overthrow Iran's Islamic Republic.

The clerical regime murders its opponents beyond, as well as inside, Iran. Most of the latter were shot on the streets during demonstrations or judicially murdered after torture and sham trials. But there have also been assassinations. Victims included the Shah's nephew, Shahriar Mustapha Chafik, a young former naval officer who was shot dead in December 1979 outside his Paris apartment by a man wearing a motorbike helmet. General Hussein Fardust, the Republic's security chief, had been in the city days before.[27] Another victim was the Shah's last relatively liberal Prime Minister, Shapour Bakhtiar, a seventy-seven-year-old veteran of the Spanish Civil War and of the French Resistance.

After fleeing Iran, Bakhtiar lived in France under heavy police protection. He survived the first attempt on his life on 18 July 1980, though a police guard was killed. Eleven years later, in August 1991, three men in their thirties led by his trusted aide, Farydoun Boyerahmadi, were frisked before entering the villa, where one of them killed Bakhtiar with a karate blow to the throat. They then used kitchen knives to slash his body to pieces and walked out past the police guards, despite their clothing being saturated with blood. The three were Iranian agents despatched by Ali Fallahian, Minister of Intelligence. The Islamic Revolution was also notorious for devouring its own children. Iran's first elected republican President, Abolhassan Banisadr, was the target of three assassination attempts by Islamic radicals while still in office, and then in exile after he fled in June 1981. A more recent example of the long reach of the Ayatollahs was the shooting of three Kurdish nationalists in a Berlin restaurant in 1992, for which the German government held the head of Iranian intelligence responsible.

However, it is important to register that the new Islamic regime was itself the victim of multiple assassinations, almost all of which involved Kurdish nationalist groups or the murky Mujahedin-e-Khalq (MEK).

In May 1979, both the former head of the Artesh – Iran's armed forces – and Ayatollah Morteza Motahhari, a member of the Revolutionary Council, were murdered by ethnic Kurdish separatists.

On 28 June 1981, Ayatollah Mohammed Beheshti, Chief Justice of Iran, the Ministers of the Environment, Transport and Power, and the Deputy Head of Commerce were killed in a bomb attack on the Islamic Republic Party headquarters. Seventy people perished, including twenty-three members of Iran's parliament.

On 5 August of that year, the co-founder of the Islamic Republic Party was shot dead; on the 30th of the same month, Mohammed Ali Rajai (President of the Republic), Hojatolislam Bahonar (the Prime Minister) and Colonel Houshang Datsgerdi (the Police Chief) were killed at a meeting of the security council, when an aide opened a briefcase containing a bomb.

On 11 September 1981, Ayatollah Assadollah Madani, an aide of Ayatollah Khomeini and a member of the Assembly of Experts, was killed in a mosque with a concealed hand grenade, detonated as the killer asked the Ayatollah to pray for him.

And on 29 September, the Defence Minister Mussa Namja, the acting Chief of Staff Valiollah Falahi, the former Air Force General Javad Fakuri and the IRGC chief Mohsen-Rahim Koladoz died together in a suspicious plane crash.

Most killings of senior Iranian figures were the handiwork of the MEK. Originally this was part of a much broader opposition movement that had been appalled by the Anglo-American coup against Prime Minister Mohammad Mosaddeq in 1953. It originated in discussions in the mid-1960s between middle-class and urban engineers and scientists from traditional family homes. One of the main theoretical influences was the public intellectual Ali Shariati, whose own eclectic sources of inspiration included French Social Catholicism and liberation theology, as well as Marxism and Shia Islam.

The MEK sought to fuse revolutionary Shiism with revolutionary Marxism, as practised and propagated throughout what was coming to be called the Third World. One of their slogans was 'May America be Annihilated', a common sentiment around the world at the time. Their emblem combined a gun, anvil and sickle, encircled by exhortations from the Koran. Adopting a cellular organization, the movement sent members to PLO training camps in Jordan and Lebanon. On 8 February 1971, they carried out a raid on an Iranian gendarmerie post and tried to sabotage the Shah's extravagant celebrations of 2,500 years of the Persian monarchy.

The MEK came to wider notice through mass trials of its leaders during 1972, when the defendants were allowed to make lengthy speeches. In response to the resulting thirteen executions, the MEK launched attacks on police stations, prison officials and pro-government newspapers. In line with the spirit of the age, these attacks focused on the American corporate presence: General Motors, PanAm and Pepsi-Cola, as well as senior US military 'advisers', of whom there were 6,000 in the country. The group murdered seven Americans based in Iran, and General Taheri, head of Tehran's police, was another prominent casualty.

The mujahedin graduated to full-blown gun battles with the Shah's police on the streets of the capital, though they invariably came off worst.[28] Although they admired the earliest manifest-ations of what they dubbed 'Red Shiism', an uprising against corrupt early medieval caliphs, they deplored what they called 'Black Shiism', a contemporary reactionary clergy that was subservient to the Shah.

In contrast to the MEK, there were very few clerical martyrs, despite their Shia faith being based on ostentatious martyrdom. When the MEK attempted to make common cause with those few clerics who were opponents of the Shah, they were bitterly disappointed.

These Islamo-Marxists also suffered an internal schism: the majority of mujahedin moved closer to other parties of the left, while the more religious broke away. In May 1975 this rift led to a gun battle, in which the movement's religious leaders were slaughtered. The majority retained the MEK's emblem, dropping the slogan 'In the Name of God', while the mujahedin survived mainly within prisons under its leader Masud Rajavi. Both groups separately continued attacks on the Shah's regime and US business interests.

As the Shah was losing his grip on Iran, he freed many political prisoners, mainly under pressure from Western human-rights lobbyists. The freed MEK ones retrieved their hidden weapons and played a crucial role in neutralizing the regime's demoralized forces, amidst the strikes and demonstrations that led to the Shah's flight.

However, the MEK's leaders lacked the imagination to grasp how events might proceed, not least because they viewed them through the prism of the Bolshevik Revolution. They overlooked the crucial role of the returned Imam Khomeini, whose goal was a populist theocracy and who was idolized despite only being present in Iran through audiotapes of his sermons.

Khomeini coldly out-manoeuvred his secular opponents and established his own Islamic Republican Party, revolutionary guards, revolutionary tribunals and new secret police. The clerics elaborated a unique dual-institutional control over state institutions, while subjecting parliamentary candidates to their own Council of Guardians for vetting. The confiscated wealth of exiles flooded into clerical charitable foundations, some of it being given to the increasing number of dependents of martyrs who died in the war with Iraq after 1980. Constant reference to a world of external and internal enemies further consolidated support for the embattled regime.

In 1979 the MEK boycotted the referendum on the new constitution of an Islamic Republic that replaced the 1906 one. The clerics then managed to exclude most MEK candidates from the ensuing elections, and in 1981 the MEK were banned. On 20 June 1981 the MEK staged an uprising, in alliance with the ousted President Banisadr. This was comprehensively and brutally crushed. The victims included Ashraf Rabi'i, Rajavi's wife, who was killed in a raid on a safehouse by the Revolutionary Guard. The number of executions rose from 600 in September 1981 to 1,700 that October and 2,500 in December. In scenes not seen since the 1910s, the corpses of those hanged were left dangling at public execution sites.

From his refuge in Paris, the MEK leader Masud Rajavi declared war on the clerical regime. In addition to the assassination of those government officials mentioned earlier, a number of imams were killed in suicide attacks. On 8 December 1981, a twenty-one-year-old woman blew up Imam Jom'eh in Shiraz with a grenade hidden under her chador. Jojjat al-Islam Mostawfi, head of the Society of the Militant Clergy of Tehran, was shot dead while concluding his sermon at Friday prayers. In 1981 there were three such attacks per day, declining to five a week in early 1982 and five per month by the end of the year.[29] Some 12,500 political dissidents were executed or slain, too.

Rajavi ran the MEK from a heavily fortified base in Paris, with forward operations and a radio station at Sar Dasht in Iraqi Kurdistan, where Saddam Hussein regarded the group as a priceless asset in his war with Iran. The MEK took part in Iraqi attacks into Iran, culminating in Operation Eternal Light, when they embarked on a suicidal mission six weeks after a peace had been signed. 1,301 of them were killed, and another 1,100 returned to Iraq. Khomeini took the opportunity to execute 4,500 imprisoned MEK supporters and other Leftists. After the Second Gulf War, in which Iraqi forces were expelled from Kuwait, the MEK joined Saddam's Republican Guards in the vicious suppression of the Kurdish uprising in 1991.

To the unthinking Left, the MEK was just another popular Third World cause. Rajavi extended diplomatic feelers to Hani al-Hasan of the PLO, Walid Jumblatt (the Lebanese Druze leader) and Ahmed Ben Bella (former leader of Algeria's FLN), as well as to countless political parties, including Britain's Labour Party and Germany's Christian Democrats. For a short time, he managed to rally other Iranian opposition groups, but they fell away because of his dictatorial style and dependence on the patronage of Saddam Hussein.

As it became apparent that the Iranian clerical regime theocracy was not about to collapse, Rajavi turned the MEK into a totalitarian sect. Each MEK household acquired a 'supervisor' who reported to a higher one and then to Rajavi himself. Members had to surrender their money, and account for every hour of the day, until the final chant of 'Greetings to the Chairman' at lights out.

These controls included the hierarchical allocation of daily tasks, what clothes one wore, and permission to marry. Mehdi Abrishhamchi, a close comrade, was prevailed upon to divorce his wife Maryam Azodanlu, who then married Rajavi under the auspices of the sect's thirty-four-strong Central Committee. Maryam was appointed his co-equal leader as a gesture to feminism, though she had no qualifications for such a role. Soon the MEK's slogan was 'Rajavi is Iran, Iran is Rajavi', odd for a movement claiming to seek a democratic Islamic revolution. In 1987, and by now expelled from France to Camp Ashraf in Iraq, Rajavi adopted the titles Rahbar, or 'Guide', and worse, 'The Present Imam'.

In 1990 he insisted that all members divorce, so as to focus their minds on fighting. They were obliged to exchange their wedding rings for pendants engraved with his face, while their children were 'adopted' by MEK supporters in Europe. The unencumbered women were supposed to supply Rajavi with sexual services and were coerced into doing so if they declined his advances. Meanwhile, his older brother Kazem was shot dead near Geneva by Iranian agents in 1990; six years later, his widow was murdered in Turkey.

Western countries classified the MEK as a proscribed terrorist group, but with Iran added to an imaginary 'Axis of Evil', things changed. A 5,000-strong terrorist group based in a camp outside American-occupied Baghdad was allowed to conduct extensive lobbying operations in the US, while off-the-books US 'contractors' took some of the MEK to Nevada for training. This arrangement was finally terminated by Iraq's Shia Premier Nouri al-Malaki, who expelled the MEK to oblige his Iranian patrons.

With US connivance, 2,700 MEK members were sent to Albania between 2014 and 2016. The main attraction for the Albanian government was that the MEK afforded it high-level political contacts in the US, though the group's presence in Albania was resented by people who had spent half a century under the tyranny of the dictator Enver Hoxha between 1944 and 1985. Albania's rulers were delighted that by hosting the MEK, American scrutiny of organized crime links to its politicians was less robust.[30]

Rajavi is presumed to have died in around 2003, but his widow Maryam retains an iron grip on the sect. The MEK can, and does, intimidate Albanian journalists, while fugitives from the group are tracked down and brought back. It is assumed that most external MEK funding derives from Saudi Arabia and the UAE, which regarded the sect as a useful weapon to deploy against Iran.[31]

Few Iranians under sixty can directly remember the MEK, let alone desire to be ruled by such an organization, were the clerical regime to fall to internal unrest driven by its corruption and economic incompetence. The Iranian regime has not forgotten or forgiven the MEK either. On 11 December 2015, a fifty-six-year-old Iranian expat electrician called Ali Motamed was shot as he left his home in Almere, near Amsterdam. Two contract killers had been hired by a gangster who was serving an eighteen-year prison sentence. Motamed's real name was

Mohammed Reza Kolahi Samadi, and he was the MEK bomber who killed seventy Iranian politicians in 1981. The Iranians who set up the contract killing had not forgotten him.[32]

But there is another side of MEK activity which reconnects this story with Israel. From the 1990s onwards, the Jewish state feared that the Iranians were trying to develop nuclear weapons to fuse with their already sophisticated ballistic-missile programmes. This would have breached non-proliferation treaties, which Iran had signed, but which Israel has not.

This was partly because any sustained assault on Iran's diffuse nuclear facilities was beyond the IDF's capacity – not least in aerial refuelling – so the Americans would have to be involved. But there was a hitch. In 2007 the US National Intelligence Estimate (a summation of what has been discovered by seventeen US agencies including the CIA and NSA) determined that Iran had conducted clandestine nuclear activity in 2002–03, but then halted the programme. That was also when Iran elected to cooperate with the International Atomic Energy Agency (IAEA) and with the European 'Big Three'. No surprises then that in 2003 alleged documents from that programme began surfacing at the IAEA and in the Western media. At first, they were said to be from a laptop stolen from an Iranian scientist by German intelligence. But as flaws in the documents began to be revealed, the source shifted to unspecified Iranians who had presented the documents to US intelligence. This was most likely the MEK and the documents they 'presented' were in fact Israeli forgeries. That explained both the crude attempts to link Iranian companies with military research projects and 'exposure' of designs for a nuclear warhead, which the Iranians had already superseded.

The Obama administration sought to coerce Iran with economic sanctions, a policy which ultimately paid off when Tehran agreed to the 5+1 de-nuclearization talks, which led to the international 'JCPOA' agreement of 2015 for it also involved China, Russia and three European medium powers. Throughout, the Israeli response to Great Powers going above their heads was to beat the war drums, while abandoning any pretence at political bi-partisanship in the US. Prime Minister Bibi

Netanyahu and President Barack Obama became thinly veiled foes (Obama could not stand being in the same room with him), as Israeli lobbyists, thinktanks and journalistic shills went into overdrive by rummaging through the cliché box about Hitler and Appeasement.

But the Israelis also decided to take more direct action against Iran. One route, in collaboration with US spy agencies, was the 2012 'Olympic Games' viral assault on the Siemens-built operating computers controlling nuclear centrifuges, which is popularly known as the 'Stuxnet worm'. They were temporarily damaged after being remotely spun out of control.

Mossad cannot operate easily inside Iran, which has sophisticated intelligence services, so the MEK were the logical proxy, since as Iranian nationals they could. The MEK have also had decades of experience in killing Iranian officials.

Apparently, fifteen Iranian scientists were listed for assassination, the aim being to deter others from working on the programme, unless they and their families were prepared to live under constant police guard.[33] From 2007 onwards, at least four Iranian nuclear scientists were assassinated inside Iran with one gravely wounded. For example, on 11 January 2012, Mostafa Ahmadi Roshan, the director of a uranium enrichment facility at Natanz, died when two motorcyclists attached a small magnetic shaped charge to his car. This followed a bomb attack on Massoud Ali-Mohammadi, who was blown up by a motorcycle parked outside his Tehran home, an attack on Majid Shahriari, victim of another motorcycle bombing, and the wounding of Fereydoun Abbasi-Davani, head of Iran's Atomic Energy Organization. In 2011 Darioush Rezaeinejad and his wife were shot dead after two motorcyclists drew alongside their car as they set off to pick up their five-year-old daughter from school. A twenty-four-year-old kickboxer was charged with being the mastermind of these attacks; he confessed to have been trained in Tel Aviv after being flown there from Azerbaijan. He was hanged in 2012.

The aim of this Israeli campaign of indirect state terrorism was to deter Iranian scientists and engineers from working on any nuclear programme, though Iran is entitled to a civil one for medical research or electricity generation.[34] While much of the world's conservative press simply treated this as a further example of Mossad's can-do spirit, Netanyahu refused to stop there. His eagerness for military strikes on Iran appalled Meir Dagan, who resigned as Mossad chief, while the relationship with US Democrats deteriorated further because of Netanyahu's bumptious treatment of Obama, who was a lot steelier than he looked.

After President Donald Trump unilaterally withdrew the US from the nuclear deal, the European powers struggled to sustain it using special financial instruments to enable Iran to still export oil. This makes it odd that, in 2018, alleged Iranian agents should have tried to bomb the annual rally of the MEK in a Paris suburb, and seek to kill the leader of an alleged Arab Struggle Movement for the Liberation of Ahwaz in Denmark. This group had killed twenty-four people at a military parade in this predominantly ethnic Arab part of Iran. These conspiracies were detected just before Iran's President Rouhani was due to visit Austria, as part of his attempt to re-engage the Europeans in the failing nuclear deal. It is not inconceivable that they were themselves part of a false-flag operation to undermine this, as Israel and Iran pursue their shadowy vendettas, and Trump ratcheted up the war talk against the Islamic Republic even as he befriended the North Korean dictator Kim Jong-un, who has functioning rather than theoretical nuclear bombs.[35]

10

Snipers in the Skies?
Targeted Assassinations

In 1975, members of the US Senate's Church Committee on assassination were tantalized as they handled an item of physical evidence: a modified Colt automatic. This handgun was equipped with a telescopic sight and fired electrically. It passed from the chairman, Democrat Senator Frank Church, to the hawk-like Republican Barry Goldwater.

The purposes of this gun were drily described by the CIA Director William Colby during his testimony. He spoke of a weapons programme codenamed 'M. K. Naomi' of which this 'nondiscernible microbionoculator' was an example. The 'poison dart gun' fired a projectile with a pellet containing frozen shell-fish toxin to a range of one hundred metres, after a shoulder stock and barrel extension were added. The dart would puncture clothing and enter the victim's bloodstream, causing the heart to stop and leaving nothing more than a small red dot on the skin, the size of an insect bite. There would be no trace of the poison in the target's body.[1]

The background for the Committee's investigation was the political killings which had taken the thirty-fifth President, his brother Bobby and Dr Martin Luther King, and revelations that the CIA had tried to kill foreign leaders. The country's main intelligence agencies were in the doghouse after the Watergate scandal had revealed that the CIA did not exclusively operate overseas, as was its remit. The National Security Agency also kept various people under electronic surveillance, which was completely illegal. The effect was akin to the contents of a sewer seeping onto a street.

Commencing in January 1975, Church and his colleagues heard testimony regarding CIA attempts to assassinate not only Cuba's Fidel Castro or the Congolese militant Patrice Lumumba, but Dominican dictator Rafael Trujillo and Chile's commander in chief General René Schneider. A stickler for constitutional proprieties, Schneider was murdered on 25 October during a botched kidnap attempt by those involved in a coup against Salvador Allende. The Church Committee absolved the CIA of murdering Schneider, though it had armed the plotters with automatic weapons.[2]

Many of these US senators were appalled by the paramilitary activities of the CIA, and viewed much of the evidence for this activity as 'distasteful'. They concluded that US government employees were directly implicated in the attempted assassination of Castro and the assassination of Trujillo. In the three other cases, while US agents were linked to events, there was no direct evidence that they had attempted these assassinations. They were incorrect about Lumumba. Behind these specific cases also lurked the fear of what is nowadays called 'blowback'. John Kennedy himself had once remarked of assassination, 'We can't get into that kind of thing or we would all be targets.'[3]

Determining who ultimately authorized lethal violence was easier said than done, despite the hard evidence for assassination attempts. The top players, Dwight Eisenhower and John Kennedy, were dead and had been clever enough never to commit murderous intent to paper, though others left meetings with that understanding. The CIA chiefs who testified were much more coldly laconic than some of their florid subordinates, who tantalized the senators with tales of rogues and rough stuff. Partly this was because the top CIA men believed in keeping secrets as part of their professional code; partly they were fearful of making enemies.

Practically, it helped that they controlled whatever documentary evidence found its way to the Committee, which meant they talked to the specifics of a text rather than adding anything that was not in it. The senators' staffers could not make copies nor pursue internal references, while documents the senators demanded were thoroughly sieved at the White House for anything that might incriminate dead Presidents.[4]

The Committee focused its attentions on ambiguities in authorizing such actions. Was it because some CIA officials had gone rogue, or had they operated within a system crafted so as to allow plausible deniability at the executive level? Such a system enabled the President and senior officials to deny knowledge of any operation that might come to light, but also created confusion about the exact nature of any order given and the legality of the action taken.

With bizarre assassinations plots being aired in the press, the CIA took pre-emptive action some years before the Church Committee convened. On 6 March 1972, Director Richard Helms sent a memo to his deputies ordering, 'I direct that no such activity or operations be undertaken, assisted or suggested by any of our personnel.' After an internal review of such past 'questionable' operations, on 29 August 1973 his successor William Colby reiterated: 'The CIA will not engage in assassination nor induce, assist or suggest to others that assassination be employed.'

While the Church Committee heard evidence, President Gerald Ford offered to prohibit US intelligence agencies from engaging in assassinations, while also pleading with the Committee to keep their report secret from the general public lest it damage US foreign policy and reputation. Only the sections on Chile initially saw the light of day, but the final detailed report was leaked to the press in January 1976.

The following month Ford issued Executive Order 11,905. This stated: 'No employee of the United States Government shall engage in, or conspire to engage in, political assassination.' In January 1978 President Carter extended this executive order to include persons 'employed by or acting on behalf of the US', which President Ronald Reagan adopted in Executive Order 12,333. George H. W. Bush and all later US Presidents have affirmed this prohibition. Although it seemed to oblige Congressional demands to do something to clean up the CIA's act, in reality it imposed minimal constraints on what Presidents could do themselves. The appetite for covert operations and killings comes and goes, the tempo dictated by the wider inter-national context as well as the balance of power *within* intelligence agencies.[5]

The Church Committee had sought a statute banning assas-sination backed up with federal criminal penalties, and they were not happy with CIA self-policing. They wrote: 'Administrations change, CIA directors change, and someday in the future what was tried in the past may once again be a temptation . . . Laws express our nation's values; they deter those who might be tempted to ignore those values and stiffen the will of those who want to resist.'[6]

The Church Committee wanted such a law to extend to all foreign officials, including the leaders of political parties or insurgencies of which the US disapproved, provided the US armed forces were not at war. In 1978 a group of senators introduced a bill banning assassination on pain of imprisonment. The attempt failed, as did a repeat effort in spring 1980, largely because by then President Carter was involved in the real-time complexities of Afghanistan and Iran, where the CIA might need some slack.

Congressional attempts to ban assassinations by statute grad-ually petered out and the American public lost interest once the more lurid CIA schemes had been aired in the press. The House and Senate committees on intelligence operated differently – and the latter had close relations with the White House. It did not help that Vice-President Nelson Rockefeller encouraged Colby to give away as little as possible to the committee that Rockefeller chaired, nor that at least one CIA station chief was assassinated by Greek terrorists as a result of classified information being inadvertently disclosed by the Church Committee.

To those not familiar with the US constitution, Executive Orders might seem like tablets of stone, but rather than asking how Executive Order 12,333 could have been entrenched in law, successive administrations were more interested in how it could be circumvented or disregarded. The laws of war proved helpful.

There is no unitary law governing military conflict; rather there is an untidy mess of international and national laws and each country's military governance. A presidential or congressional declaration of war massively enhances the scope for all kinds of killing, though both the US Army's General Orders (1863) and the 1907 international Hague Convention prohibited treacherous assaults on enemy commanders. What happened if the assault force arrived wearing enemy uniforms but then changed into their own? Was that treacherous?

Article 51 of the UN Charter allows states the right to individual or collective self-defence in the event of an actual or imminent attack. That threat could come from sovereign states, or in the case of terrorism, from non-state actors. The length of time between the attack and the response should also be short, since reprisals were also illegal under the Charter. This ceased to be academic in April 1986, when the NSA intercepted messages from Libya that may have led to the bombing of the La Belle discotheque in West Berlin, in which two of the three dead and 79 of the 229 wounded were off-duty US servicemen. On 14 April eighteen US F-111 jets flew to Tripoli and bombed Colonel Qaddafi's home, killing his fifteen-month-old daughter. Subsequent attempts to legislate so as to authorize the killing of foreign leaders involved in acts of terrorism failed in Congress, partly because the term was elastic.

Alternatively, creative government lawyers could 'park' the ill-defined word assassination and explore how the absence of a ban on encouraging coups might 'inadvertently' result in the death of a hostile leader. Assassinations could also occur during military operations, which were legal in wartime. It made no odds if the target were a large concrete building housing the general staff or intelligence service, or one of the fleet of Winnebagos Saddam Hussein travelled in. From there it was a short jump to Bill Clinton's retaliatory cruise-missile strikes on the dictator after he conspired to assassinate former President George H. W. Bush.

Finally, Presidents can simply overwrite earlier Executive Orders. Those EOs that apply to government employees do not have to be published, especially when they pertain to national security. Following the 9/11 attacks, legality was not a high priority in a climate of shock that such a crime could be committed against the most powerful nation on earth. Vice-President Dick Cheney lowered any obstacles to the no-holds-barred war he wished to wage. The 'one per cent doctrine' allowed virtually anything, provided it removed even the smallest risk of America suffering another attack.

Shortly after 9/11, Cheney said: 'It's going to be vital for us to use any means at our disposal, basically, to achieve our objective. It is a mean, nasty, dangerous, dirty business out there, and we have to operate in that arena. I'm convinced we can do it. We can do it successfully. But we need to make certain that we have not tied our hands, if you will, of our intelligence communities in terms of accomplishing their mission.'[7] Hardmen came in and out of the Oval Office, openly boasting that soon America's enemies would 'have flies on their eye-balls', though ironically, a large number of senior Al-Qaeda operatives responsible for 9/11 were traced and detained by what amounted to good detective work.[8]

On 18 September 2001 Congress issued a Joint Resolution on the use of force under the War Powers Act. The key clause read: 'the President is authorized to use all necessary and appropriate force against those nations, organizations, or persons he determines planned, authorized, committed, or aided the terrorist attacks that occurred on September 11, 2001, or harbored such organizations or persons, in order to prevent any future acts of international terrorism against the United States by such nations, organizations or persons.'[9] A separate intelligence finding sanctioned the sustained use of deadly force to eliminate the threat from that organization. In theory that did not contravene the ban on assassination in Executive Order 12,333, since targeting Al-Qaeda's chain of command would be legal under Article 51 of the UN Charter on legitimate self-defence by the state under attack.

A particular difficulty arose because enemy combatants wore no uniforms and blended into civilian populations in countries with which the US was not at war. In wartime, enemy soldiers can be killed, regardless of what they are doing. They have no right to a warning of imminent attack and minimizing their casualties is not a prime consideration. In domestic law enforcement, the opposite is true; policemen are not allowed to shoot criminals when they pose no threat or if there is the slightest risk that innocent people might be shot too. After 9/11, the US adopted 'targeted killing', which blended the identifiable guilt of individuals with quintessentially military tactics.

In the military and intelligence worlds, lawyers are omni-present. In the search to justify this new approach, the Bush administration revisited an advisory opinion issued in 1989 by Judge Advocate General of the Army W. Hays Parks. While he upheld the ban on political assassination and extended it to ordinary citizens who might be killed for political motives, he also said that the wartime killing of enemy combatants could be extended to specific individuals who posed a direct threat to US citizens or national security. Parks also argued that deadly force could be employed in self-defence in cases where the local government refused to deal with the problem.[10]

In such a febrile climate, few asked whether 'decapitation' actually worked, in the sense of collapsing terrorist organizations by 'taking out' their leaders. Such thoughts required empirical study of whether terrorist organizations are hierarchically or laterally organized; whether they rely on one leader's charisma; how long they have existed; whether they are motivated by religion or ideology. The answers to those questions are not as straightforward as many might imagine; there is a body of evidence that terrorist organizations tend to collapse more quickly by not assassinating their leaders, because of internal factionalism or war-weariness. Terror groups with older leaders are also more likely to negotiate than ones where younger people are in charge.

In fact, the rate of decline for those whose leadership were killed was twenty per cent *less* than for those that were left alone. Capturing leaders alive was smarter, since interrogations would help unravel either hierarchies or dispersed networks. The most obvious example of how removing a key man made a negative difference came after the US crowed at killing the notorious Jordanian-Palestinian jihadist Abu Musab al-Zarqawi in 2006. Within five years, his mini-rendition of an Islamic state reappeared as ISIS, which ended up running a state 45,000 square kilometres in extent and which required a fresh cycle of killing.[11]

In sum, Executive Order 12,333 was a nuisance rather than a permanent obstacle to US Presidents ordering assassinations. What seemed like an absolute prohibition was retained largely in the interest of America's self-image, which in turn influenced its ability to build coalitions of the willing. The term 'targeted killing' meant the US had reverted to assassination, but simply avoided calling it that.[12]

•

Several elements of this story come together with an unmanned aerial vehicle that has become the West's weapon of choice in the global war on terror and for battlefield surveillance in other conflicts. Drones are ubiquitous, with the US arsenal rising from 167 to twelve thousand between 2002 and 2012, with the budget rising from $550 million in 2002 to $5 billion in 2011. In 2005 they constituted 5 per cent of all US military aircraft; they are currently 33 per cent of the total and rising.[13]

A Predator drone costs $10.5 million, fourteen times less than an F-22 Raptor stealth fighter, which has hardly seen action since its inception in the 1980s. The Predator's successor, the armed MQ-R Reaper, costs about $20 million, but it can carry the same armament load as an F-16 manned fighter, stay airborne ten times longer at roughly forty hours or so and fly at 50,000 feet, higher than combat jets.[14]

Drones give the illusion of an omnipresent superpower, though nowadays fifty other countries manufacture and deploy them. The big players include China and Russia as well as Israel, Iran and Turkey, which has deployed them to great effect in the civil war in Libya. Non-state actors can 3D-print them or adapt those they buy from Amazon. People who think about the future of warfare imagine that swarms of killer drones will soon be controlled by AI so that algorithms will decide who is killed.

Drones are not the first 'autonomous' weapons. Take land-mines, which are placed so that a person or vehicle is blown up on contact. What if they were programmed only to explode if a person of adult weight or bearing a metallic gun stepped on them? Or if the mine could identify a specific target? Or if it could be programmed to deactivate itself? Sea mines are set to explode when certain types of ships are near, for example aircraft carriers rather than trawlers. In the case of drones, a human pilot presses a button to kill, on behalf of other humans who made that decision.

Ever since the dawn of military aviation, intrepid minds turned to eliminating the fatigue-prone human pilot, to create pilotless flying bombs. These weapons never lived up to their billing in terms of lethality. Instead, after the First World War, the main use of pilotless aircraft was to improve the skills of anti-aircraft batteries. But the dream of remote-controlled flying bombs continued.

However, the pecking order within the world's air forces ensured that nothing much came of drones. From the Great War onwards, glamour accrued to highly trained combat pilots, and the select few who during the Cold War flew very high-altitude spy planes like the U2, developed with CIA funding. There were also the test pilots for the incipient American manned space programme.

Military drones continued to be used mainly for target practice, but by the 1960s they were successfully equipped with cameras, for reconnaissance and surveillance. Versions of the Ryan Firebee were released from big fixed-wing aircraft in their thousands over Vietnam, and were recovered in mid-air with long hooks by helicopters while descending by parachute when they ran out of fuel.

The key technical advances were made by the Israeli aeronautical engineer Abraham Karem to satisfy Israel's need for real-time aerial surveillance technology. In 1977 he moved from Israel to California, where he tinkered with unmanned aerial vehicles in his garage. In 1980 he succeeded in keeping a drone called the Albatross aloft over Utah for fifty-six hours. The Defense Advanced Research Projects Agency (DARPA) took an interest in funding his work, as did the CIA. It contracted his Leading Systems company to manufacture two types of surveillance drone, one of which had the characteristic inverted-V tailfin of the later Predator.[15]

When Karem proved incapable of manufacturing at scale, in 1991 two extremely wealthy brothers, Neal and Linden Blue, acquired his bankrupt company and services. They had long combined an interest in aviation with businesses ranging from farming to uranium mining. They owned land in Nicaragua, which had brought them into the orbit of the CIA, since they were friendly with the dictator Luis Somoza Debayle. The new venture was called General Atomics. The CIA was not the only interested customer, though it brought much technical expertise to what the Blues and Karem were doing.

The civil war in Yugoslavia during the 1990s raised a number of tactical problems for the US Air Force. Cloud conditions over the Balkans made flying difficult, and fast jets were of limited use for reconnaissance. What the military and the CIA needed was something that could hover over a target area, often as low as 1,000 feet, relaying images that could result in rapid air strikes by combat jets.[16]

General Atomics drones, by now renamed Predators, began to be deployed by US Air Force pilots in Hungary and CIA pilots in Albania. Relaying their images took time since they had to go to a manned aircraft, then to a ground base station and finally via satellite to CIA headquarters in Langley, Virginia.

The addition of satellite communications and GPS navigational technology drastically improved the speed of delivery while making it possible to fly surveillance drones from thousands of miles away. Creech Air Force base in Nevada became the air force command centre for these Predators; GPS positioning equipment and laser beam target designation systems meant they could light up targets that combat aircraft or helicopters then destroyed. The final evolution was to turn drones into armed weapons. The incentive to do this arose from the developing war against Al-Qaeda, which in 1998 killed hundreds of people in two bomb attacks on US embassies in Nairobi and Dar-es-Salaam.

On 7 September 2000, the CIA and air force mounted a joint surveillance mission called 'Afghan Eyes' to find Al-Qaeda's leader, Osama bin Laden. On 25 September the drone involved relayed images of a tall man in white robes identified as bin

Laden, walking around a complex called Tarnak Farms near Kandahar. The problem was that the nearest cruise missiles were on US submarines stationed in the Arabian Sea. By the time these missiles reached Tarnak Farms, bin Laden might well have moved on.

The solution would be to arm the drone itself, which was done by adding Lockheed Martin Hellfire missiles to the drone's long wings. Although this new weapon only worked in optimal weather conditions, the imperatives created by the Al-Qaeda attacks on 9/11 meant that the armed Predators were sent off to war. Armed drones had three major advantages apart from their relative low cost and the fact that they never went blind on their orbit but rather could loiter for a couple of days at a time. Nowhere is beyond their reach, though major powers can shoot them down. There is never a risk of losing the pilot or having to mount costly search-and-rescue missions. Finally, these drones solved at a stroke the legal complexities which arose after 9/11 over irregular enemy captives, many of whom were taken alive by regular law-enforcement processes.

The captives were held at the US exclave at Guantánamo Bay, Cuba, and proliferating black sites scattered from Romania to Thailand. Detainees were also quietly 'rendered' in hired jets to Egypt, Jordan and Morocco, where terrible things were done to them while CIA officers posed the questions. But sooner or later there would have to be trials, and debates about the legality of testimony extracted with torture would delay court proceedings for decades. While drone killings raised a separate subset of legal questions – for example when US citizens were the targets, or if a person was killed as a favour to a foreign government – they also rendered a lot of the legal argument around prisoners academic.[17]

It would be misleading to imagine that armed drones were universally popular within the CIA, and not just because it had about 1 per cent of the Pentagon's budget and lacked its network of bases from which to launch such missions. By the new millennium, the Agency had swollen to about 17,000 personnel, only a thousand of whom served abroad. Officers in the overseas stations were mindful of how Agency drone operations played with touchy host governments; their people often resented the Western power dispensing death from the skies.

The most basic division within the CIA had long been between cerebral academic analysts and those often described as 'knuckle-draggers'. The Agency had evolved into an intelligence-gathering organization, without ever quite shedding the culture of the knife and gun. From February 1986 onwards, the more robust staff had their own department at Langley, called the Counterterrorism Center (CTC). The 9/11 attacks ensured that this outfit grew, from 300 to 2,000 personnel or 12 per cent of the entire workforce, even as the CIA's reputation plummeted because of its failure to prevent these attacks, to find Osama bin Laden and its involvement in confabulating the existence of Weapons of Mass Destruction in Iraq before the 2003 invasion.[18]

These new CTC officers were the rugged soulmates of the equally marginal Special Operations Command in the Pentagon, which was founded a year later. Many military top brass were sceptical of the special forces. SOC could draw upon tiny numbers of such elite troops, the army's Delta Force and the navy's SEAL Team Six, but both units were only trained for very short operational bursts such as hostage rescue. There were major cultural impediments to spies becoming soldiers or soldiers acting like spies.

At a senior level, many CIA officials had internalized the routinely reissued 1975 executive ban on assassination. They regarded intelligence collection and its analysis as the CIA's primary task, and were dismissive of the more swashbuckling types who had got the Agency into much trouble. Indeed, at the time the US was deeply critical of how the Israelis had blurred a youth protest movement and terrorism to carry out targeted assassinations of Palestinian militants in Gaza which killed 455 people, including 177 non-combatants.[19]

This was also the view of the 9/11 Commission, which recommended that all paramilitary functions should migrate from the CIA to the Pentagon, though this did not happen. Another bureaucratic fix was to appoint an overall Director of National Intelligence for all seventeen US agencies, the first appointee being the Greek-American diplomat John Negroponte.

Whereas it would be hard to name any of his successors, it is easy enough to list CIA directors, an indication that this new umbrella role did not work very well – none of the agencies welcomed the creation of an overall supremo.

The terror attacks on 9/11 were a massive blow to the US national security establishment as well as a crisis for the CIA. The top decision-makers were in a state of fury and shock. There was also Bush's statement to congressional leaders in the Cabinet Room: 'We will answer the bloodlust of the American people that is rightly on the boil.' They received relentless briefings about possible nuclear or biological attacks as the CIA's collective imaginations ran riot, and every day seemed to bring a new threat. Friends like Britain's Tony Blair were joined by new allies, such as Vladimir Putin, whose generals supplied the Americans with Soviet-era battleplans in Afghanistan. This was also a time of opportunity for opportunists within and beyond the government apparatus.[20]

Since the army's botched Iran hostage rescue operation in 1980, the Pentagon had experimented with its own in-house spies so as to avoid such disasters arising from patchy local intelligence. The Defense Intelligence Agency had been established in 1961 by Robert McNamara in the Kennedy administration to consolidate all military-related intelligence, and grew into a vast new agency. It also spawned an organization called the Field Operations Group, soon changed to Intelligence Support Activity (ISA).

After 9/11, such groups had a powerful champion in Defense Secretary Donald Rumsfeld. Sceptical of the CIA's more politically sensitive approach to intelligence, not least the need to cooperate with foreign governments, Rumsfeld encouraged the mushrooming of US Joint Special Forces Command as a new pro-consulate in the American empire. Its manpower rose from 1,800 in 2001 to 25,000 in 2011, and there were 72,000 special forces troops under its command in 2020, just short of the total strength of the entire British army.

Now Rumsfeld had soldiers who acted like spies, sometimes appearing in countries where neither the US ambassadors nor CIA station chiefs knew they were there. The sheer scale of the globalized wars the US embarked on, and the vast sums of money required to fight them, also meant the growth of a huge private military sector. Many of these 'contractors' were ex-intelligence officers and soldiers who never really retired. It also signified that part of this global war was being conducted beyond the formal legalities of government departments and agencies or their soldiers and spies. There were many of these contractors compared with ground troops: 163,446 in Iraq in 2008, compared with 146,800 troops, and 104,101 in Afghanistan in 2009 compared with 63,950 regulars.

By the dawn of the campaign against the Afghan Taliban in late 2001, the CIA disposed of its own modest Predator drone fleet, while inserting around 110 officers on the ground to liaise with indigenous anti-Taliban forces in a new style of campaign fought on horseback using high tech. Yet the air force was not going to easily relinquish its role operating drones. CIA drones were flown by air force pilots from the 32nd Expeditionary Air Intelligence Squadron out of trailers at the Langley headquarters until they acquired a separate base at Indian Springs in Nevada. This unit played a modest role in the larger US air campaign over Afghanistan, which within about half an hour wiped out any significant command and control or air defences the Taliban regime had. Al-Qaeda's mountain redoubts were hit by massive bombardments from B-52s while drones hunted the leaders. One early victim of a drone strike, in November 2001, was Al-Qaeda's military supremo Muhammad Atef. Amidst the debris of his house near Kabul, investigators found materials for a future attack on American interests in Singapore. But bin Laden, Ayman al-Zawahiri and the Taliban's Mullah Omar proved more elusive.

With the Taliban and Al-Qaeda dispersed, Agency-controlled drones were deployed to kill fleetingly glimpsed Afghans whose height approximated to that of bin Laden. In 2002 two tall men who appeared to be supervising bearded Afghans on an old airstrip came within minutes of being obliterated by a Predator drone. Luckily the mission controller called the CIA, for otherwise the two CIA agents who were building an airstrip would have been obliterated, along with their Afghan work-force.[21]

In 2002 thirty-one-year-old Daraz Khan and two young friends were climbing a mountain near Khost to collect scrap metal from an old Soviet munitions dump that had been repeatedly pulverized by recent US bombing strikes. A reconnaissance drone showed they were wearing robes and that 'Tall Man Khan', as he was known to the local villagers, was loftier than his companions. They were all killed. This was long before any policy was agreed to carry out strikes based on the 'signature behaviour' of the targets, for drone strikes were supposed to be led by rigorous identification of known 'personalities'.[22]

Under its commander Stanley McChrystal, JSOC acquired its own drone capacity, with dedicated air force pilots from the 3rd Special Operations Squadron in Nevada. CIA missions were controlled by the CTC headquarters at Tyson's Corner in Virginia, with the drones operated from air bases in Pakistan.

Since Al-Qaeda was an international terrorist organization, the war on terror involved hunting its operatives in countries with which the US was not formally at war. Leaving aside active battlefields, like Afghanistan and Iraq, drones have been deployed in Pakistan, Yemen, Syria, Somalia, Mali and Libya. One danger of using them was that a terror organization like Al-Qaeda shifted shape, with the greatest threat to the US displaced from Afghanistan to the Arabian peninsula. The Bureau of Investigative Journalism in London has calculated that since 2010, drones have been used to kill between 7,584 and 10,918 people, including between 751 and 1,555 civilians.[23]

These countries' leaders were prevailed upon to accept limited drone strikes within their territories, either with veiled threats or after payment of aid money. However, in all these cases there were significant areas in which the central government had minimal authority compared with that of tribal leaders. The Federally Administered Tribal Areas (FATA) in Pakistan consisted of seven tribal areas bordering Afghanistan; in 2018 it was renamed Khyber Pakhtunkhwa. The Pakistani army could only operate within metres of designated roads, after which tribal chiefs made the rules.

The Afghan Taliban use these wild places as a base; they are home to the Pakistani Taliban too, as well as 'Arab' Al-Qaeda elements who are like parasites on a more or less willing host. Pakistan's government forces and more proprietary terror brands like the Haqqani network were also active in the area, with civilians stuck in the middle of these rival forces. In Somalia, the central Islamic Courts Union government was actively hostile towards the US and engaged in a civil war against various warlords, some of whom were involved in thwarting the US-led UN Operation Restore Hope in the early 1990s.[24]

While international law on armed conflict covered inter-state wars, civil wars and insurgencies within states, there was little provision for outside armed intervention in someone else's war. In some failed states like Pakistan, orderly and disorderly juris-dictions co-existed. Teeming cities like Karachi presented a further set of problems, with Islamists thriving in lawless parts of them.

US relations with these states had a visible but also a submerged aspect involving intelligence and military interactions between their services and agencies, with tension between the two. Moreover, given that local governments could control 'popular' protests, US soft power was always playing catch up with a military tactic that was never publicly acknowledged.

Some foreign leaders did not object to US operations over parts of their territory, not least since they might slip their own enemies onto America's burgeoning kill lists. Others combined moralizing posturing about US infringements of their national sovereignty with private desires to kill every Islamist militant the US could feasibly target. Many folk quietly rejoiced every time violent Islamist thugs who terrorized local people were killed, especially if they were Arabs, Chechens or Uighurs.[25]

In November 2002, officers in the Counterterrorism Center watched a Toyota Land Cruiser bump along a dusty road in Yemen. Inside was Qa'id Salim Sinan al-Harethi, who the CIA had identified as one of the Al-Qaeda terrorists responsible for bombing the USS *Cole* at Aden in 2000, killing seventeen sailors.[26]

Attempts by the Yemeni police to capture Harethi alive had left eighteen officers dead, for he was well-protected. Military intelligence officers from ISA acquired some of the mobile telephone numbers he used, which were passed to the NSA's in-country Cryptological Support Group. Whenever he made or received a call, it was intercepted by NSA satellites operated by its Geolocational Cell. While he spoke to a caller, an armed Predator came on station from a secret CIA base in Djibouti. Once his voice had been identified back in Maryland, commanders at the CTC and the CENTCOM commander Tommy Franks at Tampa authorized the drone operators in Djibouti to launch the drone's missile. Harethi and his five companions were killed; he was identified by a distinctive mark on his severed leg.

While the autocratic ruler of Yemen, Ali Abdullah Saleh, kept the Americans on a tight leash, in Pakistan former general and President Pervez Musharraf had a tricky dilemma. True, Pakistan derived significant aid from the US for its cooperation in the war on terror, as an alternative to being bombed back to the Stone Age – as the threat went after 9/11.[27] But Islamist hatred of the Americans was endemic there. Its Inter-Services Intelligence agency, or ISI, was engaged in double-dealing with the Afghan Taliban, who also acquired a Pakistani offshoot. This is why Musharraf routinely attributed US drone strikes to mystery 'explosions' or claimed credit for the violent deaths of militants at the hands of Pakistan's own armed forces. What else could he do, since the US administrations never publicly acknowledged drone strikes? When Hillary Clinton paid her first official visit to Pakistan as Secretary of State in October 2009, she put herself in the awkward position of fielding aggressive questions about drones that she was not allowed to answer since drone strikes were classified.[28]

One man the Pakistanis wanted dead was the Pakistani Taliban commander Baitullah Mehsud, who in 2007 declared war on Pakistan itself. Two years later his 'very brave boys' assassinated Benazir Bhutto, leaving her corrupt widower to take up her political baton. Mehsud's followers also regularly attacked US supply convoys winding their way into Afghanistan.

In June 2009 the CIA learned that Mehsud would attend a funeral for slain Taliban leaders in South Waziristan. Drones were despatched to kill everyone at the funeral, and around sixty people died. Unfortunately, Mehsud had decided not to attend that day, but eighteen villagers who had were killed. In August 2009 the CIA tried again, tracking him to his father-in-law's house where he was laid up with diabetes. The drone operators saw a man on the roof hooked up to a drip, with a gaggle of bodyguards around him, and fired a missile. Initially the Taliban claimed it killed Mehsud's wife, but they later acknowledged that he was dead. Few Pakistanis mourned him, since he was responsible for 80 per cent of the suicide bombings in the country between 2007 and 2009.[29]

But virtually every strike in Afghanistan or Pakistan came with other costs – and sometimes the victims were not militants at all. On 24 October 2012 people tending fields in Gundha Kala noticed several drones cruising overhead. Suddenly one of them fired two Hellfire missiles into a field, killing a sixty-eight-year-old grandmother, Mamana Bibi, while she tended her okra crop. As her young grandchildren ran to help her, two more missiles slammed into the site, badly injuring them with shrapnel, while a three-year-child old injured himself after falling from a roof. There was no conceivable reason for the attack, save that a Talib had driven past the fields ten minutes earlier, leaving a ghostly phone signature.

Not all such attacks were so small-scale. On 6 July 2012, drones fired four missiles into a group of eighteen labourers in a field outside Zowi Sidgi. The first blast killed eight, while the second killed another ten men who had rushed to help the wounded.[30]

One strike on a school in Chenegai in 2006 killed eighty people, the majority boys and young men. Worse, attempts by journalists to investigate civilian deaths can prove lethal. After a house was destroyed in a mystery explosion, a Pakistani free-lance journalist called Hayatullah Khan went to investigate in a village in North Waziristan. He photographed a missile fragment stamped 'GUIDED MISSILE, SURFACE ATTACK, ADM-114', indicating that a Hellfire missile had been used. On 5 December 2005 he was kidnapped, and his body was found in June 2006. He had been shot in the head, allegedly by Al-Qaeda. A year later, after his widow insisted he had been murdered by the ISI, she was slain by a bomb outside her house.[31]

George W. Bush kept a chart of leading terrorists on his desk, crossing them off as they were killed. He compared them to rattlesnakes in a hole, adding that he'd deal with the foreign leaders who tolerated them, too. But in reality it was his successor Barack Obama who took drone-targeted killings to a new level.

Obama wanted to end America's involvement in Bush's war in Iraq to concentrate on Afghanistan, from where Al-Qaeda had plotted attacks on the West. He also sought to return the US from the dark side into which Cheney had so eagerly crossed. Although he would not say so explicitly, his disapproval of torture at secret sites and desire to extricate the US from costly Middle Eastern wars left him few logical alternatives if he also needed to counter parallel claims that he was soft on terrorism and sympathetic to Islam.

The number of drone strikes rose from 46 in Bush's final term to 542 under Obama. These resulted in 3,797 fatalities, of which 324 were civilians. As he ruefully recognized, he became 'the drone President'.

Only in Obama's second term after 2012 did he seek to give drone strikes a patina of judicial process, after disquiet from both the Left and the libertarian Right about these extra-judicial killings spread in the US itself. Obama publicly wrestled with his own dilemmas, first to a younger audience on YouTube, and then in a speech on 23 May 2013 to the National Defense University at Fort McNair. The following passage dealt with extending oversight of drone-strike decision-making:

> Going forward, I've asked my administration to review proposals to extend oversight of lethal actions outside of warzones that go beyond our reporting to Congress. Each option has virtues in theory, but poses difficulties in practice. For example, the establishment of a special court to evaluate and authorize lethal action has the benefit of bringing a third branch of government into the process, but raises serious constitutional issues about presidential and judicial authority.
>
> Another idea that's been suggested – the establishment of an independent oversight board in the executive branch

– avoids those problems, but may introduce a layer of
bureaucracy into national security decision-making, without
inspiring additional public confidence in the process. But
despite these challenges, I look forward to actively engaging
Congress to explore these and other options for increased
oversight.

I believe, however, that the use of force must be seen as
part of a larger discussion we need to have about a comprehensive counterterrorism strategy – because for all the focus
on the use of force, force alone cannot make us safe. We
cannot use force everywhere that a radical ideology takes
root; and in the absence of a strategy that reduces the well-
spring of extremism, a perpetual war – through drones or
Special Forces or troop deployments – will prove self-
defeating, and alter our country in troubling ways.[32]

Obama insisted that he would approve every such strike,
after inspection of evidence from several sources and with
lawyerly input. He expected people to put trust in his counter-
terrorism advisor and National Security chief John Brennan, a
flinty Irish-American who would go on in 2013 to direct the
CIA, in which he had spent twenty-five years of his career as
an analyst and station chief in Riyadh.

Brennan insisted on nominations to a 'kill list' based on prior
CIA or Pentagon intelligence. After processing up their respective
hierarchies, the list would have to be signed off by Obama, with
advice from Brennan himself. These pseudo-legalistic processes
did not involve judges, and the only lawyers present were the
ones who justified such strikes. Nearer the operational level,
practical steps were taken to improve target accuracy, with the
aid of more spies recruited on the ground and use of homing
chips that could be left in houses or vehicles to guide the Hellfire
missiles to their targets. Voice-recognition software was also
deployed to identify targets by voice patterns.[33]

By 2012, some elements in the CIA had become soldiers
while some of the military were acting as spies, creating obvious
disadvantages for other parts of the US government. The drone
strikes often cut across the State Department's mission. A

striking example came when Senator John Kerry secretly visited Islamabad to retrieve the tailfin of one of the stealth helicopters abandoned during the bin Laden raid the previous year. Mission accomplished, Kerry was horrified to learn that the CIA had struck with a drone almost as he boarded his flight in Islamabad.[34]

At the highest level, this fusion was evident when Obama switched his CIA chief Leon Panetta to the Pentagon, while four-star general David Petraeus was moved to command the CIA. Moreover, burly men of unknown provenance cropped up in odd places, like the 'consultant' Raymond Davis who in 2011 was arrested in Lahore after shooting dead two would-be street robbers. The vehicle he summoned from the US consulate to extract him itself killed a motorcyclist after it hurtled the wrong way along a one-way street. Since Davis had paid multiple clandestine visits to Waziristan, it is presumed he was liaising with the local agents who fingered terrorists for the CIA strikes. The US and Pakistan eventually negotiated a $2 million compensation deal for the families of the dead men, but two days after Davis was flown out, the CIA carried out a drone attack that killed forty-four people in a quest to kill a single militant. This was payback for the very public detention of Davis.[35]

Army officers lacked the political smarts of CIA field officers, and it took a long time for some of them to learn that not shooting someone might be the better strategy. The CIA was transformed into a macho organization partly to survive budgetary predations. Killing people kept the money flowing – drone strikes made it seem as if they were doing something. The Agency's failures, from Al-Qaeda to the 2011 Arab Spring, reflected the atrophy of its founding objectives.[36]

•

The bureaucratic politics of drone warfare should not distract from the reality of young men and women sitting in trailers steering drones with a joystick and pressing a button to kill people seven or eight thousand miles away. Thousands of men and women have flown drones. A few of them have written or spoken about what they do.

One important caveat in discussing drone pilots is that those who spoke to journalists may not be representative of the silent majority, and it is against the law to discuss classified activities. The critical literature is the work of lawyers, philosophers and others, divorced from the messy reality.

Though they are mostly professional pilots, drone operators are not on their own like combat jet pilots, whose missions normally last a couple of intense hours before they return to a base or aircraft carrier. Ground troops or fighter pilots do not re-enter home life after every shift, as drone crews do.

Normally there are three personnel in the drone-flying trailer, and they are in constant communication with up to twenty people – like any bureaucracy engaged in killing, responsibility is compartmentalized and dispersed. Rather than being the man or woman who simply presses the button to launch a missile, some drone pilots view themselves as 'orchestrators' of incoming and outgoing information. Someone much higher up the 'kill chain' decides when a 'high-value target' must be killed or if an attack is called off.[37]

High-value 'personality' targets were an elusive objective and limited in number. There was usually positive voice identification on them from eavesdropping. They would then be classified as JPEL – on the Joint Prioritized Effects List, which meant they would soon be dead.

So many of these high-value targets were killed that the emphasis shifted towards a new approach based on 'signature' patterns of behaviour; detailed biographical knowledge about a target was replaced by the lifestyle of anonymous groups of enemy fighters. The risk of inadvertently killing innocent civilians or civilians with whom militants interacted increased, notably at such events as weddings.

Such inflation was not without inherent problems in cultures that were entirely alien. At its most basic, while a group of men with Kalashnikov assault rifles would arouse suspicion in most Western societies, in many contexts men are routinely armed. Firing guns into the air may also be normative on festive occasions. How does one interpret the purpose of a gathering without hearing what is said at it? The fact that US authorities were often relieved to find the corpse of a known terrorist among the dead spoke chapters.[38]

These drone teams work twelve-hour shifts, which can be scheduled so that they see the target country in daylight while it is night outside in Nevada. The most common feeling among drone crews is tedium interspersed with brief adrenaline rushes. It takes time for a Predator or Reaper to go on station, and then it can circle for hours at a time at a cruising speed of 100 mph. Why not leave the unmanned aircraft on autopilot and play a computer game? That led to one unfortunate incident when a virus infected the drone's operating systems after jumping across from the computer game.[39]

After going off duty, these crews return to their families, so that they might be bathing their children within forty minutes of killing a stranger in a foreign country. Although some civilians probably regard drone killing as akin to a computer game, nothing can be further from the reality. Even those who start off dull to the differences and relish each 'bugsplat' soon realize that real people are being hurt, even if death has no smell in remote air-conditioned trailers.

A term like 'bugsplat' is a gift to civilian critics of drones, but in reality it derives from a computer programme designed to *mitigate* the collateral effects of explosions. Likewise, civilian critics forget that some apparently dubious terms mean something else entirely in the jargon of military communications. For example, people rushing out of a building after a firefight are referred to as 'squirters', referring to the effect of dispersal.[40]

The most recent technical development involves adaptation of the missiles fired by drones. President Obama sought to reduce collateral casualties by finding a new type of warhead for Hellfire missiles. The solution, called R9X, was an inert warhead that sends about 100 pounds of metal at enormous velocity but instead of exploding releases six sharp knives. It was used in June 2020 to kill Khaled al-Aruri, the head of Al-Qaeda's operations in Syria.[41]

Few soldiers on any battlefield spend entire days, let alone weeks, stalking someone they have orders to kill. Classic studies show that the majority of soldiers fire in a general direction and probably do not hit anyone; sniping is something else, deliberate and cold-blooded. Contemporary snipers avail themselves of various kinds of data, including software that compares a person's facial features or gait with records in electronic data-banks. Scientists working for the Department of Defense will soon equip them with the fruits of the Jetson Project, which registers minute heart vibrations. A laser vibrometer will be used to compare a target's unique heartbeat signature with stored data.[42]

But snipers are also liable to be shot themselves and can be directly blamed by their victims' surviving comrades. Being a sniper is not as risk-free as flying a drone. Drone pilots get to know their targets, which may explain why they allegedly suffer from disproportionate stress. Drone pilots can see their targets so immediately that they become fascinated by their social inter-actions, which in any Third World village are complex.

Drone pilots are reliant on someone telling them that a target is who they say it is, though high-value targets often prove elusive, since they are conscious about using mobile phones or travelling in the same vehicles. Furthermore, the staring eye does not avert itself after a Hellfire missile has ripped the target apart. Drone pilots see what they have done once any smoke has cleared, not least to verify that the strike does not have to be repeated. They might see women and children who wandered into the wrong place at the wrong time but who are now in pieces. There have also been claims that after one drone strike, rescuers have been targeted – it is called 'double tapping' – since they might include comrades of the victims. This means adopting tactics which are normative to many terrorist organizations, such as planting two bombs in delayed sequences.[43]

Combat stress can creep up on those doing this kind of killing, despite the systems designed to preclude it. A drone pilot may see more death and destruction than a soldier who moves on, let alone a remote artillery gunner or pilot hurtling by at hundreds of miles per hour. Drone pilots have no opportunities to be personally brave, since their targets can never shoot back. Ubiquitous images of collapsing towers on 9/11 or occasional vivid glimpses of the barbarity of Al-Qaeda and the Taliban did not always counter the feeling that this high-tech type of warfare was fundamentally unfair.

This is also reflected in the distribution of rewards. For a long time, flying drones did not result in medals for distinguished service or rapid promotions, since the top brass regard drone work as akin to a desk job involving no personal danger. Defense Secretary Chuck Hagel apparently vetoed the idea of awarding drone pilots the Distinguished Warfare Medal. There is also a high burnout rate from intense repetition of the same tasks six days a week, and as people grow older they lose the hand-to-eye coordination required. There are few jobs open to burned-out drone pilots, especially if they have been psychologically damaged.

People who are 'corporately' devalued tend to maudlin thoughts about life's injustices. Long days and nights in small cabins surrounded by instrument panels also result in uneasy reflection as well as bad dreams. This can involve the moral damage of this one-sided war, for the victims do not stand a chance once a missile hurtles in. Most people recoil at the thought of hunting a deer, lion or elephant with a machine gun from an SUV. This remote slaughter involves human beings; sometimes including collateral damage like the sixty-eight-year-old grandmother Mamana Bibi.

Among those drone crews who suffer from PTSD, and between 7 and 30 per cent allegedly do, there are also a few who wondered about the economics of this forever war in an expanding number of global theatres. Do the makers of drones and their armaments have a vested interest in perpetual conflict, to keep their shareholders' dividends flowing? A visit to any major arms fair reveals an enormous range of equipment; even the drone pilots' chairs are ergonomically designed to prevent back ache. And naturally, after studies showed that drone pilots were experiencing PTSD, teams of chaplains and psychiatrists were installed at American drone bases.[44]

While drone killings have resulted in the deaths of many known terrorists, responsible for appalling violence themselves, even those most involved in ordering such killings have doubts about the unforeseen effects. Not all of these are geopolitical.

Drones circling overhead create an atmosphere of fear for those living below, especially in what are not declared war zones, even if it also means that militants and terrorists are too frightened to sit down together or to use a mobile phone. Ordinary people began to shun their company lest it result in silent death, for a Hellfire missile flies faster than the speed of sound.

Drones affect how people regard the United States. Unlike Israel, whose enemies lurk in the occupied territories or in neighbouring states, the US is a global power with more allies and friends than enemies, a few of which have become havens for terrorists. By no stretch of the imagination could it use the excuse of being besieged.[45]

Thanks to drones, the US is seen by some as a sinister deus ex machina with an asymmetric war machine, rather than the land of opportunity. As Pakistan's former ambassador to the US Husain Haqqani once remarked: 'When the drone strikes killed people that Pakistan didn't want killed, there were protests. When the drone strikes killed people that Pakistan didn't mind being killed, there were no protests.' The urban protestors seem not to note that militants and terrorists extort from or shoot village elders while forcing village girls to become jihadi brides. Terrible tortures were also inflicted by the Taliban on anyone suspected of being an American or government spy.[46]

The US war to win hearts and minds had few successes. In February 2010 Anne Patterson, then US ambassador to Islamabad, reported that 80 per cent of Pakistanis had a more negative view of the US than of India, largely because of drone strikes.[47] Earlier she had reported that 'Increased unilateral operations in these areas risk destabilizing the Pakistani state, alienating both the civilian government and military leadership, provoking a broader governance crisis in Pakistan, without finally achieving the goal' of eliminating the Al-Qaeda and Taliban leadership.[48]

Drones can also become a mindless substitute for strategic thinking about the conduct of US foreign and security policy, especially as they appeal to primitive instincts in the American psyche. Even attempts to mitigate civilian casualties with warheads that protrude sharp blades as they hit a target pander to the same instincts and distract from the larger questions. Just keep killing terrorists by expanding the target pool, even if this increases the number of militants, rather than pondering whether the US needs to make remote warfare at all. When you have a hammer, every problem becomes a nail. That was the result of Obama elevating a tactic into a strategy in order to remove America's big bootprint from troubled Muslim parts of the world so as to focus on domestic reform and economic growth.

Against this, some argue that if the US withdrew from various fragile states it would mean entrusting or sub-contracting their future security to highly volatile regimes. Huge industrial concerns and their lobbyists ensure that the defensist view prevails among those who control national defence budgets, with retired generals revolving lucratively onto the boards of the companies concerned, to ensure it remains so.[49]

A further problem about drones has become increasingly apparent. At least eight countries, notably China, Russia, Israel and Turkey, have their own sophisticated drone industries, and dozens more can put a rudimentary kind of drone in the skies. At the time of writing, the Turkish army has used both large drones and swarms of small 'kamikazi' ones to repel the rebel general Khalifa Haftar's forces from Tripoli. They were then used to destroy Armenian armour in the short war with Azerbaijan, Turkey's ally. The most sophisticated militant groups also employ drones, especially with the technical help of Iran and cheap Chinese components. In late 2019 a major Saudi Aramco oil-processing plant at Abqaiq was put out of commission when Houthi drones hit multiple storage tanks, causing panic on world oil markets. The drones cost about $15,000 each to manufacture, and the Houthi were trained to use them by Iranian Revolutionary Guards.

The most striking recent example of military drone use comes from Ukraine, which in Soviet times was a hub of the arms industry and more importantly produces a lot of technically gifted graduates. After Russian-backed separatists went to war in 2014, hundreds of garage-based Ukrainian enthusiasts re-visited their hobby aircraft skills to manufacture drones. Many of the components came from China. These unmanned aerial vehicles are all over the skies of eastern Ukraine, mainly spotting

Russian-backed separatist troop movements, though they might also be equipped to drop munitions or for kamikaze runs against ammunition dumps and command posts. Their cameras record images on a memory card that is retrieved when the drone returns to base. Although there have been attempts to regulate drone use, notably by the EU, they are so useful as a weapon that it seems unlikely they will be subject to the same regulation as cluster munitions, chemical weapons or land mines.[50]

•

Late on Friday 3 January 2020, Major-General Qassem Soleimani flew from Damascus to Baghdad International Airport for a meeting with Iraq's Prime Minister, Adil Abdul-Mahdi. Anyone could have tracked his Cham Wings plane with the aid of online commercial flight trackers. Doubtless the Americans and Israelis had agents reporting his whereabouts, as well as the capability of tracking phones used by his entourage.

Soleimani's ostensible purpose in visiting Baghdad was to deliver Iran's response to a letter from the Saudis to the Iraqi premier, as part of joint ongoing efforts to de-escalate the crisis between the two powers. Equally, he could have been involved in orchestrating local Shia proxies to prise the US out of Iraq. Soleimani was accompanied by four senior Revolutionary Guard commanders. At the airport he met Abu Mahdi al-Muhandis and four aides from Kata'ib Hezbollah.

Born in southern Basra, Muhandis had gone to Iran to fight with the IRGC during the war with Iraq in the 1980s, where he had met Soleimani. His Iraqi militia was one of the Shia groups that comprised the 100,000-strong Popular Mobilization Units (PMUs). These units had fought ISIS after the regular Iraqi army ran away in 2014 and were in the throes of being integrated into Iraq's armed forces. Ironically, his ability to dispense state money meant that he was in a position to control the wilder Shia militias, which meant that his murder was bad news for the fragile stability of Iraq. It is likely that Muhandis had visions of a reverse takeover, just as Hezbollah seemed to be doing with the national army in Lebanon. His Kata'ib militia was certainly also active in Syria, where it had a headquarters at Albukamal, helping to establish Iranian logistic routes towards Hezbollah so as to menace Israel.[51]

Ten men boarded two SUVs that headed out of the airport, but they were all killed by three Hellfire missiles fired from a US MQ-9 Reaper drone noiselessly circling overhead. Soleimani was identified by the large garnet in a silver ring he habitually wore on his left hand. The justification for this strike related to a sudden sequence of events in Iraq, though the motives were deeper than that.

On 27 December 2019, Kata'ib fighters launched a rocket attack on the American K-1 Air Base near Baghdad, killing a single US contractor. The US responded with air strikes on a Kata'ib Hezbollah base that killed twenty-five fighters. This resulted in angry protests outside the entrance to the Green Zone in Baghdad, which includes the US embassy

At his Mar-a-Lago resort complex in Florida, Trump darkly imagined a re-run of the 2012 storming of the US consulate in Benghazi in Libya where the US ambassador, Chris Stevens, had died. Trump had used that scandal as a black mark against former Secretary of State Hillary Clinton in the US election campaign; this time he was also facing imminent impeachment proceedings. When presented with options to strike at Iran, which Trump held responsible for this grave development, he decided upon Soleimani, perhaps needing a target as high-profile as Osama bin Laden. Some of his military advisors were horrified; this was the most extreme option, customarily the one Presidents are supposed to reject. Not Trump. It helped that in April 2018, Trump had redesignated the entire IRGC as a terrorist organization. He had also been riled as Iran's leaders traded Twitter insults with him.

Soleimani was not a terrorist but rather a senior officer in the Iranian state apparatus. Such people are usually off-limits when it comes to killing unless in time of war, especially as the regime encouraged rumours that one day he might become President of Iran. Soleimani had many Shia admirers, but there were powerful people who had long hated him. Many British or US generals who served in Iraq after 2003 link him with the lethal IEDs that militias used to rip into armoured vehicles and kill their troops.

After Soleimani went on a long mission to Lebanon, he wrote to US generals on his return: 'I hope you have been enjoying the peace and quiet in Baghdad. I've been busy in Beirut.' He also texted General David Petraeus as a military equal.[52]

Soleimani's detractors have less to say about his subsequent role in combating ISIS, a greater existential challenge to Iranian Shia than to Western troops in Iraq. The Israelis dubbed him 'the teeth in the mouth of the Iranian snake', for Iran is the one regional power that Israel genuinely fears. It is a populous and proper country, with a strong scientific base, not one sketched on a map by British or French colonialists and ruled by corrupt autocrats.

Soleimani was born in 1953 into a poor farming family in mountainous Kerman, about five hundred miles from Tehran. He left school at thirteen, and after the 1979 Revolution worked briefly for a municipal water authority. His real vocation was as a soldier. He first rose to prominence as a young IRGC officer during Iran's long defensive war against Saddam Hussein between 1980 and 1988, in which a million people died. His war ended commanding the IRGC's elite 41st Combat Division.

After three years repressing drug-traffickers in his native Kerman, from 1997 Soleimani headed the Quds (Jerusalem) Force of the Revolutionary Guard. This expeditionary elite of political soldiers was (and is) active in Lebanon, in Syria and in Yemen. Iran also has sympathetic armed militias in Iraq, whose politics are febrile at the best of times. One of Soleimani's ancillary roles was to mediate between rival political factions.

Soleimani was a small, dapper man with iron-grey hair. Theatrically modest in style, he was not personally corrupt, as many IRGC officers and clerics certainly are, and he rarely raised his voice. In late 1998, he took charge after the Afghan Taliban murdered Shia Hazaras in Mazar-i-Sharif, including nine Iranian intelligence agents. He chose to boost a rival proxy force, the Northern Alliance, after 9/11, sharing Iranian intelligence on the Taliban with his shadowy US counterparts. Little of this figures in many Western accounts of Soleimani's life, and those writing about it in our media would also neglect Soleimani's crucial role in destroying ISIS.[53]

After a lifetime living in the shadows as a diplomat, soldier and spy, Soleimani's main role was in coordinating Iran's regional foreign proxy forces and in helping to smooth relations between Iraq's complex ethno-religious factions. There was a grand strategic vision: Syria would become the mid-point of a Shia crescent, enabling Iran to hit back at Israel via Hezbollah and Hamas, for Iran regards Israel as its most deadly foe in the region. However, the lure of celebrity was Soleimani's undoing. He had at least ten dedicated Instagram accounts filled with images of himself and was portrayed in a feature film made by one of Iran's top directors. He grew over-enamoured of PR opportunities and selfies as he popped up amidst the proxy forces he coordinated to keep Iran's enemies off-balance.

The fact that successive American Presidents had declined to kill him when they had the chance probably gave him a sense of inviolability. Equally, his Shia admirers referred to him as a 'living martyr' who could be killed at any moment. There are rumoured to have been several plots against his life, some organized by the Israelis.[54]

President Obama declined to kill Soleimani because of the overriding priority of securing a nuclear deal with Iran in 2015. Including any further issues would have been a non starter for a process which required much trust building. Clandestine talks with the Iranians commenced in a military officers' club on the Omani coast.[55]

Following the eruption of ISIS, Soleimani was first on the ground in Iraqi Kurdistan, where he organized ammunition and weapons that enabled the Kurdish peshmerga to hold off ISIS's assaults. His hastily organized PMUs also repulsed ISIS from Baghdad itself, whose defence he organized. This is rarely mentioned by Soleimani's Western critics, nor the ways in which Iran repelled ISIS from its own borders with Iraq.

However, the election of Donald Trump in November 2016 changed the calculus. Having come to power to satisfy a popular US desire to disengage from costly wars in the Middle East, Trump betrayed his own supporters by actions that re-engaged the US, notably on behalf of the corrupt and murderous Saudi regime. He abandoned the Obama-era attempt to regulate use of drones, delegating their use to military commanders who could strike without referring to the White House – without even attempting to counterfeit the appearance of legality.[56]

Iran was always going to be in his sights. What patient diplomacy had created, Trump tore down in a day. Trump withdrew the US from the nuclear deal and initiated a campaign of 'maximum pressure' on Iran, through stringent sanctions that reduced its oil exports to below two million barrels per day. Egged on by Israel, some of Trump's more hawkish advisors thought the clerical regime might collapse if only they could incite enough domestic popular unrest. This was not the first or last example of Western 'magical thinking' about the Middle East, where unintended consequences are ignored.[57]

Soleimani's week-long funeral in Iran occasioned mass shows of emotion and unity, as crowds waved his photograph and sought to touch his coffin. His admirers extended far beyond the fervent, perhaps an indication that as President he might have won over secular nationalists to the regime. The Supreme Leader Ayatollah Ali Khamenei wept at the loss of this most distinguished son of the Islamic Revolution, while Russian officers attended a parallel memorial service in Damascus for the man who had visited Moscow and brokered Putin's 2015 intervention on behalf of Assad.

Iran responded almost immediately, with ballistic missile strikes against US bases in Iraq. Iranians saw TV images of their fiery trails lighting up the night sky as they ascended. US soldiers suffered severe concussion but no fatalities. The Iranians were doubtless bucked up more when Iraq's Shia-dominated parliament passed a resolution ordering US forces to depart.[58]

Within hours of his death, Ayatollah Khamenei had appointed Soleimani's successor and boosted the Quds Force budget by $233 million. Major General Esmail Ghaani, Soleimani's deputy since 2007, is known as the 'Damascene General' because he has spent the last decade propping up Assad, with the aid of Shia fighters from Afghanistan, Iraq, Lebanon and even Pakistan. Before that he spent twelve years dealing with Afghanistan. But unlike Soleimani, Ghaani is not an Arabist, which makes a nonsense of US Secretary of State Mike Pompeo's claim that Americans in the region were much safer after Soleimani's demise.

It is significant that his own department immediately urged all Americans to vacate Iraq by land, sea or air and to stay away from their own embassy in Baghdad.[59]

On paper Iran's Artesh or armed forces are no match for the US, should either side take missteps resulting in war. True, they number 545,000 personnel, including 125,000 Revolutionary Guards, but the Americans could easily destroy Iran's aged air force and its larger surface ships within hours. Experts are unsure about multiple attacks by Iranian swift boats on Gulf shipping and oil installations. General Ghaani could also take Shia PMU pressure off ISIS remnants in eastern Syria, which Covid-19 is also enabling to regroup while the Western world is in turmoil.

Iran is a nation rich in engineers and scientists, and its cyber-warfare units could mount electronic attacks, most obviously on Saudi oil facilities. In 2012 they wiped all the data on the systems of oil giant Saudi Aramco and in 2018 they attacked a major petrochemical plant remotely. Iran has also used the computing power of poorly protected US private sector 'cloud' servers to mount attacks on US banks and the NY Stock Exchange. So far they have not managed to penetrate any vital US systems like the electricity grid, which could have life-threatening consequences for ordinary Americans.

As happened at the two oil installations Abqaiq and Khurais in 2019, far more damage can be done to the Saudi oil industry with conventional drone and cruise missile attacks which hit storage tanks dead centre. The attack was claimed by the Yemeni Houthi, who have been fighting a Saudi and UAE-led invasion, but there is little doubt who supplied the weapons that flew under the kingdom's US-supplied air defence systems.

Since Europe gets most of its oil not from the Gulf but from Russia, Kazakhstan and Norway, and while the US has its enormous domestic shale reserves, interference with maritime traffic through the Strait of Hormuz would be felt mainly in Asia. Still, it would impact on global prices, and in a fragile world economy could deepen the depression caused by Covid-19. Although many commentators are fixated on what Iran might do to disrupt global oil supplies, Iran itself depends on oil exports for most of its revenues. Given the domestic impact of draconian US sanctions, Iran's rulers cannot afford to further diminish the living standards of their own citizens.

Killing Soleimani was an act of war with Iran, though it has yet to be formally declared as such. In June 2020 the UN's Human Rights Council's special rapporteur officially declared that this was an arbitrary and illegal killing in a sovereign state (Iraq) based on no evidence that Soleimani was planning any imminent attacks. The act delivered little for Donald Trump and nothing for US strategy in a region that was already upset by Trump's transactional brand of international diplomacy. It served to dampen protests in Iraq or Lebanon against Iran's influence and may have hastened the exodus of US forces from Iraq, after they had already disengaged from Syria and Afghanistan. The fact that Iraq's new Prime Minister, Mustafa al-Kadhimi, had to win the approval of Hassan Nasrullah in Beirut may be more consequential than that the Saudis and US approve of him too.[60] Soleimani's death also consolidated enough support around the Iranian regime to enable it to weather socio-economic protests that had extended to the $100–200 million a year which Tehran showers on proxy forces like Hezbollah.

Rarely can such a high-profile assassination of a leading member of a foreign government have yielded so little for its perpetrators in terms of improving their strategic position. They will live with the consequences and the 'hard revenge' Iran will probably exact for years. The one thing that held Trump back from a full-blown war with Iran was that more cautious voices were asking about the endgame. Invading Iran would merely have repeated the war in Iraq on a grander scale.[61]

•

If 2020 began with the killing of an Iranian general, it ended with the murder of one of its most prominent scientists. On Friday 27 November 2020 the sixty-year-old Iranian scientific manager Mohsen Fakrizadeh set off to visit his in-laws in the bucolic town of Absard, about sixty kilometres east of Tehran. At a highway junction his convoy of non-armoured SUVs was halted by what Israeli sources claim was remotely controlled machine-gun fire from a small Nissan truck parked at the roadside. According to the *Jewish Chronicle* the Nissan truck was then blown up by a 'one tonne bomb' attached to the gun, which had been smuggled into Iran in pieces, damaging overhead powerlines. Much was made of failures by Iran's security services and the technological prowess of a Mossad team which may have had twenty members, many of them Iranians, though a one tonne bomb would surely have caused a massive explosion.

However, initial Iranian sources had reported a number of gunmen appearing from SUVs and on motorbikes who raked the halted cars with automatic fire. Fakrizadeh's bodyguards were wounded and the man himself fatally shot three times. He died in a helicopter taking him to hospital in Tehran, after rescuers discovered that at the nearest local hospital the power supply had conveniently gone down.

It was glaringly obvious that Israel's Mossad was responsible. Though officially Israel was silent about the subject, many journalists more or less licensed by Mossad to circumvent censorship have indicated as much.[62]

On paper Fakrizadeh was an academic (and long-standing IRGC member) at Tehran's Imam Hussein University. He doubled up as head of the Physics Research Centre and then SPND, the Ministry of Defence's Research and Innovation Organization. Some describe him as 'the father of the Iranian bomb', an Iranian Robert Oppenheimer, who was a kind of impresario-manager for the efforts of many other scientists and engineers. To call Fakrizadeh 'brigadier-general' is snide and misleading. After all, Oppenheimer was commissioned as a lieutenant-colonel and had the uniform designed, but we don't refer to him as one but as a physicist. Certainly, during 2020 Fakrizadeh's public profile increased as he was filmed standing near the Supreme Leader. In a break with convention, his body was photographed. After the loss of General Soleimani, Iran needs all the public heroes it can get. At his funeral he was shown wrapped in an Iranian flag and with his face exposed, both of which are un-Islamic. Proximity to the leadership may partly explain why both Soleimani and Fakrizadeh were killed.[63]

Fakrizadeh's cards were marked since a 2018 Mossad raid on a Tehran archive which yielded about 5,000 pages of sensitive documents (some of which have since been shown to have been 'doctored' by the Israelis). Posing on TV before a cabinet of box files, Israeli Prime Minister 'Bibi' Netanyahu openly remarked when announcing this coup de théâtre: 'Remember that name, Fakrizadeh.' This televised stunt was typical of a leader who throughout his career has realized that the Americans are addicted to television sensations, for they were his real audience.

Fakrizadeh joins a list of half a dozen Iranian scientists and engineers who have been shot or blown up by Mossad agents, starting with one who in 2007 dropped down dead in his laboratory after being poisoned.

Quite what Fakrizadeh did for a living is complex and the subject of rival disinformation efforts. According to all US intelligence agencies, Iran stopped its active nuclear weapons programme in 2003, after the US invaded Iraq and Tehran feared it might be next on an American list of so-called 'rogue regimes' which also included North Korea. Perhaps Iran had by then accumulated the scientific knowledge, and the multiple processes, with which they could in theory build nuclear warheads, though whether to 'break out' as an active nuclear power like India or Pakistan was and remains a decision which the Supreme Leader has demonstrably not taken. Iran claims that at the time, Fakrizadeh was using his organizational skills to help Iran develop a coronavirus vaccine, for the virus has had terrible consequences in Iran.

Leaving aside whether an Iranian bomb might actually create greater stability in the Middle East, as Ken Waltz has argued, the 2015 JCPOA six-power nuclear agreement introduced stringent 24/7 IAEA monitoring by fixed cameras and ad hoc inspections on all known nuclear installations (Iran has a single functioning reactor) so as to freeze Iranian nuclear research until 2031. Some claim that Fakrizadeh, who ran a programme called Amad, or 'Hope', continued to explore dual-use technologies which could be applied to miniaturizing a nuclear bomb on top of a ballistic missile and dealing with warhead re-entry problems. It was also the case that since the Trump administration pulled out of the JCPOA, and applied 'massive pressure' sanctions which have hurt ordinary Iranians, Iran has sought to increase its low-yield uranium stockpile (that is enriched to 4–5 per cent), and in 2020 resumed enrichment to 20 per cent, partly in response to Trump's multiple hostile provocations in the run up to the anniversary of Soleimani's murder. From there it is a short step to further enrichment to 90 per cent, which is bomb grade, though much else has to be perfected before a bomb can be attached to a ballistic missile warhead, of which Iran has many.[64]

That does not mean that the Iranians have resumed the quest to make nuclear bombs. Rather it shows that the nuclear issue is a politically sensitive one in Iran. Like other states Iran is fully entitled to civil nuclear energy, and unlike Israel, it is a signatory to international nuclear non-proliferation agreements. If the current pragmatic government did nothing to respond to US and Israeli aggression, hard-liners would soon have them out. A decision to acquire nuclear weapons requires authorization by the Supreme Leader, but he has his own religious scruples about these devices. Nor does it mean that having the technical capacity to make such bombs means that Iran will do so, not least because it would lead to speedy proliferation with among others Egypt, Saudi Arabia and Turkey following not far behind, and their command-and-control systems might well be worse than those of Iran or the rival nuclear powers India and Pakistan.

Iran's scientific capabilities are such that killing one man is unlikely to make much difference. He was comparable to Oppenheimer in this respect, since killing Oppenheimer during the war would not have made much difference. Plenty of others have Fakrizadeh's scientific skill set in a country which produces 150,000 science graduates a year. Like General Soleimani, Fakrizadeh may have been a 'key man' but neither were indispensable.

Instead, Fakrizadeh's murder (for that is what this was) was intended to signal that even those Iranians at the top of the tree are highly vulnerable to attack and that Iran's counter-intelligence services are not what they should be. Threatening 'the night is long and we are awake' (as the main IRGC candidate for president Hossein Dehghan warned) is all very well, but the assassins should have been stopped long before Fakrizadeh reached that road junction. Indeed it was ironic that the Iranian security services leapt on the remote high-tech aspect of the Mossad operation since it effectively absolved them of failing to prevent a ground-based and human assault.[65]

This murder follows on from the joint US–Israeli drone strike murder of General Soleimani outside Baghdad airport in January 2020, and the shooting of Al-Qaeda Numbr 2 Abu Mohammad al-Masri and his wife on a Tehran street in August. The latter had 'progressed' from long years of detention to house arrest before he was slain in what may have been a joint effort by Mossad and the CIA. As so-called heretics, Shiite Iranians have no love for Sunni terrorist organizations, but the regime is sufficiently cynical and realistic to know that everyone has their uses.

These later events coincided with the opening of the trial in Brussels of Iranian diplomat (and a Belgian-Iranian couple) Assadollah Assadi who had been filmed handing the latter a small TATP bomb and detonator in a Luxembourg Pizza Hut restaurant. They were allegedly to plant this device at a rally of the National Council of Resistance in Iran, the latest incarnation of the MEK – the Albania-based Marxist-Islamist terror organization. The rally was held in Villepinte near Paris on 30 June, probably with such foreign enthusiasts as John Bolton, Rudi Giuliani and British MP Theresa Villiers invited. The Belgian-Iranian couple are former MEK members who were allegedly recruited by Assadi – allegedly Iran's top intelligence officer in Europe – as far back as 2012. In February 2021 Assadi was jailed for twenty years for this plot.[66]

But if we need a more strategic view of the killing of Fakrizadeh then it was Israel's attempt to queer the pitch for the then incoming President Joe Biden's ability to return the US to the JCPOA which had been signed into international law under the Obama administration. Just to be clear, a US client state (Israel) carried out an illegal act in a state with which it is not at war (Iraq) in order to influence the future foreign policy of the incoming US administration, at the real risk of sparking a regional conflagration. The outgoing Trump administration may have colluded in this policy, which would certainly fit the future presidential ambitions of Secretary of State Mike Pompeo and even a returning Donald Trump in 2024.

So far President Biden has not indicated what (if any) conditions he intends to attach to this step, or whether he will alleviate sanctions on Iran, which Trump and Pompeo (a Christian Zionist) sought to pile on every week until Trump left office. Speaking of Trump, in November 2020 he sought Pentagon approval of air strikes on the enrichment facility at Natanz despite his administration claiming he did not want to trigger a war in the Middle East as he endeavoured to draw down troops from Afghanistan, Somalia and Syria before leaving the White House. The killing of the Al-Qaeda leader was probably the lesser option proposed by nervous generals fearful of triggering a wider Middle Eastern war.

Killing such a prominent Iranian scientist was also an unsubtle attempt by Netanyahu to wag the dog's tail, by helping Iran's hard-liners to return to power in presidential elections due in June 2021. It distracted from Netanyahu's own corruption trials and related attempts to intimidate judges, prosecutors and government witnesses with 'semi-Stalinist' tactics according to one (former Mossad) person involved.

Iran's hardliners argue that the US and Israel are hand in glove, not to mention with the Saudi murderer MbS with whom Pompeo and Netanyahu met on a two-hour flying visit to the burgeoning city of 'Neom' on the Red Sea just before the assassination. The man Netanyahu would like to succeed him, the head of Mossad Yossi Cohen, accompanied his Prime Minister. While the Saudis are unlikely to join the recently contrived Abraham Accord alliance between Israel and the Gulf monarchies, they already have covert dealings with Israel's intelligence agencies and its murky private technology companies who supply surveillance equipment to prepress dissidents at home and abroad. MbS wants to confront Biden with an enhanced alliance in which Israel will provide him with political cover.

As Netanyahu's former National Security Advisor, Cohen and the Prime Minister are very close. Indeed Cohen is one of two men who Netanyahu respects as possible successors after the 2010 PR disaster in Dubai when Mossad agents were caught on hotel CCTV in the process of killing the Hamas armourer Mahmoud al-Mabhouh – eleven of the team also had their iris prints taken going through the airport using their cloned foreign passports.[67] This was a black mark against Mossad chief Tamir Pardo, who between 2011 and 2016 undertook fewer such operations. His successor Cohen was more au fait with the new world of CCTV and digital technology. He prefers to use foreign nationals to kill Israel's enemies. In December 2016 a large team were involved in shooting the drone expert Mohamed Zaouri (forty-nine) in the Tunisian town of Sfax. The main assassins were a Bosnian and a Croat who were flown in at the last minute, and who did not know their support teams who provided them with silenced pistols. Their home governments have refused to extradite them to Tunisia.[68]

In the past, such assassinations involved deep deliberations by Israeli leaders who had some moral awareness. In his obsessional focus on Iran, Netanyahu has dispensed with any of what in any case does not conform with his crude commando view of things. The satirist Sacha Baron Cohen has turned such a macho viewpoint into a global joke with the gun-obsessed character of Colonel Erran Morad. Netanyahu did not consult his co-Prime Minister General Benny Gantz or General Aviv Kochavi, the chief of staff of the IDF, about either his 'not so secret' trip to Neom or helping the UAE acquire F-35 fighters from the US – potentially a security threat to Israel itself. Netanyahu regards most of the generals as treacherous 'Leftists' and cuts them out of the loop whenever he can. This is completely outrageous since it is their job to weigh up the profit and loss of each operation, including how the Iranians might react and how the wider world beyond the US will regard Israel.

Netanyahu's animus towards the Israeli generals runs deep. One distinguished former general Ehud Barak thwarted his re-election bid and others have challenged his hold on power over the years; among them are such former IDF Chiefs of Staff as Shaul Mofaz, Yitzhak Mordechai, and more recently Moshe 'Boogie' Yaalon, Gantz and the current Foreign Minister Gabi Ashkenazi, a former CGS too. The current IDF chief of staff

Kochavi is a former paratrooper who was a regimental protégé of Gantz's. Having grudgingly accepted a joint power sharing regime with Gantz, Netanyahu sought to destroy the former general and his failing Blue and White party before the general elections were held, thereby reneging on the deal whereby Gantz was to become Prime Minister in November 2021. Remaining Prime Minister will also assist Netanyahu in dodging several imminent corruption trials involving bribes from German submarine manufacturers as well as free suits and cigars. No wonder, given this background, that many generals and former Mossad spies attend the weekly anti-corruption demonstrations outside Netanyahu's Balfour Street residence shouting 'Enough', a slogan common to the protestors during the Arab Spring.

The Iranians have so far refused to fall into the trap which Trump and Netanyahu set for them which, at the time of writing, could well result in US strikes on Iran by a president showing signs of derangement. Hard-line Iranians called for missile strikes on Haifa, or attacks by such proxies as Hizbollah and Palestinian Islamic Jihad, with the Yemeni Houthi bombarding oil installations in Saudi Arabia. It is likely that Rouhani will bide his time until Biden and Secretary of State Antony Blinken decide whether rescinding sanctions is a price worth paying for America's return to the nuclear deal.

Meanwhile, the US has made no official response to the killing of Fakrizadeh. The EU and some Western foreign ministers have, notably Germany's Heiko Maas. The former CIA Director John Brennan called it a 'criminal act', which shows the depths of loathing of Netanyahu among Democrats, after he flagrantly broke with US bipartisan support for Israel by criticising Obama in public. Lesser powers tend to be cautious with Israel. A former UK Foreign Secretary reports that whenever he condemned similar lethal Israeli actions, which involved cloning the passports of UK nationals, British Likud supporters 'would be straight on the phone to Tony' to rein him in.

The Trump–Netanyahu attempt to thwart Biden's future relations with Iran – which are designed to impede acquisition of a bomb – may even strengthen Biden's attempts to restore Obama's legacy achievement. It will also shape how Biden responds to other controversial Israeli policies towards the Palestinians, who are not without friends among the Democrats. Above all, the assassination of Fakrizadeh further muddies Israel's international image, while bringing the risk that Iran or its proxies may turn their thoughts to prominent Israeli scientists. So on every level the assassination may have been another 'tactical' triumph for Netanyahu and Mossad, but a longer term strategic failure.[69]

.

Given increased Western reluctance to lose soldiers on distant battlefields, the future of armed conflict will be dominated by drones of one size or another. As was already evident in Afghanistan, the kill lists could be extended to include drug barons, on the grounds that their opium harvests indirectly helped fund the Taliban who taxed their profits. Ironically some of the traffickers had earlier worked for the CIA against the Taliban and Al-Qaeda. Why not kill Colombian or Mexican cartel bosses with drones too?

Several science-fiction books and films have shown us a world with robots running amok, or being programmed to enslave or kill our species. Robotically enhanced UniSols, or Universal Soldiers, have long been on our screens, and companies like Boston Dynamics have in the interim manufactured robots that can carry heavy loads or fire weapons. It is conceivable that soldiers will regard them like valued 'companions' as they currently regard their sniffer dogs. Other machines will soon do things that are risky for humans, like mine detection.[70]

But most level-headed studies of future warfare foresee a cooperative 'win-win' for man and machine mirroring what is likely to happen in peaceful industries. Even the most advanced AI systems will need humans to go the last mile where our infinitely more sophisticated consciousness kicks in, and algorithms cannot 'process' intractable moral problems. It will ultimately be humans who program armed robots to, for example, wound rather than kill enemy fighters, for they are not subject to the anger, fear or vengeful emotions that humans routinely show in warfare.[71]

Ethicists might like to revisit assassination in the age of drones. A friend who once served in a Western intelligence agency suggested hiring two Afghan lads to shoot a Taliban commander for a couple of thousand dollars. Their horrified bosses were appalled at this gross moral turpitude, indignantly rejecting assassination when the occasional politician suggested this solution. Instead the bosses opted for a 'targeted extrajudicial killing' and slew the Taliban commander with a drone and a $115,000 Hellfire missile. He was not the only victim.

The age of drones does not mean that political assassinations no longer occur. There have been several notorious recent cases, a mixture of killings by agents of states and those carried out by murderous outsiders in a climate of intensified political polarization. As long as anger is the defining characteristic of a resurgent populist politics, it is likely that some angry people will turn to symbolic violence, as has been the fate recently of some democratic politicians. Those who contribute to this climate bear a heavy responsibility for the mood they have created by word and deed.

11

The Phantom, Two Stooges and Murder in Istanbul: Assassination as a Contagious Disease

Some assassinations have become enduring mysteries that obsess people who might otherwise collect coins or stamps. The killing of Olof Palme in 1986 is still being investigated, thirty-six years after it occurred. A report by the Swedish Prosecutor Krister Petterson published in late 2020 threw little new light on that tragedy; as we shall see, Petterson's name is unfortunate.

On 26 October 1986, the Swedish Prime Minister Olof Palme and his wife Lisbet Beck-Friis went to Stockholm's Grand Cinema to see *The Mozart Brothers*, a silly Swedish comedy. Palme did not bother with bodyguards; Sweden is, after all, one of the most orderly societies in the world. There was also a certain class arrogance involved since he came from a well-heeled background and his wife was Swedish nobility. He looked rather impish and was ferocious in argument, though it was his psychologist wife who wore the trousers in their relationship.

Swedish politics had been dominated by the Social Democrats from 1932. Their durability rested on the successful blending of nationalism and communitarian socialism. Like his deputy Ingvar Carlsson, Palme served a long political apprenticeship under Tage Erlander. Palme was Prime Minister from 1969 to 1976 after his esteemed boss died of a heart attack. Following a six-year hiatus when the opposition was in charge, Palme's second term began in 1982.[1]

Palme was responsible for much of the socially controlling, high-tax and generous welfare system with which Sweden was associated, but his real passion was foreign policy. He was a big figure on the international scene, exchanging Sweden's dubiously profitable wartime neutrality for that of Nordic moral champion abroad. Though educated in the US he was a vociferous critic of the Vietnam War, and he took up several Third World causes popular with the Left. Many conservative Swedes hated him, and not just because of high levels of taxation.

After bidding farewell to their son Marten, Olof and Lisbet decided to walk the mile and a half to their home, first along Sveavägen, one of Stockholm's main streets. It was 11.20 p.m. and the streets were lightly covered with ice and snow. A tall man approached the couple from behind. He put one hand on Olof's shoulder and shot the fifty-nine-year-old Prime Minister in the back with the other. A second bullet grazed Lisbet. Although passers-by tried to aid Palme, the bullet had severed his spinal cord and punctured the aorta. He was rushed to hospital but died at midnight. The assassin disappeared into the night.[2]

This crime deeply shocked Swedes, though some rejoiced at Palme's death, and church attendance rose sharply. Since the chief of Stockholm County Police was out of town on a skiing trip, the initial investigation was comprehensively botched. A perimeter at the crime scene was too narrowly cast, and passers-by bearing memorial flowers trampled over it. No one thought to include passing motorists in the call for witnesses. Only two days after the shooting did a civilian find one of the bullets on the street, though no gun was ever found. It was presumed to have been a powerful .357 magnum, since the bullets were large and armour-piercing. No attempts were made to lock down roads, ports, railway stations or the airport.

The police assembled a composite image of the alleged killer, a Nordic-looking man with a long nose and thin lips who was christened 'The Phantom' in the Swedish press. But the investigation took another direction when the police chief, Hans Holmer, suspected the Kurdish terror group PKK, whose leaders Palme had recently placed under close restrictions. They are certainly extremely violent and deeply involved in drug-smuggling and other crimes. By March 1987, Holmer was forced to resign, after the press compared him to Peter Sellers's Inspector Clouseau in the *Pink Panther* movies.

By the summer of 1986, the testimony of another eyewitness led the police and press to move on from The Phantom to another suspect dubbed The Shadow. The quest proved equally fruitless, though for a time suspicion fell on a hapless thirty-three-year-old teacher called Viktor Gunnarson. Even heavy interrogation did not break Gunnarson's alibi; he had been to the Rigoletto Cinema to see *Rocky IV* and then for a burger.

A year later, the police thought they had found their man. Three acquaintances of one Christer Petterson thought he resembled the suspect and added that they thought him capable of murder. Witnesses confirmed seeing him loitering in the foyer of the cinema, while others claimed to have seen him burning his clothes on the balcony of his flat after the police mentioned gunshot residues on TV. Whether this chronically unfit man could bound up eighty-eight steps as part of his getaway struck some as doubtful.

Raised in a middle-class family, Petterson had descended with the aid of drugs into a life of crime. His criminal record fitted the bill, revealing dark depths under the placid surface.[3] In 1969 he served a short jail sentence for theft. In December 1970, when two men accidentally knocked over his Christmas shopping in a department store, Petterson went berserk and chased one of them into an alley, where he stabbed him to death with a bayonet. After spending only six months in a psychiatric clinic he was allowed to move in with his therapist; he duly beat her up and left. Petterson then took up 'rolling' petty drug-dealers – using an accomplice to set up deals and then robbing the dealers.

In 1973 Petterson got into a bar fight and hit his opponent on the head with an iron bar. In 1974–75 he committed two stabbings with his bayonet. In 1977, and fresh out of jail, he used an axe in a fight, stabbed another man with the bayonet and slashed someone else with a knife. That November he stabbed a drug-dealer who had tried to short-change him. Petterson was jailed for five years and released in early 1983, having stretched Swedish tolerance to its limits. Though described as 'a dangerous psychopath', he had never used a gun in the course of committing a crime, even if it would have been easy to acquire one.[4]

After he emerged from prison, he would visit state liquor stores and order a large bottle of Absolut vodka. After a pause he would ask for an expensive bottle of wine. When the assistant went to fetch it, Petterson would dash out of the store with the vodka, earning the nickname 'The Dasher'. Soon he spent his days in parks on the benches with winos. After being put under surveillance, Petterson was detained on 14 December 1988 and Lisbet Palme identified him as the killer after watching a video line-up. Her testimony as a cool and collected witness was undone when others testified that she had been hysterical at the scene of the crime. However, following a seven-week trial, Petterson was convicted of murder and jailed for life.

In the event, Petterson did not remain in jail for long. It transpired that the police had pre-identified him in the line-up by saying that he was an alcoholic. That is why Lisbet Palme said: 'Number eight matches my description, you can see who is the alcoholic.' Petterson was released, richer by £38,000 in compensation, some of which he immediately spent on alcohol. A mix of Bailey's Irish Cream and vodka became known in bars as 'The Killer', his favourite tipple. Lisbet Palme was so furious at the acquittal that she attacked a press photographer outside her home.

Over the last thirty years, 130 crackpots have confessed to slaying Palme. The case has generated huge quantities of files, including transcripts of 10,000 police interviews. While police interest waxed and waned, a large number of amateur sleuths have developed wild conspiracy theories, some of which alighted upon the unhappy Lisbet herself.

More seriously, some critics of the police revisited claims that this was a political killing, linked to Palme's criticism of South African apartheid and his support for Nelson Mandela. The South African regime routinely murdered people at home and abroad, and their secret police struck at exiled or foreign supporters of the ANC through 'Operation Long Reach'.

In 1991 Adrian Guelke was a forty-four-year-old scholar of

apartheid who had moved to Queen's University Belfast to teach comparative politics. Masked gunmen shot him in his bed at 4 a.m. as he slept next to his wife Brigid, though left when their gun jammed after one shot. Guelke had police bodyguards in hospital – this was unlikely to be the last attempt.

Prior to the hit, Leon Flores, an agent of South African military intelligence in London, had flown to Belfast with doctored 'evidence' that substituted Guelke's name for that of another academic who was allegedly the pivotal contact between the ANC and Sinn Féin. Flores passed this 'evidence' to loyalist paramilitaries and identified where Guelke lived in South Belfast. In fact, Guelke had no connections with Republican political groups of any kind and was critical of their violence.[5]

Something resembling this plot could conceivably have happened in the murder of Olof Palme. The crime writer Stieg Larsson was obsessed with the case and thought that South African secret agents may have contracted Palme's assassination to one of the far-right groups that abound in Sweden. He came to believe that a former mercenary called Bertil Wedin had worked for the South Africans and may have pulled the trigger, something Wedin denied. Equally, suspicion subsequently fell on Stig Engstrom, who worked at the offices of Skandia, Sweden's largest insurance company. He was politically conservative, with military training, and had left the Skandia building two minutes before Palme was shot, though nothing else connected him to the murder. He committed suicide in 2000.

Although Petterson was retroactively acquitted, plenty of policemen and prosecutors thought he was guilty. His life was so rackety that he could not resist selling interviews to eager journalists. Moreover, many of his criminal associates saw a chance to make money by either fingering him for the crime or revealing what he had told them in prison. His best friend inside was Lars Tingstrom, who had used explosive devices to kill various people, and revealed a 'plot' to kill the King of Sweden and then Palme. Television producers tricked Petterson into appearing on a live TV show. Having been bribed by the producers to sign a confession, he simply replied 'Fuck off' when asked to endorse it on air. Given his daily intake of moonshine vodka, Petterson's end was inevitable. In 2004 he got into an altercation on a park bench; the police dislocated his arm in a brawl and he died in hospital of an intercranial haemorrhage.[6]

•

The Democratic Republic of North Korea is one of the most totalitarian societies on earth. It has been ruled by three generations of the Kim dynasty, who claim mystical heavenly origins.

The first dictator, Kim Sung-il, was a tough Stalinist who fought the Japanese before being imposed on North Korea by the Soviets. His heir, Kim Jong-il, was a more madcap character, whose habits included kidnapping famous exiled actors to star in lavish movies. The current incumbent is Kim Jong-un, who after his succession in 2011 killed several senior people to secure his grip on power, including his own uncle.[7]

Reluctantly propped up economically by China, Kim has been deft in exploiting his 'friendship' with President Trump to ensure the survival of his nuclear-armed state.[8] Since he came to power, North Korean agents have assassinated five exiled dissidents using poisons delivered with a syringe or on the blade of a knife.[9] In the past, North Korea used to send its hit men to commit political murder in the South; nowadays they have 'thousands' of agents embedded there, some of whom can be activated to murder defectors and critics.[10]

The old generals who run North Korea intend to remain in the saddle, and any challenge against Kim Jong-un is likely to involve a member of his family. Though Kim's sister Kim Yo-jong is capable, usurpation would most likely involve a male relative. Kim has two older brothers. His full sibling Kim Jong-chul was passed over, since his father regarded him as being 'like a little girl'. He lives quietly in Pyongyang and plays guitar in a rock band.

Kim's louche older half-brother Kim Jong-nam was the son of Kim Jong-il's favourite mistress. As a youth he was detained while travelling to Japan on a false Chinese passport in order to visit Disneyland, and his furious father exiled him permanently.

Kim Jong-nam became a fixture in the casinos of Asia, which may be where he met a mysterious Korean-American who was probably working for the CIA. Money changed hands and Kim Jong-nam handed over a laptop containing encrypted files, which the other man downloaded. Cash in hand, Kim Jong-nam flew to Kuala Lumpur, without a care in the world.

On 13 February 2017, airport CCTV showed Kim Jong-nam in faded blue jeans, a blue T-shirt and grey jacket. He was carrying a black rucksack filled with $145,000, a laptop whose memory had been wiped and phials of antidote for nerve agents. He would never get the chance to use them. As he scanned the departure signs for his flight home to Macau via Singapore, two young women rushed up to him and smeared on his face what they believed to be baby oil with their hands. Within minutes, Kim felt unwell, though not so bad that he couldn't point towards the two culprits, who were detained. Security guards took him to the airport medical centre where a photo shows him sprawled in an armchair, sweating profusely, with his belly sticking out of his shirt and one arm outstretched. 'Very painful, I was sprayed liquid,' he groaned in English. Within twenty minutes, he was dead.[11]

The 'assassins' were an improbable pair. Months before, North Korean agents had combed Kuala Lumpur in search of pretty foreign prostitutes. They alighted upon Siti Aisyah, a twenty-five-year-old Indonesian single mother, and twenty-seven-year-old Duong Thi Houng, who was from Vietnam. Siti had worked since 2016 in the Flamingo Hotel spa as a masseuse, with a second job as a call-girl in the Beach Club bar. On 5 January 2017 she was recruited by a Malaysian taxi driver called 'John' to take part in a prank, which would be posted on YouTube. 'John' introduced Siti to 'James', who claimed to be Japanese but was a North Korean agent. Meanwhile, Houng had worked as a prostitute in Hanoi since late 2016. She was also tantalized by fame, and had had a brief experience of it on *Vietnam Idol*. These two young women never met until the day of the attack on Kim.

The women were offered $100 each to ambush hapless victims in public transport venues. James accompanied Siti to Phnom Penh, where she carried out the prank three times. She was next flown to Macau, but then suddenly told to fly to Kuala Lumpur. She celebrated her twenty-fifth birthday in the Hard

Rock Café, before the women were each told the next job was at Kuala Lumpur international airport. They were warned that the 'client' might be grumpy at being ambushed since he was the firm's boss. Kim died after he was taken from the medical centre, where one of four North Korean agents was filmed loitering outside. They were to smear the oil in his eyes, from the fattier and tougher lower parts of their palms. Then they must wash it off rapidly.

When the Malaysian police raided the hotel spa where Siti worked the following evening, she thought it was just another practical joke. Huong was arrested the following day at KL Airport after she went in search of her promised $100 fee. Both women became distressed when they were shown newspapers reporting the death of Kim Jong-nam from their prank; meanwhile, experts in protective suits cordoned off large parts of KL Airport.

'James' and his three North Korean accomplices took refuge in the North Korean embassy in Kuala Lumpur. After Pyongyang detained several Malaysians on trumped-up charges, the four North Korean agents were quietly flown home, while Siti and Huong faced lesser charges. After protests from Indonesia and Vietnam about the two women being charged at all while the real perpetrators were allowed to depart, both women were released, though Huong spent two years in prison and pleaded guilty to causing hurt with a dangerous weapon. Dressed to the nines for the last day in court, their tears were replaced by smiles of joy, as they enjoyed their moment in the limelight. They now live under police protection in their respective homelands, lest James and his sinister friends decide to target the main eyewitnesses to North Korea's crimes. Incredibly, the Malaysians repatriated Kim Jong-nam's body to North Korea, whose young ruler now knows that he can assassinate people and get away with it. The habit of murdering critics would prove contagious.[12]

•

Until the rise of a new Saudi crown prince, the Saudi autocracy would not have bothered to murder a difficult journalist, let alone one living in a foreign country with US residency. It is only because they botched the job that we know a great deal about what happened and who was responsible.

The Saudi journalist Jamal Khashoggi walked along lines that could be blurred, and there were real dangers lurking on either side. Like many journalists, he pushed the boundaries of what he could get away with publishing, which could result in more than a slap on the wrist from his editor or proprietor. His life was entangled too, with the rich men who ruled Saudi Arabia.

Khashoggi's family were comfortable businessmen in Medina, but with connections to people such as Adnan Khashoggi, the billionaire international arms dealer. Jamal Khashoggi weaved his way among this elite throughout his life without being an insider, but he also subscribed to Western notions of journalistic integrity.

The young Jamal developed an early enthusiasm for the Muslim Brotherhood and politically organized religious fundamentalism. While visiting Jeddah, he became acquainted with the young Osama bin Laden, a slightly older but much richer adopter of a rigorous form of Islam. But in the interim, he spent five years studying business management in Indiana, before returning home to work in a bookshop. From there he got his first breaks in journalism, which became his life's passion.

He ventured off in 1988 to report on his first war, visiting the international mujahedeen in Afghanistan who were battling the Soviets. The West backed and armed a much broader spectrum of Afghans to fight the Soviets and then the militant Islamist Taliban. Khashoggi re-encountered bin Laden, who was acting as patron-in-chief to some of these groups whose ranks were bolstered with Chechens and Central Asians as they gradually metamorphosed into Al-Qaeda. Bin Laden was graduating from a role that was still just about acceptable in Riyadh to one that would lead the Saudis to declare him stateless. In 1992 he relocated with his four wives and seventeen children to Khartoum in Sudan. Khashoggi flew to visit him, but this time as an unofficial emissary sent to try to persuade bin Laden to change his errant ways.

Khashoggi established himself as a leading commentator on Arab affairs, but also acted as a communications specialist for whichever Saudi royals he could latch onto. Although he was sacked from the Saudi newspaper *Al-Watan* for crossing unwritten boundaries, he was hired by the former head of the kingdom's General Intelligence Directorate, Prince Turki al-Faisal, as a PR man when he became ambassador to London in 2003 and he duly followed the Prince to Washington DC two years later. Turki found himself constantly undermined by his predecessor Prince Bandar bin Sultan and did not last long; by then Khashoggi was married with four children, though in 2010 he was fired a second time by *Al-Watan*.

The 2011 Arab Spring uprisings meant that Khashoggi's sympathy with the Muslim Brotherhood conflicted with his loyalty to Saudi princely patrons. He could get away with this ambivalent stance so long as older royals were in charge; their 'desert wisdom' was supple and they moved cautiously, even in repression. That was not the case with the millennial thruster who was en route to becoming the most powerful man in Saudi Arabia.

This was Prince Mohammed bin Salman bin Abdulaziz Al Saud, colloquially known as MbS. He was the sixth son of King Salman, who as the twenty-fifth son of the kingdom's founder succeeded Abdullah in 2015. A lot of other men had to die before Salman succeeded; they did so since their lifestyle was unhealthy, despite their privilege. That gave MbS ideas too – the boy who wanted to be like Alexander the Great never relinquished his ambition. It did not help that he was a bearded provincial or that he enjoyed video games like *Call of Duty*. The intellectually snobbish Khashoggi called him 'a PlayStation king, a WhatsApp ruler'.

A recent biography of MbS has little to say about his childhood, save that he was a spoiled brat and indulged by his father. His mother was of lower status than Salman's first wife, but the traditionalist Salman doted on his son, believing that he was more authentically Saudi because he lacked social graces and Western polish. This happily chimed with the ascendant world leaders who drew support from the honestly ignorant masses in their struggle against 'globalizing elites'.[13] Outsiders were not convinced; a deliberately leaked German intelligence report warned that MbS was impulsive and reckless. They were right.

Once his father became King following the death of Abdullah from lung cancer in 2015, MbS encouraged him to change the line of succession. Salman's mental focus was intermittent, and he obliged his dynamic son, who took to dictating his talking points on an Apple iPad. Two of Abdullah's sons, Turki and Mishaal, were replaced as Governors of Riyadh and Mecca, and Salman replaced his own brother Muqrin as Crown Prince with his fifty-five-year-old nephew Prince Mohammed bin Nayef. The CIA rated Nayef highly as a strong and reliable partner in counter-terrorism, but he had a less illustrious matrilineal pedigree, which made him vulnerable whenever MbS decided to move against him.

The twenty-nine-year-old MbS was appointed deputy Crown Prince but also Defence and Economy Minister, as well as head of Saudi Aramco's oversight board. However, this family settlement proved temporary: in 2017 Mohammed bin Nayef – who allegedly had an opioid problem – was bundled out and replaced by his cousin. Nayef was held at his palace in Jeddah, where he remains today, having been stripped of his fortune, and MbS was made Crown Prince. His grip on the kingdom was further evident when in April 2017 he secured the appointment of his younger brother Khalid as ambassador to the US at the age of twenty-nine.

MbS had also acquired an older mentor in Prince Mohammed bin Zayad (MbZ) of Abu Dhabi. Together they launched a war against the insurgent Yemeni Houthi, who they regarded as puppets of Iran. Their forces committed serial war crimes, as 'smart' US and UK bombs were dropped on factories and meeting halls as well as school buses.

Thuggishness was also evident in Saudi 'diplomacy'. In late 2017 the Lebanese Prime Minister, Saad Hariri, son of the assassinated Rafik, was badly roughed up on a visit to Riyadh, during which he resigned live on television. The Saudis wanted him out and his older brother Baha in, to engineer the reduction of Hezbollah (and hence Iranian) influence in Beirut. An outraged President Macron of France secured Hariri's return home. A few months earlier, MbS and MbZ combined to quarantine Qatar, thereby destroying the cohesion of the Gulf Cooperation Council.

Qatar is rich in natural gas, and its Wahhabi emirs combined zero tolerance of domestic dissent with generous hosting for exiled Egyptian and Palestinian members of the Muslim Brotherhood. Worse, the Qatari satellite channel al-Jazeera broadcast throughout the Arab world, with its Arabic version being more politically controversial than the English-language one that most Westerners see. The rulers of Abu Dhabi and Dubai were also horrified when Qatar won the right to stage the 2022 FIFA World Cup, for they viewed Doha as a rival centre of air traffic, shopping and tourism.

All trade and air traffic with Qatar was halted, though a rumoured Saudi invasion was checked when the Turkish President Erdoğan pointedly reinforced a garrison there. Though MbS and MbZ hit Qatar with a thirteen-point ultimatum designed to be as insulting as the one Austria-Hungary delivered to Serbia in 1914, the Qataris resisted their bullying neighbours, and were helped to do so by Iran, Oman and Turkey.

Khashoggi's ability to manoeuvre in this polarized regional climate was severely curtailed, though he enjoyed an official pension and wanted rich princes to subsidize his various TV ventures. MbS did not tolerate 'advice', let alone constructive criticism. Worse, he had an entourage of advisors, of whom the most sinister was his communications chief Saud al-Qahtani, who ran internet surveillance and had a mini-army of vicious online trolls among his 1.3 million Twitter followers. Qahtani's forte was issuing sinister threats and blackmail, and from there it was a short jump to abducting people, who found themselves incarcerated in disused royal palaces where electrocution and threats of rape were common. Reports of these practices found their way to the CIA.[14]

Qahtani hated Khashoggi and resolved to destroy him. He was banned from using social media and then prevented from publishing his journalism, but not before he'd used his last *Al-Hayat* newspaper column – it is published in Arabic in London – to criticize the corporate nature of MbS's Saudi Vision 2030. In late summer 2017 he decided to leave for Virginia, where he had bought a modest apartment when he was earning a diplomatic salary. Unfortunately, the Saudi government does not regard going into exile as the end of the matter, especially as Khashoggi alighted upon a really influential platform.

Khashoggi had enough contacts to help him get freelance work as a journalist with the *Washington Post*, which had recently been acquired by the Amazon boss Jeff Bezos. The paper grew in importance with Trump in the White House since it opposed his bullying and corrupt regime with a passion that the proprietor shared.

That corruption extended to Saudi Arabia, since Trump effectively delegated his entire Middle East policy to his ambitious son-in-law Jared Kushner. As another spoiled millennial, Kushner quickly established a rapport with MbS. Though he lacked diplomatic experience, Kushner imagined he would resolve the problems of the Middle East, starting with the Israeli-Palestinian conflict that had existed for half a century. It helped that MbS cared little about the Palestinians, though his father had more conventional views.

By then, Riyadh had worked out what really animated Trump and Kushner: money. Both men were inordinately impressed by Saudi wealth. Trump had bought his first yacht from Adnan Khashoggi and sold it to Prince Alaweed bin Talal. Riyadh was the world's fifth biggest purchaser of arms. The Saudis also bought luxury apartments in Manhattan's Trump Tower and spent lavishly at Trump's hotels, including the latest addition in the US capital.

The British have their own Camel Corps of former diplomats, spies and generals who always had an eye for an opportunity in the Gulf, provided a hefty fee and first-class travel were involved. Fawning sycophancy was much in evidence when the Saudis came to town. When MbS visited the UK, hoardings welcomed his arrival in London, with black taxis bearing photos of his smiling face. The conservative press obliged with supportive copy heralding this new reformer, in return for lucrative full-page adverts.

The Saudis were good at nodding enthusiastically when arms contracts were outlined, though their follow-through was invariably more modest. They also excelled at spreading large sums of money around DC, lobbying shops to ensure favourable coverage, though after 9/11 most ordinary Americans deplored these 'allies'. Fifteen of the suicide hijackers were Saudis and Americans suspected Saudi connivance through so-called 'religious diplomats' in the US. Although the Obama administration tried to stop a new bill enabling American families of the victims of these attacks to sue the Saudi government, Congress got its way.

MbS was also clever enough to couple the prospect of generational change and limited reform with enhanced domestic repression. The grim swordsmen went into overdrive in Riyadh's notorious 'Chop Chop Square', especially in the case of persecuted Shiites in the kingdom's oil-rich Eastern Province. He also single-handedly revised the history of Saudi Arabia by claiming that all extremism was an Iranian import from after 1979, which rather ignored the bloody history of Wahhabism since the eighteenth century and the Sauds' enthusiastic sponsorship of armed Islamist militancy.

MbS was right to seek to diversify a hydrocarbon-reliant economy that employed more foreign technicians than native Saudis. He curbed the intrusion of the religious police, and hoped to boost entertainment and sports. Young Saudis could go to cinemas and pop concerts. A vast high-tech resort city called Neom would appear on the Red Sea, at a projected cost of $500 billion. All of this 'reform', which never included political liberalization, was to be financed by selling 5 per cent of the giant state oil concern Saudi Aramco, assuming a market valuation of around $2 trillion.

MbS had also learned from Presidents Vladimir Putin and Xi Jinping that anti-corruption campaigns could be used both to purge high-level rivals and to coerce the too-rich-to-fall oligarchy. Putin had done that with the likes of Berezovsky and Ukos oil company billionaire Mikhail Khodorkovsy, the one dead and the other jailed in a remote prison camp, while Xi removed hundreds of thousands of corrupt generals and Party functionaries. MbS mounted his own 'sheikh down'.

MbS and Qahtani converted the glitzy ballroom of the Ritz Carlton Hotel in Riyadh into a plush prison. Among the 350 men held there were Prince Miteb bin Abdullah, the head of the National Guard; his brother Prince Turki, the former Governor of Riyadh; and Major General Ali al-Qahtani, Turki's military aide. The National Guard is the most powerful security force in Saudi Arabia, so neutralizing its commanders was important to MbS's onward ascent.

Languishing on mattresses behind locked doors, these rich men were threatened and strong-armed into relinquishing $106 billion of allegedly corruptly acquired assets. In General Qahtani's case, the strong-arming went too far and this fit fifty-five-year-old died of abuse. In May 2016 he had joined other top Saudis at a meeting in Georgetown with former CIA and State Department officials to express their disquiet about MbS. Older captives who refused to sign over their assets were so pressured that they ended up in prison hospitals after suffering heart trouble and the like. If their children went abroad, they had to leave their own offspring behind as a guarantee of good behaviour. Ordinary Saudis rejoiced as the arrogant and rich experienced the arbitrariness to which they were exposed themselves.[15]

MbS did not soil his own hands. That was left to Saud al-Qahtani and his henchman Brigadier General Maher Abdulaziz Mutreb, who headed a new security detail called the Rapid Intervention Force. A visiting Canadian businessman in Riyadh recalled Qahtani 'boasting to me that they slapped and hung some detainees upside down'. Wives and daughters were intimidated to put pressure on their menfolk. Whether they lived in Saudi Arabia or abroad, they were seriously frightened and sensed that Saudi agents were lurking never far away. One young Saudi, Ghanem al-Dosari, was beaten up by three Saudi agents outside Harrods in London early one evening.[16] Khashoggi's rich patron Prince Alaweed bin Talal, who emerged from detention claiming that he had been treated well, looked tired and distressed when he announced this on television.[17]

It was against this ominous background that the sixty-year-old Jamal Khashoggi fell in love with Hatice Cenghiz, a thirty-six-year-old Turkish academic he had met at a conference in Istanbul.[18] There was one impediment to their relationship:

in order to marry Hatice, Khashoggi had to get confirmation that he was no longer married to anyone else. Cenghiz's father was worried about casual Saudi polygamy, and he was right to be suspicious – and not only about Khashoggi's wife back in the kingdom who he had never divorced.

Before Khashoggi's relationship with Cenghiz, on 2 June 2018 he had married a fifty-year-old Egyptian air stewardess in Virginia. Their wedding was never officially registered. She had been a faithful companion during the darkest times in Khashoggi's life, but given her profession, an episodic one. He repaid her by divorcing her a few weeks after the marriage, having decided that his future lay with Cenghiz.

This was why Khashoggi needed an official document from the Saudis to confirm his single status. When in Washington he took the elementary precaution of texting a friend 'in' or 'out' when he visited the Saudi embassy, but in Istanbul he was less cautious.

On 28 September 2018 he ventured into the Saudi consulate. After an initial surprise, the staff recognized him as a famous fellow countryman, but were not sure how he was regarded by their bosses in Riyadh. To that end, even while a relieved Khashoggi flew off for a long weekend in London, an intelligence officer in the consulate telephoned Riyadh. Unfortunately for him, Turkey's MIT intelligence service had bugged the consulate and its phones.

More urgent calls ensued that Friday. They were from the Saudi intelligence officer in Istanbul and forty-seven-year-old Brigadier Mutreb, Qahtani's pitbull. Between 2002 and 2007, Mutreb had served as Deputy Chief of Intelligence in Saudi Arabia's embassy in London. He had often joined Khashoggi at Friday prayers and tea in Mayfair. After returning to Riyadh he went on various training programmes run by US private security firms. Another key team member was Thaar Ghaleb Alharbi, a lieutenant in the royal guard, who in October 2017 shot dead Mansour al-Amri as he tried to storm MbS's Al-Salam Palace in Jeddah.[19]

The officer in Istanbul offered video footage of Khashoggi entering and leaving, and vouchsafed when Khashoggi would return to collect his documentation. Mutreb spoke darkly of 'chopping off heads'. More calls followed, between Riyadh and the Istanbul Consul General, Mohammed al-Otaibi.[20]

They urgently requested that an intelligence officer be despatched to Riyadh to be briefed about an urgent assignment from the head of Saudi state security. That man flew to Riyadh for four days, for the 'top secret' assignment that was being developed 'rapidly'. He was followed later by four other security men who, having amateurishly debugged the consulate, arrived to explain its internal layout.

While Khashoggi socialized with old friends in London and gave talks about what an Israeli-Palestinian peace plan cooked up by Kushner and MbS might look like, three members of a Rapid Intervention Group advance team flew into Istanbul. They booked three suites and seven rooms at the Movenpick hotel, insisting on sea views. Clearly they were expecting company.

On 2 October, Khashoggi's flight from Heathrow landed in Istanbul at around 4 a.m. He was eager to see Hatice, but had no idea that a Gulf Stream jet – chartered from Sky Prime Aviation, which the Saudi regime often used – had landed at the same airport from Riyadh at 3.13 a.m.[21]

The passengers were a squad of Rapid Intervention men led by Brigadier Mutreb. In total fifteen Saudis came to Turkey, the majority with army and intelligence backgrounds. They were dubbed 'the tiger team'. While most of this squad were tough guys, there was also a forty-seven-year-old military doctor, Colonel Salah Mohammed al-Tubaigy, a professional forensic pathologist. There can be no doubt why he was present.

At 1.14 p.m. on 2 October 2018, Khashoggi and Hatice went to the visa section of the Saudi consulate. She waited outside holding his mobile phone, for it was common knowledge that the Saudis had acquired spyware from the Israeli company NSO that could reveal its contents and turn the speaker and camera on, without the owner being aware. Other Israeli equipment could derange dissident websites with multiple remote attacks whose sources could not be identified.[22]

Khashoggi went inside and immediately was surrounded by ten men. As would later be revealed by bugs, the leader Mutreb announced that Khashoggi was being taken back to Saudi Arabia under an Interpol warrant, which Khashoggi knew did not exist. 'I am being kidnapped,' he cried against a background noise of scuffling. Mutreb enquired about Khashoggi's phone that was outside with Hatice. He was handed another one and told to text his son in Saudi Arabia something to the effect of 'I'm in Istanbul, don't worry if you don't hear from me.' He refused. At 1.33 things turned violent. The men jumped on Khashoggi and tried to inject him with a sedative while tasering him, before using a plastic bag to suffocate him. Khashoggi's final words were, 'I have asthma. Do not do it, you will suffocate me.'[23]

By 1.39 Khashoggi's dead body was stripped naked and laid out on plastic sheeting. Dr al-Tubaigy went to work with an electric saw, observing that he normally listened to music while he worked. Khashoggi was cut into multiple pieces. From the walls, portraits of Ibn Saud, King Salman and Crown Prince Mohammed gazed down impassively on this blood bath.

Mutreb made calls to Riyadh to announce that 'The thing is done.' He was probably bringing Qahtani up to speed. National Security Agency computers probably logged these calls, but would only explore the content if certain words or phrases were mentioned. Indeed, in 2017 MbS had triggered such American analysis of a call in which he used the trigger word 'bullet' in connection with Jamal Khashoggi. Like 'big wedding', a favoured terrorist code for a spectacular attack, 'bullets' were among the trigger words. The Americans also established that before and after Khashoggi was killed, MbS and Qahtani – who was in direct contact with Mutreb – exchanged a flurry of fifteen or so text messages, though their content was opaque to whoever logged this traffic.

At 3 p.m., various black vehicles left the consulate. One of them contained RIGF men bearing black plastic rubbish sacks and a large suitcase on wheels. They disappeared into the consul's residence, a mere 500 metres away.

Shortly before that, a Khashoggi lookalike left the consulate's back door, wearing his clothes and making sure the CCTV cameras noted him. This was Brigadier Mustafa al-Madani, who was wearing a beard that he had not had when he arrived that morning. Khashoggi's glasses were perched on his nose. One major error was that he was wearing his own trainers and not Khashoggi's shiny black shoes, since the size was wrong. He was also not wearing Khashoggi's big Apple Watch. He and a companion went to the Blue Mosque where Madani switched clothes in a cafe, dumping a bag with Khashoggi's into a skip and removing the beard. Among the items removed from the consulate was the server onto which external CCTV footage was recorded, though they missed the gatehouse cameras that caught their comings and goings.

The killers then headed to the airport for their flights back to Riyadh on a private jet which had arrived from there at 3.11 p.m. Meanwhile, Hatice Cenghiz was desperate about why Khashoggi had never re-emerged from the consulate. Having ventured in and told that everybody had left for the day, Hatice made urgent phone calls to friends and acquaintances, including to Yasin Aktay, an advisor to President Erdoğan. Aktay phoned the Saudi ambassador to Ankara. The next call he made was to Hakan Fidan, the capable chief of Turkey's MIT intelligence service. Soon President Erdoğan, who had met Khashoggi, became aware that something grave had happened in Istanbul.[24] The Turkish government later interviewed the ambassador, Waleed A. Elkhereiji, about Khashoggi's disappearance in the consulate. He claimed to know nothing and the Turks did not include him (later deputy Saudi Foreign Minister) in the list of twenty people they suspected of being involved in the murder.

The first Saudi jet took off at 6.30 p.m. The airport security officers who X-rayed the luggage did not wonder why it contained multiple phones, taser devices, walkie talkies and various cutting tools including a scalpel. In the event these killers flew to Cairo, lingered there for twenty-four hours and then flew to Saudi Arabia. Another jet carrying Dr al-Tubaigy departed at 10.45 p.m. By that time, the Turkish authorities were sufficiently exercised to have it held in a holding pattern over eastern Anatolia, but then it flew to the UAE and on to Riyadh. The last two members of the murder squad, the body double Madani and his companion, left on a regular Turkish Airlines flight to Saudi Arabia.

Although only two members of this assassination team had diplomatic passports, the Turkish authorities were cautious about what was legally sovereign Saudi territory. The Turks and Sauds have had a fraught relationship ever since the Ottomans were the regional imperial power and thought nothing of beheading some of the al-Sauds' tribal predecessors. Erdoğan's sympathy for the Muslim Brotherhood set them at loggerheads after the Arab risings of 2011 and when Erdogan helped thwart the isolation of Qatar. But as a pious Muslim, he was mindful that the Saudi Kings are custodians of Mecca and Medina and he respected King Salman. Relations with MbS were very cool, however; Erdoğan had little time for him and smelled his ambition. It should be stressed that his own treatment of the media is disgraceful. Furthermore, many other foreigners have been assassinated there without so much fuss being made.[25]

An army of reporters gathered at the scene of Khashoggi's disappearance. Al-Otaibi, the Saudi consul, brazenly invited in the TV cameras and went about opening cupboards and doors to prove Khashoggi was not inside. Hesitation by the Turks enabled the Saudis to send their own team of 'judicial investigators' to inspect the scene. They were followed by a large contract cleaning squad armed with quantities of bleach and paint to cover the walls. Eventually, after a fortnight, Turkish forensic officers gained access.

Though these Turkish officers noted that something had been sprayed around the floor, they were unable to identify it as blood because of the bleach. The Saudis had also cleaned their vehicles and left them parked out in the rain. The Turks moved on to the consul's house, noting a deep well and a kebab oven. It remains unknown whether that is where Khashoggi's body parts were disposed of. A wider trawl of recent CCTV footage revealed some of the same vehicles at Saudi-owned villas several miles distant from Istanbul and usually surrounded by dense woods, but it is more probable that his severed head and torso were contained in the five items of large luggage when his killers returned to Saudi Arabia.

Initially, the Saudi government denied everything described above, while their PR men smeared Khashoggi as an active member of the Muslim Brotherhood, which he had never joined. He was allegedly an agent of the Qataris too, for which there is no evidence, though some British journalists eagerly recycled these claims, at least until their proprietors developed better business relations with Doha.

But as it became clear that outrage extended to important US senators, Riyadh's story shifted. Trump initially refused to believe ill of an important ally for his gathering confrontation with Iran, and one which spent billions on US-manufactured and serviced arms, but gradually even he had to recognize that Khashoggi was dead. He despatched Secretary of State Mike Pompeo to Riyadh for what was billed as a stern conversation with MbS, though footage shows a very amicable session. By this time, the CIA determined that Khashoggi had been murdered after Turkey's MIT shared its covert tapes. But while Gina Haspel, the new CIA director, talked Trump through the transcripts, he refused to listen to the actual recordings. He would have made no sense of them anyway, in Arabic. It was striking that though the CIA had picked up threats against Khashoggi, they did not act on their 'duty to warn' him, even though he was a US resident.[26]

With Erdogan and the MIT indirectly drip-feeding more titbits to the international press, the Saudis dropped their claim that Khashoggi had disappeared and changed their story. An attempt to abduct Khashoggi, ordered by the deputy GID chief, General Ahmed Al-Asiri, had degenerated into a fight in which Khashoggi had accidentally died.

A sixty-year-old overweight man with no unarmed combat training does not have a chance against ten fit men half his age, and why would an autopsy specialist be there too, equipped with mechanical saws? To incline the Turks to this new view, the Saudis despatched an elderly prince to Ankara to offer the debt-laden Erdoğan government what amounted to an economic bribe, which the President refused.

Meanwhile, MbS was appointed head of a commission to investigate Khashoggi's murder. Riyadh duly announced that eighteen people had been arrested, though only eleven would stand trial. They included Mutreb, but not Qahtani or al-Otaibi, the Saudi consul. Five of the eleven faced capital charges in a secret court, although the regime was already pacifying Khashoggi's sons by forcing them into an uncomfortable televised rendezvous with MbS. Expensive houses in Jeddah, unimpeded travel and $10,000 per month government stipends were to follow, so that, by the time of writing in May 2020, they had publicly forgiven those convicted of their father's murder. This mattered in a Sharia system in which the relatives of victims determine penalties. In the event, eight low-level operatives were sentenced to prison terms of seven to twenty years after a secret trial which a UN investigator called 'a parody of justice'. Those convicted were not even named.

While MbS was widely condemned by many civilized countries as a murderer, many corporate leaders flew to his 'Davos in the Desert' to win business, staying in the same Ritz Carlton where rich Saudis had been subject to extortion. MbS also continued to privately commune with Kushner, as well as with President Vladimir Putin, whose GRU agents had tried to kill Sergei Skripal in Salisbury. Indeed, that brazen act may have encouraged MbS to go down this route of killing dissidents abroad in the first place.

At a G20 summit in Argentina, Putin and MbS high-fived each other, while a cowardly Trump avoided a public meeting with the berobed Saudi. Group photos in which MbS stood alone on the platform masked a more fundamental reality: the vastly wealthy Saudis could use the threat of pivoting to China or Russia to counter those in the US who wanted 'Crown Prince Bone Saw' isolated and sanctioned. Discussions with the Russians about buying their S-400 surface-to-air missiles portended that way, as would Chinese medical help in countering the Covid-19 virus.

Trump, an amoral and narcissistic man for whom everything is about money and all human relationships are transactional, had long decided that the strategic relationship with the kingdom outweighed any human rights concerns. He claimed that Saudi Arabia might implode without the Sauds so MbS had to remain in place, which was also the view of the US deep state. 'I saved his ass,' Trump crudely averred. He also blocked senatorial attempts to invoke the 2016 Global Magnitsky Act, which would have required a formal investigation of Khashoggi's murder and a report to Congress. This was despite the fact that both the CIA and the Senate Foreign Relations Committee had held MbS responsible for ordering his murder. Trump also vetoed a congressional block on US arms sales to Saudi Arabia despite the murderous air war in Yemen.[27]

Trump's insistence that 'the world is a very, very vicious place' chimed with the implicit Saudi claim that every country kills people. The British government of Theresa May opted for the usual private 'admonitions' from Foreign Secretary Jeremy Hunt, coupled with ongoing greedy pursuit of Typhoon jet contracts to sustain thousands of jobs in Lancashire and the kickbacks and perks the British elites received from dealing with the Gulf States.

MbS hosted the online post-Covid G20 in Riyadh in November 2020, hoping it would begin his return to respectability, before his imminent succession to the Saudi throne. Some called it the 'Impunity Summit'. The international community already treats him as if he is King, and amoral corporate leaders continue to flock to Riyadh in search of deals. He is a worrying example of how assassination can become contagious, for he seems to have caught the habit from the Russians, though Trump contributed to a climate in which leaders like him thrive. Ignoring the murderousness of a close ally is a part of the return of Social Darwinian disorder in global affairs.[28]

While people rejoice that Saudi women can now drive cars unescorted, the reality is that there has been no political reform in a kingdom that still executes dissidents with depressing frequency and jails many critics. Although many members of the Saudi royal family and the oligarch class privately hate and fear MbS, none of them are likely to oppose him when he succeeds his father because they rely on handouts rumoured to amount to $2 billion a year. Although Qahtani had to relinquish his official post, he is still operating within MbS's palaces. Meanwhile, the price of oil has collapsed and the kingdom's finances are not as healthy as they once were. Foreign investment plunged to $1.4 billion in 2017 and many rich Saudis took their money offshore.

While MbS can in theory look forward to fifty years or so on the throne, he has made a lot of powerful enemies. Trump sulked out of the White House on 20 January 2021, and the Biden administration has frozen offensive arms sales to the Kingdom. When the Democrat Senator Bernie Sanders and the Republican Mike Lee ventured this in the Senate in March 2018, it only lost by a margin of 55 to 44. The only card MbS has to play is to withhold formalising relations with Israel, as other Gulf states and Morocco did in 2020, in order to curry favour with Biden and using Israel as a kind of shield. The release of a CIA report directly blaming MbS for Khashoggi's murder in February 2021 leaves the US in the quandary of how to deal with a future leader who it has denounced as a murderer. In an ideal world, the ramified Saudi royal family in which MbS has many enemies would change the current succession arrangements.

•

Murdering journalists is not an exclusively Saudi affair; it also occurs in the heart of Europe. Malta is one of those countries that cause the EU sleepless nights, along with Bulgaria, Croatia, Hungary, Poland and Slovakia, because of corruption or illiberalism. A former British colony which became independent in 1964, Maltese politics was dominated by a highly repressive and Eurosceptic Labour Party, which long after Malta joined the EU in 2003, reversed its hostility membership. On the afternoon of 16 October 2017, the fifty-three-year-old investigative journalist Daphne Caruana Galizia set off to meet her bank manager because her accounts had been frozen in the wake of multiple libel actions. In 2008 her collie had its throat slit before being dumped on her doorstep. A terrier was also poisoned and another collie was killed with a shotgun. Then came an attempt to burn down the family home with gasoline-soaked tyres. The family built a wall around their house, and added a fierce Neapolitan mastiff to their elderly Staffordshire for security.

From 2013 Daphne wrote a sensational blog called *Running Commentary*. With up to half a million views, it had a wider readership than all of Malta's print newspapers combined. Daphne was a combative personality who made many enemies. She did not always check the veracity of what she published, relying on moral obloquy to silence her victims.

Following the international press release of the Panama
Papers, Daphne wrote that two senior politicians, Keith Schembri
il-Kasco, the Chief of Staff to Labour Prime Minister Joseph
Muscat, and Konrad Mizzi, the Energy Minister, had used the
Panamanian law firm Mossack Fonseca to open offshore
accounts within days of taking office. Venturing boldly where
few would go, she also claimed that there was another account
in the name of Muscat's wife Michelle. Next she claimed that
a fellow Maltese had seen the Economy Minister visiting a
brothel in Germany while on an official visit. These claims
resulted in a flurry of libel actions and the blocking of her bank
account so that Daphne's husband had to write blank cheques
whenever his wife needed cash.[29]

Daphne was blown to pieces shortly after she left her house
by a bomb hidden under the seat of her leased Peugeot. One of
her sons was just eighty metres away. Her funeral was attended
by Antonio Tajani, the President of the European Parliament,
and conducted by the Archbishop of Malta.

Malta's police and security service were unused to dealing
with complex conspiracies involving money laundering and the
like. More usually they deal with cases like the old man in Gozo
who used a fish to hit his wife so that she fell down the stairs
and died, before he consumed the main evidence. But so great
was the outrage about Daphne's killing that this time the FBI lent
a hand. They established that the bomb had been detonated by
a text REL1=ON sent to a mobile phone being used on a yacht
to the bomb which was concealed in a shoe box they placed
under the driver's seat and that multiple phone mast 'pings'
revealed Daphne had been under surveillance for several weeks.
The phone mast evidence led to two gangsters, the brothers Alfred
'The Chinese' and George 'The Bean' Degiorgio, who had stupidly
taken their mobile phones as well as disposable burners to watch
Daphne. They had thrown the burner phones in the sea. The
police then wondered why the two brothers (who were arrested)
were able to afford some of Malta's most expensive lawyers,
though that was solved when they realised that their visitors in
jail were bringing in large amounts of cash. Taps on their jail
phone calls to a third brother, revealed that after exchanging

pleasantries he passed his phone to a third man, one Melvin Theuma, who the police then followed. He was a twenty-nine-year-old taxi driver who was a willing factotum of a very rich and politically connected thirty-eight-year-old businessman called Yorgen Fenech. Theuma was increasingly not reassured by Fenech's version of how the police investigation into Daphne's murder was going, for Fenech had long hobnobbed with senior officers. It being typical of Malta that such a man would regularly receive confidential information about what the police detectives knew or did not know. Theuma began to secretly record his patron's conversations, obviously fearing that he might be murdered himself, a real possibility since Fenech researched on the 'dark web' where to get guns and cyanide.[30] Theuma did a deal with the authorities and admitted commissioning the Degiorgio brothers to kill Daphne for a fee of €150,000, with thirty thousand paid up front. So did a third accused called Vincent Muscat who in exchange for a fifteen-year jail sentence revealed that he had acquired the bomb used to kill Daphne. His testimony incriminated two brothers for supplying the explosives. Initially the killers wanted to shoot Daphne with a rifle equipped with a telescopic sight, but this plan was abandoned and exchanged for a bomb, both items courtesy of the Italian Mafia. The outstanding balance on the contract to kill Daphne was delivered in the village of Ramla Taz-Zietun ten days after the murder.[31]

With the Degiorgios behind bars, and Theuma cooperating with the police, Fenech sought to flee to Sicily on one of his yacht's but was stopped at sea by armed troops. Fenech accused Schembri and Prime Minister Joseph Muscat of being behind Daphne's murder.[32]

The motive went beyond her spraying accusations against all and sundry. Malta had always depended on burning heavy and polluted imported fuel oil to generate electricity, though a power cable to Sicily was designed to rectify that. This made it strange that Muscat should give the go ahead to building a gas-fired power station which relied on LNG imported via an Azeri energy company. With the help of whistleblowers, Daphne began looking into the corporate structures of the consortium which won the supply contracts. The Panama Papers further enabled her to uncover a complex web of shell companies linked to government ministers, as well as one in Dubai called 17 Black which was owned by Fenech. Despite only having four employees, this entity took huge success fees running into millions whenever some (meaningless) milestone was reached with the power station. Huge sums of money were pumped into the power station, which then disappeared via places like Azerbaijan, before winding up in the accounts of obscure entities registered in Panama, accounts which appeared to be in the names of Maltese ministers.[33]

A report on the rule of law in Malta by the Council of Europe cited these complex transactions as examples of more pervasive financial improprieties on the island.[34] While Malta became the Eurozone's fastest-growing economy, it also suffered from chronic flaws.[35] The report outlined what was rotten in the state of Malta. The rule of law had been eroded in favour of the rule by one party, Labour in this case. The office of Prime Minister is extremely powerful, appointing judges, senior civil servants and police chiefs. Members of the parliament worked part-time and were poorly paid, hence they were eager to be awarded extra work as contractors. Financial regulation is extremely weak and politically malleable. Dodgy Russians and Iranians could easily acquire residency visas.[36] In the event, after mass protests, Joseph Muscat resigned as Prime Minister, along with Schembri and Mizzi. As for the power plant, when a ship's anchor damaged the electricity cable from Sicily, the island was solely reliant on the new power station for the first time. The lights flickered and then went out across the island.

Malta is now subject to increased scrutiny by European institutions. Perhaps more importantly, a large international consortium of journalists collaborated in highlighting what had happened to Daphne Caruana Galizia. A French documentary filmmaker established Forbidden Stories, a website dedicated to continuing the work of reporters imprisoned or killed during investigative work.[37] This is more necessary than ever; in Slovakia an investigative reporter called Ján Kuciak and his fiancée Martina Kušnirová were murdered in February 2019. He was twenty-seven. At the time Kuciak was working on a story that the Calabrian 'Ndrangheta had set up in eastern Slovakia to traffic drugs from this quiet backwater. A businessman they were investigating was acquitted of the crime, though a former soldier, was convicted of being the shooter. The killings led 60,000 people to protest on the streets and to the downfall of Prime Minister Robert Fico. The general public may not seem to rate journalists very highly, but they care passionately when they are killed.[38]

•

Among the members of the Sandershausen shooting club, forty-five-year-old Stephan Ernst was known as 'a quiet type who never lost his cool'. He was the club's head of bow and arrow shooting, and was not one of the four club members who had access to its firearms.[39]

Ernst lived in a suburb of eastern Kassel, where the sound of lawnmowers almost drowned out the autobahn traffic nearby. To neighbours he was a model citizen who spent much of his time on DIY. Ernst worked shifts at a dental firm so was often invisible. His wife worked in a pharmacy. They had two children.[40]

This image of suburban normalcy changed at 2 a.m. one Saturday in 2019, when dozens of police vans and cars appeared outside Ernst's house. He was arrested and taken away. His DNA had been matched to skin tissue found at the home of Christian Democrat politician Walter Lübcke in Wolfhagen-Istha, a small village with 890 inhabitants; Lübcke's villa was a handsome white affair, with two wrap-around terraces where he and his wife could sit. The house was well-lit at night and open to the street. On 2 June, they were looking up last-minute walking holidays on an iPad. At 23.17 they stopped. His body was found on the lower terrace shortly after midnight. The sixty-five-year-old Lübcke had been shot in the head, the first German politician to be assassinated since the Second World War.

The victim, a big man with a droopy moustache, had achieved national salience during the 2015 migration crisis after Chancellor Angela Merkel announced, 'We can do it,' meaning receiving migrants in Germany who had trekked through the Balkans. He was scathing in his criticism of those who objected, on one occasion saying that if these people did not like government policy they should live somewhere else. Following repeated death threats, the police offered Lübcke intermittent protection; he declined this, since he thought that voters needed to know their MPs.[41]

Among those who responded to a surge in extremist propaganda, much of it online but also diluted in the right-wing press, was forty-five-year old Stephan Ernst. Though he did not have neo-Nazi banners fluttering outside his home, he was not an ordinary neighbour. In November 1992, he was convicted of attempted murder after stabbing a migrant in the lavatory at Wiesbaden central station. He was nineteen at the time, which may explain why he was free a year later to attempt a pipe-bombing on an asylum centre in Hohenstein-Steckenroth, for which he was given six years in custody. He made no attempt to disguise his hatred of migrants.

From here it was a short journey into the dark far-right scene. Ernst was active in the National Democratic Party of Germany, which brought him into Combat 18, an armed neo-Nazi group, and 'Blood and Honour', part of a self-styled National Socialist Underground. Between 2000 and 2007, this small group murdered ten people in an armed rampage across six German cities. When two members of the cell killed themselves after botching a robbery in Eisenach, the remaining members were convicted of these murders.[42]

In 2009 Ernst was jailed again, for being part of a 400-strong far-right attack on a German trade union congress meeting in Dortmund. Then came the migrant crisis. Ernst allegedly stabbed a young Iraqi in the back on 6 January 2016, on the grounds that he might be a supporter of Islamic State. During the police search of his house in 2019, a knife with the victim's DNA was found in the basement.[43]

During a four-hour interrogation, Ernst admitted shooting Lübcke, as well as the earlier attack on the Iraqi. He had made a note of Lübcke's name after he spoke at a meeting when a hostel for asylum-seekers was being mooted; he used a phone camera to film the politician and posted an edited version on YouTube. Ernst conflated migrants with ISIS terrorists, who had recently beheaded two Scandinavian tourists in Morocco.

Ernst repeated this confession at the opening day of his trial as his new defence lawyer sought to blame everyone from Ernst's alcoholic father down to his co-accused and mentor 'H'. Investigating magistrates established how the assassination had been prepared, starting with shooting practice in a wood using Chancellor Merkel's image as the target. Ernst had repeatedly driven the thirty kilometres to Wolfhagen-Istha. He usually took a camera in addition to the one on the dashboard of his VW Caddy, and on one occasion Ernst filmed the victim's car with his wife sitting behind the wheel.[44]

The night before the shooting, Ernst used a retractable fifteen-centimetre-long thermal-imaging telescope to survey Lübcke's home. The telescope was linked to his Flir Scout TK Compact camera, which was found in a black rucksack in the boot of his car. To create an alibi, Ernst did a lot of social media chatting on his phone and then used specialist software to remove the dates and times when the calls occurred.

Ernst also led detectives to a hidden arsenal of guns, one of which he had taken with him on the last visit to Wolfhagen-Istha. This arsenal included an Uzi machine pistol, and everything had been bought on the black market.[45]

That night, Ernst parked his car and waited in a paddock opposite the house. When he saw the glow of Lübcke's iPad fade, he walked across to the house and shot him with a revolver loaded with .38 Special calibre bullets. The fatal bullet went into the victim's head just above his right ear. Ernst's trial commenced in June 2020. On 28 January 2021 he was sentenced to life imprisonment for Lubcke's murder, with H merely convicted of illegal weapons' possession.[46]

Perhaps because Lübcke was a local rather than a national politician, his death failed to trigger the large-scale protests seen in Malta. There was a minute's silence in the Bundestag, although the far-right Alternativ für Deutschland members refused to respect it. After all, they more than anyone else had polarized the political climate, and an 'eastern' wing of the party were neo-Nazi sympathisers. One (former) party spokesman talked openly in September 2020 of shooting or gassing illegal migrants. That is where we have arrived at.[47]

Many German politicians have reported death threats from the far-right. The case of the young Labour politician Jo Cox MP in Britain was remarkably similar, though her age and gender gave her killing a wider European resonance.

Germany's domestic security agency needs to improve how it deals with these far-right groups, and the sentences for membership of illegal organizations and weapons possession should be weightier. But far more could also be done to hold up a mirror to society in general, along the lines successfully attempted by Israeli psychologists in a working-class Tel Aviv suburb where denizens pride themselves as being 'right of Genghiz Khan'. Instead of the usual moralizing admonitions about racism, the psychologists accentuated existing beliefs, to the point where many people felt uneasy with what they had become. After a year of such exposure to an exaggerated version of themselves, their views changed.

Unless something like that is undertaken, politicians will continue to be slain, not in random events, but as the logical outcome of a mindset that has murderous violence at its core. Otherwise assassination may become more frequent in Western societies that have been deliberately polarized by mainstream populist actors beyond the long familiar neo-Nazi underground which in various new guises is becoming disturbingly visible. At the start of 2021 we all watched American far-right extremists occupy the US Congress. In addition to the horned helmets and Confederate flags, there were explicit threats to murder by bullet or noose both senior Democrats and the handful of Republicans who rejected the claims of President Trump that the November 2020 election was fraudulent. 'The storm is coming,' they cried, and it might be all too likely that assassins will be at the epicentre of it.

Afterword

Mankind has always sought to divine purpose behind assassinations. Plutarch thought that the assassination of Caesar had cosmic effects since the sun shone feebly for the year following his murder, which had been intimated in advance by comets and strange celestial portents. Crops withered and failed as it remained too cool because of the absent sun. The Victorian statesman Benjamin Disraeli was unconvinced. Addressing the Commons in 1865 after the death of Abraham Lincoln, he said: 'Assassination has never changed the history of the world.' He mentioned the deaths of William the Silent and Henri IV as well as Caesar and Lincoln with which we began. Superficially he was right, for emperors and kings are succeeded by their heirs, and Presidents and Prime Ministers by surrogates who might be better or worse than the victims. Disraeli was wrong about Caesar since Rome ceased to be a republic, and one could argue that Lincoln's successor contributed to the indelible stain of racism which still disfigures US society and politics. Whether assassinations are failed (Jair Bolsonaro) or successful (Benazir Bhutto) can have very tangible political effects in what are notional democracies. We may no longer believe like Plutarch in the cosmic effects of assassination, but we have seen several examples of how the social and cultural 'portents' are almost as visible, the material of novelists, filmmakers and social scientists. This book has sought to marry up these various approaches, for the last is too desiccated and the others very often too speculative.

It is easy enough to statistically tabulate assassinations on whether they succeeded or not, once one omits gangland slayings and the like, which are part of the eternal business model of organized crime, though this can 'jump spark' into the political realm too as it did in Cuba and Sicily. It is also possible to trace the ways in which intelligent people, including philosophers and theologians, have sought to justify political killing, often as doing God's will and sometimes as a clean alternative to mass wars. The claim that assassinations can be 'good politics' is actually as old as the Koran, which avers: 'If two Khalifs live, one should be murdered, for murder is better than disorder'. The same logic had informed the Roman Emperor Octavian when he had Cleopatra's boy Caesarion murdered. One can also identify times in which assassination is more or less likely, or ages in which by general consensus rulers have decided to forgo this easy solution to a hated rival. There is much to recommend such fastidious restraint in this narrow field as well as in foreign policy in general.

A wave of high-level killings ended as the early modern wars of religion petered out; the Enlightenment era saw attempts to legally constrain the conduct of war, including sneak attacks on fellow rulers. As in the wars of religion, the advent of modern pseudo-religious ideologies licensed any number of symbolic murders (in which there was often much collateral damage) which targeted monarchs, Prime Ministers, judges and policemen as well as such symbols as opera houses and stock exchanges. When these ideologies captured powerful states, then the number of assassinations skyrocketed since states have many murderers at their disposal and their rulers sometimes operate with a different morality from that of ordinary men and women. In some cases, the Jacobin journalist-terrorist Jean-Paul Marat being one, Lenin another, those who lived by the sword died by it, or at least as near as damn it in Lenin's case. Secret agents became the preferred instruments by which these states extended their long reach against their enemies as we saw in the international operations of the NKVD and its KGB successors.

Democracies acquired such apparatuses too though in most cases their agents are under greater control. This ceases to be the case when the spies become militarized. The United States resorted to political killing, often in the hot peripheral theatres of the Cold War and incorporating assassination into how it fought the Vietcong and then more diffuse international Islamist terror organizations after 9/11. Over time, the means has shifted from men with guns, bombs and toxins to armed drones which are deployed in countries with which the US is not at war. This is despite a kind of fastidious American official disapproval of the one state which has elevated targeted killing into a normative procedure – Israel – though other regional actors have gone down that road too. The ill effects on Iraq of the assassinations of Soleimani and Muhandis clearly show that what seems a bold stroke at the time can have disastrous consequences. The American experience also shows a kind of blowback, in which extreme political polarization amidst a deranged ambient cultural and media noise provides almost ideal climactic conditions for politically motivated killing at home. If people want to minimize the frequency of assassinations then a more general reduction of societal anger, much of which is deliberately engineered, might be a start, though one is not optimistic these days especially in the case of politicians who bravely champion the rights of migrants.

The US is not the world, though it often imagines it is. Our clear and present danger is that the more general undermining of international rules by a galaxy of so-called 'strongmen' will result in this practice becoming contagious, as is most glaringly evident in the cases of Russia and Saudi Arabia. Our gentler democracies need to become very hard-faced whenever the violence of cowboy states is visited on persons on our own streets. Chucking out a few token Russian spies is hardly an adequate answer, and sanctions are blunted by the fact that Russia's state finances are actually pretty well managed with a decently run central bank and a huge sovereign-wealth fund to mitigate their effects. That, presumably, is why the Russian opposition figure Alexei Navalny was poisoned with the nerve agent Novichok – secreted inside his boxer shorts – before an August 2020 flight from Omsk to Moscow, as confirmed by testing laboratories in France, Germany, Holland and Sweden. Putin's mocking denial in December 2020 that if the secret agencies were involved Navalny would have died, was hardly reassuring. Rather than ejecting a few Russian spies, it might be better to also clearly explain the rules of road to the ambassadors of such states as Saudi Arabia or Israel, while also banning any company peddling dubious offensive 'security technologies' on our shores. In that respect a more populist and less elite foreign policy might be advantageous since it is these elites who are most keen on being friendly with the lords of the deserts.

Some assassinations were clearly the result of long-planned conspiracies – for example against Caesar, de Gaulle or the President of Rwanda – but conspiracies have the inherent flaws which centuries ago Machiavelli alluded to, however attractive they may be to minds needing to find 'deeper' explanations for banal events. In many more cases we are left with the strange odysseys of lone individuals who on their special day carried out something extraordinary. A few of them may or may not have been insane (though equally as we saw in South Africa they had coherent and heartfelt political reasons for killing the architect of apartheid) but in several cases they simply sought to make their mark on History before old age swallowed them into Time's oblivion. While many sought the limelight, others – for example whoever shot Olaf Palme – were content with taking their special secret to the grave unless they met with a fatal accident. In most cases what they did on their big day had no real consequences other than to temporarily discombobulate a society with an act bound up with their own life stories and personalities. Very little in a 900-page biography of Lee Harvey Oswald by one of America's leading authors actually remains memorable save that he died aged just twenty-four after shooting a flawed greater man as well as a lowly Dallas policeman. The slightly deranged feel of modern American life, with its obsessions with conspiracies and guns and murderous racial undercurrents, remains another matter. Assassins hearing the voice of God will always be with us, as Mr Bolsonaro discovered. But, more widely, as long as men (and many fewer women) are deluded enough to think that a single act of symbolic violence can alter the course of History, and the media connives at giving them 'exposure' for doing so, then we are going to live with assassination. Perhaps better the oblivion which the more sophisticated states like Norway or New Zealand are now using to erase all memory of vicious terrorists?

Acknowledgements

This book would not have been possible without much advice and help from friends. I warmly thank Vernon Bogdanor, Philip Bobbit, Niall Ferguson, Sir Roderick Braithwaite, Robert Service, Luke Harding and Mark Urban for stimulating discussions and key bibliographical recommendations. Bob Service in particular went way beyond the call of duty in helping me navigate Russia past and present. Alphabetical order and a long waiting time fortuitously meant an hour-long tutorial on Julius Caesar with Professor Dame Mary Beard while waiting for a WWI commemorative service to start in the choir of Westminster Abbey.

I owe so much to George Walden that I cannot adequately express it. During the extended Covid-19 lockdown he read each chapter, making helpful suggestions while always being encouraging and wise. Paul Ritchie gave me the benefit of his deep experience as he too read the whole book as it evolved. So did Clovis Meath-Baker, who helped with insights into the legal aspects of drone warfare. I am grateful to another comrade, General Sir Cedric Delves, for crucial clarification of the meaning of 'hard arrests'. Bryan Appleyard was also kind enough to read through the manuscript to lighten it up where it was needed and to introduce more signposts for readers.

This book owes much to the nine months I spent as Engelsberg Chair at LSE Ideas, for which I am grateful to the Ax:Johnson Foundation in Stockholm. For that privilege I owe an enormous debt to Professors Christopher Coker and Mick Cox, with whom I was privileged to enjoy weekly discussions on many of the subjects dealt with in the book. I am also grateful to Dr Emilia Knight and to Dr Mihnea 'Vlad' Zigarov, Transylvanian prince of researchers, for every conceivable technical assistance and a lot of fun in both London and Romania. Halfway through, Mr Stuart Austin did sterling work for me among law journals relating to subjects like Executive Order 12,333, to which legal scholars bring such orderly minds where I merely chronicle the messy realities.

I must also thank Andy Duff, Paul Lay, John Ray, Mike Smith, Nancy Sladek, Nick Pyke, Shmuel Bar, and Tobie Mathew for very useful advice. Dr Nathaniel Morris was incredibly knowledgeable about Mexico, and Dr Iavor Rangelov helped with Bulgarian materials for the Ağca story. Michael Dynes guided me through the complexities of Rwanda, for which I am deeply grateful.

My agent Natasha Fairweather at Rogers, Coleridge and White still thinks I am hopeless at writing outline proposals. She is right, but I hope Natasha is satisfied with the book itself.

This is one of several books I have published with Macmillan, and once again it was commissioned and edited by my dear friend George Morley at Picador with the aid of Nick Humphrey and Nicholas Blake. It has been a journey which started in the late 1990s, with plenty of fun along the way.

From March 2020 onwards my wife Linden found herself in the weird position of guarding my health, with the combined zeal of a prison warder and a tigress. During lockdown I dread to think how many times her evenings were further agitated by the latest revelations from upstairs about political killings, even as people were being scythed down by a virus throughout the UK.

Finally, this book was conceived around the time of the Saudi assassination of the exiled journalist Jamal Khashoggi, about which I wrote much at the time – though not with the skill of Jonathan Rugman. Despite strange things happening to my mobile phone after I published critical things about MbS before that horror happened, I refuse to accept that such heinous deeds are normal to most states at all times, which is why I wrote the book in the first place. They are not, and I hope I have shown why, before the habit becomes as endemic as a virus, though this is not a polemical or proselytizing work but one just about killers and their victims on what for both was always a fateful day.

Michael Burleigh
London 2021

Endnotes

Chapter 1

1 Mary Beard, *SPQR. A History of Ancient Rome* (London 2016) pp. 442–8 on housing. Although it excludes assassination in favour of death by natural causes, there is much of interest in Benjamin Jones, Benjamin Olken, 'Do Leaders Matter? National Leadership and Growth Since World War II', *Quarterly Journal of Economics* (August 2005), pp. 835–64. I am grateful to Vernon Bogdanor for this reference. For a fascinating study of fictional accounts of assassins by Ambler, Fleming and Forsyth see my late friend Hans-Peter Schwarz's *Phantastische Wirklichkeit. Das 20 Jahrhundert im Spiegel des Polit-Thrillers* (Munich 2006).

2 Ward Thomas, 'Norms and Security: The Case of International Assassination', *International Security* (2000) 25, pp. 108–109.

3 Plutarch, *Roman Lives*, translated Robin Waterfield (Oxford World Classics 1999), p. 354.

4 See Mary Beard, *SPQR. A History of Ancient Rome*, p. 256. Professor Beard gave me a very memorable private tutorial on this subject in 2018.

5 Suetonius, *The Twelve Caesars*, translated by Robert Graves (London 1957 revised edition 2007) p. 35. Lupercali were societies of men who wore goatskins at this fertility festival in mid-February.

6 On this question see Colin Campbell, 'The Assassination of Julius Caesar. The Bodyguard Paradox Cost Him His Life', *The Collector*, 1 December 2020 https://www.thecollector.com/julius-caesar-assassination/

7 Appian, *The Civil Wars*, translated John Carter (London 1996), p. 127.

8 Kathryn Tempest, *Brutus. The Noble Conspirator* (New Haven 2017), pp. 101–103.

9 *Julius Caesar* in *The Arden Shakespeare Complete Works* (ed. Richard Proudfoot et al., London 1998), Act 2:1, p. 340. See also

Stephen Greenblatt's thought-provoking *Tyrant. Shakespeare on Power* (London 2018).

10 Shannon K. Brincat, ' "Death to Tyrants": The Political Philosophy of Tyrannicide – Part 1', *Journal of International Political Theory* (2008) 4, pp. 214–220.

11 For a finely written recent account of the conspirators and their motives see Peter Stothard, *The Last Assassin. The Hunt for the Killers of Julius Caesar* (London 2020), pp. 24ff.

12 Heinrich Schlange-Schöningen, 'Harmodios und Aristogeiton, die Tyrannenmörder von 514 v. Chr.', in Alexander Demandt (ed.), *Das Attentat in der Geschichte* (Darmstadt 2019), pp. 29–56 is compelling and comprehensive.

13 Here I rely on B. M. Lavelle, 'The Nature of Hipparchos' Insult to Harmodios', *American Journal of Philology* (1986) 107, pp. 318–331.

14 Thucydides, *History of the Peloponnesian War*, trans. Rex Warner (London 1954), pp. 442–446.

15 Josiah Ober, 'Tyrant Killing as Therapeutic Stasis: A Political Debate in Images and Texts', in Kathryn A. Morgan (ed.), *Popular Tyranny: Sovereignty and its Discontents in Ancient Greece* (Austin, Texas 2003), pp. 217ff.

16 See the lucid discussion by Francisco Pina Polo, 'The Tyrant Must Die: Preventive Tyrannicide in Roman Political Thought', in Francisco Marco Simòn, Francisco Pina Polo and José Remesal Rodríguez (eds), *Repúblicas y Ciudadanos: Modelos de Participación Cívica en el Mundo Antiguo* (Barcelona 2006), pp. 71–100.

17 Barry Strauss, *The Death of Caesar* (New York 2015), pp. 81–86. [Octavian was never called that since his name was Gaius Octavian. He would become Gaius Julius Caesar and then Augustus after he became emperor.]

18 Stothard, *The Last Assassin*, p. 62.

19 On the role of ordinary citizens in these events see T. P. Wiseman, 'After the Ides of March', in his *Remembering the Roman People. Essays on Late-Republican Politics and Literature* (Oxford 2009), pp. 211ff.

20 Stothard, *The Last Assassin*, pp. 88–95.

21 Herodotus, *The Histories*, translated Aubrey de Selincourt (London 1957, revised by John Marincola, London 1972), p. 331: Book 5/55.

22 Richard White, *The Republic For Which It Stands. The United States During Reconstruction and the Gilded Age, 1865–1896* (Oxford 2017), p. 28 on the cost of artificial limbs.

23 For what did not find its way into the congressional record see Stephen E. Maizlish, *A Strife of Tongues: The Compromise of 1850*

and the Ideological Foundations of the American Civil War (Virginia 2019).

24 James M. McPherson, *Battle Cry of Freedom. The American Civil War* (London 1990).

25 Bertram Wyatt-Brown, *Southern Honor. Ethics & Behavior in the Old South* (Oxford 2007), p. 108.

26 C. Vann Woodward, 'John Brown's Private War', in his *The Burden of Southern History* (3rd edition, Baton Rouge 2008), pp. 41ff.

27 Among many studies of Lincoln see Jay Winik, *April 1865. The Month That Saved America* (New York 2001), pp. 230ff.

28 Bertram Wyatt-Brown, *The Shaping of Southern Culture. Honor, Grace, and War 1760s–1880s* (Chapel Hill, NC 2001), pp. 245–246.

29 Walt Whitman, 'Specimen Days', in Walt Whitman, *Complete Prose Works* (originally 1882, Amazon reprint without date), pp. 25ff.

30 Michael Kauffman, *American Brutus. John Wilkes Booth and the Lincoln Conspiracies* (New York 2004), p. 383.

31 Kauffmann, *American Brutus*, p. 400.

32 James L. Swanson, *Manhunt. The 12-Day Chase for Abraham Lincoln's Killer* (London 2006), is a thrilling read.

33 White, *The Republic For Which It Stands*, p. 62.

34 All ably explained by David W. Blight, 'The Reconstruction of America: Justice, Power, and the Civil War's Unfinished Business', *Foreign Affairs*, vol. 100 (January/February 2021), pp. 44–50.

35 Adam Gopnik, 'The Takeback', *New Yorker*, 8 April 2019, pp. 76ff. is enlightening on Reconstruction.

36 A point excellently made by Steven Levitsky, Daniel Ziblatt, *How Democracies Die. What History Reveals About Our Future* (London 2019), pp. 89–92.

37 https://lynchinginamerica.eji.org/drupal/sites/default/files/2019–08/lynching-in-america-3d-ed-080219.pdf

38 Mehmet Ali Ağca, *Mi avevano promesso il paradiso. La mia vita e la verità sull'attentato al papa* (Milan 2013).

39 Christopher Andrew, Vasili Mitrokhin, *The Mitrokhin Archive. The KGB in Europe and the West* (London 1999), pp. 662ff. Unless otherwise indicated, this is the source for Politburo and KGB thinking. When he was exfiltrated by SIS to Britain in 1992, Mitrokhin brought a treasure trove of KGB documentation.

40 Christopher Coker, *The Rise of the Civilizational State* (Cambridge 2019); although this deals with China and Russia it equally applies to Turkey. See also Burak Kaderan, 'The Year of the Grey Wolf: The Rise of Turkey's New Ultranationalism', *War on the Rocks*, 16 July 2018, which is good on the wider and longer political context,

and Tom Stevenson, 'Our bodies are Turkish, our Souls are Islamic!. The Rise of Turkey's ultra-nationalists', *Middle Eastern Eye*, 21 July 2018, which is vivid on the wolf symbolism.

41 Jeffrey Bale, 'The Ultranationalist Right in Turkey and the Attempted Assassination of Pope John Paul II', *Turkish Studies Association Bulletin* (1991) 15, p. 28. Bale is excellent on the context of Ağca's life. On Ağca's background see also https://www.washingtonpost.com/archive/politics/1984/10/14/child-of-turkish-slum-finds-way-in-crime/59f513c6-e532-4acb-bf97-b422bf98e54a/.

42 For some of these details on Ağca's peculiar movements see 'The Plot to Kill Pope John Paul II', *Newsweek*, 3 January 1982.

43 Ağca, *Mi avevano promesso il paradiso*, pp. 161–72.

44 https://www.washingtonpost.com/national/on-faith/vatican-shoots-down-claim-that-iran-backed-john-paul-assassination-attempt/2013/02/01/bc0ae828–6caf-11e2–8f4f-2abd96162ba8_story.html

45 The Italian indictment is recorded in Claire Sterling, 'Bulgaria Hired Agca To Kill Pope, Report of Italian Prosecutors Says', *New York Times*, 10 June 1984.

46 For a good account see https://www.independent.co.uk/news/world/europe/shooting-of-john-paul-ii-the-man-who-nearly-killed-the-pope-6111856.html.

47 https://www.upi.com/Defense-News/2002/05/26/Pope-John-Paul-II-ends-visit-to-Bulgaria/24221022435343/ which mentions he did not blame Bulgaria for this taint.

48 Andrew Mitrokhin, *The Mitrokhin Archive*, p. 674, citing a Polish admiral.

49 Matthew Day, 'CIA "tried to frame Bulgaria for John Paul II assassination attempt" ', *Daily Telegraph*, 20 April 2010.

50 For these passages I am indebted to local research by my LSE colleague Dr Iavor Rangelov, who translated key Bulgarian accounts and spoke with surviving friends and relatives of the three Bulgarians named. See https://m.bgdnes.bg/Article/5409552 (Bulgaria Dnes), a Bulgarian account from 2016.

51 Roy Godson, James J. Wirtz (eds), *Strategic Denial and Deception: the Twenty-First Century Challenge* (New York 2017), is an account of CIA psy-ops by the CIA officer who ran that section. Roy is the older brother of Dean Godson, the director of British right-wing think tank Policy Exchange.

52 Armin Führer, 'Viele Spuren ins Nichts: Ali Ağca und das Attentat auf Papst Johannes Paul II', in Alexander Demandt (ed.), *Das Attentat in der Geschichte* (Darmstadt 2019), pp. 455–70.

53 Bale, 'The Ultranationalist Right', p. 33 for the letter.

Chapter 2

1 See the neglected study by Pitirim Sorokin and Walter Lunden, *Power & Morality. Who Shall Guard the Guardians?* (Boston 1959), p. 65.

2 Cary J. Nederman, 'A Duty to Kill: John of Salisbury's Theory of Tyrannicide', *Review of Politics* (1988), vol. 50, no. 3, pp. 365–89.

3 Shannon Brincat, ' "Death to Tyrants": The Political Philosophy of Tyrannicide', *Journal of International Political Theory*, vol. 4 (2008), pp. 212–40.

4 Niccolò Machiavelli, *The Discourses*, translated by Leslie Walker SJ (London 1970), Book Three 6, 'On Conspiracies', pp. 398–424. I am hugely indebted to Erica Benner and her *Machiavelli's Ethics* (Princeton, NJ 2009), pp. 273ff. for advice on this subject.

5 Horatio Robert Forbes Brown, *Studies in the History of Venice*, vol. 1 (London 1908), pp. 216–54, is a marvellous antiquarian guide to this theme.

6 Ward Thomas, 'Norms and Security: The Case of International Assassination', *International Security* (2000) 25, pp. 109–10.

7 Marshall G. S. Hodgson, *The Secret Order of Assassins. The Struggle of the Early Nizârî Ismâ'îlîs Against the Islamic World* (Philadelphia 2005), pp. 79–80.

8 Bernard Lewis, *The Assassins: A Radical Sect in Islam* (Oxford 1987), p. 58.

9 Gérard Chaliand, Arnaud Blin (eds), *The History of Terrorism. From Antiquity to Al Qaeda* (Berkeley, CA 2007), pp. 61ff.

10 A point well made by Franklin Ford, *Political Murder. From Tyrannicide to Terrorism* (Cambridge, MA 1985), p. 104 against the arguments of Bernard Lewis.

11 Ford, *Political Murder* p. 156.

12 Vincent J. Pitts, *Henri IV of France. His Reign and Age* (Baltimore, MD 2009), pp. 63–4.

13 Lisa Jardine, *The Awful End of Prince William the Silent. The First Assassination of a Head of State with a Handgun* (London 2006), p. 60.

14 Motley, *History of the United Netherlands From the Death of William the Silent to the Twelve Years' Truce 1609* (Cambridge 1867) pp. 206–209 for the quotation from Philip, and Geoffrey Parker, *Imprudent King. A New Life of Philip II* (New Haven 2014), pp. 247ff. I would like to thank Christopher Coker for the reference to Motley.

15 Roland Mousnier, *The Assassination of Henry IV. The Tyrannicide*

Problem and the Consolidation of the French Absolute Monarchy in the Early 17th Century (London 1973), pp. 86–105.

16 James Sharpe, *Remember, Remember the Fifth of November. Guy Fawkes and the Gunpowder Plot* (London 2005), pp. 46ff., is the best modern account.

17 Antonia Fraser, *The Gunpowder Plot. Terror and Faith in 1605* (London 1996), p. 232.

18 Stephen Greenblatt, *Will in the World. How Shakespeare became Shakespeare* (London 2014), pp. 333–55.

19 Pitts, *Henri IV of France*, pp. 136–42.

20 Mousnier, *The Assassination of Henry IV*, pp. 110–16.

21 Anita Walker, Edmund Dickermann, 'Mind of an Assassin: Ravaillac and the Murder of Henri IV of France', *Canadian Journal of History* (1995) 30, pp. 210–29.

22 Franklin L. Ford, *Political Murder. From Tyrannicide to Terrorism* (Cambridge, MA 1985), pp. 186–8 for these documents.

23 On Wallenstein's murder see Peter H. Wilson's excellent *Europe's Tragedy. A New History of the Thirty Years War* (London 2009), pp. 539–41.

24 Ward Thomas, 'Norms and Security', pp. 118–21.

Chapter 3

1 Lindsay Porter, *Assassination. A History of Political Murder* (London 2010), pp. 73–90. For an excellent account of one notorious assassination see Martin Connolly, *The Murder of Prime Minister Spencer Percival: A Portrait of the Assassin* (Yorkshire 2018).

2 Abraham Ascher, *P. A. Stolypin. The Search for Stability in Late Imperial Russia* (Stanford, CA 2001), p. 138.

3 Friedrich von Holstein, diary entry 15 February 1882 in *Die geheimen Papiere Friedrich von Holsteins, Tagebuchblätter*, ed. Norman Rich and M. H. Fischer (Göttingen 1956–63), vol. 2, p. 5. See also Rachel G. Hoffman, 'The Age of Assassination: Monarchy and Nation in Nineteenth-Century Europe', in Nikolaus Wachsmann, Jan Rüger (eds.), *Rewriting German History: New Perspectives on Modern Germany* (Basingstoke 2015), p. 127.

4 Michaela Vocelka and Karl Vocelka, *Franz Joseph I. Kaiser von Österreich und König von Ungarn 1830–1916. Eine Biografie* (Munich 2015), pp. 308–312.

5 James Joll, *The Anarchists* (London 1964), p. 148.

6 For example Martin Conway, Robert Gerwarth, 'Revolution and

Counter-Revolution', in Donald Bloxham, Robert Gerwarth (eds.), *Political Violence in Twentieth-Century Europe* (Cambridge 2011), p. 147.

7 Ronald Hingley, *Nihilists. Russian Radicals and Revolutionaries in the Reign of Alexander II, 1855–81* (London 1967), pp. 57–58.

8 On Tkachev see Franco Venturi, *Roots of Revolution. A History of the Populist and Socialist Movements in Nineteenth-Century Russia* (Chicago 1983), pp. 389–428.

9 Mark Leier, *Bakunin. The Creative Passion* (New York 2006), p. 235.

10 Michael Burleigh, *Blood and Rage. A Cultural History of Terrorism* (London 2008), pp. 70–73.

11 The best biography is Giuseppe Galzerano, *Giovanni Passannante. La vita, l'attentato, il processo, la condanna a morte, la grazia 'regale' e gli anni di galera del cuoco lucano che nel 1878 ruppe l'incantesimo monarchico* (Salerno, 2004).

12 Scott Miller, *The President and the Assassin. McKinley, Terror, and Empire at the Dawn of the American Century* (New York 2011), p. 108, for the numbers of labour disputes.

13 Sidney Fine, 'Anarchism and the Assassination of McKinley', *American Historical Review* (1955) vol. 60, pp. 777–99.

14 LeRoy Parker, 'The Trial of the Anarchist Murderer Czolgosz', *Yale Law Journal* (1901) 11, pp. 80–94.

15 'John Fowler et al., 'Official Report of the Experts for the People in the Case of the People v. Leon F. Czolgosz (1901)', in John D. Dawson (ed.), *American State Trials* (St Louis 1923), vol. 14, pp. 169–70.

16 Elizabeth White, *The Socialist Alternative to Bolshevik Russia. The Socialist Revolutionary Party 1921–1939* (London 2011), pp. 7–14.

17 Ordinary people as opposed to sundry intellectuals are missing from Pankaj Mishra's derivative *Age of Anger. A History of the Present* (London 2017).

18 White, *The Socialist Alternative to Bolshevik Russia*, pp. 7–14.

19 Orlando Figes, *A People's Tragedy. The Russian Revolution 1891–1924* (London 1996), p. 136.

20 Adam Ulam, *Prophets and Conspirators in Prerevolutionary Russia* (New Brunswick 1998), p. 251, and p. 327 for the membership numbers of these sects.

21 W. E. Mosse, *Alexander II and the Modernization of Russia* (London 1992), p. 176.

22 For a sympathetic discussion of the evolution of radical violence see Vera Broido, *Apostles into Terrorists. Women and the*

Revolutionary Movement in the Russia of Alexander II (London 1977).

23 There is an almost incomprehensibly pretentious biography of Karakozov by Claudia Verhoeven, *The Odd Man Karakozov. Imperial Russia, Modernity, and the Birth of Terrorism* (Cornell 2009).

24 Verhoeven, *The Odd Man Karakozov*, pp. 66–84.

25 Alex Butterworth, *The World That Never Was. A True Story of Dreamers, Schemers, Anarchists, and Secret Agents* (London 2011), pp. 142–6.

26 Venturi, *Roots of Revolution*, pp. 542–3.

27 Dariya Tyutcheva to her sister Ekaterina, 6 February 1880. I am immensely grateful to Tobie Mathew, who owns the original letter, which is in German, and for recommended reading on terrorism in Tsarist Russia.

28 Hingley, *Nihilism*, pp. 104–117.

29 See the excellent account by Norman Naimark, *Terrorists and Social Democrats. The Russian Revolutionary Movement Under Alexander III* (Cambridge, MA 1983), pp. 14–19.

30 Charles Lowe, *Alexander III of Russia* (London 1895), p. 171.

31 Lowe, *Alexander III*, pp. 141ff. and Robert Service's remarkable *Lenin. A Biography* (London 2000), pp. 47ff.

32 Yves Ternon, 'Russian Terrorism, 1878–1908', in Gérard Chaliand, Arnaud Blin (eds), *The History of Terrorism from Antiquity to Al Qaeda* (Berkeley 2007), p. 157.

33 Ascher, *P. A. Stolypin*, p. 144.

34 Anna Geifman, *Entangled in Terror. The Azef Affair and the Russian Revolution* (Wilmington, DE 2000), p. 135.

35 Geifman, *Entangled in Terror*, pp. 143ff.

36 Mark Mazower, *The Balkans. From the End of Byzantium To the Present Day* (London 2000), p. 102.

37 Christopher Clark, *The Sleepwalkers. How Europe Went To War In 1914* (London 2013), pp. 242ff.

38 David MacKenzie, *Apis, The Congenial Conspirator. The Life of Colonel Dragutin T. Dimitrijević* (Boulder, CO 1989).

39 MacKenzie, *Apis*, p. 74; see also Danilo Šarenac, 'Why did nobody control Apis? Serbian military intelligence and the Sarajevo assassinations', in Mark Cornwall (ed.), *Sarajevo 1914. Sparking the First World War* (London 2020), pp. 125ff., and the correspondence occasioned by Mark Cornwall's 'Who caused the war?', *Times Literary Supplement*, 3 August 2020, which resumed in subsequent issues.

40 Vladimir Dedijer, *The Road to Sarajevo* (London 1967), p. 204.

41 Tim Butcher, *The Trigger. Hunting the Assassin who Brought the World to War* (London 2014), pp. 200–201.
42 MacKenzie, *Apis*, pp. 100ff.
43 Lisa Traynor, *Archduke Franz Ferdinand and the Era of Assassination* (Leeds 2018), pp. 21–6.
44 Noel Malcolm, *Bosnia. A Short History* (London 1994), p. 154.
45 Dedijer, *The Road to Sarajevo*, pp. 393–5.
46 Vocelka and Vocelka, *Franz Joseph I*, pp. 341–5.
47 See especially Mark Cornwall's excellent essay 'Serbia' in Keith Wilson (ed.), *Decisions for War, 1914* (London 1995), pp. 77ff., and his edited collection *Sarajevo 1914.*

Chapter 4

1 See René Girard, *Violence and the Sacred* (Baltimore 1979), p. 145.
2 James McMillan, 'War', in Donald Bloxham, Robert Gerwarth (eds), *Political Violence in Twentieth-Century Europe* (Cambridge 2011), pp. 63–68. For an overview see also Robert Gerwarth, *The Vanquished. Why the First World War Failed to End, 1917–1923* (London 2016).
3 Michael T. Foy, *Michael Collins's Intelligence War. The Struggle Between the British and the IRA 1919–1921* (London 2008), p. 120, for these and other details.
4 Anne Dolan and William Murphy, *Michael Collins. The Man and the Revolution* (Cork 2018).
5 Andrew Gordon, *A Modern History of Japan. From Tokugawa Times To The Present* (New York 2003), pp. 187–9.
6 Gérard Chaliand, Arnaud Blin, 'Lenin, Stalin, and State Terrorism', in Gérard Chaliand, Arnaud Blin (eds), *The History of Terrorism from Antiquity to Al Qaeda* (Berkeley 2007), pp. 198–203.
7 Mauro Canali, 'The Matteotti murder and the origins of Mussolini's totalitarian Fascist regime in Italy', *Journal of Modern Italian Studies* (2009) 14, no. 2, pp. 143–67. See also Christopher Duggan's fine *The Force of Destiny. A History of Italy since 1796* (London 2007), pp. 433ff.
8 Luca de Caprariis, '"Fascism for Export?" The Rise and Eclipse of the Fasci Italiani all'Estero', *Journal of Contemporary History* (2000) 35, no. 2, p. 163.
9 Stanislao G. Pugliese','Death in Exile: The Assassination of Carlo Rosselli', *Journal of Contemporary History* (1997) 32, no. 3, pp. 305–19.

10 Martin Sabrow, 'Mord und Mythos. Das Komplott gegen Walther Rathenau 1922', in Alexander Demandt (ed.), *Das Attentat in der Geschichte* (Darmstadt 2019), pp. 323–4.

11 Robert Service, *Spies & Commissars. Bolshevik Russia and the West* (London 2011), pp. 294–6.

12 Martin Conway, Robert Gerwarth, 'Revolution and Counter-Revolution', in Bloxham, Gerwarth (eds), *Political Violence*, p. 155.

13 Christian Streifler, *Kampf um die Macht. Kommunisten und Nationalsozialisten am Ende der Weimarer Republik* (Frankfurt am Main 1993), pp. 283ff.

14 Streifler, *Kampf um die Macht*, pp. 256–9.

15 Eric Voegelin, *Hitler and the Germans*, in Detlev Clemens, Brendan Purcell (eds), *The Collected Works of Eric Voegelin* vol. 31 (Colombia, Missouri 1999), p. 88 and p. 118 for these points.

16 Jeremy Noakes, Geoffrey Pridham (eds), *Nazism 1919–1945. A Documentary Reader*, vol. 1 (Exeter 1983), doc. nr. 125, p. 181.

17 Gottfried Karl Kindermann, *Hitlers Niederlage in Österreich. Bewaffneter NS-Putsch, Kanzlermord und Österreichs Abwehrsieg von 1934* (Hamburg 1984).

18 See above all Amy Knight, *Who Killed Kirov? The Kremlin's Greatest Mystery* (New York 1999), pp. 201–205.

19 The day of Kirov's death is best described by Stephen Kotkin, *Stalin*, vol. II: *Waiting for Hitler, 1929–1941* (London 2017), pp. 200–204.

20 Robert Conquest, *The Great Terror* (London 1968), pp. 78–9, for the text of the Kirov Law.

21 Knight, *Who Killed Kirov?*, pp. 212–13.

22 J. Arch Getty, Oleg Naumov, *Yezhov. The Rise of Stalin's 'Iron Fist'* (New Haven 2008), pp. 143ff.

23 I am much indebted to Boris Volodarsky's brilliant *Stalin's Secret Agent. The Life & Death of Alexander Orlov* (Oxford 2015), pp. 157–61, pp. 198ff.

24 Volodarsky, *Stalin's Secret Agent*, pp. 345–9, for a copy of Orlov's letter.

25 Philip Stein, *Siqueiros. His Life and Works* (New York 1994), pp. 102ff.

26 Nicholas Mosley, *The Assassination of Trotsky* (London 1972), p. 139.

27 Isaac Don Levine, *The Mind of An Assassin* (New York 1959), pp. 43ff.

28 Robert Service, *Trotsky. A Biography* (London 2009), p. 49.

29 Andrei Soldatov, Irina Borogan, *The Compatriots. The Brutal and*

Chaotic History of Russia's Exiles, Emigrés, and Agents Abroad (New York 2019), is excellent on Eitignon.

30 Levine, *The Mind of an Assassin*, pp. 149ff. summarizes the findings of the Mexican criminologists.

31 Mikrofilm T 175 Roll 490, p. 2254 (IfZ MA 649) and Peter Hoffmann, 'Hitler's Personal Security', in George L. Mosse (ed.), *Police Forces in History* (London 1975), pp. 151ff.

32 Sabine Behrenbeck, *Der Kult um die toten Helden. Nationalsozialistische Mythen, Riten und Symbole 1923 bis 1945* (Greifswald 1996) is definitive. See also Michael Burleigh, *The Third Reich: A New History* (London 2000) for the wider cult.

33 Keith Jeffery, *MI6. The History of the Secret Intelligence Service, 1909–1949* (London 2010), pp. 383–7.

34 All details are from the Gestapo's *Vernehmungsprotokoll* dated 19 November 1939, which is reproduced in Anton Hoch, Lothar Gruchmann, *Georg Elser: Der Attentäter aus dem Volke* (Frankfurt am Main 1980), pp. 55–154.

35 Peter Hoffmann, 'Maurice Bavaud's Attempt to Assassinate Hitler in 1938', in Mosse (ed.), *Police Forces in History*, pp. 173–204.

36 Hellmut Haasis, *'Den Hitler jag' ich in die Luft': der Attentäter Georg Elser. Eine Biographie* (Berlin 1999), p. 185.

37 The reconstructed bomb is depicted front and side view in Haasis, *'Den Hitler jag' ich in die Luft'*, pp. 204–5.

38 Joachim Fest, *Plotting Hitler's Death. The German Resistance to Hitler, 1933–1945* (trans. Bruce Little, London 1996), pp. 3–4 for these figures. There is no mention of Elser in the index.

39 *'Vernehmungsprotokoll'*, pp. 153–4.

Chapter 5

1 See R. W. Johnson, *South Africa. The First Man, The Last Nation* (London 2004), especially pp. 62–74.

2 Christopher Saunders, Iain Smith, 'Southern Africa, 1795–1910', in Andrew Porter (ed.), *The Oxford History of the British Empire* Vol. 3, *The Nineteenth Century* (Oxford 1999), pp. 597ff.

3 Deidre McMahon, 'Ireland, the Empire and the Commonwealth', in Kevin Kenny (ed.), *Ireland and the British Empire* (Oxford 2004), pp. 192–5. I owe this reference to Dr Simon King.

4 These details are mainly from Henry Kenney, *Architect of Apartheid. H.F. Verwoerd – An Appraisal* (Johannesburg 1980).

5 See the excellent account by Saul Dubow, *Apartheid, 1948–1994* (Oxford 2014), especially pp. 10ff.

6 Johnson, *South Africa*, pp. 141–4.

7 Thomas J. Noer, *Cold War and Black Liberation. The United States and White Rule in Africa, 1948–1968* (Columbia, MO 1985), pp. 46–7.

8 See the extremely fine memoir by Pratt's daughter Suzie Cazenove, *An Unwitting Assassin* (Cape Town 2019), p. 168.

9 For the Verwoerd quotation from 1962 see Harris Dousemetzis, *The Man Who Killed Apartheid. The Life of Dmitri Tsafendas* (Auckland Park, SA 2018), p. 7. I have drawn heavily on this fine biography.

10 These biographical details are from Henk van Woerden, *A Mouthful of Glass. The Man Who Killed The Father of Apartheid* (trans. and ed. Dan Jacobson: London 2001).

11 Dousemetzis, *The Man Who Killed Apartheid*, pp. 198–9 for the dinner.

12 For the background see Adam Hochschild, *King Leopold's Ghost. A Story of Greed, Terror and Heroism in Colonial Africa* (London 1998); there is also a useful recent history of the Congo within Martin Meredith's outstanding *The State of Africa. A History of the Continent Since Independence* (London 2011), pp. 93ff.

13 Emmanuel Gerard, Bruce Kuklick, *Death in the Congo. Murdering Patrice Lumumba* (Cambridge, MA 2015), p. 14.

14 For these biographical details see mainly Leo Zeilig, *Lumumba. Africa's Lost Leader* (London 2008).

15 Georges Nzongola-Ntalaja, *The Congo from Leopold to Kabila. A People's History* (London 2002), pp. 81ff.

16 Colin Legum, *Congo Disaster* (Harmondsworth 1961), pp. 75–6.

17 Nzongola-Ntalaja, *The Congo*, p. 89.

18 Guy Vanthemsche, *Belgium and the Congo, 1885–1980* (trans. Alice Cameron and Stephen Windross, Cambridge 2012), pp. 208–11.

19 For a good account of UN policy see Susan Williams, *Who Killed Hammarskjöld? The UN, the Cold War and White Supremacy in South Africa* (London 2011).

20 The cable is dated 19 July 1960 and is in Madeleine G. Kalb, *The Congo Cables. The Cold War in Africa – from Eisenhower to Kennedy* (New York 1982), pp. 26–8; see also Gerard, Kulick, *Death in the Congo*, pp. 60–65 and 68–70.

21 John Ranelagh, *The Agency: The Rise and Decline of the CIA* (New York 1986), pp. 276–285, and Charles Cogan, Ernest R. May, 'The Congo, 1960–63: Weighing Worst Choices', in Ernest R. May, Philip D. Zelikow (eds), *Dealing with Dictators. Dilemmas of US Diplomacy and Intelligence Analysis, 1945–1990* (Cambridge, MA 2006), pp. 55.

22 Kalb, *The Congo Cables*, pp. 53–5.

23 Kris Hollington, *Wolves, Jackals, and Foxes. The Assassins Who Changed History* (New York 2013), pp. 34ff. Gottlieb would also work on LSD-induced psychoses in project MK-ULTRA. Despite his foot he was an enthusiastic dancer who worked as an aid worker in his retirement.

24 Kulick, *Death in the Congo*, pp. 154–5.

25 Church Committee, *Alleged Assassination Plots Involving Foreign Leaders. 1975 US Senate Report on CIA Covert Operations to Kill Fidel Castro, Ngo Dinh Diem, and Others* (Washington, DC 1975), p. 51.

26 Kalb, *The Congo Cables*, p. 133 for the cable cited and Larry Devlin, *Chief of Station, Congo. Fighting the Cold War in a Hot Zone* (New York 2007), pp. 94–7.

27 Ludo de Witte, *The Assassination of Lumumba* (trans. Ann Wright and Renée Fenby, London 2001), pp. 23–4; see also the earlier Jacques Brassinne, Jean Kestergat, *Qui a tué Patrice Lumumba?* (Paris 1991).

28 Zeilig, *Lumumba*, p. 121 for the speech.

29 Zeilig, *Lumumba*, pp. 122–4 for this letter.

30 De Witte, *Assassination of Lumumba*, p. 117.

31 Jennifer Rankin, 'Belgium mulls charges over 1961 killing of Congo's first elected leader', *Guardian*, 1 July 2020.

32 Meredith, *The State of Africa*, pp. 157–61.

33 See the stunning account by Philip Gourevitch, *We Wish To Inform You That Tomorrow We Will Be Killed With Our Families. Stories From Rwanda* (New York 1998), p. 83.

34 *Tribunal Pénal International pour le Rwanda Jugement and Sentence* (2003), pp. 46–7 for the Commandments.

35 Linda Melvern, *Conspiracy to Murder. The Rwandan Genocide* (London 2006), pp. 20ff. is excellent on so-called Hutu self-defence.

36 Melvern, *Conspiracy to Murder*, p. 114.

37 https://www.theguardian.com/world/2004/mar/31/usa.rwanda using declassified documents under FIA rules.

38 Pierre Péan, *L'Homme de l'Ombre* (Paris 1990).

39 Melvern, *Conspiracy to Murder*, p. 41.

40 See Allan Thompson (ed.), *The Media and the Rwanda Genocide* (London 2007), for a comprehensive account.

41 Roméo Dallaire, *Shake Hands With The Devil. The Failure of Humanity in Rwanda* (London 2004), pp. 88ff.

42 Gourevitch, *We Wish To Inform You*, pp. 185ff. is excellent on the Hutu Power dictatorship in refugee camps.

43 Raymond Bonner, 'Unsolved Rwanda Mystery: The President's Plane Crash', *New York Times*, 12 November 1994.

44 Melvern, *Conspiracy to Murder*, pp. 51–2.

45 https://www.bbc.co.uk/news/world-africa-46687492.

46 Michela Wong, 'Suspects in murder of ex-Rwandan spy chief "directly linked to Kigali" inquest', *Guardian*, 18 April 2019.

Chapter 6

1 https://nsarchive2.gwu.edu/NSAEBB/NSAEBB4/ciaguat2.html for the transcribed text. Declassified in 1997, the manual is called 'A Study of Assassinations'. It includes several examples of successful and unsuccessful attempts and handy sequential diagrams for anyone wanting to enter a conference room and kill everyone in it. Tom Stevenson, 'Finer points of murder', *TLS*, 11 January 2019, pp. 8–9, is an excellent guide to this document.

2 Alex von Tunzelmann, *Red Heat: Conspiracy, Murder and the Cold War in the Caribbean* (London 2011), is essential to the wider context.

3 Victor Marchetti, John Marks, *The CIA and the Cult of Intelligence* (London 1974), pp. 52–5.

4 William Colby, Testimony for the House Committee on Government Operations, Prepared Statement July 1971, p. 3, and Seymour Hersh, *The Price of Power: Kissinger in the Nixon White House* (New York 1997), p. 547 for the Nixon quote.

5 Walter A. McDougall, *Promised Land, Crusader State. The American Encounter with the World since 1776* (New York 1997), pp. 183–92, is excellent on the global meliorist 'sociology' of the Vietnam War.

6 Joshua Kurlantzick, *A Great Place to Have a War. America in Laos and the Birth of a Military CIA* (New York 2017), p. 8.

7 For a good portrait of Diem see Frances FitzGerald, *Fire in the Lake. The Vietnamese and the Americans in Vietnam* (New York 1972), pp. 72–137.

8 Seth Jacobs, *Cold War Mandarin. Ngo Dinh Diem and the Origins of America's War in Vietnam, 1950–1963* (Lanham, MD 2006), pp. 46–51.

9 The best account of Diem's beliefs is Edward Miller, *Misalliance. Ngo Dinh Diem, the United States, and the Fate of South Vietnam* (Cambridge, MA 2013).

10 The latest biography of Lansdale is Max Boot, *The Road Not Taken. Edward Lansdale and the American Tragedy in Vietnam*

(New York 2018), but see also Jonathan Nashel, *Edward Lansdale's Cold War* (Amherst 2005), and Cecil B. Currey, *Edward Lansdale. The Unquiet American* (Washington 1998).

11 David Talbot, *The Devil's Chessboard. Allen Dulles, the CIA, and the Rise of America's Secret Government* (London 2015), p. 569, citing Truman's op-ed in the *Washington Post*.

12 See Fredrik Logevall's outstanding *Embers of War. The Fall of an Empire and the Making of America's Vietnam* (New York 2012), pp. 684–5.

13 Richard Schultz, 'The Limits of Terrorism in Insurgency Warfare: The Case of the Viet Cong', *Polity* (1978), vol. 11, pp. 67–91.

14 Mark Moyar, *Phoenix and the Birds of Prey. Counterinsurgency and Counterterrorism in Vietnam* (Lincoln, NB 2007), pp. 11ff.

15 Howard Jones, *Death of a Generation. How the assassinations of Diem and JFK Prolonged the Vietnam War* (Oxford 2003) p. 271.

16 Miller, *Misalliance*, p. 311.

17 On Madame Nhu's US tour see Jacobs, *Cold War Mandarin*, p. 172.

18 Kai Bird, *The Color of Truth. McGeorge Bundy and William Bundy, Brothers in Arms: Biography* (New York 1998) p. 282.

19 McDougall, *Promised Land, Crusader State*, p. 191.

20 Robert Dallek, *Lyndon B. Johnson. Portrait of a President* (London 2004), pp. 160–62.

21 Douglas Valentine, *The Phoenix Program* (Lincoln, NB 2000), pp. 100–141 for the evolution of ICEX.

22 William Rosenau, Austin Long, 'The Phoenix Program and Contemporary Counterinsurgency', RAND National Defense Research Institute Occasional Paper (Santa Monica 2009), p. 15 for the details.

23 Nick Turse, *Kill Anything That Moves. The Real American War in Vietnam* (New York 2013), p. 190.

24 John L. Cook, *The Advisor. The Phoenix Program in Vietnam* (Atglen, PA 1997), pp. 84–5.

25 Stanley Karnow, *Vietnam. A History* (London 1994), p. 617.

26 Max Hastings, *Vietnam. An Epic Tragedy 1945–75* (London 2019), pp. 488–92.

27 Heather Stur, 'The Viet Cong Committed Atrocities Too', *New York Times*, 19 December 2017.

28 Truong Nhu Tang, *A Viet Cong Memoir* (New York 1986), pp. 158–9.

29 Moyar, *Phoenix and the Birds of Prey*, pp. 86ff.

30 Valentine, *The Phoenix Program*, pp. 221–2.

31 Cook, *The Advisor*, pp. 212–215.

32 https://www.reddit.com/r/aznidentity/comments/jd4vdz/must_read_history_the_phoenix_program_the_Cias, which quotes Okamoto

33 Memo for the Office of Special Assistant for Vietnamese Affairs, HQ CIA, subject 'The Geneva Conventions and the Phoenix Program', dated 30 August 1971, CIA Archives, Langley VA. It is interesting that this memo was not dated 1968 when the program was being hatched, rather than when it was being investigated by the House.

Chapter 7

1 Paul Henissart, *Wolves in the City: the Death of French Algeria* (London 1971), pp. 38ff. for the founding of the OAS.

2 Christian Plume, Pierre Démaret, *Target de Gaulle* (trans. Richard Barry, London 1976), pp. 125–139.

3 Julian Jackson, *A Certain Idea of France. The Life of Charles de Gaulle* (London 2019), p. 557.

4 Plume, Démaret, *Target de Gaulle*, p. 266.

5 Ted Morgan, 'His only regret – not to have killed de Gaulle', *New York Times*, 2 September 1973 is a revealing interview with Tocnaye. See also his memoir *Comment je n'ai pas tué de Gaulle* (Paris 1969). His witty last wish on death row was 'to learn Chinese'. He never got the chance.

6 Henry Kamm, 'TNT in Toulon Flowerpot Hints Plot on de Gaulle', *New York Times*, 29 August 1965.

7 Alain Peyrefitte, *C'était de Gaulle* (Paris 1997), pp. 42–5.

8 For this line of argument see David Talbot, *The Devil's Chessboard. Allen Dulles, the CIA, and the Rise of America's Secret Government* (London 2015), pp. 412–24.

9 Norman Mailer, *Oswald's Tale. An American Mystery* (New York 1995), pp. 498–516.

10 David A. Rothstein, 'Presidential Assassination Syndrome: A Psychiatric Study of the Threat, the Deed, and the Message', in William J Crotty (ed.), *Assassinations and the Political Order* (New York 1971), pp. 161ff.

11 Robert Dallek, *John F. Kennedy. An Unfinished Life, 1917–1963* (London 2003), p. 694.

12 Here I diverge from Norman Mailer's *Oswald's Tale*, pp. 733ff., which suggests that Ruby was instructed to kill Oswald.

13 'Jim Leavelle' obituary, *The Times*, 10 October 2019, p. 53.

14 Rothstein, 'Presidential Assassination Syndrome', p. 191.

15 Mailer, *Oswald's Tale*. This contains many of the Minsk KGB transcripts of the Oswalds talking in the apartment.

16 Paul Gregory, 'Lee Harvey Oswald Was My Friend', *New York Times*, 7 November 2013 (Gregory paid Marina for Russian lessons. He is a top historian of Russia at Stanford's Hoover Institution nowadays). Robert Service kindly gave me this reference.

17 Gerald Posner, *Case Closed. Lee Harvey Oswald and the Assassination of JFK* (New York 1993), p. 89.

18 Posner, *Case Closed*, p. 438.

19 See Jefferson Morley, *Our Man in Mexico. Winston Scott and the Hidden History of the CIA* (Lawrence, KS 2008), pp. 153ff.

20 *The Warren Commission Report*, pp. 340ff. for Oswald's relationship with Marina.

21 Morley, *Our Man in Mexico*, pp. 219ff.

22 Morley, *Our Man in Mexico*, pp. 212–13.

23 'JFK', *Newsweek*, 22 November 1993.

24 Peter Grose, *Allen Dulles: Spymaster. The Life & Times of the First Civilian Director of the CIA* (London 2006), pp. 540–4.

25 Posner, *Case Closed*, p. 445.

26 Louis A. Pérez, *Cuba in the American Imagination. Metaphor and the Imperial Ethos* (Chapel Hill, NC 2008), p. 235.

27 See also Chapter 5 for the Congolese angle to ZR/RIFLE.

28 Bayard Stockton, *Flawed Patriot. The Rise and Fall of CIA Legend Bill Harvey* (Washington DC 2006), pp. 152–8 for texts of these notes and papers.

29 *Report of the Select Committee on Assassinations US House of Representatives* (Washington DC 1979), pp. 165–6.

30 Posner, *Case Closed*, pp. 462–5.

31 For the details see the CIA's own review, 'Material Reviewed at CIA HQ by House Select Committee on Assassinations Staff Members' (originally 1978 but only released in sanitized form in 1997), plus supplementary materials released in 2017 on the orders of the Trump administration. See also Thomas Maier, 'Inside the CIA's plot to kill Fidel Castro – with mafia help', *Politico*, 25 February 2018.

32 See Max Boot, *The Road Not Taken. Edward Lansdale and the American Tragedy in Vietnam* (New York 2018), pp. 396–7.

33 Diane Kunz, 'Camelot Continued. What If John F. Kennedy Had Lived?', in Niall Ferguson (ed.), *Virtual History: Alternatives and Counterfactuals* (London 1967), pp. 377–91.

34 Knud Krakau, 'John F. Kennedy 22 November 1963', in Alexander Demandt (ed.), *Das Attentat in der Geschichte* (Darmstadt 2019), pp. 429ff., is good on the search for meaning through myriad

conspiracy theories. See the essential David Aaronovitch's *Voodoo Histories. The Role of Conspiracy Theories in Shaping Modern History* (London 2010).

35 James T. Patterson, *Grand Expectations. The United States 1945–1974* (Oxford 1996), p. 663.

36 Kunz, 'Camelot Continued', p. 373; see also Steven Livingstone, *Kennedy and King. The President, the Pastor, and the Battle Over Civil Rights* (New York 2017).

37 Livingstone, *Kennedy and King*, pp. 547–8.

38 Extract from the transcript 'I've Been To the Mountaintop', Address Delivered at Bishop Charles Mason Temple in Memphis 3rd April 1968, The Martin Luther King Jr. Research and Education Institute, King Papers Stanford.

39 See above all Gerald Posner, *Killing the Dream. James Earl Ray and the Assassination of Martin Luther King, Jr.* (New York 1998), pp. 77ff.

40 Kris Hollington, *Wolves, Jackals, and Foxes. The Assassins Who Changed History* (New York 2007), pp. 155–69 for the details.

41 For the political narrative that follows I have relied on Ramachandra Guha's *India After Gandhi. The History of the World's Largest Democracy* (London 2017 revised edition), pp. 35ff.

42 Judith Brown, *Nehru. A Political Life* (New Haven 2003), pp. 177–80.

43 Larry Collins and Dominique Lapierre, *Freedom at Midnight. The Epic Drama of India's Struggle for Independence* (London 1997), p. 496.

44 For a fine appreciation of Gandhi see Gitika Bhardwaj, 'Gandhi shares his vision for India', *World Today*, 8 April 2020.

45 Guha, *India After Gandhi*, p. 566.

46 M. R. Narayan Swamy, *Inside an Elusive Mind. Prabhakaran* (Colombo 2008), pp. 222–30.

47 Michael Roberts, 'Killing Rajiv Gandhi: Dhanu's sacrificial metamorphosis in death', *South Asian History and Culture* (2009) 1, pp. 25–41, includes some of the photographs taken by Hari Babu before he died.

48 Narayan Swamy, *Inside an Elusive Mind*, pp. 239–40.

Chapter 8

1 See the neglected study by Pitirim Sorokin and Walter Lunden, *Power & Morality. Who Shall Guard the Guardians?* (Boston 1959), p. 65.

2 Pavel Sudoplatov, *Special Tasks* (Boston 1995), pp. 246–8.

3 Christopher Andrew, Vasili Mitrokhin, *The Mitrokhin Archive. The KGB in Europe and the West* (London 2000), pp. 466–7.

4 Kevin Ruffner, *Cold War Allies: The Origins of the CIA's Relationship with Ukrainian Nationalists. Fifty Years of the CIA* (1998) https://www.cia.gov/library/readingroom/docs/ STUDIES%20IN%20INTELLIGENCE%20NAZI%20-%20 RELATED%20ARTICLES_0015.pdf.

5 Sudoplatov, *Special Tasks*, pp. 334ff.

6 For these details see the marvellous study by Boris Volodarsky, *Stalin's Agent. The Life and Death of Alexander Orlov* (Oxford 2015), pp. 376–82.

7 Rodric Braithwaite, *Afgantsy. The Russians in Afghanistan, 1978–89* (London 2012), pp. 56–7.

8 Odd Arne Westad, *The Global Cold War* (Cambridge 2007), p. 316, is excellent on the wider geopolitical backdrop.

9 William Taubman, *Gorbachev. His Life and Times* (London 2017), p. 173.

10 Andrew Monaghan's excellent *The New Politics of Russia. Interpreting Change* (Manchester 2016), pp. 44–8, is essential reading.

11 Amy Knight, *Orders to Kill. The Putin Regime and Political Murder* (London 2018), pp. 263–4.

12 Ben Judah, *Fragile Empire. How Russia Fell In and Out of Love with Vladimir Putin* (New Haven 2013), pp. 209–11, makes much of the expense of a tuna sandwich Nemtsov focused on during what was supposed to be an interview.

13 For these details see the remarkable study by John B. Dunlop, 'The February 2015 Assassination of Boris Nemtsov and the Flawed Trial of his Alleged Killers. An Exploration of Russia's Crime of the 21st Century', in Andreas Umland (ed.), *Soviet and Post-Soviet Politics and Society*, vol. 185 (Stuttgart 2019).

14 Joshua Yaffa, 'Putin's Dragon', *New Yorker*, 31 January 2016, p. 22.

15 Commission on Security and Cooperation in Europe (ed.), *Boris Nemtsov, 1959–2015: Seeking Justice, Securing His Legacy* (Washington DC 2018), p. 6.

16 Knight, *Orders to Kill*, p. 49.

17 Kathrin Hille, 'Boris Nemtsov FT interview days before he was murdered', *Financial Times*, 1 March 2015 https://www.ft.com/ content/e288978c-c024-11e4-a71e-00144feab7de.

18 This is one of the main themes of Catherine Belton's outstanding *Putin's People. How the KGB Took Back Russia and Then Took On the West* (London 2020).

19 Steven Lee Myers, *The New Tsar. The Rise and Reign of Vladimir Putin* (New York 2015), pp. 14–16.

20 Michel Eltchaninoff, *Inside the Mind of Vladimir Putin* (trans. James Ferguson, London 2017).

21 See Richard Sakwa, *Russia's Futures* (Cambridge 2019), p. 21.

22 For the above see Yuri Felshtinsky, *The Putin Corporation. The Story of Russia's Secret Takeover* (London 2012), p. 77 for scandium prices.

23 Luke Harding, *A Very Expensive Poison* (London 2016), pp. 9–12.

24 Mark Urban, *The Skripal Files. The Life and Near Death of a Russian Spy* (London 2018), pp. 94–5.

25 Andrei Soldatov, Irina Borogan, *The New Nobility* (Philadelphia 2010), pp. 13ff., is excellent on the reorganization.

26 These and other details on Litvinenko are from the Litvinenko Inquiry chaired by Sir Robert Owen into his murder (London 2016) see https://webarchive.nationalarchives.gov. uk/20160613090757/https://www.litvinenkoinquiry.org/files/ Litvinenko-Inquiry-Report-print-version.pdf.

27 See Richard Sakwa's important *Russia's Futures*, p. 31 for this distinction.

28 Olga Kryshtanovskaya, Stephen White, 'Putin's Militocracy', *Post-Soviet Affairs* (2003), vol. 19, p. 291.

29 The most exhaustive investigation of the Moscow bombings is John Dunlop, *The Moscow Bombings of September 1999. Examinations of Russian Terrorist Attacks at the Onset of Vladimir Putin's Rule* (Stuttgart 2014); I am grateful to Robert Service for the reference.

30 Monaghan, *Power in Modern Russia*, pp. 44–5.

31 Charles Clover, *Black Wind, White Snow. The Rise of Russia's New Nationalism* (New Haven 2016), p. 252.

32 'The new musketeers', *The Economist*, 22 June 2019, p. 29 details the political careers of Putin's bodyguards.

33 Soldatov, Borogan, *The New Nobility*, pp. 193–206, is the best account of these out of area deaths.

34 Matthew Karnitschnig, 'Berlin hit job could blight German-Russian relations', Politico eu, 30 August 2019, and Max Seddon, 'String of murders chills Chechen exiles in Europe', *Financial Times*, 11 July 2020. See also https://www.bellingcat.com/news/uk-and-europe/ 2019/12/03/identifying-the-berlin-bicycle-assassin-part-1-from-moscow-to-berlin/ for Sokolov's real identity.

35 Angus Roxburgh, *The Strongman. Vladimir Putin and the Struggle for Russia* (London 2013), p. 177.

36 Myers, *The New Tsar*, p. 306.

37 On Petrov see https://www.theatlantic.com/international/
archive/2017/11/russian-mob-mallorca-spain/545504/. The Spanish
granted him bail in 2012. He promptly fled to Russia from where
it is impossible to extradite him.

38 Robert Service, 'Report for the Litvinenko Inquiry', document INO
019146, especially the final section on Patrushev and Putin.

39 https://www.theguardian.com/news/2018/dec/26/skripal-
poisonings-bungled-assassination-kremlin-putin-salisbury.

40 https://www.bellingcat.com/news/uk-and-europe/2019/02/14/third-
suspect-in-skripal-poisoning-identified-as-denis-sergeev-high-
ranking-gru-officer/. See Eliot Higgins, *We are Bellingcat. An
intelligence agency for the people* (London 2021), pp. 180ff.

41 Franklin Foer, 'It's Putin's World', *Atlantic Monthly*, March 2017.

Chapter 9

1 James Barr, *A Line in the Sand* (London 2011), is an excellent
account of British and French geopolitical map-making.

2 Donald Reid, 'Political Assassination in Egypt, 1910–1954',
International Journal of African Historical Studies (1982) 15 no. 4,
pp. 625–51.

3 On the general political context see Yoram Peri, 'The Assassination:
Causes, Meaning, Outcomes', in Peri (ed.), *The Assassination of
Yitzhak Rabin* (Stanford 2000), pp. 42–57.

4 Vered Vinitzky-Seroussi, *Yitzhak Rabin's Assassination and the
Dilemmas of Commemoration* (New York 2009).

5 Ehud Sprinzak, 'Israel's Radical Right and the Countdown to the
Rabin Assassination', in Peri (ed.), *The Assassination of Yitzhak
Rabin*, p. 120.

6 Fine accounts of Amir and Rabin's assassination include Barton
Gellman, Laura Blumenfeld, 'Israel's Mainstream Brings Forth A
Killer', *Washington Post*, 12 November 1995, and Michael Karpin
and Ina Friedman, *Murder In The Name of God. The Plot to Kill
Yitzhak Rabin* (New York 1998). See most recently the fine piece
(and BBC radio programme) by the *Guardian's* Jonathan Freedland
https://www.theguardian.com/world/2020/oct/31/assassination-
yitzhak-rabin-never-knew-his-people-shot-him-in-back.

7 For a good portrait of Amir see Natan Odenheimer, 'Trying to
Understand Yigal Amir 21 Years On', *Jerusalem Post*, 10
November 2016.

8 https://www.newyorker.com/magazine/2015/10/26/shot-in-the-
heart.

9   See Hannes Baumann, *Citizen Hariri. Lebanon's Neoliberal Reconstruction* (London 2016).

10 Robert Bosco, 'The Assassination of Rafik Hariri: Foreign Policy Perspectives', *International Political Science Review* (2009) 30, no. 4, p. 352.

11 Sergio Catignani, 'Israeli counter-insurgency strategy and the quest for security in the Israeli-Lebanese conflict area', in Clive Jones, Sergio Catignani (eds), *Israel and the Hizbollah: An asymmetric conflict in historical and comparative perspective* (London 2010), pp. 70–86, is an excellent account of this campaign.

12 UNSC S/2005/203, 24 March 2005, 'Report of the Fact-Finding Mission to Lebanon Inquiring into the Causes, Circumstances and Consequences of the Assassination of Former Prime Minister Rafik Hariri'.

13 The best account of the event is Nicholas Blanford's *Killing Mr Lebanon. The Assassination of Rafik Hariri and its Impact on the Middle East* (London 2009).

14 On Captain Eid see Neil Macdonald, 'CBC Investigation: Who killed Lebanon's Rafik Hariri?', 21 November 2010, https://www.cbc.ca/news/world/cbc-investigation-who-killed-lebanon-s-rafik-hariri-1.874820.

15 Shira Rubin, 'Israel's top-secret Mossad looks to recruit via Netflix, Hulu and Apple TV', *Washington Post*, 18 December 2020 https://www.washingtonpost.com/world/middle_east/israel-mossad-spies-netflix/2020/12/18/a48745d4-3f88-11eb-b58b-1623f6267960_story.html. It is apparently unproblematic in *NCIS* that the Mossad agent is a professional *foreign* assassin who does indeed shoot people, even though the real NCIS tends to handle investigations into, for example, American sailors involved in arms or drug smuggling.

16 Tamir Libel, 'Looking for Meaning: Lessons from Mossad's failed adaptation to the post-Cold War era, 1991–2013', *Journal of Intelligence History* (2015) 14, no. 2, pp. 83–95.

17 Ronen Bergman, 'Israel-Morocco Deal Follows History of Cooperation in Arms', *New York Times*, 10 December 2020. The subject became salient in 2020 after Morocco joined Gulf Arab regimes in formally recognizing Israel.

18 The third was Ehud Barak, Prime Minister from 1999 to 2001 and a former elite commando.

19 Ronen Bergman, *Rise and Kill First. The Secret History of Israel's Targeted Assassinations* (trans. Ronnie Hope, London 2018), pp. 61–85.

20 Catignani, 'Israeli counter-insurgency strategy', p. 81.

21 Adam Goldman, Ellen Nakashima, 'CIA and Mossad killed senior

Hezbollah figure in car bombing', *Washington Post*, 30 January 2015.

22 Daniel Bynum, 'Do Targeted Killings Work?', *Foreign Affairs* (2006) 85, pp. 102–4.

23 Gordon, *Gideon's Spies*, p 125.

24 See Efraim Halevy, *Man in the Shadows. Inside the Middle East Crisis with a Man Who Led the Mossad* (London 2006), pp. 164–77.

25 Jeff Stein, 'How the CIA Took Down Hizbollah's Top Terrorist' https://www.newsweek.com/2015/02/13/imad-mugniyah-cia-mossad-303483.html.

26 For the details see Adam Entous and Evan Osnos, 'Last Man Standing', *New Yorker*, 10 February 2020, pp. 40–51.

27 https://www.nytimes.com/1979/12/09/archives/paris-killing-linked-to-iran-police-aide-lawyer-ties-slaying-of-the.html.

28 Ervand Abrahamian, *The Iranian Mojahedin* (New Haven, CT 1989), pp. 139–42.

29 Abrahamian, *The Iranian Mojahedin*, p. 223.

30 Robert Fantina, 'The MEK in Albania', *Counterpunch*, 27 December 2019.

31 Arron Merat, 'Terrorists, cultists – or champions of Iranian democracy? The wild wild story of the MEK', *Guardian*, 9 November 2018, is a brilliant investigative account of sinister MEK activities in Albania.

32 Daniel Boffey, Martin Chulov, 'Death of an electrician: how luck ran out for dissident who fled Iran in 1981', *Guardian*, 14 January 2019.

33 Ronen Bergman, 'When Israel Hatched a Secret Plan to Assassinate Iranian Scientists', *Politico*, 5 March 2018.

34 Mehdi Marizad, 'Israel teams with terror group to kill Iran's nuclear scientists, US officials tell *NBC News*', 9 February 2012.

35 Mohammad Ali Shabani, 'Terror accusations undermine Iran-Europe engagement at worst possible time', *Al Monitor*, 6 August 2018: https://www.al-monitor.com/pulse/originals/2018/11/iran-denmark-france-bomb-assassination-plot-israel-jcpoa.html.

Chapter 10

1 https://www.nytimes.com/1975/09/17/archives/colby-describes-cia-poison-work-he-tells-senate-panel-of-secret.html.

2 *US Senate Report on CIA Covert Operations to Kill Fidel Castro, Ngo Dinh Diem, and Others 1975 Alleged Assassination Plots Involving Foreign Leaders* (Washington DC 1975), p. 11.

3 *US Senate Report on CIA Covert Operations*, p. 284.

4 For a brilliant account of the mindset of top CIA officers see Thomas Powers, *The Man Who Kept the Secrets. Richard Helms and the CIA* (New York 1978), especially, pp. 378–82.

5 For some of what follows see Boyd M. Johnson III, 'Executive Order 12,333: The Permissibility of an American Assassination of a Foreign Leader', *Cornell International Law Journal* (1992) 25, no. 2, pp. 401–35.

6 *US Senate Report on CIA Covert Operations*, p. 285.

7 Peter Baker, *Days of Fire. Bush and Cheney in the White House* (New York 2013), p. 146.

8 Ron Suskind, *The One Percent Doctrine. Deep Inside America's Pursuit of its Enemies Since 9/11* (London 2007), pp. 62ff.

9 https://www.congress.gov/107/plaws/publ40/PLAW-107publ40.pdf.

10 Gabriella Blum, Philip Heymann, 'Law and Policy of Targeted Killing', *Harvard National Security Journal* (2010) 1, no. 1, pp. 155–63.

11 Jenna Jordan, 'When Heads Roll: Assessing the Effectiveness of Leadership Decapitation', *Security Studies* (2009) 18, no. 4, pp. 719–55.

12 Howard A. Wachtel, 'Targeting Osama bin Laden: Examining the Legality of Assassination as a Tool of U.S. Foreign Policy', *Duke Law Journal* (2005) 55, no. 3, pp. 677–710.

13 The figures for the US drone fleets and their costs come from Ahmed S. Hashim and Grégoire Patte, ' "What is that Buzz?" The Rise of Drone Warfare', *Counter Terrorist Trends and Analyses* (2012) 4, no. 9, p. 8.

14 Brian Glyn Williams, *Predators. The CIA's Drone War on al Qaeda* (Washington DC 2013), pp. 70–71.

15 Peter Finn, 'Rise of the drone: From Calif. Garage to multibillion-dollar defense industry', *Washington Post*, 23 December 2011.

16 See https://www.nytimes.com/1999/06/03/world/crisis-balkans-drones-they-re-unmanned-they-fly-low-they-get-picture.html for an early account of drones on military operations in former Yugoslavia.

17 Mark Mazzetti, *The Way of the Knife. The CIA, a Secret Army, and a War at the Ends of the Earth* (New York 2014), p. 92.

18 See Tim Weiner, *Legacy of Ashes. The History of the CIA* (London 2007), pp. 448ff., and Williams, *Predators*, p. 232 for CTC numbers of personnel.

19 Chris Woods, *Sudden Justice. America's Secret Drone Wars* (London 2015), p. 52.

20 See the outstanding account by Baker, *Days of Fire*, especially, pp. 119ff.

21 Steve Coll, *Directorate S: the C.I.A. and America's secret wars in Afghanistan and Pakistan* (New York 2018), p. 83.

22 https://www.nytimes.com/2002/02/17/world/a-nation-challenged-the-manhunt-us-leapt-before-looking-angry-villagers-say.html.

23 Eyal Press, 'The Wounds of the Drone Warrior', *New York Times Magazine*, 13 June 2018.

24 See Hassan Abbas (ed.), *Pakistan's Troubled Frontier* (Washington DC 2009), for a good account of each of these seven areas.

25 Seumas Miller, 'The Ethics of Targeted Killing: Osama bin Laden, Drones, and Counter-Terrorism', *Public Affairs Quarterly* (2014) 28, pp. 317–340, is good on disorderly and orderly jurisdictions.

26 Ramzy Mardini (ed.), *The Battle for Yemen. Al-Qaeda and the Struggle for Stability* (Washington DC 2010).

27 See Victoria Clark's excellent *Yemen: Dancing on the Heads of Snakes* (London 2010).

28 See the fine account by Mark Landler, *Alter Egos. Hillary Clinton, Barack Obama, and the Twilight Struggle Over American Power* (London 2016), pp. 109–14.

29 Williams, *Predators*, pp. 2–9.

30 For the full Amnesty USA report see https://www.amnestyusa.org/files/asa330132013en.pdf.

31 Woods, *Sudden Justice*, pp. 104–5.

32 https://obamawhitehouse.archives.gov/the-press-office/2013/05/23/remarks-president-national-defense-university.

33 Amy Davidson Sorkin, 'John Brennan's Kill List', *New Yorker*, 7 January 2013.

34 Lander, *Alter Egos*, p. 116.

35 Lander, *Alter Egos*, pp. 117–18.

36 Many claim that the CIA also failed to see the disintegration of the Soviet Union, though others dispute this. See Bruce Berkowitz, 'U.S. Intelligence Estimates of the Soviet Collapse: Reality and Perception', *International Journal of Intelligence and Counterintelligence* (2008) 21, no. 2, pp. 237–50.

37 Thomas E. Ricks, 'Interview with a US Air Force drone pilot: It is, oddly, war at a very intimate level', *Foreign Policy*, 6 November 2014.

38 Woods, *Sudden Justice*, pp. 114–118.

39 Noah Schachtman, 'Computer Virus Hits Drone Fleet''', *Wired*, 7 October 2011 https://www.wired.com/2011/10/virus-hits-drone-fleet/.

40 For a spirited and intelligent view of civilian perceptions of drone

warfare see Joe Chapa, ' "Drone Ethics" and the Civil–Military Gap', *War on the Rocks*, 28 June 2017.

41 https://www.nytimes.com/2020/06/24/world/middleeast/syria-qaeda-r9x-hellfire-missile.html?referringSource=articleShare.

42 'Finding it in one's heart', *The Economist*, 25 January 2020, pp. 72–3.

43 https://www.nytimes.com/2012/02/06/world/asia/us-drone-strikes-are-said-to-target-rescuers.html.

44 https://www.nytimes.com/2013/02/23/us/drone-pilots-found-to-get-stress-disorders-much-as-those-in-combat-do.html.

45 As pointed out by Bynum, 'Do Targeted Killings Work?', pp. 95ff.

46 Williams, *Predators*, pp. 104ff for spies, fate of.

47 'US embassy cables: Imran Khan criticises "dangerous" US policy. Wikileaks cables 247596 (2 February 2010), *Guardian*.

48 Cable quoted in the excellent account by Anatol Lieven, *Pakistan. A Hard Country* (New York 2011), pp. 478–9.

49 https://rendezvous.blogs.nytimes.com/2012/08/22/sizing-up-the-effects-of-u-s-drone-attacks/.

50 John Wendle, 'The Fighting Drones of Ukraine', *Air & Space*, February 2018.

51 Seth Frantzman, 'Who was Abu Mahdi al-Muhandis, killed in US airstrike with Soleimani?', *Jerusalem Post*, 6 January 2020. On the deleterious effects of Muhandis's assassination see https://www.brookings.edu/blog/order-from-chaos/2020/03/03/what-will-happen-to-iraqi-shiite-militias-after-one-key-leaders-death/.

52 Dexter Filkins, 'The Shadow Commander', *New Yorker*, 30 September 2013 https://www.newyorker.com/magazine/2013/09/30/the-shadow-commander.

53 Ali Soufan, 'Qassem Soleimani and Iran's Unique Regional Strategy', *Combating Terrorism Center West Point* (2018), p. 11.

54 The best profile of the general is by Filkins, 'The Shadow Commander', *New Yorker*.

55 See William J. Burns, *The Back Channel. American Diplomacy in a Disordered World* (London 2019), pp. 337ff.

56 Daniel J. Rosenthal, Loren Schulman', 'Trump's Secret War on Terror', *Atlantic*, 10 August 2018.

57 See the important piece by William J. Burns, Jake Sullivan, 'Soleimani's Ultimate Revenge', *Atlantic*, 6 January 2012.

58 On the political consequences of Soleimani's assassination see Maysam Behravesh, 'Soleimani Was More Valuable In Politics Than In War', *Foreign Affairs*, 8 January 2020.

59 George Packer, 'Killing Soleimani Was Worse Than a Crime', *Atlantic*, 3 January 2020.

60 https://www.theguardian.com/world/2020/may/09/iran-iraq-khadimi-control-middle-east-suleimani.

61 On some of these points see Shmuel Bar, *Middle East Strategic Outlook* (April 2020), especially p. 4, and Ali Hashem, 'What Iran lost with Soleimani's killing', *Al-Monitor*, 3 January 2020.

62 David Kirkpatrick, Ronen Bergman, Farnaz Fassihi, 'Brazen Killings Expose Iran's Vulnerabilities as it Struggles to Respond', *New York Times*, 29 November 2020.

63 Adam Taylor, 'Who is Mohsen Fakhiizadeh, the Iranian nuclear scientist killed in attack outside Tehran?', *Washington Post*, 27 November 2020. See also https://www.thejc.com/news/world/world-exclusive-truth-behind-killing-of-iran-nuclear-scientist-mohsen-fakhrizadeh-revealed-1.511653.

64 For a discussion of the nuclear issue see Gideon Rose and Jonathan Tepperman (eds), *Iran and the Bomb. Solving the Persian Puzzle* (New York 2012). Ken Waltz's article is pp. 121–6.

65 First reported by David Hambling in *Forbes Magazine* on 30 November 2020 (see https://www.forbes.com/sites/davidhambling/2020/11/30/why-a-remote-controlled-machinegun-was-the-perfect-weapon-for-iranian-assassination/) then Roger Boyes, 'The era of AI assassinations has arrived', *The Times*, 9 December 2020. More recently see https://www.thejc.com/news/world/world-exclusive-truth-behind-killing-of-iran-nuclear-scientist-mohsen-fakhrizadeh-revealed-1.511653. In fact drones have used the same technologies for years and so have ground-based remote gun platforms and artillery batteries, not to speak of the CROW systems on armoured vehicles (to prevent roof gunners from being hit by snipers) and cruder remote guns used by among others the Free Syrian Army. See Christopher Coker, *Future War* (Cambridge 2015), on the technical and ethical issues involved. Talk of a 'one tonne bomb' seems implausible since it would have killed everyone within 80 metres and seriously injured everyone at 840 metres. Yet Mrs Fakrizadeh and his bodyguards and driver survived?

66 Peter Conradi, 'Iran's deadly Pizza Hut delivery – a bomb meant to massacre foes in Paris', *Sunday Times*, 15 November 2020 and https://www.bbc.co.uk/news/world-europe-55931633 for the 2021 verdicts. The Iranian couple received long sentences in Antwerp too.

67 See Haviv Rettig Gur, 'Why Mossad's Yossi Cohen, shadow warrior against Iran, is PM's chosen successor', *Times of Israel*, 2 December 2020, https://www.timesofisrael.com/why-mossads-yossi-cohen-shadow-warrior-against-iran-is-pms-chosen-successor/.

68 'Hamas accuses Israel of killing its Tunisian drone expert', *BBC News*, 17 December 2016.

69 See the excellent article by Shlomo Bron and Shimon Stein, 'Does the Cost of the Fakrizadeh Assassination Outweigh the Benefits?', *INSS Insight*, Nr 1410, 2 December 2020; and on the US angle see Daniel Larison, 'Israel Tries To Kill The Nuclear Deal', *American Conservative*, 2 December 2020. I would like to acknowledge insights which Larison's blog on that site has provided over many years.

70 Christopher Coker's forthcoming *Why War?* is a good guide to AI, robots and warfare that pours cold water on much of the techno-babble.

71 Craig Whitlock, 'US targets Afghan drug traffickers', *Washington Post*, 24 October 2009 https://www.washingtonpost.com/wp-dyn/content/article/2009/10/23/AR2009102303709.html.

Chapter 11

1 Olof Ruin, 'Three Swedish Prime Ministers: Tage Erlanger, Olof Palme and Ingvar Carlsson', *West European Politics* (1991) 14, no. 3, pp. 58–82, deftly explains the role of these Prime Ministers in this very stable system.

2 Imogen West-Knights, 'Who Killed the Prime Minister', *Guardian*, 16 May 2019, is a well-researched account.

3 See Kajsa Norman, *Sweden's Dark Soul. The Unravelling of a Utopia* (London 2018), for the underbelly.

4 For these details of Petterson's criminal career see Jan Bondeson, *Blood on the Snow. The Killing of Olof Palme* (Ithaca, NY 2005), pp. 117–118.

5 Adrian Guelke, 'A Flawed Account of Why I was Shot', *Fortnight* (May 2004), Nr. 425, p. 24. Having collaborated with Professor Guelke in an LSE Ideas pamphlet, I was able to ask him about this near-death experience. The chapter on Africa above also owes much to his work on apartheid.

6 Bondeson, *Blood on the Snow*, pp. 148–50.

7 The 2016 movie *The Lovers & The Despot* deals with the most notorious kidnapping.

8 See Anna Fifield's excellent *The Great Successor. The Secret Rise and Rule of Kim Jong Un* (London 2019).

9 https://www.nbcnews.com/news/north-korea/north-korea-has-history-assassination-attempts-foreign-soil-n823016.

10 https://thediplomat.com/2011/10/north-koreas-clumsy-assassins/.

11 The best accounts of the assassination include Farik Zolkepli, Austin Camoens, Jo Timbuong and Justin Zack, 'The Assassination

of Kim Jong-nam', *Star*, 13 February 2020, and Simin Parry, Frankie d'Cruz, 'The World's Most Unlikely (and Gullible) Assassins', *Mail on Sunday*, 19 May 2019.

12 https://thediplomat.com/2020/02/3-years-ago-kim-jong-un-got-away-with-murder/.

13 See Ben Hubbard, *MBS. The Rise to Power of Mohammed bin Salman* (London 2020), upon which I rely for some of these details about MbS.

14 Mark Mazzetti, Ben Hubbard, 'It Wasn't Just Khashoggi: A Saudi Prince's Brutal Drive to Crush Dissent', *New York Times*, 17 March 2019.

15 David Ignatius, 'The Khashoggi killing had roots in a cutthroat Saudi family feud', *Washington Post*, 27 November 2018.

16 https://www.thetimes.co.uk/article/saudi-leader-mohammad-bin-salmans-agents-attacked-me-outside-harrods-says-activist-ghanem-al-dosari-wd279tn77.

17 Jonathan Rugman, *The Killing in the Consulate. Investigating the Life and Death of Jamal Khashoggi* (London 2020), especially pp. 87ff. I would like to acknowledge this fine book as the main source on Khashoggi's killing.

18 See Roula Khalaf, 'Khashoggi fiancée Hatice Cengiz', *Lunch with The FT*, 26 July 2019.

19 https://www.aljazeera.com/news/2017/10/reports-attack-foiled-saudi-palace-jeddah-171007113614609.html.

20 David Ignatius, 'How the mysteries of Khashoggi's murder have rocked the U.S.–Saudi partnership', *Washington Post*, 29 March 2019.

21 David Kirkpatrick, Carlotta Gall, 'Turkish Officials Say Khashoggi Was Killed on Order of Saudi Leadership', *New York Times*, 9 October 2018.

22 See the excellent *Financial Times* report on NSO, https://www.ft.com/content/95b91412-a946–11e9-b6ee-3cdf3174eb89. NSO is owned by a British private equity group called Novalpina Capital.

23 'Khashoggi's murder: One year on, here's what we know', *Al Jazeera News Report*, 1 October 2019.

24 'Massive intel headquarters open in Ankara', *Duvar English*, 6 January 2020.

25 Melik Kaylan, 'The Secret History of the Saudi Consulate Affair: Turkey's Counter-Attack', *Forbes*, 10 October 2018.

26 A point made by David Ignatius in 'What did U.S. spy agencies know about threats on Khashoggi – and when?', *Washington Post*, 18 October 2018.

27 Sherif Mansour, Michael De Dora, 'Two Years After Khashoggi's

Murder, the Fight for Justice Isn't Over', *World Politics Review*, 29 September 2020, and Shane Harris, Greg Miller and Josh Dawney, 'CIA concludes Saudi Crown Prince ordered Jamal Khashoggi's assassination', *Washington Post*, 16 November 2018.

28 https://www.wsj.com/articles/america-first-doesnt-mean-america-alone-1496187426.

29 These claims are reported by Stephen Grey, 'The Silencing of Daphne', *Reuters Investigation*, 17 April 2018. I make no claims regarding their veracity and they have been disputed. Stephen Grey is an outstanding reporter.

30 See Ben Taub, 'Murder in Malta', *New Yorker*, 21 December 2020, pp. 38–49 for some of these details of the crime.

31 Stephen Grey, 'Daphne's murder accused details plot to kill for 150,000 euros', *Reuters*, 28 November 2019. For the latest developments in the courts see https://www.theguardian.com/world/2021/feb/23/man-accused-daphne-caruana-galizia-assassination-pleads-guilty-vincent-muscat. See also https://www.theguardian.com/world/2021/mar/11/daphne-caruana-galizia-killer-lays-out-plot-in-court?.

32 https://timesofmalta.com/articles/view/caruana-galizia-family-writes-to-siemens-to-rescind-power-station.789881.

33 https://timesofmalta.com/articles/view/caruana-galizia-family-writes-to-siemens-to-rescind-power-station.789881.

34 Council of Europe Parliamentary Assembly Resolution 2293 (2019) 'Daphne Caruana Galizia's assassination and the rule of law in Malta and beyond: ensuring that the whole truth emerges'.

35 https://www.telegraph.co.uk/business/2019/08/25/malta-model-economy-money-launderer-everyone-has-issues-london/. I am grateful to Jeremy Warner for a discussion of this report on Malta, which he wrote about for the *Daily Telegraph*.

36 Roderick Pace, 'Will the Assassination of Daphne Caruana Galizia lead to wholesale institutional reform in Malta?', *LSE European Politics and Policy Blog*, 7 November 2017.

37 Juliette Garside, 'Exposing Malta's dark side: "Daphne's story is far from over" ', *Guardian*, 8 February 2020.

38 James Shotter, 'Slovak murders put political elite on trial', *Financial Times*, 10 December 2019.

39 On this club see Lars Wienand, 'Verdächtiger Stephan E. hat lange Neonazi Vergangenheit', *T-online*, 17 June 2019.

40 https://www.sueddeutsche.de/politik/mord-luebcke-gestaendnis-regierungspraesident-kassel-1.4515112.

41 https://www.theguardian.com/world/2019/jul/02/germany-slow-to-hear-alarm-bells-in-killing-of-walter-lubcke.

42 https://www.dw.com/en/neo-nazi-nsu-member-beate-zschäpe-
     found-guilty-of-murder-sentenced-to-life-in-prison/a-44626859.

43 Peter Maxwill, Mattias Bartsch, Max Holscher, 'Die Welt des
     Stephan E.', *Der Spiegel*, 17 June 2019.

44 Hannelore Crolly, 'Für Schießübungen eine Zielscheibe mit Merkels
     Konterfei', *Die Welt*, 5 August 2020.

45 https://www.sueddeutsche.de/politik/luebcke-mord-waffen-
     rechtsextreme-waffenrecht-1.4581706

46 Martin Steinhagen, 'Walter Lübckes letzte Nacht', *Die Zeit*, 27
     May 2020, is based on the federal prosecutors' statement of the
     facts. On the verdict see https://www.welt.de/regionales/hessen/
     article225195071/Lebenslang-fuer-Moerder-Enttaeuschung-ueber-
     zweites-Urteil.html?cid=onsite.onsitesearch. Ernst was deemed not
     guilty of the earlier stabbing of the Iraqi but the crime is being
     reinvestigated.

47 https://edition.cnn.com/2020/09/29/europe/germany-afd-migrants-
     christian-luth-intl/index.html.

Index

Assassins (including unsuccessful assassins) are shown by an obelus (†) and victims (including those who survived) by an asterisk (*).